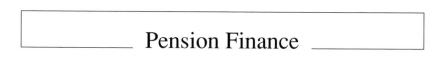

Pension Finance

Pension Finance

David Blake

John Wiley & Sons, Ltd

Published by   John Wiley & Sons Ltd, The Atrium, Southern Gate, Chichester,
                      West Sussex PO19 8SQ, England

                      Telephone   (+44) 1243 779777

Email (for orders and customer service enquiries): cs-books@wiley.co.uk
Visit our Home Page on www.wiley.com

Other Wiley Editorial Offices

John Wiley & Sons Inc., 111 River Street, Hoboken, NJ 07030, USA

Jossey-Bass, 989 Market Street, San Francisco, CA 94103-1741, USA

Wiley-VCH Verlag GmbH, Boschstr. 12, D-69469 Weinheim, Germany

John Wiley & Sons Australia Ltd, 42 McDougall Street, Milton, Queensland 4064, Australia

John Wiley & Sons (Asia) Pte Ltd, 2 Clementi Loop #02-01, Jin Xing Distripark, Singapore 129809

John Wiley & Sons Canada Ltd, 6045 Freemont Blvd, Mississauga, ONT, L5R 4J3, Canada

Wiley also publishes its books in a variety of electronic formats. Some content that appears in print
may not be available in electronic books.

Library of Congress Cataloging-in-Publication Data

Blake, David, 1954-
  Pension finance / David Blake.
    p. cm.
  ISBN-13: 978-0-470-05843-5 (alk. paper)
  ISBN-10: 0-470-05843-9 (alk. paper)
  1. Pension trusts–Management.   2. Pension trusts–Investments.
3. Portfolio management.   I. Title.

  HD7105.4B6 2006
  332.67'254–dc22

                                              2006020145

British Library Cataloguing in Publication Data

A catalogue record for this book is available from the British Library

ISBN 13 978-0-470-05843-5 (HB)
ISBN 10 0-470-05843-9 (HB)

Typeset in 11/13pt Times by TechBooks, New Delhi, India
Printed and bound in Great Britain by TJ International Ltd, Padstow, Cornwall, UK
This book is printed on acid-free paper responsibly manufactured from sustainable forestry
in which at least two trees are planted for each one used for paper production.

For M.L.T.

Contents

Preface

With many countries in the world facing an existing or looming pension crisis, there could not be a more opportune moment to launch a new series of books on pensions. Countries around the globe are fast waking up to the fact that they have a major challenge on their hands with their state-run pension schemes. The combination of a rapidly changing population and fertility rates well below replacement rates has led to a striking increase in the dependency ratios in many countries. At the same time, many private sector schemes are facing severe funding difficulties as a result of poor stock market returns, falling interest rates and increasing longevity.

Pensions problems are becoming highly complex, and although there are many people with expertise in pensions, their expertise tends to be one dimensional. They might be a pension lawyer with a deep understanding of pension rules and regulations, but their understanding of the role of pensions in lifecycle financial planning might be poor. They might be a pension actuary with an indepth knowledge of how to calculate pension liabilities in a number of different ways, but their understanding of the financial risks in pension funds might be inadequate. They might be a skilled investment manager, but have little comprehension of how pension liabilities respond to macroeconomic or demographic shocks. They might be a pension accountant familiar with all the global pension accounting standards, but have little understanding of how these standards affect corporate dividend and investment policy. All these professions might know very little about the social dimension of pensions in their own country or about the pensions systems operating in other countries.

What is clearly needed is a well-trained group of professionals capable of providing appropriate and sustainable pensions solutions to complex pension problems. In short, there is a need for a new class of professional, the *pension scientist*. This is someone who can competently deal with the multi-disciplinary nature of pension problems. The development of a common body of knowledge is the first step in this process.

The Pensions Institute was started by economists. But we soon became aware of the limits of our knowledge in the pensions field. We found that actuaries, accountants and lawyers were talking about pensions in a language that was at the same time both strange and familiar. It was strange because of the new terms they used. It was also strange because terms familiar to us had subtly different meanings to them. For us to be able to deepen our understanding of the complexities of pensions, we needed to begin to understand the way that these different professional groups thought about pensions.

In the process of doing this, we realised just how multi-disciplinary a thorough understanding of pensions needs to be. To use a mountaineering analogy, we felt as though we were talking to different groups of skilled mountaineers who had climbed different sides of the same mountain. While each group was an expert at climbing its own side, they knew very little about the other sides of the mountain. We felt that was time to look at the pensions mountain from all sides.

That is why at the Pensions Institute we have started to write a series of books that will look at pensions from each of the different side of the pensions mountain. The first two books in the series are:

- Pension economics
- Pension finance

In due course we hope to have the following additional books:

- Actuarial principles for pensions
- Pension accounting
- Pension law
- Comparative pensions systems and regulation
- Social policy and ageing populations

These books are aimed at those currently working as, or seeking to work as:

- a pension regulator
- a pension policymaker
- a pension scheme manager
- an employee benefit consultant

- a client relationship manager
- a pension lawyer
- a pension scheme auditor
- a pension accountant
- an investment manager
- an investment consultant
- a pension economist

David Blake, Director of the Pensions Institute and Professor of Pension Economics at Cass Business School, London

1
Investment Assets
Held by Pension Funds

In this chapter we consider the full range of assets in which a pension fund might consider investing. These comprise financial assets (principally money-market securities, bonds and loans, shares and collective investment vehicles), real assets, derivatives and alternative investments. We also examine how these assets are valued or priced.[1] Finally, we review the different characteristics of the different assets and how the assets are used in pension fund portfolios.

1.1 MONEY-MARKET SECURITIES

Money-market securities are short-term instruments with maturities of less than one year. There are two main classes: those that are quoted on a *yield basis* and those that are quoted on a *discount basis*.

The most important examples of money-market securities that are quoted on a yield basis are money-market deposits and negotiable certificates of deposit. Such instruments are always issued at par. *Money-market deposits* are fixed-interest, fixed-term deposits of up to one year with banks. The deposits can be for the following terms: overnight, 1 week, or 1, 2, 3, 4, 5, 6, 9 or 12 months. They are not negotiable, so cannot be liquidated before maturity. The interest rates on the deposits are fixed for the term and are related to LIBID (the London inter-bank bid rate) of the same term. The interest and capital are paid in one lump sum on the maturity day.

Negotiable certificates of deposit (CDs) are receipts from banks for deposits that have been made with them. The deposits themselves carry a fixed interest rate related to LIBID and have a fixed term to maturity, so cannot be withdrawn before maturity. But the certificates or receipts on those deposits can be traded in a secondary market; that is, they are negotiable. CDs are, therefore, very similar to negotiable money-market

---

[1] Further details of the pricing of the instruments considered below can be found in Blake (2000).

deposits, although the yields are about 0.25% below the equivalent-term deposit rates because of the added benefit of liquidity. The maturities of CDs are generally between one and three months, although some CDs have maturities in excess of one year (e.g. five years). Interest is paid at maturity, except for CDs lasting longer than a year, in which case interest is paid annually. While most CDs are fixed-rate, some have variable interest rates. For example, a 6-month CD could have a 30-day roll-over; this means that the interest rate on the CD is related to 6-month LIBID and is fixed for 30 days, and it will change every 30 days if LIBID has changed. Pension funds hold CDs in sterling and the major overseas currencies.

Another money-market security quoted on a yield basis is a *repurchase agreement* (or repo). This involves lending cash using a government bond as collateral for a specified term; that is, the bond is sold for cash with an agreement to repurchase it at a later date. The transaction from the counterparty's position is known as a *reverse* (or reverse repo).

Treasury bills, local-authority bills, bills of exchange, bankers' acceptances and commercial paper are the most important examples of money-market securities that are quoted on a discount basis; that is, they are sold on the basis of a discount to par.

Treasury bills (*TBs*) are short-term UK Government IOUs of 3 months' duration. On maturity the holder is paid the par value of the bill from the National Loans Fund. *Local-authority bills* are similar to TBs but are issued by local authorities. *Bills of exchange* (or *trade bills* or *commercial bills*) are also similar to TBs but are issued by private companies against the sale of goods. They are used to finance trade in the short term.

Bankers' acceptances are written promises issued by borrowers to banks to repay borrowed funds. The lending bank lends funds and in return accepts the bankers' acceptance. The acceptance is negotiable and can be sold in a secondary market. The investor who buys the acceptance can collect the loan on the day that repayment is due. If the borrower should default, the investor has legal recourse to the bank that made the first acceptance.

Commercial paper (CP) comprises unsecured promissory notes issued by large corporations. The notes are not backed by any collateral, rather, they rely on the high credit rating of the issuing corporation. Such corporations also tend to maintain credit lines with their banks sufficient to repay all their outstanding commercial paper. CP is therefore a quickly and easily arranged alternative to a bank loan. The sterling commercial-paper market began in 1986. *Medium-term notes* (MTNs) are unsecured notes with durations of between 9 months and 40 years whose issuance is underwritten by an investment bank.

All these securities are sold at a discount to their par value. On maturity the investor receives the par value. Explicit interest is not paid on discount instruments. However, interest is reflected implicitly in the difference between the discounted issue price and the par value received at maturity.

Money-market funds are pooled portfolios of money-market instruments offering safety and liquidity combined with yield. The instruments must be at least A1/P1 quality, have a weighted average maturity of no more than 60 days, have no more than 10% invested in the instruments of any one issuer and no more than 20% in repurchase agreements, and have daily dealing and same-day settlement. There must also be a complete separation between fund manager and custodian.

Pension fund trustees are monitoring the returns from cash more intently than in the past: it is no longer acceptable for administrators and fund managers to simply leave surplus cash, arising from contributions and dividends etc., in a bank account with the custodian.

We will illustrate the valuation or pricing of money-market instruments, using TBs as an example. TBs are quoted on the basis of a *discount rate*. The issue price of TBs is determined as the difference between the face value and the *discount*. Given the discount rate, d, the discount is found as follows:

$$\text{Discount} = 100 \times d \times (Nim/365) \qquad (1.1)$$

where *Nim* is the number of days between issue and maturity. From this we can find the issue price as:

$$
\begin{aligned}
P^{TB} &= 100 - \text{Discount} \\
&= 100 \times \left[1 - d \left(\frac{Nim}{365} \right) \right] \qquad (1.2)
\end{aligned}
$$

If we know that the discount rate on a 91-day £100 TB is 10%, then we can calculate the issue price as:

$$
\begin{aligned}
P^{TB} &= 100 \times \left[1 - 0.10 \left(\frac{91}{365} \right) \right] \\
&= 97.51
\end{aligned}
$$

implying a discount of £2.49.

The *equivalent yield*, r, on the TB is given by:

$$r = \frac{\text{Discount}}{P^{TB}} \times \frac{365}{Nim}$$

$$= \frac{d}{1 - d(Nim/365)} \tag{1.3}$$

For the TB given here:

$$r = \frac{0.10}{1 - 0.10(91/365)}$$
$$= 0.1026 \quad (10.26\%)$$

The alternative way of pricing the TB is to substitute the yield into a standard present value formula[2]:

$$P^{TB} = \frac{100}{[1 + r\,(Nim/365)]}$$

$$= \frac{100}{[1 + 0.1026\,(91/365)]}$$

$$= 97.51. \tag{1.4}$$

This means that £97.51 is the present value of £100 to be received in 91 days' time when the yield is 10.26%. This is because if we invested £97.51 for 91 days when the annual interest rate is 10.26%, we would end up with exactly £100.

The important point to note is that with all discount securities the yield is always greater than the discount rate; i.e. $r > d$. This follows precisely because the securities trade at a discount: the return of £2.49 is achieved with an investment of only £97.51, not £100; the yield is based on £97.51, whereas the discount is based on £100.

Equation (1.4) is an example of a *discounted cash flow pricing model*: the future cash flows on the security (in this case just the principal repayment on the maturity date of the Treasury bill) are discounted (using an appropriate yield or discount rate) to the current date and then summed to derive the present value of the security. The financial markets use discounted cash flow models to value securities that generate future cash flows.

---

[2] Present values are explained in Appendix A of the book.

1.2   BONDS AND LOANS

Bonds are capital-market securities and as such have maturities in excess of one year. They are negotiable debt instruments. There are many different types of bonds that can be issued. The most common type is the *straight bond*. This is a bond paying a regular (usually semi-annual), fixed coupon over a fixed period to maturity or redemption, with the return of principal (that is, the par or nominal value of the bond) on the maturity date. All other bonds will be variations on this. The frequency of coupon payments can differ between bonds: for example, some bonds pay coupons quarterly, others pay annual coupons. The coupon-payment terms can differ between bonds: for example, some bonds might not pay coupons at all (such bonds are called *zero-coupon bonds* and they sell at a *deep discount* to their par values, since all the reward from holding the bond comes in the form of capital gain rather than income); some bonds make coupon payments that change over time, for example, because they are linked to current market interest rates (*variable-rate bonds* or *floating-rate notes*), and some bonds make coupon payments only if the income generated by the firm that issued the bond is sufficient (such bonds are known as *income bonds*; unlike other bond-holders, an income-bond holder cannot put the issuing company into liquidation if a coupon payment is not paid). The redemption terms can differ between bonds: some bonds have a range of possible redemption dates (such bonds are known as *double-date bonds*) and sometimes the actual date of redemption is chosen by the issuer (*callable bonds*) and sometimes it is chosen by the holder (*puttable bonds*); some bonds have no redemption date at all, so that interest on them will be paid indefinitely (such bonds are known variously as *irredeemables, perpetuals* or *consols*). Some bonds have option features attached to them: callable and puttable bonds are examples of this, as are *convertible bonds* (bonds that can be converted into other types of bonds or into equity) and *bonds with warrants* attached to them.

Bonds can also be differentiated by their issuer. Most bonds in the UK are issued by the British Government in order to finance and manage the national debt; they are commonly known as *gilts*. Then there are bonds that are issued by UK public authorities, especially local authorities. Such bonds are secured on the revenues of the local authorities and are generally not guaranteed by the government. The duration of local-authority bonds is typically between one and five years, although most are for one year and are known as *yearling bonds*.

Private companies also issue bonds, known as *corporate bonds*. There are several classes of corporate bonds. *Debentures* are the most secured form of corporate debt (unlike in the USA, where debentures are unsecured corporate obligations). They are secured by either a *fixed* or a *floating charge* against the assets of the company. *Fixed-charge debentures* specify certain specific assets that are chargeable as security and the company is not permitted to dispose of them; in the event of default, the assets are sold and the proceeds used to repay the debenture-holders. *Floating-charge debentures* are secured by a general charge on all the assets of the company. The company is able to dispose freely of assets until a default crystallises the floating charge, at which time the charge fixes on the assets of the company that are not secured by a fixed charge. Fixed-charge debentures rank above floating-charge debentures in the event of default, but only floating-charge debenture-holders can ask for a company to be declared insolvent under the 1986 Insolvency Act.

Unsecured loan stocks are corporate bonds that are not secured by either a fixed or floating charge. In the event of liquidation, loan-stock holders rank beneath debenture-holders and preferential creditors (such as Her Majesty's Customs and Revenue (HMRC), formerly the Inland Revenue). *Guaranteed loan stocks* are corporate bonds that are not secured by a fixed or a floating charge but are guaranteed by a third party, typically the parent company of the issuer.

Asset-backed bonds are bonds backed by assets which generate predictable cash flows, such as rents and interest on mortgages, loans and credit cards (the process of issuing asset-backed bonds is sometimes known as *securitisation*).

Corporate bonds tend to be less liquid than gilts; partly this is because many bonds are held to maturity and hence not traded. Corporate bond price indices are provided by iBoxx, a consortium of investment banks.

Bonds can also be distinguished by the currency of denomination. Bonds issued in the UK in sterling by domestic issuers or foreign issuers are known as *domestic* and *foreign* (or *bulldog*) *bonds,* respectively. The coupons on domestic bonds are generally paid net of UK basic-rate income tax, whereas the coupons on bulldogs do not generally have tax deducted.

Bonds issued and/or traded in the UK in a currency other than sterling are known as *eurobonds* or *international bonds* (the introduction of the euro as a currency has changed the use of the term eurobond to avoid confusion with euro-denominated bonds). The first eurobond was issued in 1963 by the Italian company Autostrada with a coupon of 5.5% and an issue size of $15m. *Eurosterling bonds* were first issued in 1972; they have all the characteristics of eurobonds, rather than those of domestic or bulldog bonds, and the main issuers have been UK building societies seeking long-term funds to finance their home loans. The main currencies of issue of eurobonds are US dollars, euros and Japanese yen. They are generally issued by multinational companies, international agencies (such as the World Bank) and sovereign governments, and are generally unsecured. New issues are underwritten and placed with investors by a syndicate of international banks led by a *lead manager bank* (such as UBS, Merrill Lynch or JP Morgan). The size of a eurobond issue usually lies between $50m and $100m, with a maturity of about six or seven years. Eurobonds are principally in bearer form, transferable by delivery with no record of holder. The bond certificates have detachable coupon claim tokens and coupon payments are generally paid annually free of UK income tax and withholding tax. Eurobonds are usually listed on the London or Luxembourg stock markets.

The international bond market has been the most innovative of all bond markets in designing new types of bond, in terms of both coupon payments and redemption proceeds. For example, there are: *dual-currency bonds*, where the coupon payments are in one currency and the redemption proceeds are in another; *currency-change bonds*, where coupons are first paid in one currency and then in another; *deferred-coupon bonds*, where there is a delay in the payment of the first coupon; *multiple-coupon bonds*, where the coupon payments change over the life of the bond (although in a predetermined manner); *fixed-then-floating bonds*, where the coupons change from being fixed-rate to floating-rate; *floating-then-zero bonds*, where the bonds change from being floating-rate coupon bonds to zero-coupon bonds; and *missing-coupon bonds*, where a coupon payment is missed whenever a dividend payment on the issuing corporation's shares is missed.

With *index-linked* or *indexed bonds*, the coupon and principal are linked to a particular index, such as the retail price index (RPI), a commodity price index (for example, oil) or a stock-market index. Index-linked government bonds were first introduced in the UK in March 1981. These bonds are linked to the RPI and are therefore designed to give a constant *real* yield. Initially, only pension funds could invest in them, because pension funds had (partially) index-linked pensions to deliver to their pensioners. However, since March 1982, any investor can hold index-linked gilts. Most of the index-linked stocks that have been issued have annual coupon payments of 2% or 2.5%: this is designed to reflect the fact that the long-run real rate of return on the UK capital stock has been between 2 and 2.5%.

Finally, bonds can be classified according to their default risk. UK Government bonds have a negligible risk of default, whereas the unsecured loan stock of private corporations has a much higher risk of default. The *default risk* (or *credit risk*) on a bond is usually assessed in the form of a *credit rating*. There are two main services providing credit ratings: Moody's and Standard & Poor's. These are shown in Table 1.1.

Table 1.1 Credit ratings on bonds

Moody's			Standard & Poor's
Investment grade			
Smallest degree of risk – gilt-edged	Aaa	AAA	Highest rating: capacity to pay interest and repay capital extremely strong
High quality	Aa	AA	Strong capacity to service debt
Upper-medium grade: elements suggest possible future weakness	A	A	Strong capacity to service debt but susceptible to adverse changes in circumstances or economic conditions
Adequate security at present but may be unreliable over time; has speculative characteristics	Baa	BBB	Adequate capacity to service debt over time but adverse conditions likely to weaken capacity to service debt
Non-investment grade			
Speculative: uncertain future	Ba	BB	Lowest degree of speculation
No desirable investment characteristics	B	B	Speculative
Poor standing: in default or in danger of going into default	Caa	CCC	Speculative
Highly speculative	Ca	CC	Highly speculative
Lowest rated: poor prospect of ever attaining investment grade	C	C	No interest is being paid
		D	In default
(Grades B to Aa can be modified by 1, 2 or 3)			*(Grades B to AAA can be modified by '+'or '−')*

Pension funds hold all these types of bonds as well as overseas bonds; that is, foreign-currency domestic bonds issued by governments, municipal corporations and companies. However, some pension funds are prevented by their trust deeds from holding bearer bonds (which have no official record of ownership) or non-investment grade bonds.

Loans are non-negotiable debt instruments. Pension funds make long-term loans to local authorities, public and private corporations and other financial institutions. One such type of loan is a *mortgage*, which is used to finance property purchase. Loans are almost always secured with collateral provided by some form of lien. The loan can be on either a fixed or variable interest-rate basis. The term of the loan can be fixed; alternatively, there might be provision for early repayment.

We will illustrate the valuation of a bond using a straight government bond. A *straight bond* is a security that promises to pay a fixed interest or coupon payment every half-year, together with the return of principal or par value of the bond at maturity. For example, 8.75% Treasury Loan Stock 1997 was issued on 9 March 1987 and made 20 coupon payments of 4.375 on 1 September and 1 March each year together with a final payment of 104.375 on 1 September 1997.

The *fair price* of such a bond is given by the discounted present value of the cash flow stream, using the market-determined discount rate for a bond of this maturity and risk class (and also using *semi-annual* discounting)[3]:

$$
\begin{aligned}
P_0^B &= \frac{d/2}{(1 + \frac{r}{2})} + \frac{d/2}{(1 + \frac{r}{2})^2} + \cdots + \frac{d/2}{(1 + \frac{r}{2})^{2T-1}} + \frac{d/2}{(1 + \frac{r}{2})^{2T}} \\
&\quad + \frac{B}{(1 + \frac{r}{2})^{2T}} \\
&= \sum_{t=1}^{2T} \frac{d/2}{(1 + \frac{r}{2})^t} + \frac{B}{(1 + \frac{r}{2})^{2T}} \\
&= \frac{d}{r} \left[1 - \frac{1}{(1 + \frac{r}{2})^{2T}} \right] + \frac{B}{(1 + \frac{r}{2})^{2T}}
\end{aligned}
\tag{1.5}
$$

where:

P_0^B = fair price of the bond
d = annual fixed coupon payment

---

[3] The first term in the last row of Equation (1.5) is the formula for the present value of a T-year annuity making semi-annual payments. For a derivation of the present value of an annuity making annual payments, see Appendix A of the book.

B = par value of the bond

T = number of *complete* years to maturity

r = market-determined discount rate or required rate of return on a bond with this risk class and maturity (as a proportion).

For Treasury Loan Stock 8.75% 1997, we have:

d = 8.75 per 100 nominal

B = 100

T = 9 years (i.e. the date of the calculation is 1 September 1988)

r = 9.54 (assumption).

The fair price of this bond is:

$$P_0^B = \frac{8.75}{0.0954}\left\{1 - \frac{1}{\left[1 + \frac{1}{2}(0.0954)\right]^{18}}\right\} + \frac{100}{\left[1 + \frac{1}{2}(0.0954)\right]^{18}}$$

$$= 52.07 + 43.23$$

$$= 95.30.$$

The fair price of £95.30 is composed of the sum of the present value of the stream of coupon payments (£52.07) and the present value of the return of principal (£43.23).

The fair price of a perpetual or irredeemable bond (or consol) is given from (1.5) by setting $T = \infty$:

$$P_0^B = \frac{d}{r}. \tag{1.6}$$

1.3   SHARES

There are several types of shares that can be held in the firm, as specified in the *memorandum* and *articles of association*. The most important type is *ordinary shares* (also called *common stock* or *equity*). Ordinary shareholders are the legal owners of the firm and have voting privileges, the right to receive dividends and subscription privileges in the event of new shares being issued. When a firm is first established, a certain number of shares will be *authorised*. They will have a *par value*, which in the UK is typically 25p. Some or all of the authorised shares will be issued to shareholders (and are called *issued shares* or *called-up shares*), with an issue price which can exceed the par value but cannot be less than the par value. Any shares that are authorised but not issued are called *unissued shares*. All the issued shares will remain *outstanding* unless they are repurchased by the firm. Large firms will have their ordinary shares listed on the stock market, while the shares of smaller firms may be unlisted.

Most UK pension funds will hold most of their equity portfolios in UK *listed* shares (i.e. shares listed on the London Stock Exchange or the Alternative Investment Market (AIM)), but in recent years funds have begun investing in *unlisted* or *unquoted* shares. In some cases the risks are great, but so are the potential long-term rewards.

Pension funds have also invested heavily abroad since the ending of exchange controls in 1979. Initially, this was in overseas domestic equity markets, but in the second half of the 1980s, an international equity market began to develop and this has been used by pension funds. More than 600 shares worldwide have a significant international market. In the UK, equities are bought and sold on trading platforms called SETS (used for large-cap securities), SEAQ (for mid-cap securities) and SEATS plus (for small-cap and AIM securities).

The other important class of shares is *preferred shares*. Preferred shares have many of the characteristics of bonds. In particular, preferred shares offer a fixed dividend, like bonds and unlike ordinary shares. But preferred shares do not guarantee to deliver the dividend payment, and a preferred dividend need not be paid if the firm's earnings are not sufficient to fund it. But if this situation arises, preferred shareholders do not have the right to have the firm declared insolvent, unlike bond-holders. It is this fact that makes preference shareholders legal owners of the firm (along with ordinary shareholders). There are several types of preferred shares. With *cumulative preferred shares*, all unpaid dividend payments cumulate and are paid when earnings are sufficient, unlike standard preferred shares where a dividend is lost if it is not paid in any given year. *Participating preferred shareholders* have the right to have their dividends increased above the fixed rate if the firm makes large profits. There are also *redeemable preferred* and *convertible preferred shares* (which are convertible into equity).

The most commonly used method for valuing shares is the *dividend discount model* (another example of a discounted cash flow model). Suppose that a firm pays dividends once a year. In reality they usually make two dividend payments per year: an interim and a final dividend. Suppose also that an investor intends to buy the share, hold it for one year and then sell it at the end of the year. He expects to receive a dividend at the end of the year as well as the price for the share at that time. In order to make this return, he will be prepared to pay the following fair price for the share today:

$$P_0^S = \frac{E(d_1)}{1+r} + \frac{E(P_1^S)}{1+r} \tag{1.7}$$

where:

P_0^S = fair price of the share

$E(d_1)$ = expected (or forecast) annual dividend per share at the end of year 1

$E(P_1^S)$ = expected (or forecast) price of the share at the end of year 1

$E(\ )$ = expectations operator based on all current information (the average across all market participants)

r = market-determined discount rate or cost of capital or required rate of return on a firm with this risk class.

In (1.7), the return on the shareholding comprises an income element (d_1) and a capital gain element $(P_1^S - P_0^S)$. Clearly, if the return is constant, then the higher the income element, the lower the capital gain and vice versa.

It must also be the case that:

$$E(P_1^S) = \frac{E(d_2)}{1+r} + \frac{E(P_2^S)}{1+r} \tag{1.8}$$

By substituting (1.8) into (1.7) we get:

$$P_0^S = \frac{E(d_1)}{(1+r)} + \frac{E(d_2)}{(1+r)^2} + \frac{E(P_2^S)}{(1+r)^2} \tag{1.9}$$

By repeatedly substituting equations like (1.8) for $E(P_2^S)$, $E(P_3^S)$, etc., into (1.9), we get:

$$P_0^S = \sum_{t=1}^{T} \frac{E(d_t)}{(1+r)^t} + \frac{E(P_T^S)}{(1+r)^T} \tag{1.10}$$

where d_t is the dividend per share in year t. As $T \to \infty$, (1.10) becomes:

$$P_0^S = \sum_{t=1}^{\infty} \frac{E(d_t)}{(1+r)^t} \tag{1.11}$$

since we assume that the second term on the right-hand side of (1.10) vanishes as $T \to \infty$, which will occur if $E(P_\infty^S)$ is finite (i.e. we rule out *speculative bubbles* of the kind that led to the dot.com boom in the late 1990s).

For preferred shares where the preferred dividend is known, (1.11) becomes:

$$P_0^S = \frac{d}{r} \qquad (1.12)$$

which is identical to the formula for valuing perpetual bonds given in (1.6).

1.4　COLLECTIVE INVESTMENT VEHICLES

The following are the principal types of collective investment vehicle.

1.4.1　Unit trusts and open-ended investment vehicles

A *unit trust*, is a financial institution which invests in the securities of other companies. Its operations are subject to trust law rather than company law. A unit trust is formed by a trust deed made between the managers and the trustee. The managers operate and manage the unit trust's investments and charge a fee for doing so. The trustee, typically a bank or an insurance company, takes custody of the assets and keeps a register of unit-trust holders. A unit trust is not permitted to borrow funds to invest in securities; that is, it cannot engage in gearing.

The unit trust issues units, which represent claims on the assets of the unit trust. The units must be priced to equal the net asset value per unit in the unit trust. Unit trusts are *open-ended funds*, which means that they can create or cancel units as demand conditions permit. Unit trusts can specialise in different sectors of the market (e.g. shares or bonds, UK or Far East) or pursue different investment objectives (e.g. income, value or growth). Alternatively, a *balanced* unit trust will be widely invested across sectors and will aim to achieve high income with some capital appreciation.

In the past, authorised unit trusts could only invest in bonds and shares that were quoted on an approved market. The approved markets are the listed and unlisted securities markets of Europe, North America and the Far East. The investment powers of unit trusts were extended by the 1986 Financial Services Act. Authorised unit trusts can now invest in property, options, futures and commodities. Previously, only unauthorised offshore unit trusts could make such investments. Unit trusts must still abide by any restrictions contained in their trust deeds. For example, typically no more than 5% of the fund can be invested in any one investment, and the fund can typically hold no more than 10% of the issued share capital of any company.

Pension funds will tend to invest in *exempt unit trusts*; that is, trusts that are exempt from both corporation tax and capital gains tax. Exempt unit trusts are a suitable investment vehicle for small pension funds, since this enables them to get the maximum benefits from diversification at the lowest cost. A particularly suitable vehicle that enables a small, or even medium-sized, fund to invest in property is the *exempt property unit trust*. Property is a 'lumpy' investment, and a unit trust is effectively the only way for a small fund to get a weighting in this sector.

Pension fund pooling vehicles (PFPVs) are unauthorised unit trusts approved by HMRC for managing the assets of both UK and overseas pension schemes. They are generally established by trust deed and require both a trustee and a custodian. They have not been authorised by the Financial Services Authority for sale to the general public, so they can be marketed to the trustees of exempt approved pension schemes, but not to individuals through personal pension schemes (Financial Services (Promotion of Unregulated Schemes) Regulations 1991)). Their purpose is to create a tax-efficient common investment fund: investors can transfer assets (other than land or buildings) into or out of a PFPV without incurring a liability to stamp duty or stamp duty reserve tax. This is not the case with standard unit or investment trusts. As gross funds, PFPVs are priced gross on a daily basis and they also have the advantage of accruing tax credits on a daily basis, which makes it easy to calculate the tax credits due to members both active and deferred. However, providers of PFPVs are not able to give investment advice. Group personal pension schemes (GPPSs) cannot be offered via PFPVs. PFPVs were designed specifically for multinational employers running defined benefit schemes.

Open-ended investment companies (OEICs) are like unit trusts but are based on company law rather than trust law. They are eligible, under the European Union UCITS Directive on collective investments in transferable securities, for sale on the continent, where trust law is unknown. The manager of an OEIC is known as an authorised corporate direct (ACD).

1.4.2   Investment trusts

An *investment trust* is, like a unit trust, a financial institution which invests in the securities of other companies. But, unlike a unit trust, it is not a trust at all; rather, it is a company, subject, as with all other companies, to the provisions of the Companies Acts. In particular, the 1980 Companies Act created a new type of public company, namely the *investment company*, and an investment trust is an example of one of these, since it issues shares to the public.

Investment trusts use their capital and reserves to invest directly in the securities of other companies. A shareholder in an investment trust, therefore, has an indirect interest in the underlying portfolio of securities. As with unit trusts, different investment trusts specialise in different sectors of the market or pursue different investment objectives.

In 1965, the *split-level investment trust* was introduced with two types of equity capital, *income shares* and *capital shares* (usually in the form of *zero-dividend preference shares*), and a fixed life (often of twenty years). During the life of the investment trust, the income shares receive all the income from the underlying portfolio and the capital shares are entitled to all the assets. When the company is liquidated, the income shares are paid out at their par value and the remaining value is paid out to the capital shareholders.

The main differences between investment trusts and unit trusts are as follows. Investment trusts are *closed-end funds*; that is, they have a fixed number of shares which can only be increased through a rights issue. Investment trusts can engage in *gearing* (i.e., borrowing to buy more securities), whereas unit trusts are not allowed to borrow. The prices of shares in investment trusts are determined by market forces, as with the shares of all companies. The prices of unit-trust units, in contrast, are set equal to the net asset value of the underlying portfolio. The prices of investment-trust shares can differ quite substantially from their net asset value. Typically they trade at a substantial discount to net asset value. Unit trusts generally distribute all their income, whereas investment trusts declare dividends, which may be low enough to leave some retained earnings in the company.

Investment trusts provide an alternative to unit trusts as a vehicle for pension funds, especially small pension funds, to engage in low-cost diversification. In addition, the discount to net asset value of most investment-trust share prices makes them a cheap way of buying securities.

1.4.3 Insurance products

Insured funds (or *life funds*) are the collective investment vehicles of life offices. Insured funds are used to invest the premiums of life office defined contribution pension schemes and other life products such as endowment policies. A number of financial services companies have established life offices in order to run their DC pension schemes, including GPPSs. The main advantage of doing this was to accrue for future tax credits on a daily basis within the unit price of the insured fund. However, a life office can only make tax reclaims on a quarterly basis, less frequently than a PFPV, which can also accrue tax credits on a daily basis. On the other hand, life offices enjoy full value-added tax (VAT) exemption on fund management fees and administrative charges, which is not the case with PFPVs. The life office route allows a provider to offer a wider range of services such as guaranteed funds, life cover and annuities. Nevertheless, life offices face certain investment restrictions, for example, they are unable to invest in unquoted securities, and they can only accept pensions business from UK exempt approved schemes.

Endowment policies are a combination of an accumulation fund and a term life assurance policy. The accumulation fund has returns allocated in the form of annual bonuses, which, once awarded, cannot be removed, and a terminal bonus, which generally represents a large proportion of the total return. Insured funds and endowment policies have the protection of the Financial Services Compensation Scheme, which will pay up to 90% of the policy value in the event of an insurance company becoming insolvent.

Traded endowment policies (TEPs) have recently begun to appear in the portfolios of small pension funds. Only around one-third of endowment policies reach maturity, the rest are usually cashed in early with the result that the remaining annual bonuses, as well as the terminal value of the policy, are lost. Traded endowments are a way of capturing the terminal value by assigning the benefits to a new investor for a fee, with the new investor continuing to make the premiums until maturity. The transfer of ownership takes place at auctions or via dealers. The policies are also tradable in a tertiary market with a bid-offer spread of around 6%. The proceeds at maturity are tax free to exempt approved schemes.

An *insurance bond* operates in a very similar way, depending on its structure, to either a unit trust or a with-profit policy. In the first case, premiums are paid into the bond and these are used to buy a number of units in a fund that invests in a particular stock market or sector. The price of the bond is related to the total value of assets in the fund and will therefore rise and fall in line with movements in the market or sector. In the second case, the premiums earn cumulative smoothed returns through the allocation of annual bonuses (i.e., the 'profits' in 'with profits'), which cannot normally be withdrawn once they have been declared. However, in exceptional circumstances such as a stock market crash, a *market-value adjustment* (MVA) might be applied, which would lower the surrender value if the bond were encashed just after the crash.

The bonds are issued by insurance companies and come in two main types: *single-premium bonds* for lump sum investments and *regular-premium bonds*. A variation on the single-premium bond is the *distribution bond*, which pays an income, usually half yearly. Regular-premium bonds typically have two components: *initial* (or *capital*) units and *accumulation* (or *ordinary*) units. The initial units are used as a means of imposing a front-end charge of between 4 and 5%. This is achieved by cancelling the initial units. With accumulation units, all the income from the assets is reinvested; there is also an annual management charge. It is possible to switch between bonds offered by the same insurance company on a bid-price-to-bid-price basis. If a bond is surrendered before the end of the original term, its value will be calculated on the basis of the ruling bid price less a surrender penalty. The income and capital gains on insurance bonds are taxed at the basic rate. Higher rate taxpayers can take tax-free withdrawals of up to 5% a year on a cumulative basis for up to 20 years, but if the bond is cashed, any profit is taxed at a rate equal to the difference between the higher and basic rates of tax. Insurance bonds can be used by pension schemes, but pension contributions will be placed in *exempt units*, which will be free of income and capital gains taxes. Lump-sum pension contributions can also be placed in single-premium bonds, but not those that make distributions.

1.4.4 Exchange-traded funds and guaranteed growth funds

Exchange-traded funds (ETFs) are tracker funds with shares traded on the stock exchange. They began in the USA in 1993. There is no stamp duty payable and management fees are in the range 0.35–0.50% per annum, which is higher than a typical institutional investor would have to pay for index tracking (about 0.2% per annum). Barclays Global Investors calls its EFTs iShares: iFTSE 100 and iFTSE ex UK.

Guaranteed growth funds (or *guaranteed funds*) guarantee to return a minimum fund value (e.g. 98% of the original investment) whatever happens to the value of the underlying investments. They come in two types. The first type is a cash- or bond-based investment that uses part of the initial investment, together with the income generated by the cash or bond portfolio, to buy call options on an equity index, such as the FTSE 100 index; in this form the product is sometimes called an *equitised cash portfolio*. The combination of the bonds plus the call options gives complete downside protection against falls in the value of the stock market, but leaves open some upside potential if the stock market rises. The second type of guaranteed fund is equity-based and uses part of the initial investment, together with the income generated by the equity portfolio, to buy put options on an equity index, such as the FTSE 100 index. The combination of the underlying equities plus the put options on the stock market index gives complete downside protection against falls in the value of the stock market, but leaves open some upside potential if the stock market rises. The value of the guaranteed equity product in this second case equals the sum of the values of the equities and the put options held in the portfolio.

1.5   REAL ASSETS

So far we have examined the main *financial assets* that a pension fund might hold in its portfolio. But it can also invest in *real assets*: principally property, land and collectibles.

1.5.1   Property

The main classes of *property* that pension funds invest in are industrial, commercial and office property. They do not tend to invest in residential property. Large funds prefer direct property investment, whereas small funds prefer indirect investment through exempt *property unit trusts* (e.g. the Pension Fund Property Unit Trust).

The main objectives of direct property investment are the attainment of a stable rental income and an appreciation of capital value. Large funds tend to select their investments to meet the latter objective, whereas small funds appear to be more concerned with the former. All funds prefer to let their property to substantial tenants, mainly public companies and public authorities, and this preference influences the type of property invested in. In other words, the tenant is as important as the property from the investment viewpoint.

Originally, pension funds invested in the equity of property companies, but since the 1960s they have begun to invest directly in property, preferably freehold property, but leasehold property with good capital-appreciation prospects is also acceptable. Direct investment offers more influence over both the type of property purchased and the subsequent management of the property than does investment in property-company shares. Also initially, property holdings were confined to the UK, but with the ending of exchange controls in 1979, pension funds started investing in property overseas, especially in the USA.

In contrast with financial assets, real assets are differentiated by a large number of characteristics. The differences between the shares in two different companies are usually quite small, but the differences between two buildings can be enormous. It is, therefore, important to specify the set of characteristics underlying property investment. Location, design and type and conditions of tenure are three of the most important characteristics of any property. Of these, location is by far the most significant factor in letting property. If the location of a building is good, it can be let even if the design is inadequate. Similarly, a building can become difficult to let because the centre of gravity of activity has shifted in relation to its location. A typical example is the building of a new shopping centre, which reduces the popularity of a traditional shopping zone. The design of a building (both internal and external) also has an important influence on rental values. This is because a poorly designed building or, just as important, a building with an out-of-date design, might have to be internally or externally restructured if it is to be let. Rental values also depend on the types and conditions of tenure: freehold or leasehold, length and nature of leasehold, rental review periods, and so on.

Depending on its location, design and tenure conditions, property is categorised as either prime or secondary. *Prime property* is in the best location, is well-designed and in excellent condition, is freehold and let to a first-class tenant on a lease with frequent review periods. At any one time only about 1–2% of property on the market is prime property; the remainder is *secondary property*, and so is, to some extent, less desirable in terms of these three characteristics. This will be reflected in lower rental values.

Offices, shops and industrial property have different factors that should be considered when designing the investment property portfolio. With offices, the most important factor is ease of access for staff. More than one-quarter of UK workers work in offices, and half of these are in the Southeast. Proximity to transport routes has a large effect on rental values. Good design is also essential, the most important factors being: modern and sound construction, good lateral and vertical communication, efficient heating and ventilation, flexibility in terms of use of space and adequate servicing, including computing and telecommunications facilities. With shops, the most important factors are: ease of access for customers and delivery vehicles and good storage capabilities. The location restrictions for shops are less severe than for offices, since profitable shopping sites are not confined to central urban locations. With shopping types ranging from hypermarkets down to individual units, the most important type, from the investment viewpoint, is the multiple-shop complex occupied by national chain-store tenants. Specific features of such complexes that contribute to the property's value are good customer access (e.g. car-parking facilities), good pedestrian flow (otherwise customers are not attracted to shopping units on upper levels), good tenant mix (e.g. cafeteria services attract customers to the complex even though they do not maximise rental income on a unit basis), good shape, layout and upper-level access (rectangular units with wide frontage attract the most walk-in customers, while escalators and lifts are needed to attract customers to upper levels; atriums give a sense of openness, even though they are otherwise a 'waste of space') and good access by delivery, refuse and other services.

Industrial property covers light-industrial premises, heavy-industrial buildings and warehouses. Only the first and last categories make suitable investments for pension funds. Heavy-industrial buildings are generally purpose-built by the companies that intend to use them for production purposes. The main criterion for industrial property is the ease with which raw materials can be moved in and finished goods moved out. This suggests that light-industrial property and warehouses with good rail and road connections close to conurbations will make the most desirable investments for pension funds.

Given the heterogeneous nature of property, it is probably not surprising that the property portfolios of pension funds also tend to be very diverse. While many have a general mix of property, some concentrate on office and retail property, with yet others specialising in industrial property.

Property has advantages and disadvantages compared with other investments. The main disadvantages are liquidity and management time and costs. Direct purchasing of property costs 5.5% (including stamp duty), while spreads with property unit trusts are 6–8%. The main advantages of property compared with other assets are high income returns protected by upward-only rental reviews, low volatility of returns and low, or even negative, correlation with other assets, making property an excellent asset for diversification purposes.

Property is valued by discounting projected rental income. The discount rate used is typically linked to that of a high-quality corporate bond.

1.5.2   Land

In the 1970s, pension funds were substantial investors in *agricultural land*, especially in the rented sector rather than the vacant-possession sector. They acquired farms with sitting tenants and entered into sale and lease-back agreements.

Agricultural land tends to be an attractive investment when inflation is high: the appreciation in land values more than adequately compensates for the low net yields experienced with this type of investment. But if the rate of inflation falls, financial assets tend to generate higher real returns than land, and without the problems associated with managing farm tenants. This has tended to reduce the attractiveness of investing in agricultural land, and some pension funds have unloaded some of the lower-quality land from their portfolios.

1.5.3   Collectibles

Collectibles is the name given to small physical assets whose value is expected to increase over time. Collectibles therefore include works of art, precious metals, porcelain, jewellery, carpets, furniture, rare stamps and coins, antiquities, vintage wines, and so on. Collectibles, mainly in the form of works of art, have been a controversial part of pension fund portfolios ever since they first started to be collected in the 1970s. The most notable collector was the British Rail Pension Fund, which invested £40m (or 2% of its funds) in 2300 items from twenty-two categories, mainly paintings, coins, china and silver, between 1974 and 1978, and hence earned a reputation for being 'one of Europe's greatest art patrons since the Medici' (Godfrey Barker, *Daily Telegraph*, 28 February 1987).

The British Rail Pension Fund's art collection began in 1974, during the depth of the London equity-market crash, with exchange controls preventing investment abroad, no index-linked gilts available to insulate the fund from soaring inflation at home and an increase in salaries of 31%. The art collection was an attempt to generate the real returns from physical assets that had apparently disappeared from the holding of financial assets. It was, in the words of the art consultant to the fund, 'a dramatic measure taken in a moment of crisis'.

Despite being copied by many companies throughout Europe and the USA, the British Rail Pension Fund art collection has had a controversial history. First, there was the issue about whether the collection constituted trading or investment. Under HMRC rules, pension funds can only get tax relief on investments, not on trading. The collection was eventually accepted as an investment for the purposes of obtaining tax relief. Second, there are the costs of storage and insurance, which are much higher than for financial assets. Third, there is the risk of making poor investment choices that are subsequently difficult to undo. The British Rail fund subsequently admitted that it felt it had diversified into too many fields. Fourth, collectibles cannot be disposed of very rapidly, making them a relatively illiquid investment. Fifth, there are uncertainties about valuation. These investments generate no income, and the return comes entirely from capital appreciation. Given the costs of holding them, the gross return on collectibles has to exceed that on financial assets by a sizeable margin before it dominates the return on financial assets.

The BR Pension Fund decided to sell its collection, beginning in 1987, mainly for the reasons just discussed. In the event it achieved a compound rate of return of 15% per annum. This compared with an average return on all pension-fund investments over the same period of 15.1% per annum and a return on equities of 18.7% per annum. It turned out that equities had been the better investment, but BR argued that this could not have been known in 1974.

1.6   DERIVATIVES

1.6.1   Forwards and futures

Forward and futures contracts are examples of *derivative* instruments; that is, they are derivatives of an underlying *spot-* or *cash-market* security.

A *forward contract* is an agreement between two counterparties that fixes the terms of an exchange that will take place between them at some future date. The contract specifies: what is being exchanged (for example, cash for a good, cash for a service, a good for a good, a good for a service, cash for cash, and so on), the price at which the exchange takes place and the date (or range of dates) in the future at which the exchange takes place. In other words, a forward contract locks in the price today of an exchange that will take place at some future date. A forward contract is, therefore, a contract for *forward delivery* rather than a contract for immediate or *spot* or *cash delivery*, and generally no money is exchanged between the counterparties until delivery.

Forward contracts have the advantage of being tailor-made to meet the requirements of the two counterparties, in terms of both the size of the transaction and the date of forward delivery. However, one disadvantage of a forward contract is that it cannot be cancelled without the agreement of both counterparties. Similarly, the obligations of one counterparty under the contract cannot generally be transferred to a third party. In short, a forward contract is, in general, neither very liquid nor very marketable; however, some forward markets, for example the forward currency markets in London, are very liquid. Another disadvantage is that there is no guarantee that one counterparty will not default and fail to deliver his obligations under the contract. This is more likely to occur the further away the spot price is at the time of delivery from the price that was agreed at the time the contract was negotiated (that is, from the forward price). It will always be the case that it would have been better for one of the counterparties not to have taken out the forward contract but to have waited and transacted in the spot or cash market at the time called for delivery. If the spot price is higher than the forward price, the counterparty taking delivery (the buyer) gains and the counterparty making delivery (the seller) loses, and vice versa when the spot price is below the forward price. The greater the difference between the spot and forward prices, the greater the incentive for the losing counterparty to renege (that is, the greater the *credit risk*).

A *futures contract* is also an agreement between two counterparties that fixes the terms of an exchange that will take place between them at some future date. But it is very different from a forward contract and has been designed to remove many of the disadvantages of forward contracts. But the cost of achieving this has been to remove some of the advantages of forward contracts as well.

Futures contracts are standardised agreements to exchange specific types of good, in specific amounts, and at specific future delivery or maturity dates. For example, there might be only four contracts traded per year, with the following delivery months: March, June, September and December. This means that the details of the contracts are not negotiable as with forward contracts. However, the big advantage of having a standardised contract is that it can be exchanged between counterparties very easily. The number of contracts outstanding at any time is known as the *open interest* at that time.

The value of a futures or forward contract can be determined using the *cost-of-carry* (or the *cash-and-carry*) *model*. This is an example of an *arbitrage-free* or *risk-neutral pricing model*. Since futures contracts do not generate any cash flows prior to maturity, we cannot use a discounted cash flow model to value them. Instead, we use a model in which arbitrage strategies involving futures and cash-market positions are established and the fair (or arbitrage-free) futures price is such that riskless arbitrage profits cannot be made from these strategies. An *arbitrage strategy* is one in which the investor uses none of his own wealth (i.e. he borrows any funds needed to set up the investment strategy) to establish a set of investments that involve no risk and from which the investor hopes to generate a riskless positive return. In an efficient financial market, the futures price will quickly adjust to eliminate such a money machine or free lunch and we will have found the fair futures price.

Suppose that an individual can undertake one of the following two investments, one in the cash market and one in the futures market. He could borrow enough to buy an asset in the cash market, hold on to it for T years (earning any income, but bearing any *carry costs*[4], including interest on borrowed funds involved), and then sell it in the cash market and also repay the loan with interest. Alternatively, he could sell a futures contract on the asset at the current futures price and, at the end of T years, buy the asset in the cash market to deliver it into the futures market to fulfil the terms of the contract.

The profit under the second strategy is:

$$\text{Profit from strategy } 2 = P^{\text{F}} - P_T^{\text{S}} \tag{1.13}$$

where:

$P^{\text{F}} =$ current futures price for delivery of the asset in year T.
$P_T^{\text{S}} =$ spot price of the asset in year T.

Clearly, in a world with complete certainty $P^{\text{F}} = P_T^{\text{S}}$, the futures price must equal the actual future spot price. So the profit from this strategy

---

[4] Carry costs are the costs associated with buying, holding and disposing of a security, such as the bid-offer spread, brokerage costs, taxes, insurance, storage and interest on the funds borrowed to buy the asset.

will be zero on the maturity date T of the contract. There are no cash inflows or cash outflows during the life of the contract. Also, there are no carrying costs with a futures contract; all the carrying costs are associated with the cash-market transactions, but they are not incurred until the end of the period.

The profit under the first strategy is:

$$\text{Profit from strategy } 1 = P_T^S - P^S(1 + rT) + dP^S T \qquad (1.14)$$

where:

P^S = current spot price of the asset
P_T^S = spot price of the asset in year T
r = annual carry costs, including interest on loan (as a proportion)
d = gross annual yield from holding cash asset (as a proportion).

In (1.14) we assume that simple interest and not compound interest is used (otherwise we would need to use $(1 + r)^T$ rather than $(1 + rT)$) and that carry costs in the cash market are proportional to price. The cost of carry is $(r - d)$ and this can be positive or negative.

Both strategies achieve the same outcome, namely the sale of an asset in T years' time; both strategies use none of the individual's own wealth and both strategies are riskless. Two identical strategies using no wealth and involving no risk (i.e. arbitrage strategies) should, in equilibrium, generate the same profit, and that profit should be zero. We know that strategy 2 generates zero profit, and strategy 1 should also generate the same zero profit.

By equating (1.13) and (1.14), we can derive the fair futures price P_0^F:

$$\begin{aligned}
P_0^F &= [1 + (r - d)T)]P^S \\
&= P^S + (r - d)T.P^S
\end{aligned} \qquad (1.15)$$

The fair futures price is equal to the current spot price *plus* the cost of carry, and so is derivative of the spot price: this is why a futures contract is known as a derivative security. The difference between the futures and spot price is known as the *basis*, and it is clear from (1.15) that the basis, is equal to the cost of carry:

$$\begin{aligned}
\text{Basis} &= P_0^F - P^S \\
&= (r - d)T.P^S \\
&= \text{Cost of carry}
\end{aligned} \qquad (1.16)$$

The basis will be positive (this situation is known as *contango*) if the cost of carry is positive and negative (this situation is known as *backwardation*) otherwise.

1.6.2 Options, warrants and convertibles

The effect of a futures contract is to fix today the future price of some security. In other words, the price at which a security is traded in the future is locked in today. For many purposes this may be exactly what is required, but for others it is overly restrictive. An investor may be more certain of price rises than price falls, but would nevertheless like to protect against price falls. The solution in this case is to buy an option contract, in this case a put option contract.

An *option* gives to its *holder* the right, but not the obligation, to buy or sell an underlying security at a fixed price (the *exercise price* or *strike price*) at or before a specific date (the *maturity date* or *expiry date*). This right is given by the issuer or *writer* of the option. A *call* option gives the right, but not the obligation, to *buy* the security, while a *put* option gives the right, but not the obligation, to *sell* the security. In order to give effect to the right to buy or sell, the option has to be *exercised*. A *European* option can only be exercised on the expiry date, whereas an *American* option can be exercised at any time before the expiry date. In return for the insurance offered by the option, a price (called the *option premium*) has to be paid.

If, on the expiry date of the option, the option is *out-of-the-money* (which will occur in the case of a call if the price of the underlying is below the exercise price and in the case of a put if the price of the underlying is above the exercise price), it will expire worthless. If, however, on the expiry date of the option, the option is *in-the-money* (which will occur in the case of a call if the price of the underlying is above the exercise price and in the case of a put if the price of the underlying is below the exercise price), it will expire equal to its *intrinsic value* (the difference between the price of the underlying and the exercise price).

Figure 1.1 shows the profit and loss profile on two different dates of a call option on a share with an exercise price of 125p. The dashed line shows the P/L on 1 April when the underlying share is trading at 115p and the option is trading at 3p. If, on 1 April, the share price rises, so will the option price (along the dashed line) and the investment will show a

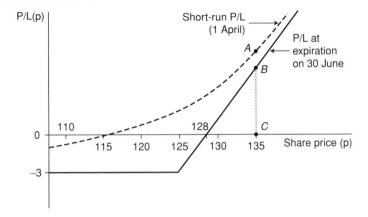

Figure 1.1   Profit and loss profile to the buyer of a call option

profit. The solid line shows the P/L on the expiry date of 30 June. If the share price is at or below 3p, the option will expire worthless and the position will show a net loss of 3p. The position breaks even with a share price of 128p and the profit on the option increases penny for penny for every penny that the share price ends up above 125p on 30 June. The vertical gap between the dashed and solid lines in Figure 1.1 is called the *time value* of the option. The option price is the sum of the intrinsic value and the time value. With the share price trading at 115p, the time value is 3p (the intrinsic value of the option is zero on 1 April, since the share is trading below the exercise price). The time value is the price that the buyer pays for the chance that the option ends up in-the-money on the expiry date of the option. The time value itself falls to zero on that date. Only intrinsic value remains and this will equal either zero if the share price is below 125p or the difference between the share price and the exercise price if the share price is above 125p. Figure 1.2 shows a similar P/L profile for a put option costing 21p on the same share.

An *equity warrant* is an option issued by a firm to purchase a given number of shares in that firm at a given exercise price, at any time before the warrant expires. If the warrant is exercised, the firm issues new shares at the exercise price and so raises additional finance. A *bond warrant* is an option to purchase more of the firm's bonds. A warrant generally has a longer maturity than a conventional option (for example, five years), and some warrants are perpetual.

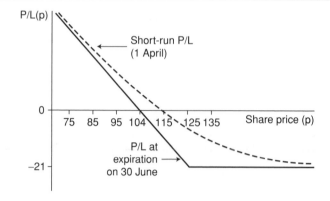

Figure 1.2   Profit and loss profile to the buyer of a put option

Warrants are usually attached to debt instruments such as bonds (known as *host bonds*). Sometimes they are detachable from these instruments and so can be traded separately; sometimes they are non-detachable. Equity warrants generally do not carry any of the rights of shareholders until they are exercised; for example, they pay no dividends and do not come with voting rights. However, warrant-holders are protected from changes to the underlying share price such as those resulting from stock splits or stock dividends through a corresponding adjustment to the exercise price of the warrant (the same is true of ordinary options). Bond warrants can either be exercised into the same class of bonds as the host bond or into a completely different class of bond.

A *convertible* is a bond (or sometimes a preferred share) that is convertible at some future date into ordinary shares (in the case where the convertible is issued by a corporation) or into another bond, known as a *conversion bond* (in the case where the issuer is a government). The conversion is at the option of the holder of the convertible, although the conversion can be forced if the convertible is also callable by the firm. A company-issued convertible is therefore a means of transforming debt into equity at some future date.

An arbitrage-free or risk-neutral model is used to value options (Cox *et al.*, 1979). Consider a European call option on a security that makes no cash payments (e.g. a non-dividend-paying share) where the security price follows a stationary binomial stochastic process, so that at the end of the period it can be higher or lower than at the start of the period, but involves no trend (i.e., is stationary over time). We assume the following notation:

P^S = current security price
p = *real world probability* that security price will rise
$1 - p$ = *real world probability* that security price will fall
r = risk-free rate of interest (e.g. $r = 0.1$)
u = multiplicative upward movement in security price, $u > 1 + r$
d = multiplicative downward movement in security price, $d < 1$

With these assumptions, the security price will increase to uP^S with probability p, or decrease to dP^S with probability $1 - p$. It is necessary that $u > (1 + r) > d$, otherwise there would be opportunities for riskless arbitrage.

Now we consider a call option on the security with an exercise price of X. The expiry value of the option has to be either $P_u^C = \max(0, uP^S - X)$ probability p or $P_d^C = \max(0, dP^S - X) = 0$ with probability $1 - p$. What is the value of the call at the beginning of the period?

To answer this question, we need to examine the return on a *riskless hedge portfolio* constructed from a long position in the underlying security and a short position in h units of the call option (where h is the *hedge ratio*). The value of the riskless hedge is given by:

$$V^H = P^S - hP^C \tag{1.17}$$

We can use the fact that a riskless hedge portfolio must have the same terminal value in all states:

$$uP^S - hP_u^C = dP^S - hP_d^C \tag{1.18}$$

in order to determine the appropriate hedge ratio, h, i.e. the number of call options to be written against the underlying security:

$$h = \frac{P^S(u - d)}{P_u^C - P_d^C} \tag{1.19}$$

The riskless hedge portfolio has a terminal value of $uP^S - hP_u^C = dP^S - hP_d^C$ in all states of the world, so that any increase in the value of the share component is always exactly offset by the fall in the value of the option component. This is why the valuation model is called a risk-neutral model: two risky securities are combined together in such a way that the combined payoff from the two securities is riskless or risk-neutral.

Because the hedge portfolio is riskless, it must be the case that the current value of the portfolio can be found by discounting the known terminal value by the riskless rate of interest:

$$P^S - hP^C = \frac{uP^S - hP_u^C}{1 + r} \tag{1.20}$$

Substituting (1.19) into (1.20) and solving for P^C, we get the fair price of the call option (P_0^C):

$$P_0^C = \frac{q.P_u^C + (1 - q).P_d^C}{1 + r} \tag{1.21}$$

where:

$$q = \frac{1 + r - d}{u - d} \tag{1.22}$$

is the *risk-neutral probability* that the security price will rise and that the option will expire worth P_u^C. Note that q does not depend on p, the real world probability that the security price will rise during the period. From (1.21), it is clear that the fair option premium is simply the discounted value of the expected expiry value of the option using risk-neutral probabilities (i.e. the discounted value of the probability-weighted sum of the values of the options in the two possible states of the world).

The option price depends on five factors: the current security price (P^S), the exercise price (X), the time to expiry ($T = 1$ in the one-period model discussed above), the risk-free interest rate (r) and the variance of the security price (σ^2). The variance of the security price, which depends on u, d and p, can be found as follows. The expected terminal value of the security price is:

$$E(P_T^S) = pP_u^S + (1 - p)P_d^S \tag{1.23}$$

and the variance is (assuming zero covariance since u and d are independent of each other):

$$\text{Var}(P_T^S) = p[P_u^S - E(P_T^S)]^2 + (1 - p)[P_d^S - E(P_T^S)]^2 \tag{1.24}$$

If the annual standard deviation[5] of the return on a security is given by σ, then the values of u and d consistent with this are given respectively

---

[5] For a definition and interpretation of standard deviation, see the appendix at the end of this chapter.

by:

$$u = e^{\sigma} \quad \text{and} \quad d = \frac{1}{u} = e^{-\sigma} \tag{1.25}$$

If the time horizon differs from one year and extends to, say, T years, then we have:

$$u = e^{\sigma\sqrt{T}} \quad \text{and} \quad d = e^{-\sigma\sqrt{T}} \tag{1.26}$$

An option is the only security whose price increases when there is an increase in risk, as represented by an increase in the standard deviation of the return on a security; this makes options very valuable trading instruments in volatile markets.

The binomial model assumes a discrete-time stationary binomial stochastic process for security price movements. In the limit, as the discrete-time period becomes infinitely small, this stochastic process becomes a *diffusion process* (also called a *continuous-time random walk* or *geometric Brownian motion*). This was the process assumed by Black and Scholes (1973) in their famous derivation of the option-pricing formula. As with the binomial model, Black and Scholes began by constructing a riskless hedge portfolio, long in the underlying security and short in call options. This portfolio generated the riskless rate of return, but the internal dynamics of the portfolio were driven by the diffusion process for the security price. The structure of the hedge portfolio could be put into a form that is identical to the heat equation in physics. Once this was recognised, the solution to the equation was easily derived.

The Black–Scholes formula for the fair price of the call option is:

$$P_0^C = P^S N(d_1) - X e^{-rT} N(d_2) \tag{1.27}$$

where:

P_0^C = fair price of call option
P^S = current price of security
X = exercise price
r = riskless rate of interest
T = time to expiry in fractions of a year (e.g. one quarter, $T = 0.25$; one year, $T = 1.00$)
σ = instantaneous standard deviation (or volatility)

$$d_1 = \frac{\ln(P^S/X) + rT}{\sigma\sqrt{T}} + \frac{1}{2}\sigma\sqrt{T} = \frac{\ln(P^S/Xe^{-rT})}{\sigma\sqrt{T}} + \frac{1}{2}\sigma\sqrt{T}$$

$$d_2 = d_1 - \sigma\sqrt{T}$$

$N(d_i)$ = cumulative probability distribution for standard normal variate from $-\infty$ to d_i.

The price of a European put option on a security that makes no cash payments is given by a relationship known as *put–call parity* (Stoll, 1969).

$$P_0^P = P_0^C - P^S + Xe^{-rT} \qquad (1.28)$$

1.6.3   Swaps

Swaps (or *contracts for differences*) are securities that involve the exchange (of cash flows) on two or more different securities. Most swaps involve combinations of two or more cash-market securities (e.g. a fixed interest-rate security combined with a floating interest-rate security, possibly also combined with a currency transaction). However, there are also swaps that involve a futures or forward component, as well as swaps that involve an option component.

Pension funds in the UK have been involved in swap agreements since the late 1960s, when they took out parallel or back-to-back currency loans to finance their overseas investments in a way that was compatible with UK exchange-control regulations then in force. The loan operated as follows. There was a matching agreement between a UK investor and an overseas counterparty, whereby the counterparty purchased overseas assets for the UK investor, who, in turn, purchased an equivalent amount of sterling assets for the foreign institution. While it involved no direct exchange of principal, this method of overseas investment was clearly very cumbersome and was made even more complicated in the period before June 1979 by additional Bank of England regulations, which required every \$100 of currency loan to be covered by \$115 of dollar assets, with the additional dollar assets being purchased with investment currency at a premium above the official rate.

The back-to-back currency loan was the precursor of the currency swap, the first example of this being between IBM and the World Bank in 1981. The swap market can be said to date from this time. The main types of swap are interest-rate swaps, basis swaps, fixed-rate currency swaps, currency-coupon swaps and asset swaps. All these swaps work on the principle that different institutions have different comparative advantages and that, as a result, there can be gains from the two institutions trading with each other. We will discuss each of them in turn.

Interest-rate swaps are the most important type of swap in terms of volume of transactions. An interest-rate swap is an agreement between two counterparties to exchange fixed interest-rate payments for floating interest-rate payments in the same currency calculated with reference to an agreed notional amount of principal (hence the alternative name, contract for differences). The principal amount, which is equivalent to the value of the underlying assets or liabilities that are 'swapped', is never physically exchanged but is used merely to calculate interest payments. The purpose of the swap is to transform a fixed-rate liability into a floating-rate liability and vice versa. The liability so transformed is, therefore, a synthetic security comprising the difference between two cash-market liabilities. The floating rate that is used in most interest-rate swaps is calculated with reference to LIBOR (the London inter-bank offer rate). Most interest-rate swaps are in US dollars, but those in yen, euros, sterling and Swiss francs are also important. Interest-rate swaps have a similar structure to interest-rate futures contracts, in the sense that the terms of the future obligations under the swap are determined today.

The motivation for an interest-rate swap is to exploit a comparative advantage and to make a gain from trade. To illustrate this, we will consider Figure 1.3, which shows the interest-rate swap established between Bank A and Bank B with funds provided by two companies, Company I and Company II. Bank A has a credit rating of AAA while B has one of BBB. The cost of borrowing directly from the companies is as shown in Table 1.2.

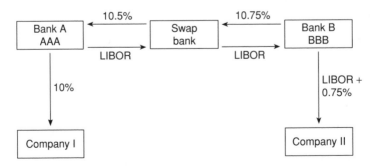

Figure 1.3   Interest-rate swap

Table 1.2 The cost of borrowing from Companies I and II

	Bank A (AAA)	Bank B (BBB)	Comparative advantage of A over B
Fixed-rate loans	10%	12%	2%
Floating-rate loans	LIBOR + 0.25%	LIBOR + 0.75%	0.5%

While A has an absolute advantage in borrowing both fixed-rate and floating-rate funds, it has a *comparative advantage* in fixed-rate loans, giving B a comparative advantage in floating-rate loans. A swap is therefore feasible if A would prefer to have a floating-rate loan and B would prefer to have a fixed-rate loan. Company I is willing to make fixed-rate loans to (or purchase the bonds of) AAA banks at a fixed rate of 10%. Company II is willing to make variable-rate loans to BBB companies at LIBOR + 0.75%.

If the swap is executed using the services of a swap bank intermediary, Bank A will make floating-rate payments to Bank B and, in return, B will make fixed-rate payments to A, as indicated in Figure 1.3. The effect of the swap on each counterparty involved might be as follows:

Bank A:	Borrows fixed at	10%
	Receives from swap bank	(10.5%)
	Pays to swap bank	LIBOR
		LIBOR − 0.5%

and so Bank A effectively borrows floating-rate funds (i.e. has created a synthetic floating-rate loan) at LIBOR − 0.5%, which is less than the rate at which it can borrow these funds directly from the market (i.e. LIBOR + 0.25%, a saving of 0.75%).

Bank B:	Borrows floating at	LIBOR + 0.75%
	Receives from swap bank	(LIBOR)
	Pays to swap bank	10.75%
		11.5%

and so Bank B effectively borrows fixed-rate funds (i.e. has created a synthetic fixed-rate loan) at 11.5%, which is less than the rate at which it could borrow such funds directly from the market (i.e. 12%, a gain from trade of 0.5%).

The swap bank:	Pays A	(10.5%)
	Receives from A	LIBOR
	Pays B	(LIBOR)
	Receives from B	10.75%
		0.25%

and so the swap bank makes 0.25% out of the deal.

Basis swaps are the same as floating/floating interest-rate swaps. This means that floating-rate payments calculated on one basis are swapped for floating-rate payments on another basis. The main examples are: the US dollar prime rate–US dollar LIBOR swap; US dollar commercial paper–US dollar LIBOR swap; and the 1-month US dollar LIBOR–6-month US dollar LIBOR swap.

Currency swaps are agreements to exchange payments in one currency for those in another. Sometimes the principal is exchanged as well as the interest payments. The structure of a currency swap is similar to a forward contract or futures contract in foreign exchange. There are two types of currency swap: fixed-rate currency swaps and currency-coupon swaps.

Fixed-rate currency swaps have three main components: the principal amounts, the exchange rate and two fixed interest rates. At the beginning of the swap, two principal amounts are 'exchanged' between the two counterparties at an agreed exchange rate. The exchange rate is usually the spot rate (the average of the bid and offer rates). This exchange of principal can either be 'notional' (no physical exchange takes place) or 'real' (a physical exchange is made). In either case, the significance of the principal is that it is used to determine both the interest payments under the swap and the re-exchange of principal when the swap matures. The interest payments that are made depend on both the principal amounts and the interest rates that are fixed at the beginning of the swap. On maturity, the principal amounts are 're-exchanged' between the two counterparties at the initial exchange rate. Fixed-rate currency swaps, therefore, allow fixed-rate liabilities in one currency to be transformed into fully-hedged fixed-rate synthetic liabilities in another currency.

The other type of currency swap is the *currency-coupon swap* or *cross-currency interest-rate*. It is a combination of an interest-rate swap and a currency swap. The format of the swap is identical to that of a fixed-rate currency swap with both initial and final exchange of principal (at the initially agreed exchange rate), but one or both of the interest payments involved are on a floating-rate basis. So, for example, fixed-rate dollars could be swapped for floating-rate sterling.

Asset swaps combine an asset and a swap to create a synthetic asset. So, for example, a fixed-rate asset can be converted into a floating-rate asset in the same currency or in a different currency.

These are the main types of swap. But other, more complicated, swaps have been executed. *Forward swaps* are swaps that are executed on a future date but the terms are agreed today. A *swaption* is an option on a swap giving the holder the right, but not the obligation, to execute the swap on a future date with the terms agreed today. A *callable swap* gives the fixed-rate payer the right to terminate the swap before the maturity date. An *index swap* is one in which the payments depend on an index, such as the retail price index, a stock index or an index of bond prices. A *zero-coupon swap* is one in which the fixed-rate payments are compounded over the life of the agreement at some agreed rate of interest and paid on the maturity date.

1.6.4 Forward-rate agreements

Forward-rate agreements (FRAs) are equivalent to forward contracts in short-term interest-rate swaps and so combine many of the features of forward or futures contracts and of swaps. In other words, FRAs are equivalent to synthetic forward-swap contracts. An FRA is a contract between two counterparties to swap short-term interest-rate payments over an agreed period at some date in the future. The buyer of an FRA locks in a fixed rate of interest, while the seller locks in a floating rate. As with a standard swap, no exchange of principal is involved. Instead, on the settlement date of the FRA, one counterparty makes a single cash payment to compensate the other counterparty for any difference between the agreed interest rate and the spot interest rate at that time.

The market in FRAs began in the early 1980s as an offshoot of the inter-bank market in forward/forward interest-rate agreements. Most FRAs (about 90%) are in sterling or dollars, although there is a growing market in euro and yen FRAs. Virtually all FRAs are quoted in LIBOR. Most are for three-sixes (that is, three-month LIBOR in three months' time), but there are other combinations available, for example, nine-fifteens (6-month LIBOR in nine months' time).

1.6.5 Synthetic securities

Derivatives can also be used to construct *synthetic securities*. These are securities constructed to replicate the payoff pattern of an underlying cash-market security.

Suppose the aim is to replicate the payoff pattern of the shares in the FTSE 100 index. This could be achieved by buying all the shares in the FTSE 100 index with the appropriate market-value weights. A much cheaper alternative would be to construct a synthetic FTSE 100 tracker using a combination of cash deposits and FTSE 100 forward contracts. This is achieved by placing, say, £1m on deposit for one year earning the one-year LIBID deposit rate of, say, 5%. At the same time, a one-year FTSE 100 forward contract is purchased at, say, 5500 from an investment bank, when the spot FTSE 100 index is 5400.

Assuming no change in the FTSE 100 index over the course of the year, the situation at the end of the year is:

- The deposit of £1m grows to £1 050 000.
- The forward expires at 5400, a loss of 100 points or £18 519 ((£1m/5400) × 100).
- A net total portfolio value of £1 031 481.

The synthetic FTSE 100 tracker has generated a return of 3.1% (which has come entirely from the cash deposit) and this will broadly compensate for the dividends that the FTSE 100 shares would have paid.

1.7 ALTERNATIVE INVESTMENTS

Alternative investments and *alternative investment strategies* (AIS) are a new class of investments/strategies that took off in the early 1990s. They are divided into three classes, according to the type of investment strategy used:

- *public market strategies*, which use exchange-traded instruments; examples are:
  - directional funds
  - hedge funds (hedge funds is a term that has become synonymous with public market strategies even though it is only one of the possible strategies)
  - arbitrage funds
  - funds of funds

- *private market* or *private equity strategies*, which use instruments that are not traded on official exchanges; examples are:
  - venture capital (venture capital is a term that has become synonymous with private market strategies even though it is only one of the possible strategies)
  - leveraged buyouts (LBOs)
  - distressed debt
- *natural resource strategies*, which involve the purchase and sale of physical, rather than financial, instruments.

The key driving force behind the growth in alternative investments has been the increasing volatility and correlation in global equity and bond markets, the principal traditional asset classes. The objective of alternative investments is to provide higher risk-adjusted returns and enhanced diversification, arising from the alternative assets' low correlation with the traditional assets that are typically held in investors' portfolios. Most of the funds discussed below have returns that have correlation coefficients with equity and bond markets in the range −0.3 to +0.3, except for long–short equity funds, which have a correlation with the equity markets of about 0.7. This has been called the quest for *decorrelation*. In principle, therefore, alternative investments are a valuable risk-reducing investment vehicle, since they offer 'structurally decorrelated performance'. In addition, alternative investments have produced some very high returns in the past. In short, the aim of alternative investments is to generate an absolute level of returns that, over time, is independent of the returns on traditional asset classes.

Alternative investments are now recognised as being one of the five main asset management styles:

- passive (index matching);
- active balanced (core);
- active specialist (satellite);
- asset–liability management (ALM);
- absolute return (alternative investments).

The first four of these strategies are discussed in detail in Chapter 7.

1.7.1   Public market strategies

We begin with *public market strategies*. The riskiest of these are *directional funds* (also known as *opportunistic funds* and *systematic trading funds*). These focus on the direction that markets are moving in and take positions based on manager opinion. The main types of directional fund are as follows (in order of decreasing risk):

- *Global macro*. Global macro managers analyse the impact of global macroeconomic variables on the principal asset classes of equities, bonds, currencies and commodities. The managers can invest in any market in the world. Strategies are usually implemented using derivatives (e.g. futures overlays), since the greater liquidity of these markets means that large positions can be established without moving the market price of the underlying security adversely. Global macro funds are, therefore, taking large directional bets (they are also sometimes known as *momentum investors*), which are also highly levered on account of the use of derivatives, with a degree of leverage of three times the fund's capital base not being uncommon. They tend to have absolute return targets and perform best when there is substantial volatility in interest rates and exchange rates. However, poor recent performance led hedge fund pioneers Julian Robertson and George Soros to close down their Tiger and Quantum global macro funds. The amount invested in these funds is now less than 5% of the total.
- *Systematic trading*. The fund manager takes a directional view of markets based on computer models that incorporate market trends and behavioural psychology.
- *Tactical trading*. The fund manager attempts to identify the principal factors (e.g. interest rates and exchange rates) determining changes in asset prices.
- *Emerging markets*. These tend to be long-only funds with significant exposure in emerging-market equities, bonds and currencies. There are two main reasons for this: a long position is difficult to hedge using emerging-market derivatives because of their poor liquidity, and short selling is generally prohibited in emerging markets. However, some emerging-market hedge funds will use main-market derivatives to at least partially hedge their exposure. Performance is usually measured against a regional market index.
- *Market timing*. These funds use technical trend-following indicators to switch out of investments that appear to be beginning a downtrend and to switch into investments that appear to be beginning an up-trend; usually the switches are between equity mutual funds and money-market funds.

- *Short selling* and *short biased*. These funds become popular during bear markets. Short positions are created by borrowing securities owned by a third party and selling them in the market (placing the received funds on deposit) with the expectation of buying the shares back at a later date, hopefully at a lower price, and returning them to the original owner in return for paying a stock-borrowing fee.
- *Active long or short*. Trend following or counter-trend following using proprietary computer models to analyse different technical factors and generate buy or sell instructions; there is no human interference with the trading decision.
- *Industry sector investing*. These funds invest in the securities of industries that are experiencing explosive growth as a result of technological or regulatory developments.
- *Long or short volatility*. These funds use option combinations to take a view on changes in the volatility of securities. For example, if volatility is expected to increase, options are purchased, while if volatility is expected to fall, options are sold.
- *Equity non-hedged*. These funds are mainly long equities, but have the ability to hedge with short sales and/or stock index options. In bull markets there is a long bias, while in bear markets there is a short bias. Also known as *stock pickers*.
- *Passive long or short*. These funds take the opposite position of commercial hedgers in order to extract an 'insurance premium'.
- *Strategic block investing*. The fund manager identifies undervalued companies, purchases a substantial block of shares in these companies and then uses these holdings to focus the attention of the incumbent management on increasing shareholder value and hence the companies' share prices.
- *Managed futures*. These use futures and options to take a directional view on market movements. They are also known as *commodity trading advisers* (CTAs). Investment horizons tend to be very short term, ranging from a few hours to no more than a couple of weeks. Some use only quantitative techniques and rely on computerised algorithms to generate buy and sell instructions. Others, known as *discretionary traders*, are more judgemental.

The most common of the alternative investments is *hedge funds*. The first hedge fund was established by Alfred Winslow Jones in the US in 1949. He created a fund that was *long* (i.e. had positive holdings) in US shares that he believed would go up in price and *short* in US shares that he believed were overvalued. The term hedge fund arises from their ability to go short and hence protect their returns from market falls. Most hedge fund managers today were formally traders from the proprietary and derivatives trading desks of the large investment banks, such as Goldman Sachs, Merrill Lynch and UBS. To cap the drain on the investment talent leaving their organisations, a number of investment banks have set up their own hedge funds: HSBC, Henderson, Gartmore, Jupiter, Martin Currie, Merrill Lynch, Alliance Capital, ABN AMRO, CSFB and SocGen. Critical to the success of a hedge fund is the fund manager's skill at identifying undervalued and overvalued securities. This skill is known as *alpha*, and good fund managers will generate positive alphas for their funds.

The main types of hedge fund are as follows (in order of decreasing risk):

- *Long–short equity*. These funds take both long and short positions in equities, hoping to profit on both sides: they are also known as *double alpha* or *market-hedged* or *equity-hedged* funds. Fundamental analysis is used to identify both undervalued and overvalued stocks. However, so-called *unengineered short positions* may need to be created, not because the fund manager believes a stock is overvalued, but only to provide capital for overweight positions. The funds tend to specialise in growth bias, value bias, small cap, large cap, sector (e.g. technology), region (e.g. Europe), long-term investing (e.g. in small-cap value companies) or short-term trading (e.g. in deteriorating growth companies). They perform best in tranquil markets where equity prices are driven by fundamental factors. Most charge a fee based on absolute return, although some charge a fee based on the outperformance of a benchmark index. This is the largest category of hedge funds with 47% of total assets.[6]
- *Event-driven*. These take advantage of pricing inefficiencies arising from corporate events. They are also known as *corporate lifestyle investing*. Examples are:
  - *Merger arbitrage funds*. These take long positions in the target company and short positions in the acquiring company. Also known as *risk arbitrage*. The fund manager's skill lies in the ability to judge the likely success of the takeover; this involves an assessment of shareholder voting intentions, regulatory reaction, the response of

---

[6] *Investments and Pensions Europe: Hedge Fund Report*, November 2001.

the incumbent management and the possibility of litigation. The takeover premium in the target's share price is likely to vanish rapidly if the merger fails.

- *Specialist credit*. These raise capital for companies that are finding it difficult to raise capital by other means. The investment vehicle is a convertible bond that is convertible into the company's equity at a discounted conversion price. Also known as *private placement arbitrage*.

- *Distressed securities funds*. As one example, the fund manager purchases convertible bonds that are trading well below par (as a result of a corporate insolvency or reorganisation combined with the distressed sale of assets) and which can be converted to equity at a later date. The market risk can be hedged by selling stock index futures. As another example, the fund manager purchases the highly collateralised senior debt of those companies in financial difficulties whose bonds have fallen from investment grade to non-investment grade (or junk) status. Institutional investors who are only able to invest in investment-grade securities must sell these bonds immediately and hence the bonds will be trading at a discount. The success of these strategies depends on the ability of the fund manager to estimate correctly the true value of the bonds in the worst-case scenario. In the second case, for example, the companies either recover and the bonds rise in value or the companies fail and the collateral backing the bonds is sold off at a price sufficient, if the fund manager's estimates were accurate, to generate a positive return to the fund.

- *Convertible arbitrage*. This involves the purchase of a convertible bond and the short sale of the underlying equity. The fund receives both the coupon on the bond and the differential between the price of the convertible and the short position. This is a bear market strategy and makes money because the gain from the short position is usually larger than the loss on the convertible. Leverage of 3–5 times the balance sheet is common.

- *Mortgage-backed securities (MBS) arbitrage*. This involves the purchase of a mortgage-backed security with credit quality and prepayment risk and the short sale of a non-prepayable US Treasury bond.

- *Long–short fixed-income*. These funds take both long and short positions in government and corporate bonds using spot, futures and swap transactions.

The term arbitrage has a very strict meaning in finance. It means buy-ing a security in one market and immediately reselling it at a higher price in another market. A pure arbitrage strategy therefore involves no risk or extended position-taking. Given the general efficiency of financial markets, it is hard in reality to find pure arbitrage strategies. In prac-tice, therefore, the term arbitrage has come to mean trading in pairs of related but mispriced securities in a way that involves as little risk as possible. The word arbitrage appeared in the description of some of the hedge funds above, but this is a misuse of the term, since the under-lying strategies involved some risk on account of having a directional bias.

The main types of arbitrage fund are as follows (in order of decreasing risk):

- *Basis trading* or *basket trading* or *portfolio trading*. The aim is to buy the underlying basket of stocks comprising an equity-market index and simultaneously sell the futures contract on the index if the basis (the difference between the futures and cash-market prices) exceeds the cost of carry (the cost of borrowing the funds to buy the basket of stocks, net of the dividends received on the stocks during the holding period when the futures contract matures); the difference between the basis and the cost of carry represents the profit on the trade at maturity when the futures contract settles and the stocks are 'delivered' against it. Leverage of 2–3 times the balance sheet is common.
- *Equity options arbitrage*. The aim is to benefit from a perceived mis-pricing of equity options by combining long positions in overpriced options and short positions in underpriced options to create synthetic payoffs.
- *Equity market-neutral* or *relative-value arbitrage*. The aim is to con-struct a portfolio with no systematic or market risk, industry bias, market capitalisation bias or geographic bias, but which is exposed to a perceived mispricing between related securities by being long relatively undervalued stocks and short relatively overvalued stocks. Leverage of 2–3 times the balance sheet is common. In theory, market-neutral portfolios have low risk and the return objective is usually to beat the risk-free rate of interest. Nevertheless, market-neutral funds tend to have a larger tracking error relative to their bench-mark, in the range 5–10%, compared with traditional funds, which tend to have tracking errors in the range 2–3%. This implies that a market-neutral fund with a tracking error of 10% that was subject to

a two-standard-deviation event (one which occurs with a probability of 5% in a given year) would deviate from its benchmark by either +20% or −20%.

- *Fixed-income or convergence arbitrage.* These exploit pricing anomalies between related fixed-income securities. Examples include: going long a 5-year bond and short a 10-year bond in the same market; going long a 5-year bond in one market and short a 5-year bond in a different market; going long and short different classes of bond of the same issuer (this is known as *capital structure arbitrage*). Again, these strategies should have low risk and the return objective is usually to beat the risk-free rate of interest. However, substantial leverage of 15–20 times the balance sheet is common.

Finally, there are *funds of funds* (FOFs). These invest in other hedge funds, typically between two and thirty, with the aim of benefiting from diversification arising from the low correlated returns of the constituent funds. For example, long–short equity funds are not likely to have returns that are correlated on the downside with convertible bond arbitrage funds. Hence, FOFs, unlike directional funds, do not depend on the market timing ability of the fund manager, an ability which empirical studies demonstrate is lacking for most fund managers (Blake *et al.*, 1999). FOFs can still specialise, say in event-driven funds, or they can choose from all types of hedge fund. They charge fees of 1–3% in addition to the fees charged by the constituent hedge funds themselves. Some funds have a performance-related component, for example, a basic fee of 1% plus a performance-related fee of 15% on gains in excess of 6%. FOFs also perform on-site due diligence when selecting the constituent funds and closely monitor their performance after selection. This is useful for investors, such as small pension funds, with low *governance budgets*; that is, low capacity to manage their investments in terms of time, expertise and organisational structure. However, there is a scarcity of hedge fund selectors and many new FOFs use hedge fund consultants to select the constituent funds. Increasingly, FOFs treat hedge funds as a talent pool rather than an asset class.

1.7.2 Private market or private equity strategies

Private market strategies, more commonly known in the UK as *private equity strategies*, are much more difficult to value than public market strategies, since, by definition, there is no liquid market in the underlying securities. The invested funds are tied up for a number of years. Such investments are therefore not suitable for investors with short-term liquidity requirements, although there is a market for secondary interests (albeit at a substantial discount to value). However, the benefit from patient investing is high long-term returns.

The *venture capital* (VC) industry began in what became Silicon Valley, south of San Francisco, and around Boston after the Second World War. A group of *venture capital partnerships* was established to invest in start-up and early-stage companies in the (computer and information) technology sector. The partnerships developed strong local networks and a high degree of internal expertise in technology. There was no such similar development of a VC industry in the UK. Subsidiaries of UK banks calling themselves venture capital firms began in the 1970s and 1980s to invest in unquoted companies, but little of this was in VC as defined in the US, mainly because of a dearth of good investment proposals. The VC industry that did develop in the UK financed a different kind of project, namely buy-outs and buy-ins of mature companies, usually the subsidiaries of quoted companies. The investee company took on substantial debt in the belief that it could be serviced from the cash flows into the company and in so doing magnify the value of the equity, hence the term leveraged buyout (LBO). In the US, VC and LBOs are separate categories of private equity, with the funding provided by different types of investor with different backgrounds. Investors tend to invest in one type or the other.

The main types of venture capital fund are:

- *Early-stage funds*. These provide seed capital for product development and initial marketing during the first three years of the life of a company.
- *Development funds*. These invest in funds in an expansion phase that are in need of capital to expand or make acquisitions.
- *Mid-management buy-out/buy-in funds*. These finance buy-outs (MBOs) of existing businesses by the current operating management or provide funds for an external management group to buy into (MBIs) an existing company, both in the range £2–£10m of invested equity.
- *Large management buy-out/buy-in funds*. These finance buy-outs and buy-ins above £10m of invested equity. These funds also finance institutional buy-outs (IBOs), where a private equity firm purchases a company with the aim of giving a stake at a later stage to the incumbent or incoming management, and leveraged build-ups (LBUs), where a

private equity firm buys a company as principal with the aim of making further related acquisitions in order to develop an enlarged business group.

- *Generalist funds.* These invest in all sizes of company at all stages of development in both the UK and globally.
- *Technology.* These specialise in the technology sector.
  Non-technology. These invest in all sectors except technology.

The typical lifecycle of a venture capital fund is ten years from initial investment to final exit, when the fund is wound up, the investments are liquidated and the gains realised. The following exit methods are used: trade sale (most common), flotation on a stock exchange (common), a share repurchase by the company or its management or a refinancing of the business (least common). Secondary purchases of the company by another private equity firm are becoming more common.

With venture capital, the biggest risk is choosing a poor fund manager, since it takes far longer than with other investments to ascertain whether the fund manager is selecting good investments or not. This is partly because of reliance on interim valuations, which can be largely subjective. The other two factors influencing returns are the valuation at acquisition and the strength of the underlying economy. In terms of valuations, price–earnings multiples have increased for large transactions where competition amongst fund providers has increased, but they are falling for small-scale transactions where competition is less aggressive.

There are a range of vehicles for investing in venture capital and private equity:

- *Venture and development capital investment trusts* (VDCITs) have the advantage of daily measurement of performance and high liquidity, and they are able to leverage up by borrowing; one of the largest funds is Schroders Ventures International Investment Trust (SVIIT).
- *Funds of funds* (FOFs) have included funds determined by a gatekeeper based on his research and knowledge of management expertise and historic performance, but there are two layers of fees, and valuations are made no more frequently than quarterly due to difficulties valuing unquoted companies prior to sale or flotation; high minimum investment of £5m.
- *Limited partnership venture capital funds* have between 10 and 30 limited partners with 10-year investment horizons, a high level of

control and accountability. They use general partners with up-to-date knowledge of venture capital fund managers to structure portfolios; general partners receive a performance fee called *carried interest* or *carry* if the performance of the fund exceeds a hurdle rate. Valuations are no more frequently than quarterly due to difficulties valuing unquoted companies prior to sale or flotation. This is the most popular investment vehicle.

- *Dedicated venture capital* or *private equity funds* are managed directly on behalf of the investor (typically an institutional investor such as a pension fund or insurance company), so there is a high level of control and accountability, but they require substantial funds to be commercially viable and to obtain good diversification.

- *Direct investment in unquoted companies.* This gives full control with direct access to companies, but requires substantial funds to be commercially viable and to obtain good diversification, a high level of staff expertise, considerable commitment and a good flow of investment opportunities (only 1% of proposals are accepted).

Another issue is *draw downs*. These are payments to the partnership by investors in order to finance investments. Funds are usually drawn down from investors on a deal-by-deal basis and investors have to budget for these calls, the timing of which is hard to predict.

Most venture capital funds are members of the British Venture Capital Association and have their performance measured by PricewaterhouseCoopers and published annually in the *BVCA Private Equity and Venture Capital Performance Measurement Surveys*. An example of a venture capital management group is CIN Venture Managers, or CINVEN, which operates the venture capital operations of the former British Coal Pension Fund and the British Rail Pension Fund. CINVEN was set up by the British Coal Pension Fund in 1976 and the pension fund has around 3% of its assets in venture capital investments. CINVEN is the second-largest venture capital management group after 3i.

1.7.3 Natural resources

These are specialist strategies with higher transaction costs than the above strategies.

Natural resource strategies involve the purchase and sale of physical, rather than financial, instruments; examples are:

- commodities;
- energy;
- timber.

Property (this is a US classification, since, in the UK, property is regarded as a mainstream asset class); examples are:

- private real estate, including farmland;
- real estate investment trusts (REITs).

1.8   SOCIALLY RESPONSIBLE INVESTMENT

In recent years, *social, environmental and ethical* (SEE) matters have had an increasing role in influencing pension fund investment decisions under the label of *socially responsible investment* (SRI). The 1995 Pensions Act requires pension funds to consider SRI matters and from July 2000 to disclose in their statements of investment principles whether they have an SRI policy, but it does not require them to adopt an SRI policy.

The Association of British Insurers (ABI) has published guidelines on how company annual reports should comply with SEE matters. The guidelines cover five areas of corporate activity: employment, the environment, human rights, communities and business relationships. Investors should expect to find answers to the following questions:

- Has the company made any reference to SEE matters? If so, does the board take these into account regularly?
- Has the company identified and assessed significant risks and opportunities affecting its short- and long-term value arising from its handling of SEE matters?
- Does the company state that it has adequate information for identification and assessment?
- Are systems in place to manage the SEE risks?
- Are the remuneration incentives relating to the handling of SEE risks included in risk-manangement systems?
- Does directors' training include SEE matters?
- Does the company disclose significant short- and long-term risks and opportunities arising from SEE matters? If so, how many different risks/opportunities are identified?

- Are policies for managing risks to the company's value described?
- Are procedures for managing risk described? If not, are reasons for non-disclosure given?
- Does the company report on the extent of its compliance with its policies and procedures?
- Are verification procedures described?

SRI investments can be made on the basis of recommendations from organisations such as the Ethical Investment Research and Information Service (EIRIS) or the Investor Responsibility Research Center (IRRC). EIRIS, for example, has a list of SRI companies, all of which are included in the FT-Actuaries All Share Index. The list contains mainly small companies and excludes companies with interests in tobacco and brewing. It also excludes the finance sector, such as banks and insurance companies. Funds based on the EIRIS list have in the past outperformed the FT-Actuaries All Share Index, so SRI does not necessarily imply low returns. There is also a FTSE4Good index of fifty qualifying FTSE 100 companies: it outperformed the FT-Actuaries All Share Index during its first year of existence beginning in October 2000.

The following fund managers run SRI funds for pension funds: Friends, Ivory & Sime (Stewardship Pension Fund, Institutional Ethical Exempt Fund and Balanced SRI Managed Pension Fund), Henderson Global Investors (Global Care Growth OEIC, Global Care Income OEIC and Global Care Asia–Pacific Fund), Jupiter Asset Management (Jupiter Ecology Fund, Jupiter Environmental Opportunities Fund and Jupiter Global Green Investment Trust), Morley Fund Management (Norwich Sustainable Future Managed Fund), Scottish Widows Investment Partnership (Scottish Widows Environment Fund and Abbey Ethical Trust) and Standard Life (Pension Ethical Fund).

1.9   GLOBAL CUSTODY

Pension funds use *global custodians* to hold the assets that they purchase. The services provided by global custodians are listed in Table 1.3.

In the past, pension funds used the custodial services provided by their fund managers, which, in a multi-manager pension fund, meant using multiple custodians using different reporting formats. During the 1990s, pension funds began to switch to a single custodian independent of these fund managers. By 2000, even fund managers were beginning to outsource their back office to custodians, since, by using the

Table 1.3   Global custody services

Service	Components	Fee type
Safe-keeping	Physical custody Registration of securities Cash forecasting	Basis points
Transactions	Settlement of trades Dividends, interest and tax reclaim Investment record-keeping (using a master record-keeping (MRK) service) Corporate actions Clean payments	£ per trade
Reports	Statutory reporting on the asset holdings on a worldwide basis (web reporting, electronic download and paper format) Accounting Taxation Custodian performance Market updates to alert trustees about regulatory changes in different markets	£ per portfolio p.a.
Corporate governance	Voting services, proxies	£ per portfolio p.a.
Value added	Performance measurement and attribution Compliance reporting Unit trust administration	£ per portfolio p.a.
Revenue added	Securities lending Foreign exchange Cash management	Mixed

Source: *Pensions Week*, 17 July 1998.

custodian's systems, a fund manager can access all the data, analyse it via a web-enabled browser application and download it into reports instantaneously.

The main global custodians are large banks, such as Northern Trust and State Street. The banks have overseas offices, which act as *sub-custodians* for pension funds' international asset holdings, thereby helping to preserve credit quality in foreign marketplaces. Standard client agreements cover negligence, fraud, wilful default and insolvency protection; the main exclusions are national intervention, acts of war, terrorism, revolution, strikes, nuclear fusion and acts of God. Pension funds with assets of £500m or more can get global custodial services for just 0.005% (half-a-basis point).

An example of the benefits of using a global custodian is the ability to monitor the efficiency of the foreign exchange transactions conducted by the fund manager against the quoted mid-market rates for the relevant currency pairs. Another example is securities lending, whereby the pension fund assets held by the global custodian are lent to other investors (say to facilitate a short sale transaction) in return for a securities lending fee, which enhances the return to the pension fund. Recent added services include voting services in response to increased awareness and involvement by pension funds in corporate governance and compliance monitoring.

1.10   DIFFERENT ASSET CHARACTERISTICS AND USES

Pension funds hold some or all of these types of assets in their portfolios. The different assets have different characteristics and different uses. In this section we examine some of these characteristics and uses.

1.10.1   Asset characteristics

The first characteristic is the *degree of liquidity*. This depends on both the marketability of a security and the transaction costs involved in the liquidation; it also depends on the relative volume of a security coming to the market at any single time. Cash and money-market securities are the most liquid of assets and property the least; between lie, in order of decreasing liquidity, gilts, ordinary shares, options, futures, debentures, loan stock, preference shares, loans and mortgages.

The second characteristic is the *degree of capital-value certainty* (also called *price risk*). Some assets, such as money-market securities, loans and mortgages, have a high degree of capital-value certainty in nominal terms. Others, such as fixed-income bonds and index-linked bonds, have capital-value certainty only at maturity – the former in nominal terms, the latter in real terms. Before maturity their capital values move inversely with nominal and real interest rates respectively (see Equations (1.5) and (1.6) and also Appendix C of the book). Other assets, shares, options and property, for example, exhibit price risk and so have no capital-value certainty at any stage.

The *degree of income certainty* is the third important characteristic of assets. Money-market securities and fixed-term fixed-income bonds and preference shares have complete, or at least a high degree of, income certainty, while fixed-rate loans and mortgages only exhibit complete income certainty if there is no early repayment. In contrast, the dividend payments on shares are not guaranteed, and derivative securities such as futures and options make no income payments at all.

The next characteristic is *inflation risk*. Only index-linked bonds offer a complete hedge against inflation. Securities such as ordinary shares, property and commodities tend to be good inflation hedges over the long term, although this is not guaranteed. Fixed-income bonds, loans, mort-gages, cash and money-market securities are poor inflation hedges, since they all lose value as the price level increases. In between lie variable-rate securities, such as floating-rate notes: if interest rates increase with inflation, the income on variable-rate securities increases to compensate for falling real capital values.

The fifth characteristic is *default risk*. Only government-guaranteed stocks and direct holdings of property are entirely free of default risk. All private-sector securities have some risk of default, unless they are backed by effective collateral. For example, mortgages are fairly safe, since they are backed by property (that is, they are *asset-backed*).

The sixth characteristic is *currency* (or *exchange-rate*) *risk*. This is the risk that affects all securities held in foreign currencies: fluctuating currency values will lead to fluctuating capital values for all overseas securities when measured in sterling.

The final characteristic is *correlation* with the returns on other assets. If an asset, such as alternative investments, has a low correlation with the returns on other assets, it is useful for diversification purposes, since it helps to reduce the volatility of the returns on the overall portfolio.

1.10.2   Asset uses

Having discussed the various characteristics that assets possess, we can consider how pension funds use assets in their portfolios. Most assets are used as part of sophisticated portfolio-management strategies, the most important of which are discussed in Chapter 7. The portfolio composition of pension funds differs depending on whether the markets are volatile or stable, and on whether the funds themselves are mature or immature.

Take, for example, money-market securities. Pension funds are, in general, very long-term investors, but they will hold short-term se-curities for one of two reasons. First, pension funds receive peri-odic cash-flow payments. These can be dividend payments on their share-holdings, coupon payments on their bond-holdings, rent on their property-holdings, as well as contribution payments from both employees and the sponsoring firm. Such receipts, although fairly predictable, will often be irregular and generally will be in small amounts. It will often be inconvenient to reinvest these payments in the capital markets the moment that they are received. Instead, they will be invested in safe but high-yielding money-market securities until a sufficient amount has been accumulated to invest in longer-term assets. Their first use will be to fund pensions in payment, however.

Secondly, money-market securities are held for the purpose of *market timing* (or tactical asset allocation). In periods when the capital markets are depressed, such as during the share-market crashes of 1974–5, October 1987 and 2000–03, pension funds will build up fairly large holdings of liquid assets for strategic reasons. This will be done either by reducing directly their holdings in shares, bonds and so on, or by refraining from investing cash inflows in such instruments. In either case, liquid-asset holdings are built up in readiness for investing in the capital markets when the bear market bottoms out and a new bull market starts.

In stable markets, immature pension funds will want to go for long-term real growth; that is, they will want to generate a real return on their investments after allowing for inflation. They will also want to maintain a fair degree of liquidity. This will be achieved by having a portfolio dominated by equity. Shares suffer from both volatility and default risks, but these can be reduced through *diversification*; that is, by holding a widely spread portfolio of shares, both domestically and overseas. Overseas assets will still suffer currency risk, but this risk can be *managed* or *hedged* using *exchange-rate futures, forwards* or *options*. Shares also suffer from capital-value uncertainty or price risk; this risk can be hedged using *stock-index futures* and *options*. In addition, over the long term, ordinary shares tend to provide good inflation hedges. The price risk associated with bond-holdings is the risk of increases in interest rates, sometimes called *interest-rate risk*; this risk can be hedged with *bond futures* and *options*. Pension funds can also write options to generate premium income: for example, during bull markets pension funds can write put options, while during bear markets they can write call options, since in neither case are the options likely to be exercised.

Real assets differ substantially from financial assets in a number of important respects. Direct holdings of real assets tend to be better long-run hedges against inflation than financial assets, even compared with those financial assets such as equity that represent indirect claims against real assets. But against this, the markets for real assets are less liquid than those of financial assets. It is simply not possible to issue new Old Masters; land can be reclaimed, but this takes time; and buildings can be rebuilt, but this also takes time as well as requiring planning permission. Similarly, real assets cannot be bought and sold in secondary markets as cheaply or as quickly as can financial assets. Related to this, real assets are not such close substitutes for each other as are financial assets. All this again tends to make real assets suitable only as long-term investments, rather than short-term, speculative investments. Indeed, in the short term, real assets can experience substantial falls in value (both nominal and real), and this risk is difficult both to predict and to hedge against.

As pension funds mature, a different investment strategy is required. Income certainty and capital certainty become more important investment objectives than real capital growth. When pension funds are immature, their long-term liabilities can be met with an asset structure dominated by equity. However, as pension funds mature, the liabilities become increasingly short-term. Pension payouts have to be paid according to a definite schedule, and short-term equity values are too volatile to guarantee meeting this payment schedule. Instead, the asset allocation has to be moved away from equity towards fixed-income and indexed bonds as pension funds mature, since the cash flows on these instruments are more reliable than those on shares. This will also have the effect of reducing the likelihood of an actuary's valuation of the pension fund's assets and liabilities revealing an actuarial deficit, with its consequences for increased contribution rates. Interest-rate and inflation swaps can be used to fill gaps in the underlying bond portfolio, as the section on liability-driven investment in Chapter 7 shows.

Related to income certainty is capital-value certainty. Pension funds must ensure that the value of their assets equals the actuarial value of their liabilities. The volatility of equity prices makes this objective much more difficult to achieve with mature funds; even if the equity-price risk can be hedged, this cannot be done without some cost. However, fixed-income bonds can be used to achieve at lower cost the desired objective with respect to capital-value certainty. This is because the volatility of bond prices is much less than that of equity prices, since bond-price movements are tied down by their known value on the maturity date. Before maturity, the bond's capital value can be hedged using *interest-rate futures, options* or *swaps*.

Swaps have a number of uses. One of the most important is as a hedging instrument. For example, a pension fund holding fixed-coupon bonds that expected interest rates to rise could execute an *asset swap* and earn a return related to LIBOR. Of course, given the capital loss that would be expected on the bonds, it might still be better for the pension fund to sell the bonds rather than undertake the swap. Another use of swaps is as an instrument for asset and liability management. On the liability side, swaps (e.g. inflation and interest-rate swaps) can be used to reduce funding costs, while on the asset side they can be used to increase returns. This last factor is of particular value to pension funds.

It is important to examine the risks involved in executing swaps. There are two main types of risk facing the swap counterparties: *credit risk* and *position* or *market risk*. Credit risk is the risk that the other counterparty defaults on his obligations. Position or market risk is the risk that market interest rates or exchange rates diverge from the rates agreed in the swap, leading to a position loss for one counterparty. While credit as such is not extended when a swap is executed, there is a risk that the promised payments and receipts under the swap are not, in fact, made. The present value of these future payments and receipts (discounted at the spot or swap interest rate[7]) represents the extent of exposure. Credit risk declines as the swap reaches maturity. Position or market risk, however, varies over the life of the swap according to the extent of movements in interest or exchange rates. The two types of risk are not unrelated. For example, a swap might be showing a position gain but the other party then defaults.

The use of derivative instruments such as futures, forwards and options by UK pension-fund managers has increased substantially since the passing of the 1990 Finance Act, which exempted them from tax on their trading income from futures, forwards and options. As a result of this change in the tax regime, turnover on the FTSE 100 stock-index futures contract on the London International Financial Futures and Options Exchange (LIFFE) increased by 40% during 1990.

Stock-index futures are the most frequently used of the derivative products. Futures involve considerably lower transaction costs than options and, for institutional investors, stock-index futures involve lower transaction costs than trades involving the underlying stocks. The most important use made of stock-index futures by active pension-fund managers is to make rapid tactical changes to asset allocation through *pre-positioning*. In other words, increased or reduced exposure in any particular market is achieved through the purchase or sale of stock-index futures, which locks in, respectively, the purchase or sale price

---

[7] Spot and swap rates are explained in more detail in Appendix B of the book.

of securities prior to buying or selling them in that market. Stock-index futures can also be used to undertake *overlay strategies*, that is, temporary adjustments in exposure without any subsequent transactions in the underlying cash portfolio. Another important use of stock-index futures is as a temporary repository of surplus cash, thereby ensuring that funds are always invested and so avoiding the risk of missing an upturn.

Forward-currency contracts are the second most frequently used of the derivative products (the size and efficiency of the forward-currency market in London destroyed its currency futures market). Forward-currency contracts are used mainly to hedge short-term exposures in foreign bond markets. They are not used to hedge long-term exposures in equity markets; indeed, currency exposure is often regarded by investors as one of the main benefits of international diversification.

While the use of derivatives is increasing amongst UK pension-fund managers, it is nevertheless still not as widespread as in the USA. The main reason for this is the reluctance of trustees to use a product that can involve unlimited losses or might involve being 'fleeced by unscrupulous floor traders' (as was proved by the Federal Bureau of Investigation in the case of the Chicago futures markets in the late 1980s). Another reason is the cost of operating computer systems that deal with the administration (clearing, settlement, marking to market, and so on), monitoring and performance of options and futures positions. Finally, there are problems in understanding the complexities of derivative products (especially options), as well as doubts about the operational effectiveness of derivative markets when they are needed most: the failure of equity futures markets during the October 1987 crash led to substantial disillusionment in the fund management profession.

The first comprehensive study of the benefits to institutional investors from using alternative investments as part of their overall portfolios was made by Schneeweis *et al.* (2000). The key findings of this study are:

- Under past (e.g. historical) market environments, a portfolio of hedge funds and managed futures offers improved risk and return opportunities when considered as an addition to both a traditional equity portfolio and a mixed portfolio (including equity, bonds and property).
- Under forecasted return relationships consistent with general market conditions, a portfolio of hedge funds and managed futures offers improved risk and return opportunities when considered as an additions to both traditional equity and mixed portfolios.

- Under alternative market conditions (e.g. extreme low/high returns of the equity and bond portfolio), the benefits of a portfolio of hedge funds and managed futures have a greater impact on risk reduction and return enhancement. More importantly, the portfolio of hedge funds and managed futures offers managed portfolio returns not obtainable through other traditional equity, bond and property investments.
- The benefits of a portfolio of hedge funds and managed futures are not sensitive to the globalisation of the equity and bond portfolio. The high correlation between international equity markets as well as the high correlation between international bond markets, especially in periods of extreme market movements, makes the results (improved risk and return opportunities) for the inclusion of a portfolio of hedge funds and managed futures consistent across a wide variety of traditional asset portfolio holdings. However, the degree of benefit will depend on the prevailing market environment and the degree to which that market environment is anticipated.

These findings have been confirmed by Jaeger (2001). He concludes:

- AIS have come a long way to satisfy the needs of institutional investors. From transparency to liquidity, strategy diversification to risk management, the industry has advanced to such a stage that it nears recognition as its own asset class. The broad range of strategies and sectors in AIS investing demonstrate very attractive risk–reward characteristics. Negative, zero and low correlations to traditional assets and to each other offer attractive capacities for diversification within the investor's global portfolio. For periods when traditional markets suffer, some AIS, in particular managed futures, display consistently positive returns. All the benefits of AIS work to improve dramatically the efficient frontier of the traditional portfolio, producing significantly higher returns with substantially lower risk.
- It is interesting to look at how AIS investors fared during times of market turmoil. Although quite diverse in their returns, hedge funds and managed futures generally showed much better performance than traditional investments during these periods. Interestingly, in difficult market environments, funds of funds have shown much worse returns than the average strategy sector (even after accounting for the extra fee level). I believe this performance pattern mirrors the fact that AIS allocators tend to behave in a pro-cyclical way and overweight the best-performing strategy sectors of the recent past. With too much money flowing into these strategies they are often the first with problems in

the next period of market turmoil. Secondly, futures strategies generally performed well during these critical periods. This justifies their presence as a 'hedge' in any multi-manager portfolio.

- As a final note, the increasing demand for AIS products from institutional investors and the generally higher level of investor sophistication render the 'black box' approach (i.e. investing in nontransparent and illiquid funds) unsuitable. A focus on increased liquidity, transparency and risk management will enable the industry to continue growing as rapidly as in recent years. The increased interest on the part of institutional investors has led to recognition that particular risks are being addressed systematically and to better awareness of the benefits of AIS in the institutional portfolio.

Alternative investment funds have some key differences compared with traditional investments:

- Lower liquidity – entry and exit are monthly or quarterly, rather than instantaneous.
- Capacity constraints – these can be reached more rapidly with some strategies than with others; strategies involving active trading have to work with less capital to avoid the risk of moving prices against the position; strategies involving substantial short positions also rapidly hit capacity constraints, unless short futures positions are used instead, since short positions have to be traded more actively, replaced more frequently and diversified more completely.
- They can engage in substantial leverage – this can increase risk and lead to substantial losses if an event (e.g. Russia's bond defaults in 1998) obliges managers to unwind positions rapidly, thereby causing spreads to widen and margin calls on futures positions to be made, which, in turn, trigger forced sales, leading to losses spiralling.
- Generally poorer price information – there is a range of providers and indices to track performance, but there is no pre-eminent provider of information and no single index has widespread acceptance in the industry.
- Misleading performance data – sometimes based not on actual performance but on reporting simulated past performance from back-testing a notional portfolio.
- Higher performance-related fees – based on a percentage of profits in the range 15–20% (plus a flat fee of 2% of assets under management).
- Offshore domicile – in less-regulated centres, such as the Virgin Islands or the Bahamas, although the managers are generally onshore,

for example in Dublin, and are subject to an established regulatory authority; Ireland permitted hedge funds to be authorised and listed in December 1999.

- Lower transparency – only limited information given on positions held.
- Restricted entry – sometimes by invitation only in order to control the growth of funds and maintain maximum flexibility in investment decision-making.
- High minimum investment.
- Relatively short lifecycles – in the range 5–10 years, so there is a danger of buying into a fund at its peak performance.

To overcome these problems, many investors invest via reputable specialist advisers, who generally recommend funds of funds in order to create a diversified structure.

There are two main types of risk with alternative investments: manager-specific risks and portfolio-specific risks. The principal manager-specific risks are:

- Style drift – the fund deviates from the stated aims.
- Excessive leverage.
- Ineffective risk management or failure to maintain market neutrality, especially in volatile markets; for example, a long–short equity fund with both a small-cap bias and a long bias (on account of the greater difficulty of shorting small-cap stocks with little free float) is susceptible to a flight to blue-chip quality in the event of a severe market stress, as happened in autumn 1998, and hence to losses on both long and short exposures.
- Poor alpha portability – a *star* fund manager skilled in one speciality is transferred unsuccessfully to manage another part of the fund.
- Poor predictability of events – for example, a stock initially believed to be overvalued is shorted and its price falls steadily, showing a profit to the position, but another investor, believing the stock to be oversold, makes a takeover bid for the whole company, causing a sharp upward movement in the stock price before the fund's short position is closed, leading to a net loss on the position.
- Poor managerial control of the fund's traders.
- Unreliable back office.
- Uncontrolled growth in assets, resulting in the fund hitting liquidity constraints.

The principal portfolio-specific risks are:

- inadequate diversification, including regional diversification;
- poor sector selection;
- hidden macro biases;
- an increase in downside correlation in a crisis (sometimes called skew risk).

Although institutional investors have been attracted to alternative investments by the promise of diversification and the very different risk–return profiles from traditional investments, they have been discouraged by the perceived risks and, in some European countries, by regulations.

To get around these problems, capital guarantees (e.g. in the form of unsubordinated structured notes from highly rated issuers) have begun to be offered with a number of public market strategies, especially hedge funds. These eliminate the risk by offering investors 100% capital protection, while enabling them to benefit from most of the upside potential. They also address regulatory concerns for investor protection. In addition, the structured notes are treated as an interest-rate security for tax, accounting and administration purposes. The annual fee for the guarantee is 1–2%. It is also possible to have greater upside participation if the investor is prepared to accept less than 100% capital protection.

Capital-guaranteed hedge funds have the same defensive features as bonds, but have the potential for higher returns. As a result, the market for these products is growing rapidly.

The most common guarantee is the *dynamic hedge* (also known as *portfolio insurance*), since this is the easiest structure for the guarantor to hedge. The guarantor monitors a *reference zero-coupon* (i.e. spot or swap) *yield curve*, which indicates the amount of capital that would have to be invested in zero-coupon bonds at each point during the holding period in order to guarantee a 100% payout at maturity. If the net asset value (NAV) of the hedge fund exceeds the amount of capital implied by the reference curve, then 100% of the investor's funds will be invested in the hedge fund. If the NAV of the hedge fund falls below the reference curve capital requirement, the guarantor will switch part of the hedge fund into zero-coupon bonds. In the extreme case, if the fall in the NAV of the hedge fund is sufficiently great, there might have to be 100% switch into zero-coupon bonds. This locks in a risk-free return for the remainder of the holding period, since it is no longer possible to switch back into the hedge fund and ensure that the guarantee can be honoured. A highly volatile hedge fund might have as much as 80% invested in zero-coupon bonds.

Other methods for securing guarantees include:

- Zero-coupon bonds with embedded call options. The capital guarantee is provided through a zero-coupon bond, while the call options provide exposure to the hedge fund.
- Total return swap. Again, the capital guarantee is provided through a zero-coupon bond; the exposure to the hedge fund comes from the total return swap with a bank (which charges a spread).
- Insurance. In this case, the capital guarantee is provided through the purchase of an insurance policy from an insurance company.

Finally, it should be noted that the existence of profitable alternative investment strategies (particularly of the market-neutral kind) is a sign of market inefficiency. The high profits should attract new entrants and the resulting competition should drive down returns: in a truly efficient market, market-neutral strategies should generate the riskless return. There appears to be some sign that this is indeed happening.

1.11   CONCLUSIONS

Pension funds invest in financial assets (principally money-market securities, bonds and loans, shares and collective investment vehicles), real assets, derivatives and alternative investments. A substantial part of the remainder of this book will be devoted to examining precisely how they do this. But before doing so, we will examine the role of pensions and pension funds in personal and corporate finance decision-making.

QUESTIONS

1. What are the main types of money-market securities?
2. How is the yield on a Treasury bill determined?
3. List the main classes of bond.
4. Explain the importance of bond credit ratings.
5. What is the difference between a bond and a loan?
6. Derive the formula for the present value of an annuity making semi-annual payments (i.e., the first term on the last line of Equation (1.5)).
7. List the main types of shares.
8. Explain the dividend discount model of share valuation.

9. Explain the difference between unit trusts and investment trusts.
10. How do split-level investment trusts work?
11. What is an insurance bond?
12. How do guaranteed growth funds work?
13. What are the most important factors to take into account when investing in property?
14. What are collectibles?
15. What are derivatives?
16. What is the difference between forwards and futures?
17. Explain the difference between the discounted cash-flow and arbitrage-free models of valuing securities.
18. Explain how futures are priced using the cost-of-carry model.
19. What are options, warrants and convertibles?
20. Explain the difference between put and call options.
21. Explain the difference between the intrinsic value and the time value of an option.
22. Explain the role of a riskless hedge portfolio in the binomial model of option valuation.
23. Explain interest-rate swaps, currency swaps and asset swaps.
24. What are forward-rate agreements?
25. What are the main types of alternative investment strategies?
26. What are the key public market strategies?
27. What are the key types of arbitrage fund?
28. What are the key types of private equity strategy?
29. What is meant by socially responsible investment?
30. What do global custodians do?
31. What are the main asset characteristics that pension funds will consider when selecting their investment portfolios?
32. How do pension funds 'use' assets in their portfolios? How does this depend on the degree of maturity of the pension fund?

APPENDIX: STANDARD DEVIATION, VALUE-AT-RISK AND CORRELATION

Standard deviation is a commonly used measure of the volatility, or risk, of a variable. It measures the extent to which the dispersion of a random variable (such as the return on a security) is concentrated around its mean or average value: if the degree of concentration is high, so that realised values of the variable are always close to the mean, then the standard deviation will be low, and vice versa.

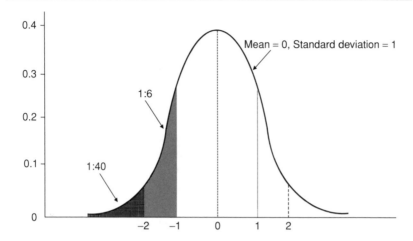

Figure 1.4 The 1-in-6 and 1-in-40 values-at-risk with the standard normal distribution

The formula for calculating the standard deviation of N values of a random variable x_i is as follows:

$$\text{Standard deviation} = \frac{\sum_{i=1}^{N} (x_i - \bar{x})^2}{N - 1}$$

where

x_i = the ith value (out of a total of N) of the variable

$\bar{x} = \dfrac{\sum_{i=1}^{N} x_i}{N} =$ the mean or average of the set of N variables

$\sum_{i=1}^{N} =$ sum over a set of variables from 1 to N.

Standard deviation is best illustrated in terms of the 1-in-6 and 1-in-40 rules, as shown in Figure 1.4. The figure shows the familiar bell-shaped curve of the standard normal distribution, which has a mean of 0 and a standard deviation of 1.

Suppose that a time-varying random variable is generated by this distribution with annual realisations of the variable. There is then a 1-in-6 chance that the realised value of this variable in a particular year will be less than one standard deviation below the mean. In other words, the area beneath the curve to the left of −1 in the figure is 1/6 of the total area under the curve. The figure –1 is also sometimes known as the 1-in-6 *value-at-risk*. Another way of expressing this is that in one year in six, we expect to see values less than one standard deviation below the mean. Similarly, there is a 1-in-40 chance that the value of the variable in a particular year (or in one year out of every 40) will be less than two standard deviations below the mean, i.e. less than –2 in Figure 1.4 (this figure is also sometimes known as the 1-in-40 value-at-risk).

Correlation measures the degree to which two variables move together. The degree of correlation lies between −1 and +1. If two variables are perfectly positively correlated (with a correlation coefficient of +1), they will move exactly in line with each other: for every one unit rise in one of the variables, there will be precisely a one-unit rise in the other variable. If two variables are perfectly negatively correlated (with a correlation coefficient of −1), they will move in exactly opposite directions: for every one-unit rise in one of the variables, there will be precisely a one-unit fall in the other variable. If two variables have a correlation coefficient of zero, they are said to be uncorrelated: the movement of one variable is unrelated to the movement in the other variable. Correlation coefficients lying between 0 and 1 indicate positive, but less than perfect, correlation between pairs of variables – the weaker the positive correlation the closer the coefficient will be to 0 and vice versa. A similar result holds for negative correlation coefficients lying between 0 and −1.

The formula for calculating the correlation between N pairs of random values of variables x_i and y_i is as follows:

$$\text{Correlation coefficient} = \frac{\sum_{i=1}^{N} (x_i - \bar{x})(y_i - \bar{y})}{\sqrt{\sum_{i=1}^{N} (x_i - \bar{x})^2 \sum_{i=1}^{N} (y_i - \bar{y})^2}}$$

REFERENCES

Black, F. and Scholes, M. (1973) The pricing of options and corporate liabilities. *Journal of Political Economy*, **81**, 637–654.

Blake, D. (2000) *Financial Market Analysis*, John Wiley & Sons, Ltd, Chichester.

Blake, D., Lehmann, B. and Timmermann, A. (1999) Allocation dynamics and pension fund performance. *Journal of Business*, **72**, 429–462.

Cox, J., Ross, S. and Rubinstein, M. (1979) Option pricing: a simplified approach. *Journal of Financial Economics*, **7**, 229–263.

Jaeger, L. (2001) *The Benefits of Alternative Investment Strategies in the Institutional Portfolio*, Swiss Alternative Investments Group, November.

Schneeweis, T., Spurgen, R. and Karvas, V. (2000) *Alternative Investments in Institutional Portfolios*, Alternative Investment Management Association, August.

Stoll, H. (1969) The relationship between put and call option prices. *Journal of Finance*, **24**, 802–824.

2

Personal Finance: The Allocation of Personal Wealth to Different Asset Classes

Pension wealth (the present value of accrued benefits in state and occupational pension schemes or the value of the accumulated assets in defined contribution schemes) is an important component of personal sector wealth. In this chapter we investigate the factors determining the allocation of aggregate personal sector wealth in the UK across five broad asset categories: net financial wealth, housing (and durable assets) wealth, state pension wealth, private pension wealth and human capital, using data constructed in Blake and Orszag (1999) and a version of Deaton and Muellbauer's (1980) AIDS (Almost Ideal Demand System) model that has been developed for modelling financial assets: the FAIDS model (Blake, 2004).

2.1   INTRODUCTION

There have been significant changes in the composition of personal sector (nonhuman) wealth in the post-war period. Figure 2.1 shows that net financial wealth (financial assets less financial liabilities such as mortgages) was the largest component of personal wealth in 1950. This was followed by net housing wealth. Total pension wealth (measured by the value of the entitlements to basic state and occupational pensions) accounted for less than one-quarter of total wealth in 1950. Figure 2.2 shows that, by 1970, both housing wealth and pension wealth had increased at the expense of net financial wealth. Figure 2.3 shows that, by 1990, total pension wealth (now also comprising personal pension and state earnings related pension scheme (SERPS) wealth) accounted for nearly half of personal wealth.

The annual changes in these shares of wealth since 1950 are presented in Figures 2.4 and 2.5. Figure 2.4 shows that the weight in net financial assets (F) fell steadily during the 1950s and 1960s from a high point of 12% to around 3%, at which level it remained throughout the

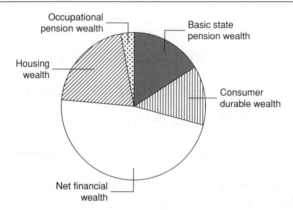

Figure 2.1   Distribution of personal (nonhuman) wealth in the UK in 1950

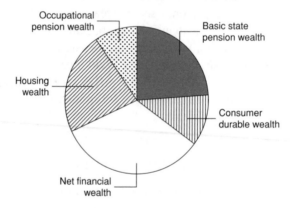

Figure 2.2   Distribution of personal (nonhuman) wealth in the UK in 1970

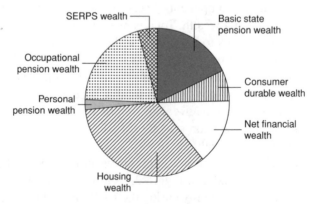

Figure 2.3   Distribution of personal (nonhuman) wealth in the UK in 1990

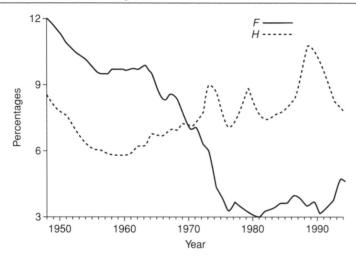

Figure 2.4   Shares of net financial wealth (F) and housing (and durable asset) wealth (H) in total personal wealth in the UK since 1950

high-inflation 1970s and 1980s, before rising to above 4% in the 1990s as inflation subsided. The weight in housing (and durable assets) wealth (H) has been on a rising trend since the late 1950s, and the impacts of the three housing booms of the early and late 1970s and late 1980s are clearly discernible. Figure 2.5 shows the growing importance in total

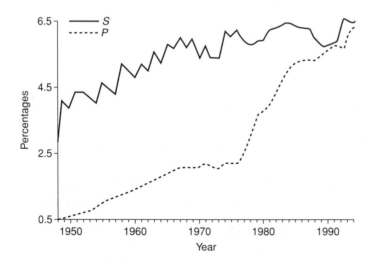

Figure 2.5   Shares of state (S) and private (P) pension wealth in total personal wealth in the UK since 1950

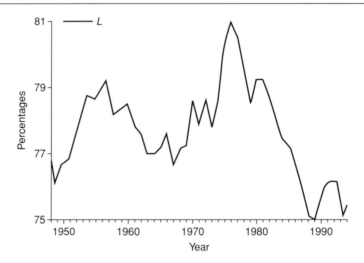

Figure 2.6   Share of human capital (*L*) in total personal wealth in the UK since 1950

wealth of the value of accrued pension rights. The share of state pension wealth (*S*) in 1948 was about 2.5%, but it rose steadily, if unevenly, until the mid 1970s,[1] after which it flattened out at about 6% of total wealth. The growth rate in the share of private pension wealth (*P*) has been even greater than this, with the share rising over the period from less than 1% to 6%: the effect of the growth in membership in these schemes from the mid 1970s is particularly noticeable. The combined weight of these four asset categories never amounted to more than 25% of total personal wealth over the sample period. Figure 2.6 explains why. The share of human capital (the expected discounted value of future career earnings, *L*) has never fallen below 75% of total wealth throughout the post-war period. It reached a peak of 81% in 1976 (largely explained by the collapse of the London stock market two years earlier), but subsequently fell steadily to around 75% by the end of the period.

2.2   MODELLING THE ALLOCATION OF PERSONAL WEALTH TO DIFFERENT ASSET CLASSES

In the FAIDS model, the objective of a representative agent is to:

$$\text{Maximise } \bar{U}(\theta_{1t}W_t, \ldots, \theta_{Nt}W_t) \tag{2.1}$$

---

[1] The jagged nature of the rise is explained by the fact that the value of the basic state pension was uprated only periodically during this period.

subject to a budget constraint (expressed in expected value form):

$$\bar{W}_{t+1} = \sum_{i=1}^{N} (1 + \bar{r}_{it})\theta_{it} W_t \qquad (2.2)$$

where bars over variables indicate expected values and where:

$U(.)$ = utility function
W_t = total real wealth at time t
θ_{it} = weight (i.e. share) in the portfolio of the ith asset category at time t
$\bar{r}_{it}$ = expected real return on the ith asset category at time t
N = number of asset categories in the portfolio.

Assuming a logarithmic functional form for the utility function in (2.1) leads to optimal (long-run) portfolio weights of the form:

$$\theta_{it}^{*} = a_i^{*} + b_i^{*} \ln W_t + b_i^{*} \ln(1 + \bar{r}_{Wt}) + \sum_{j=1}^{N} c_{ij}^{*} \ln(1 + \bar{r}_{jt}) \qquad (2.3)$$

where $\bar{r}_{Wt}$ is the weighted average return on total wealth. Asset return volatilities or risk terms, because they are subsumed in the constant terms, have a 'fixed effect' in the FAIDS model.

The standard FAIDS model predicts that the optimal portfolio weights are linear in the logarithms of total wealth and expected real asset returns, with no other variables predicted to have any significance. In practice, however, we must allow for the following possibilities. Since the capital markets are not perfect, individuals may be liquidity-constrained and these constraints may change over time as a result of, say, financial deregulation. Other variables, apart from wealth and asset expected returns, may influence the portfolio weights. Finally, individuals are unlikely to be holding optimal portfolios at all times, and there will be costs, both of adjusting actual portfolios towards optimal portfolios and of being away from optimal portfolios. We account for these possibilities in the following ways.

- *Income effects.* The effect of liquidity constraints on consumption behaviour is to introduce current income into the portfolio shares equation, just as it does in the consumption function (Flavin, 1985; Zeldes, 1989). Some investigators have included the standard deviation of current income ($YVOL$), since uncertainty about income can reduce consumption and increase precautionary asset holdings (Skinner, 1988; Caballero, 1990; Hendry, 1994). Following Hendry (1994, eqn (8)), we estimate *YVOL* as the absolute value of the residuals in the following regression equation:

$$\Delta \ln Y_t = 0.0214 + 0.4731 \Delta \ln Y_{t-1} - 0.3117 \Delta \ln P_t$$
$$+ 0.1717 \Delta \ln P_{t-1} - 0.2260 \ln YD_{t-1} \qquad (2.4)$$

where Y is real income, P is the price level and $\ln YD$ is the deviation of $\ln Y$ from a linear deterministic trend. Others have included the inflation rate, because 'nominal rather than real interest rate payments are considered to be income in the national accounts, hence in inflationary times consumers are forced to increase saving simply to keep their debt position stable' (Bayoumi, 1993, p. 1434). Hendry and von Ungern-Sternberg (1981) and Hendry (1994) use a variable that results from multiplying the value of liquid assets by the inflation rate ($\dot{P}_F$). A high value for $\dot{P}_F$ could have the following effects: it might induce individuals to increase their savings in order to maintain the real value of their liquid assets, it might encourage them to increase current consumption to avoid paying higher prices in the future, or it might induce them to switch into assets that are better inflation hedges. The first two effects influence total wealth as well as its composition, while the third influences only the composition.

- *Lifecycle factors.* The system (2.3) explains the optimal portfolio behaviour of an infinitely-lived representative agent with no bequest motive. In this framework, the portfolio composition is independent of the individual's age. Different investigators have accounted for life-cycle factors in a variety of ways. Some include the proportions of the population who are respectively young (the youth dependency ratio, *YOUTHDR*) and old (the elderly dependency ratio, *AGEDR*) (e.g. Modigliani, 1970 and Feldstein, 1980). Others include life expectancy (*LIFEXP*) (e.g. Hamermesh, 1985). If these additional M variables are denoted by Z_{jt}, the long-run FAIDS model (2.3) becomes:

$$\theta_{it}^* = a_i^* + b_i^* \ln W_t + b_i^* \ln(1 + \bar{r}_{Wt}) + \sum_{j=1}^{N} c_{ij}^* \ln(1 + \bar{r}_{jt}) + \sum_{j=1}^{M} h_{ij}^* Z_{jt}$$
$$(2.5)$$

Table 2.1 presents the long-run elasticities for the FAIDS model (2.5) estimated on UK aggregate data over the post-war period: the elasticities are with respect to absolute asset holdings (Q_F, etc.) rather than to asset weights (θ_F^*, etc.). Of particular importance are the long-run wealth

Table 2.1 Long-run asset holding elasticities

	Q_F	Q_H	Q_S	Q_P	Q_L
Wealth elasticities:	−3.1605	3.1055	0.4863	1.1700	1.0784
(t-ratios)	(5.93)	(6.93)	(1.82)	(0.78)	(32.12)
Interest-rate elasticities:					
$\bar{r}_F$	1.4334	0.2214	−0.7530	0.1429	0
	(123.91)	(2.17)	(3.69)	(1.80)	
$\bar{r}_H$	0.3552	0.7623	−0.4038	0.4347	0
	(2.17)	(35.49)	(0.94)	(1.43)	
$\bar{r}_S$	−0.9679	−0.3236	4.7416	−2.6491	0
	(3.69)	(0.94)	(59.00)	(2.48)	
$\bar{r}_P$	0.1792	0.3398	−2.5847	3.0715	0
	(1.80)	(1.43)	(2.48)	(54.93)	
Other elasticities:					
Y	4.2152	−0.3121	0.4980	0.2986	−0.3014
	(5.99)	(1.01)	(1.61)	(1.23)	(8.95)
YVOL	0.0395	0.0100	−0.0423	0.0132	−0.0011
	(1.70)	(0.96)	(3.91)	(1.51)	(0.01)
$\dot{P}_F$	−0.1262	0.0308	0.0266	−0.0028	0.0029
	(2.02)	(1.13)	(0.96)	(0.14)	(0.55)
YOUTHDR	−2.7600	0.2345	0.6289	−1.2318	0.1989
	(3.20)	(0.65)	(1.76)	(4.42)	(104.10)
AGEDR	−2.3939	−0.6995	0.1672	−1.1688	0.1224
	(0.32)	(1.13)	(0.27)	(2.51)	(34.26)
LIFEXP	−25.3563	−29.6547	7.8939	10.8258	3.1360
	(1.70)	(4.75)	(1.25)	(2.25)	(349.32)

elasticities. Net financial wealth is a wealth-inferior asset, with a long-run elasticity of −3 (i.e. a 1% increase in total wealth reduces net financial wealth by 3%). State pension wealth has a long-run wealth elasticity of around 0.5, while private pension wealth has a long-run elasticity that does not differ significantly from unity. Human capital and housing (and durable assets) are wealth-luxuries,[2] with the latter category having a long-run elasticity of 3. Turning to the interest-rate elasticities, we find that all the own-rate elasticities are positive and, with the exception of housing, exceed unity. Net financial assets complement[3] all other assets, except state pension assets; housing (and durable assets) complement private pension assets, but are a substitute[4] for state pension assets; state

---

[2] That is, have a wealth elasticity exceeding unity.
[3] That is, have a positive interest-rate cross elasticity.
[4] That is, have a negative interest-rate cross elasticity.

pension assets are long-run substitutes for all other assets, in particular, private pension assets; and private pension assets complement other categories, apart from state pensions.

The exogenous variables have the following long-run effects. Income (Y) has a statistically significant long-run effect on net financial assets and human capital. Net financial wealth is a strong income-luxury,[5] while housing (and durable assets) wealth is income-inferior[6] (although the coefficient is not statistically significant): so the income effects for these two asset categories are the opposite of the corresponding wealth effects in terms of relative size. Greater income uncertainty ($YVOL$) reduces the allocation to state pension wealth and increases it towards precautionary financial assets. The inflation loss on financial assets ($\dot{P}_F$), which is not adequately compensated in terms of higher real returns, causes a long-run shift away from financial assets.

Of the lifecycle variables, an increase in the dependency ratios of both the young and old ($YOUTHDR$ and $AGEDR$) induces greater human capital accumulation at the expense of both net financial and private pension assets, while an increase in life expectancy ($LIFEXP$) causes large switches away from financial and housing assets towards pension assets and human capital accumulation.

2.3   CONCLUSIONS

There have been substantial changes in the UK personal sector's asset allocation over the post-war period. The share of net financial wealth in total wealth has been on a falling trend, while the shares of housing and pension wealth have been on rising trends. The share of human capital has been stable within a relatively narrow band, between 75% and 81% of total wealth.

We found that wealth effects were very important for determining trend shifts in asset allocations, and certainly more important than relative returns. The main explanation for the declining portfolio weight in net financial wealth was the combination of rising per capita wealth over the post-war period and a negative long-run wealth elasticity. In contrast, positive wealth elasticities explained much of the rise in portfolio weights in the other asset categories. We found that net financial

---

[5] That is, it has an income elasticity exceeding unity.
[6] That is, it has an income elasticity below unity.

wealth, housing wealth and private pension wealth were complements, and each was a substitute for state pension wealth.

Of the exogenous variables, financial asset holdings were subject to a strong positive current income effect, while human capital was subject to a small but significant negative income effect.[7] Income volatility had little long-run impact, except to lower holdings of state pension wealth. Inflation losses on financial assets reduced the long-run holdings of financial assets without inducing any significant switch towards other assets.

Lifecycle variables were also found to be important, especially rising longevity, which induces substantial switches in the portfolio towards both pension and human capital accumulation and away from financial and housing assets.

This analysis offers some important indicators to the future composition of personal sector wealth in the UK. Rising future per capita wealth will sustain the switch from direct holdings of financial assets towards the indirect holdings of financial claims in the form of funded private pension assets and towards housing assets, although this will be attenuated by the high income elasticity on net financial assets. On the other hand, increased longevity will help to switch personal sector wealth away from financial and housing assets towards both greater human capital accumulation and pension asset accumulation. Further, given its status as a substitute, any further reduction in state pension provision will raise the demand for all assets, especially private pension assets. There will, therefore, continue to be a strong demand for financial assets, mainly by pension funds; this will encourage the supply of new financial assets.

QUESTIONS

1. What has happened to the distribution of personal (nonhuman) wealth in the UK over the last half century?
2. Define human capital.
3. What factors determine the allocation of personal wealth to different asset classes?
4. What factors determine the demand for state pension wealth in the UK?

---

[7] The stable long-run share of human capital in total wealth is explained by the combination of a long-run wealth elasticity exceeding unity and a negative long-run income elasticity.

5. What factors determine the demand for private pension wealth in the UK?

REFERENCES

Bayoumi, T. (1993) Financial deregulation and household saving. *Economic Journal*, **103**, 1432–1443.

Blake, D. (2004) Modelling the composition of personal sector wealth in the UK. *Applied Financial Economics*, **14**, 611–630.

Blake, D. and Orszag, J.M. (1999) Annual estimates of personal wealth holdings in the UK since 1948. *Applied Financial Economics*, **9**, 397–421.

Caballero, R. (1990) Consumption puzzles and precautionary savings. *Journal of Monetary Economics*, **25**, 113–136.

Deaton, A.S. and Muellbauer, J. (1980) An almost ideal demand system. *American Economic Review*, **70**, 312–326.

Feldstein, M. (1980) International differences in social security and savings. *Journal of Public Economics*, **14**, 225–244.

Flavin, M. (1985) Excess sensitivity of consumption to current income: liquidity constraints or myopia? *Canadian Journal of Economics*, **18**, 117–136.

Hamermesh, D. (1985) Expectations, life expectancy and economic behaviour. *Quarterly Journal of Economics*, **100**, 389–408.

Hendry, D.F. (1994) HUS revisited. *Oxford Review of Economic Policy*, **10**, 86–106.

Hendry, D.F. and von Ungern-Sternberg, T. (1981) Liquidity and inflation effects on consumers' expenditure, in Deaton, A.S. (Ed.) *Essays in the Theory and Measurement of Consumer Behaviour*, Cambridge University Press, Cambridge.

Modigliani, F. (1970) The life-cycle hypothesis of saving and intercountry differences in the savings ratio, in Eltis, W.A., Scott, F.G. and Wolfe, J.N. (Eds) *Induction, Growth and Trade: Essays in Honour of Sir Roy Harrod*, Clarendon Press, Oxford, pp. 197–226.

Skinner, J. (1988) Risk income, life cycle consumption and precautionary savings. *Journal of Monetary Economics*, **22**, 237–255.

Zeldes, S.P. (1989) Consumption and liquidity constraints: an empirical investigation. *Journal of Political Economy*, **97**, 305–346.

3

Corporate Pension Finance

Corporate pension finance deals with how a company pension scheme is funded and how the pension liabilities are paid. A controversial issue is how pension liabilities (especially defined benefit liabilities) should be valued: actuaries and economists differ in their approaches. There are also differences in the approaches between accountants and economists over how pension assets and liabilities should be treated in company accounts. Another important issue is the appropriate asset allocation for (i.e. the weights of the key asset classes in) the pension fund. We show that the optimal asset allocation of a pension fund depends on whether the pension fund is over or underfunded, whether or not the pension liabilities are linked to earnings growth and whether the pension fund is insured or not. Finally, the existence of a pension fund can influence the sponsoring company's profitability, credit rating and share price.

3.1 THE VALUATION OF PENSION LIABILITIES: DIFFERENCES BETWEEN THE ACTUARIAL AND ECONOMIC APPROACHES

Suppose a company has (promised) pension liabilities of L_1 (known with certainty) to be paid in a year's time. Suppose a fund of pension assets with a current market value of A_0 is available to pay these liabilities. In a year's time, the fund will be worth the (currently uncertain) amount $\tilde{A}_1 = (1 + \tilde{r})A_0$, where $\tilde{r}$ is the uncertain return on assets in the pension fund.

The pension liabilities are calculated as the present value of promised future pension payments. To do this calculation, it is necessary to choose a discount rate. There is a difference between the actuarial valuation and the economic valuation of pension liabilities.

The actuary's choice of a discount rate (say $\bar{r}$) generally reflects the past or projected future investment performance of the assets in the pension fund (i.e. $\tilde{r}$):

$$L_0 = PV(L_1) = \frac{L_1}{1+\tilde{r}} \tag{3.1}$$

Treynor (1977, p. 631) argues that this is rather odd: 'There is no more reason for looking to the return on a particular pension asset to determine how to discount the pension liability than there is for looking at the return on any other corporate assets to determine how to discount any other corporate liability – hence there is no more reason to single out pension liabilities for this bizarre treatment than, say, the employer's term loan with its local bank'. Treynor (1977, p. 632) goes on to say: 'there is no justification for the present actuarial practice of discounting pension liabilities at a rate somehow related to the historical rate of return on pension assets'.

The economist's approach (see, for example, Bagehot, 1972) is to use the riskless rate of interest (r_f):

$$L_0 = PV(L_1) = \frac{L_1}{1+r_f} \tag{3.2}$$

Treynor (1977, p. 632) argues that discounting expected future pension payments using the riskless rate 'comes close to being an objective measure of the financial burden of the company's pension liability. It is the relevant number, not only for the pension claimant, but also for private creditors of the company and, finally, for the analyst of the employer's equity shares'.

Another justification for using the riskless rate, rather than a higher one involving a risk premium, is the argument that the higher expected return on, say, equities, compared with the riskless asset, should not be credited before it has been earned. In other words, the riskless rate can be anticipated prudently, whereas the higher return on equities cannot. As Petersen (1996) argues, by using a discount rate that incorporates an equity-risk premium, the *expected value* of the pension liabilities is reduced (as if by magic, pension liabilities can be reduced by investing in riskier assets), but the *promised value* of the pension liabilities has not been and cannot be changed by changing the discount rate. The present value of a future promise should be calculated using the riskless rate. As Bagehot (1972, p. 82) says: 'If the assets available exceed the present value of future pension claims only when the latter are discounted at a higher rate, the expected proceeds from the assets will fail to meet the claims unless the assets are invested aggressively, with the attendant possibility of loss'.

3.2 PENSIONS AND THE COMPANY BALANCE SHEET: DIFFERENCES BETWEEN THE ACCOUNTING AND ECONOMIC APPROACHES

There is generally a legal separation between the company and its pension fund. The pension fund is run by a group of people, commonly called trustees, who are independent of the company. It is generally agreed that the role of the company is to fund the pension scheme, while the role of the trustees is to pay the pensions.

A key issue in corporate pension finance is whether the pension scheme's assets and liabilities should be treated as part of the company's balance sheet or not. This is particularly important in defined benefit pension schemes, where a particular pension benefit has been promised.

The conventional accounting approach is to treat the company's and the pension fund's assets and liabilities separately, as in Table 3.1. The pension assets are viewed as a separate pool to be managed in the interests of pension beneficiaries. These beneficiaries naturally will want to see the pension liabilities as fully funded as possible.

By contrast, the economist's approach is to integrate the pension fund balance sheet with that of the sponsoring company, as in Table 3.2 (Bagehot, 1972 calls this the *augmented corporate balance sheet*). As Black (1980, p. 21) states: 'A firm's pension fund is legally separate from the firm. But because pension benefits are normally independent of fund performance, pension assets impact the firm very much as if they were firm assets'. Bodie *et al.* (1985) provide evidence from the US supporting the view that companies manage their pension funds as if they are an integral part of total corporate financial policy. The pension scheme's liabilities are just one component of the firm's fixed financial liabilities. The pension assets are just one part of the firm's assets. Any pension fund surplus

Table 3.1 Company and pension funds' balance sheets: Accounting approach

Company

Assets	*Liabilities*
Corporate assets	Corporate liabilities
	Shareholder equity

Pension fund

Assets	*Liabilities*
Pension fund assets	Pension fund liabilities

Table 3.2   Combined company and pension fund
balance sheet: Financial economics approach

Assets	Liabilities
Corporate assets	Corporate liabilities
Pension fund assets	Pension fund liabilities
Pension call (= surplus)	Pension put (= deficit)
	Shareholder equity

or deficit belongs to the firm's shareholders. The company will choose
the structure of assets and liabilities to maximise shareholder value. For
example, Bodie *et al.* (1985, 1987) found that there was a positive relationship between corporate profitability and the level of pension funding
(see Section 3.4.1 below). This can be explained as follows: profitable
taxpaying companies maximise their tax savings by borrowing (interest
paid on borrowing is tax deductible) to overfund their pension schemes
and investing in the most heavily taxed securities, such as bonds.

Sharpe (1976) argues that the inclusion of the pension fund assets and
liabilities in the company balance sheet creates a *pension call* option
and a *pension put* option. The pension call corresponds to a surplus in
the pension fund and is an asset to the company to the extent that the
surplus is recoverable. The pension put corresponds to a deficit in the
pension fund and is a liability to the company.

Consider the case of a pension fund with no legal recourse to the
sponsoring company in the event of a deficiency. Suppose the company
has (promised) pension liabilities of L_1 (known with certainty) to be
paid in a year's time. Suppose a fund of pension assets with a current
market value of A_0 is available to pay these liabilities. In a year's time,
the fund will be worth the (currently uncertain) amount $\tilde{A}_1 = (1 + \tilde{r})A_0$,
where $\tilde{r}$ is the uncertain return on assets in the pension fund. Figure 3.1

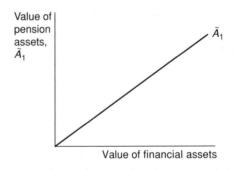

Figure 3.1   Value of the pension assets

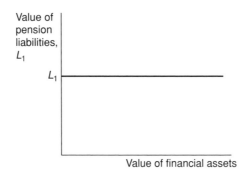

Figure 3.2   Value of the pension liabilities

shows the value of the pension assets in a year's time as a function of the value of the financial assets held in the pension fund, while Figure 3.2 shows the value of the pension liabilities. The liabilities are equivalent to a riskless bond whose value in a year's time is independent of the value of the financial assets.

If, at the end of the year, $\tilde{A}_1 > L_1$, the pension liabilities will be paid in full and the surplus $(\tilde{A}_1 - L_1)$ returned to the sponsoring company. The surplus represents the value P^C of the *pension call* (with exercise price L_1) that the company has on the pension fund assets. This is shown in Figure 3.3.

If, on the other hand, $\tilde{A}_1 < L_1$, the pension liabilities will not be paid in full, since there is a deficit in the pension fund and the pension fund has no recourse to the company. In the case where the pension fund is uninsured, the scheme members have sold a *pension put* (with exercise price L_1 and value P^P) to the sponsoring company. This is shown in Figure 3.4: the members get their pension promise honoured

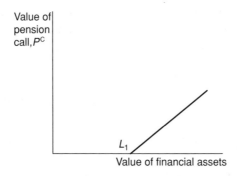

Figure 3.3   Value of the pension call

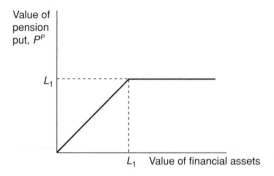

Figure 3.4 Value of the pension put

in full (if $\tilde{A}_1 > L_1$) or they get a pension based on the value of the assets (if $\tilde{A}_1 < L_1$). The value of the put is equal to the size of the terminal deficit ($L_1 - \tilde{A}_1$) and the company will exercise the put against the members if the pension fund is in deficit.

The following relationship will hold between the present values of the assets, liabilities, call and put:

$$PV(\tilde{P}_1^C) - PV(\tilde{P}_1^P) + PV(L_1) = PV(\tilde{A}_1) \qquad (3.3)$$

This is a version of the put-call parity equation (1.28). Since $PV(\tilde{A}_1) = A_0$, (3.3) can be rewritten as

$$PV(\tilde{P}_1^P) - PV(\tilde{P}_1^C) = PV(L_1) - A_0 \qquad (3.4)$$

The right-hand side is the current value of unfunded liabilities (i.e. the current deficit).

If workers are behaving rationally, they will be concerned about the total level of compensation they receive from the company, but not the form of the compensation.

Suppose the total level of compensation is W and the three components of the compensation are current wages (W_0), the promised pension ($PV(L_1)$) and the short pension put ($PV(\tilde{P}_1^P)$):

$$PV(L_1) + W_0 - PV(\tilde{P}_1^P) = W \qquad (3.5)$$

Adding W_0 to both sides of (3.4), rearranging and substituting into (3.5) gives:

$$W_0 + A_0 - PV(\tilde{P}_1^C) = PV(L_1) + W_0 - PV(\tilde{P}_1^P) = W \qquad (3.6)$$

Black and Scholes (1973) showed that the value of an option depends on the term to maturity (one year in this case), the current value of the underlying asset (A_0), the exercise price (L_1) and the standard deviation[1] of the return on assets ($\sigma(\tilde{r})$) (see Equation (1.27)). This means that (3.6) can be rewritten:

$$W_0 + A_0 - PV(\tilde{P}_1^C[A_0, L_1, \sigma(\tilde{r}), r_f, T = 1]) = W \qquad (3.7)$$

Equation (3.7) shows that corporate pension funding policy (the size of A_0) and the pension investment policy (which determines asset risk, i.e. the standard deviation of returns $\sigma(\tilde{r})$) is irrelevant so long as W is constant. Any change in funding or investment policy will change the value of the company's pension contribution (if A_0 changes) or the value of its call option (if A_0 or $\sigma(\tilde{r})$ change). But this must be matched by offsetting changes in W_0 or L_1 if W does not change. In other words, corporate funding and investment policy will change the composition of employee compensation, but not the total compensation.

The values of the pension call and put depend not only on the size of the pension fund surplus or deficit, they also depend on the asset allocation of the pension fund and the extent to which the pension fund is insured. These matters are considered below.

3.3   THE ASSET ALLOCATION OF THE PENSION FUND

Pension assets comprise the financial (and possibly nonfinancial) assets in the pension fund and the future promised pension contributions from the employer and employee.

Additional employer pension contributions, while increasing pension assets, do not change the aggregate risk of corporate assets. This is because additional employer contributions are paid for either by reducing corporate assets (which includes retained earnings) or by increasing corporate liabilities. Either way, the pension contribution leaves the combined value of corporate and pension assets that back the pension promise unchanged. As Bagehot (1972, p. 83) says: 'The corporate contribution to the pension fund merely exchanges one asset for another, leaving true corporate equity unchanged. It does not widen the pension beneficiary's margin of protection, nor is it in any true economic sense a cost to the corporation. The true pension cost incurred in an accounting period is the present value [using the riskless rate] of the additional pension obligations incurred in the period'.

---

[1] Standard deviation is defined in the appendix at the end of Chapter 1.

So, unless the pension assets are completely riskless, the pension contribution 'always increases the absolute risk characterising the underlying assets' (Treynor, 1977, p. 632). To reduce this risk, the scheme member should seek to restrict or limit dividends to shareholders in the company: the payment of dividends 'reduces the assets securing his claim'.

The optimal asset allocation of a pension fund depends on a range of factors:

- whether the pension fund is fully funded or underfunded;
- whether the pension liabilities are linked to earnings growth;
- whether the pension fund is insured, either fully or partially.

These factors will be considered in the next four subsections. However, one point can be made clear: just as the discount rate for pension liabilities should not depend on the assets in the pension fund, so the choice of pension assets should not be influenced by the choice of discount rate for pension liabilities.

3.3.1   A fully funded pension fund

Tepper and Affleck (1974), Black (1980) and Tepper (1981) show that the EET system of tax breaks[2] gives companies a strong incentive to fully fund their pension schemes and hold bonds in their pension funds. The sponsor in a funded scheme receives no tax relief when the pension is paid: this contrasts with an unfunded or pay-as-you-go scheme in which the company does get tax relief, since the pension payment, like wages, is a tax-deductible expense.

Suppose the company is liable for an infinite stream of constant pension payments (P), that the interest rate is also fixed at r and that the company faces a corporation tax rate of τ. If the company runs a PAYG scheme, its net annual cost is $(1 - \tau)P$, as shown in Table 3.3.

Suppose, instead, the company decides to pre-fund its pension obligations by establishing a pension fund. Since the pension scheme is fully funded if the level of assets is P/r (i.e. the present value of all

---

[2] The EET system of tax breaks Exempts contributions into a pension scheme from tax, Exempts investment returns on the assets in the pension scheme from tax, but Taxes the pension in payment. This system is common in the UK and US, although from 1997, the tax paid on UK dividends can no longer be reclaimed by UK pension funds.

Table 3.3 The tax advantage of funding the pension scheme

	Current cash flows	Future cash flows
PAYG scheme		
Pay pensions when due	—	$-(1-\tau)P$
Funded scheme		
1. Borrow P/r	$+P/r$	$-(1-\tau)r \times P/r = -(1-\tau)P$
2. Transfer P/r to pension fund	$-(1-\tau)P/r$	—
3. Pension fund invests in bonds	—	$r \times P/r = +P$
4. Pay pensions when due	—	$-P$
Total cash flows	$+\tau P/r$	$-(1-\tau)P$
Cash-flow advantage of funded scheme over unfunded scheme	$+\tau P/r$	—

Source: Adapted from Brealey and Myers (1991, Table 35-2).

future pension payments[3]), the company could borrow this sum in the capital markets by issuing a bond. The after-tax cost to the company is $(1-\tau)P/r$ where τ is the corporation tax rate and the tax saving (which is the net economic value of establishing a pension fund) is $\tau P/r$. If the pension fund invests the proceeds from issuing the bond also in bonds, paying an interest rate of r p.a., the pension fund receives an income of $r \times P/r = P$, just enough to pay the annual pension. The company also has to pay interest on the funds it has borrowed, which, after tax, is equal to:

$$(1-\tau)r \times P/r = (1-\tau)P \qquad (3.8)$$

Both types of scheme involve future cash payments of $(1-\tau)P$, but the funded scheme provides an immediate cash benefit of $\tau P/r$. So it is more advantageous for the company to borrow and transfer the proceeds to the pension fund to invest in bonds.

It is important to note that the benefit comes not from the decision to fund, but from the fact that the firm is able to borrow at the after-tax rate of interest, while the pension fund is able to earn the pre-tax rate of

---

[3] A pension scheme having financial assets valued at P/r and generating a return of r per year will always be able to pay out a pension equal to $r \times P/r = P$ per year.

interest. To demonstrate this, suppose that the earnings of the pension fund were taxed at the corporation tax rate τ. In the case of the funded scheme, the company now contributes $P/r(1 - \tau)$ to the pension fund. The after-tax cost is:

$$(1 - \tau) \times \frac{P}{r(1 - \tau)} = \frac{P}{r} \tag{3.9}$$

which just offsets the amount borrowed. In this case, funding has no advantage over PAYG.

As an alternative to bonds, the company could finance the pension fund using external equity. The after-tax cost to the investor remains $(1 - \tau)P/r$. However, the returns to the investor are the after-personal-tax (τ^*) stream of pension payments, discounted by the after-personal-tax rate on debt:

$$(1 - \tau)(1 - \tau^*)P \times \frac{1}{r(1 - \tau^*)} = \frac{(1 - \tau)P}{r} \tag{3.10}$$

so there is no net advantage to funding with external equity. The advantage of substituting pension scheme liabilities with corporate debt has been cancelled out by the substitution of personal leverage for the more tax-efficient corporate debt.

If the pension fund is financed from company profits that would otherwise be used to pay dividends, there is still a tax saving, as the dividends would otherwise be taxed. The value to the shareholders is the tax saving $\tau^*(1 - \tau)P/r$, but in general this will be less than $\tau P/r$.

Tepper (1981) argues that corporate defined benefit pension scheme liabilities are equivalent to corporate debt and that the pension fund's assets are corporate assets. Combine this with the EET system of tax breaks, and the optimal corporate pension policy should be one that maximises the tax shelter to the company's shareholders. This implies that a company should fully fund its pension plan and should invest the pension fund totally in bonds. Black (1980, p. 22) argues: 'greater volatility in the pension fund investments will mean greater volatility in the present value of the firm's contributions, and greater volatility in the value of the firm. Stocks in the pension fund mean more uncertainty about the firm's future cash flows than bonds in the pension fund . . . The effect of common stocks in the pension fund is to add to the firm's leverage . . . Shifting from stocks to bonds in the pension fund will reduce the firm's leverage. It will reduce the variability of the firm's earnings, the risk of the stock and the risk of default on the firm's bonds. The bond interest rate will fall, and if the shift is substantial, the firm's bond ratings should eventually go up'.

Black (1980) goes further and argues that the tax incentives encourage the company to overfund the pension plan and invest in bonds, since overfunded pension plans are less likely to default on their pension promises.

3.3.2 An underfunded pension fund

Sharpe (1976), Harrison and Sharpe (1983) and Ippolito (1986) show that a company in financial distress has an incentive to underfund its pension scheme and follow a risky investment strategy: one that invests in equities, rather than bonds. This is because the company has nothing to lose and everything to gain.

If the risky investment strategy is successful, this will reduce, and possibly even eliminate, the deficit in the pension fund. If the investment strategy is unsuccessful, the deficit will get even bigger. But this will not concern the shareholders who have limited liability towards their creditors, which include the pension fund. The shares of a company already in financial distress will be close to worthless and cannot fall below zero in value, whatever subsequently happens. The shareholders can walk away from the company, which they will do once the company has been declared insolvent, and leave the remaining assets to be divided up amongst the creditors according to the priority order for doing so. Highly secured creditors such as banks come top of the list, while unsecured creditors (which typically include the pension fund) come bottom.

3.3.3 A pension fund with liabilities linked to earnings growth

Black (1989) argues that if future wage growth is correlated with aggregate equity returns, then the non-vested, but expected, portion of the pension promise could be hedged with equities.

The argument above that pension liabilities are bond-like and that the most suitable matching asset is bonds has some justification if (a) the scheme offers no inflation uprating after the pension is in payment and (b) the pension scheme liabilities are valued on a termination or discontinuance basis, i.e. as if the scheme were about to close down, and the liabilities become crystallised with no future accruals for existing members and no new members joining (Black calls this valuation of pension liabilities the *narrow liability*). Under these circumstances, the future payments that the pension fund needs to make are indeed bond-like, in the sense that they are a regular stream of fixed payments, and fixed-income bonds are the best way of meeting these payments. Even if the pensions are subject to an inflation uprating, a termination basis of valuing the pension liabilities would justify the pension fund investing in index-linked bonds (i.e. those whose coupon payments and principal are linked to increases in the consumer price index).

However, if the pension scheme liabilities are valued on an ongoing basis, then the scheme must take into account benefits that will accrue in future, such as the future salary growth not only of current members but also of new members (Black calls this valuation of pension liabilities the *broad liability*). Black (1989, p. 10) argues: 'As a salary inflation indicator, I think that stocks do a better job than bonds... Stocks go up when it looks like times will be good. In good times, wages and salaries and benefits all tend to grow faster than usual. Thus the broader view of the pension liability, the more stocks you will need for hedging'. The argument is based on the stable long-run relationship between the share of labour and capital in national income. Since it is not possible for pension funds to invest directly in claims on labour (since slavery is illegal), then investments on claims on capital (namely equity or stocks) should provide an appropriate long-term match for pension liabilities linked to earnings growth.

There is another justification for pension funds investing in equity. In aggregate it is impossible for pension funds to invest entirely in bonds. Collectively, pension funds are too large. Pension funds can buy government bonds and also bonds issued by corporations. But total pension liabilities are larger than the total of government and corporate bonds outstanding. Companies could respond to the high demand for their bonds by buying back their shares and issuing bonds. But this would merely render the corporate bonds as risky as equity, since, as the Modigliani–Miller Theorem (1958) tells us, the total risk faced by a company (i.e. the volatility of the return on the physical capital of the company) does not change as the degree of company leverage (the proportion of bonds to equity financing the capital stock) changes.

3.3.4 An insured pension fund

In the US, the government-backed Pension Benefit Guaranty Corporation (PBGC) insures US corporate pension schemes against the insolvency of the corporate sponsor. The Pension Protection Fund performs the same role in the UK. Corporate pension policy can be influenced by the existence of such insurance schemes.

As seen above, Sharpe (1976) argues that the inclusion of the pension fund assets and liabilities in the company balance sheet creates a *pension call* option and a *pension put* option, the values of which depend on the extent to which the pension fund is insured.

A fully insured pension fund

Suppose now the company decides to insure the pension fund, so that the workers get L_1 with certainty. In exchange for a premium payable in advance, an insurance company agrees to pay any deficiency when $\tilde{A}_1 < L_1$. It is now the insurance company, rather than the workers, that has sold the put option. In a competitive market, the insurance company will charge a premium equal to the value of the put option.

Rewriting (3.6):

$$
W_0 + A_0 + PV(\tilde{P}_1^{\mathrm{P}}[A_0, L_1, \sigma(\tilde{r}), r_f, T = 1])
$$
$$
- PV(\tilde{P}_1^{\mathrm{C}}[A_0, L_1, \sigma(\tilde{r}), r_f, T = 1]) = W_0 + PV(L_1) = W
$$
$$
(3.11)
$$

The right-hand side equals the present value of total employee compensation. The left-hand side equals the total cost to the company of employing its workers (wages (W_0), contribution to the pension fund (A_0), and the premium to the insurance company ($PV(\tilde{P}_1^{\mathrm{P}}[A_0, L_1, \sigma(\tilde{r}), r_f, T = 1])$)), less the present value of the call option, $\tilde{P}_1^{\mathrm{C}}$. But the total amount equals a constant (W). Hence, any change in corporate pension funding or investment policy will not change the present value of its costs, since adjustment in other factors will keep the total constant. In other words, if the risk of underfunded pension liabilities can be fully insured, pension funding policy is irrelevant.

A partially insured pension fund

Suppose the pension fund is partially insured, as in the case of a fund insured by the US Pension Benefit Guaranty Corporation (PBGC). A company that establishes a pension fund insured by the PBGC is liable for the deficit in the pension fund, but only up to 30% of its net worth. Any excess (the contingent liability) is paid by the PBGC.

If NW_0 and $N\tilde{W}_1$ are the net worth of the company at the beginning and end of the year, the firm contributes $A_0 + 0.3NW_0$ to the fund. The total portfolio will have a return:

$$1 + \tilde{r} = \frac{\tilde{A}_1 + 0.3N\tilde{W}_1}{A_0 + 0.3NW_0} \tag{3.12}$$

or

$$\tilde{r} = \theta_A \tilde{r}_A + \theta_{NW} \tilde{r}_{NW} \tag{3.13}$$

where

$$\tilde{r}_A = \frac{\tilde{A}_1 - A_0}{A_0} \tag{3.14}$$

$$\tilde{r}_{NW} = \frac{N\tilde{W}_1 - NW_0}{NW_0} \tag{3.15}$$

$$\theta_A = \frac{A_0}{A_0 + 0.3NW_0} \tag{3.16}$$

$$\theta_{NW} = \frac{NW_0}{A_0 + 0.3NW_0} \tag{3.17}$$

The total portfolio will have a risk:

$$\sigma(\tilde{r}) = \sqrt{(\theta_A + \theta_{NW}\beta)^2 \sigma_M^2 + \theta_{NW}^2 \sigma_e^2} \tag{3.18}$$

where

β = beta of the company's shares[4]
σ_M = standard deviation of the market index
σ_e = residual standard deviation of the company's shares.

The appropriate insurance premium equals the price of the relevant put option:

$$P_0^P = PV\left(\tilde{P}_1^P[A_0 + 0.3NW_0, L_1, \sigma(\tilde{r}), r_f, T = 1]\right) \tag{3.19}$$

However, when the PBGC started in 1974, the premium was $1 per employee per year, irrespective of the degree of underfunding or the riskiness of the underlying investments.

Unlike the case of an uninsured or fully insured pension fund, there is now an optimal corporate pension funding and investment policy. This is the one that maximises the difference between the value of the put option (i.e. the value of the insurance) and the premium charged for it (i.e. the

---

[4] Beta measures the volatility of a company's share price relative to that of the whole market. It is defined formally in footnote 7 below.

cost of the insurance). A company can increase its current market value by:

- increasing pension liabilities;
- decreasing pension fund assets;
- increasing the risk of the assets held in the pension fund.

In other words, the optimal policy maximises the value of the option to default, so an underfunded pension plan should invest in equities. Indeed, as Bagehot (1972) was the first to argue, when there is partial insurance, companies have an incentive to underfund their pension schemes and invest in risky equities.

3.4   THE RELATIONSHIP BETWEEN THE PENSION FUND AND THE SPONSORING COMPANY'S PROFITABILITY, CREDIT RATING AND SHARE PRICE

A number of empirical studies have shown that there is a relationship between the assets and liabilities in a company's pension fund and its profitability, credit rating and share price. One of the key links in this relationship is through the discount rate used to value the pension liabilities. A number of studies show that corporations, especially in the US, use changes in discount rate assumptions on pension liabilities as a deliberate corporate management tool.

3.4.1   Profitability

Bodie *et al.* (1985, 1987) find that more profitable companies tend to use a lower discount rate to value their pension liabilities. This will have the effect of overstating pension liabilities compared with less profitable companies. They also find that more profitable companies have higher funding levels (i.e. more assets in relation to liabilities) than less profitable ones, despite the higher reported liabilities. Bodie *et al.* find that more profitable companies also have a larger weighting in bonds in their pension funds. So, workers tend to have more secure pension promises if they work for more profitable companies.

More profitable companies might invest their pension funds more heavily in bonds, but as we saw above, companies with underfunded pension schemes have an incentive to invest in riskier assets, especially if the pension fund is partially insured. However, in their study of US corporate pension funds, Gupta *et al.* (2000) show that this is not the case. They find that (p. 68): 'underfunded plans are generally the most conservative in their risk taking, while the most overfunded plans are the most aggressive and have amongst the greatest variability in risk profile'. The median pension fund in Gupta *et al.*'s sample had a one-year 95% *value-at-risk* (VaR)[5] of 17%. This implies that the volatility of the assets in the pension fund is such that, over the course of a year, there is a one-in-twenty chance that the assets might fall by 17% or more. This means that a pension fund that is exactly fully funded has a 5% probability that it will end the year with a funding level of 83% or less. The VaRs ranged from 9.5% to 28%, corresponding to a fund invested in a global bond portfolio and one invested in an aggressive equity growth portfolio, respectively. The degree of aggressiveness in the asset allocation was positively linked to fund size. However, most companies had risk profiles closely aligned with industry peers, except in Financials, Capital Goods and Basic Materials.

Feldstein and Mørck (1983) find that US firms with substantial pension liabilities relative to assets attempt to reduce the reported present value of their pension liabilities using a higher discount rate. By contrast, firms with large pension assets relative to liabilities tend to use a low discount rate in order to increase the tax advantages of early funding. Klumpes and Whittington (2003) find that UK firms also change their actuarial valuation method in response to a development in the pension scheme, such as the emergence of a deficit.

Godwin *et al.* (1997) find evidence that US firms increase their pension liability discount rates in response to the financial weakening of the sponsoring corporation, such as lower earnings, increasingly restrictive dividend constraints and tightening debt covenants associated with higher leverage. Klumpes and Whittington (2003) were unable to find similar behaviour in the UK: in the UK, changes in actuarial assumptions appear to be linked exclusively to events within the pension scheme and are unrelated to events within the sponsoring company.

3.4.2   Credit rating

Bodie *et al.* (1985) was one of the first studies to identify a negative relationship between the funding level in a company's pension scheme and its corporate debt ratings. The study finds that for overfunded schemes, a further increase in the funding levels improves credit ratings, while

---

[5] Value-at-risk is defined in the appendix at the end of Chapter 1.

for underfunded schemes, a further reduction in the funding levels lowers credit ratings. Carroll and Niehaus (1998) show that the response is asymmetric: the reduction in credit ratings in the second case is larger than the improvement in credit ratings in the first case. They argue that the asymmetry is consistent with the view that unfunded pension liabilities are corporate liabilities just like the debt on the company's main balance sheet, but that there are costs associated with the company's ability to extract a pension surplus (or an *excess asset reversion* as it is technically called in the US). These costs arise because the company faces pressures to enhance the pension benefits of both active and retired members, and acceding to these pressures reduces the size of the surplus. Carroll and Niehaus argue that this reduces the incentive of companies to fully fund their pension schemes.

3.4.3   Share price

Feldstein and Seligman (1981) was one of the earliest studies to investigate the effect of a firm's pension deficit on the firm's share price. They find, using a sample of US manufacturing firms, that that the emergence of a deficit is incorporated rapidly into the share price, in the sense that the share price is reduced (relative to tangible assets) by the per share size of unfunded pension liabilities. This indicates that shareholders recognise the unfunded pension liability as being equivalent to corporate debt.

Feldstein and Mørck (1983) show that company share prices reflect pension plan surpluses as well as deficits, and that the financial markets 'see through' the manipulation of pension liabilities considered above and instead value the pension liabilities of all firms at a common standard discount rate, very close to the average used across all firms. Further, there appears to be an asymmetry in the market response to whether there is a surplus or deficit. The market seems to give more weight to pension liabilities than to pension assets, and the share price responds more to variations in the size of the deficit than to variations in the size of the surplus. There is still some apparent market inconsistency, however, as Feldstein and Mørck argue that the most appropriate discount rate for pension liabilities should be the yield on long term corporate bonds with a Baa rating, rather than the much lower 'average' discount rate used by all schemes. Their idea is that the discount rate for pension liabilities should reflect the true nature of the pension promise: not risk-free, but less risky than the claims of, say, shareholders. Pension accounting standards (FAS87 in the US, FRS17 in the UK and IAS19 internationally) have settled on the yield on AA corporate bonds as the most suitable discount rate. The historical reason for this is that when US insurance companies took over the pension assets and liabilities of insolvent companies, they invested the assets mainly in AA corporate bonds.

A more recent study by Jin *et al.* (2006) also confirms that, despite arcane accounting rules for pensions, a company's equity returns do reflect the risk of its pension plan. Using the augmented balance sheet for a company:

$$\text{Assets} = OA + PA = E + D + PL = \text{Liabilities} \qquad (3.20)$$

where

OA = value of operating assets of the company
E = value of equity in the firm
D = value of debt in the firm
PA = value of pension assets
PL = value of pension liabilities
$S = PA - PL$ = pension surplus
$L = D/E$ = leverage ratio

The share price of the company in an *efficient market*[6] will reflect the true *operating risk*. This is measured by the beta[7] or systematic risk of the operating assets (β_{OA}):

$$
\begin{aligned}
\beta_{OA} &= \frac{E}{OA}\beta_E + \frac{D}{OA}\beta_D - \left[\frac{PA}{OA}\beta_{PA} - \frac{PL}{OA}\beta_{PL}\right] \\
&= \frac{E}{OA}\left(\beta_E + \beta_D\right) + \frac{D-E}{OA}\beta_D - \frac{PA}{OA}\left(\beta_{PA} - \beta_{PL}\right) - \frac{S}{OA}\beta_{PL}
\end{aligned}
$$
$$(3.21)$$

If the pension fund and its risk are ignored, then the beta of the operating assets becomes:

$$\beta'_{OA} = \frac{E}{E+D}\beta_E + \frac{D}{E+D}\beta_D \qquad (3.22)$$

---

[6] In an efficient market, share prices fully reflect all relevant information.

[7] The total risk attached to any asset or liability can be decomposed into systematic (or nondiversifiable) risk and specific (or diversifiable) risk; Equation (3.18) illustrated this decomposition. The specific risk component can be diversified away at low cost and the financial markets will not, in equilibrium, compensate investors for assuming specific risk. Only the nondiversifiable element of total risk will be priced in equilibrium. One of the most common measures of nondiversifiable risk is called beta and is defined as the ratio of the covariance between the return on the asset or liability and the return on the market to the variance of the return on the market.

Now:

$$\beta'_{OA} - \beta_{OA} = \frac{PA}{OA + S}\left(\beta_{PA} - \beta_{PL}\right) - \frac{S}{OA + S}\left(\beta_{OA} - \beta_{PL}\right) \quad (3.23)$$

This will be positive if $\beta_{PA} \geqslant \beta_{PL}$, $\beta_{OA} \geqslant \beta_{PL}$ and $S \leqslant 0$, conditions which often hold in many companies.

The company's financial capital (defined as equity plus debt) is found by rearranging (3.20):

$$E + D = OA + PA - PL = OA + S \quad (3.24)$$

and equals the value of operating assets plus the pension fund surplus. *Capital structure risk*, the systematic risk borne by the company's equity-and debt-holders, is:

$$\begin{aligned}
\beta_{E+D} &= \frac{E}{E+D}\beta_E + \frac{D}{E+D}\beta_D \\
&= \frac{PA}{E+D}\beta_{PA} - \frac{PL}{E+D}\beta_{PL} + \frac{OA}{E+D}\beta_{OA} \\
&= \beta_{PF} + \frac{OA}{E+D}\beta_{OA} \quad (3.25)
\end{aligned}$$

using (3.21) and where *pension fund risk* is defined as:

$$\beta_{PF} = \frac{PA}{E+D}\beta_{PA} - \frac{PL}{E+D}\beta_{PL} \quad (3.26)$$

Equation (3.25) shows that there is a one-to-one relationship between a company's capital structure risk and its pension fund risk.

For companies for which (3.23) is positive, the cost of capital will be overestimated if (3.22) is used instead of (3.21), since:

$$r' = r_f + \beta'_{E+D}(r_m - r_f) > r_f + \beta_{E+D}(r_m - r_f) = r \quad (3.27)$$

using the capital asset pricing model (CAPM),[8] where r_f is the risk-free rate, r_m is the return on the market index, and β'_{E+D} is given by (3.25) with β'_{OA} replacing β_{OA}. Profitable investment opportunities will be turned down if r is used as a hurdle rate rather than r'. Jin *et al.* (2006)

---

[8] The capital asset pricing model argues that the equilibrium return on a risky asset or liability is made up of two components: the risk-free return and the return needed to compensate investors for assuming systematic risk. The latter return is the product of two components: the beta of the asset or liability (which measures the 'quantity' of systematic risk assumed) and the market risk premium $(r_m - r_f)$ (which measures the 'price' of the systematic risk assumed). The CAPM is explained in more detail in Section 7.7.1 of Chapter 7 and in Blake (2000, Chapter 13).

find, using US data, that the capital structure betas of companies (3.25) (and hence share and bond prices) accurately reflect the betas of their pension funds' assets and liabilities.

Chen and D'Arcy (1986) find that the securities of US firms that use a low interest rate to discount pension liabilities outperform the securities of firms that use a high interest rate. Also, the securities of firms with relatively low pension liabilities generated positive risk-adjusted returns over the same period.

Alderson and Chen (1987) show that companies announcing plans to recover a pension surplus generally experience an abnormal rise in share price. This finding is consistent with what Alderson and Chen call the *separation hypothesis*, namely that the pension assets and liabilities are separate from those of the company, so that their recapture represents a material gain to the shareholders of the company at the expense of pension scheme beneficiaries: 'an expropriation of wealth, plain and simple' (p. 58). The finding is inconsistent with the *integration hypothesis*, namely that the markets accept the augmented balance sheet view of pension fund assets and liabilities as belonging to the sponsoring company and an excess asset reversion merely transfers assets back to their rightful owners, the company's shareholders: 'If the augmented balance sheet provides a good description of economic reality . . . there are no economic benefits from terminating the pension fund and reclaiming the excess assets. In this case, it represents nothing more than a reshuffling of assets from the pension fund to the firm' (p. 58). By contrast, Alderson and Chen find, from their sample of US companies, that those companies which engaged in excess asset reversions earned a positive risk-adjusted return of 10% from two months before the announced date of the reversion through one month after it.

3.5   CONCLUSIONS

The relationship between a company and its pension scheme is a highly complex one, especially if the pension scheme is a defined benefit one. There are also differing approaches amongst actuaries, accountants and economists as to how pension assets and liabilities should be valued and treated in company accounts. Economists, for example, take an integrated approach and argue that the assets and liabilities of a pension scheme are really part of the assets and liabilities of the company, and that the only prudent way to value liabilities is to discount the promised future pension payments using the risk-free rate. Accountants prefer to separate the assets and liabilities of the company and the pension plan, while actuaries have traditionally discounted the promised future pension payments using a discount rate related to the return on the portfolio of pension assets. This discount rate will be higher than the risk-free rate on account of the equity weighting in the portfolio of pension assets.

Economists also argue that if workers are being rational and negotiate a total compensation package, then the composition of that compensation package is irrelevant. This has powerful implications for the pension funding and pension investment policies of the company: they too become irrelevant. This follows because additional employer pension contributions, which increase the level of pension assets and hence the level of funding of the pension scheme, do not change the aggregate risk of corporate assets. Similarly, an increase in pension asset risk will increase the value of the put option that the workers have against the company, but this will be matched by offsetting changes in current wages or in the value of the promised pension in order to keep the total compensation constant.

From the company's point of view, its optimal funding and investment strategy depends on the current funding level, the tax regime and on whether or not the pension liabilities are insured. With an EET tax regime, the optimal strategy of the company is to fully fund its pension scheme and invest the pension contributions in bonds. This strategy maximises the tax shield of the company. If, on the other hand, the pension scheme is underfunded and the company is in financial distress, the optimal strategy is to invest in equities rather than bonds, since the company has nothing to lose and everything to gain. If, however, the company is solvent and future wage growth is correlated with equity returns, then the non-vested, but expected, portion of the pension promise could be hedged with equities. If the pension fund is fully insured, pension funding policy is again irrelevant, but if the pension fund is only partially insured, the optimal strategy is to maximise the difference between the value of the insurance and the premium charged for it, and this is achieved by underfunding the pension scheme and investing in risky equities.

Finally, empirical studies show a relationship between pension assets and liabilities and a company's profitability, credit rating and share price. More profitable companies have higher funding levels, despite using lower discount rates and hence reporting higher relative liabilities. Increasing the funding levels in overfunded schemes raises corporate credit ratings, while lowering the funding in underfunded schemes reduces them. Company share prices appear to reflect pension scheme surpluses and deficits.

QUESTIONS

1. Explain the differences between the actuarial and economic approaches to valuing pension liabilities.
2. Explain the difference between the expected and promised value of pension liabilities.
3. Explain the differences between the actuarial and economic approaches to accounting for pensions on company balance sheets.
4. What is the pension call?
5. What is the pension put?
6. Explain the following relationship: $PV(\tilde{P}_1^C) - PV(\tilde{P}_1^P) + PV(L_1) = PV(\tilde{A}_1)$
7. Under what circumstances are corporate pension funding policy and pension investment policy irrelevant?
8. Explain why additional employer pension contributions do not change the aggregate risk of corporate assets.
9. Why does the EET system of tax breaks give companies a strong incentive to fully fund their pension schemes and hold bonds in the pension funds?
10. Why does a company in financial distress with an underfunded pension scheme have an incentive to invest in equities rather than bonds?
11. When should a solvent company invest in equities according to Black (1989)?
12. Explain why pension funding policy is irrelevant when a pension fund's liabilities are fully insured.
13. What is the optimal corporate pension funding and investment policy when a pension fund is only partially insured?
14. According to empirical studies, what is the relationship between a company's profitability and its choice of pension liability discount rate?
15. According to empirical studies, are underfunded pension plans generally more conservative or more aggressive in their risk taking?
16. According to empirical studies, how does the funding level of its pension scheme affect a company's credit rating?
17. According to empirical studies, how do pension fund surpluses and deficits affect share prices?

18. What is the relationship between capital structure risk and pension fund risk?
19. What is the separation hypothesis? What is the integration hypothesis? Which hypothesis appears to be more consistent with empirical evidence?

REFERENCES

Alderson, M. and Chen, K. (1987) The stockholder consequences of terminating the pension plan. *Midland Corporate Finance Journal*, **4** (Winter), 55–61.

Bagehot, W. (1972) Risk and reward in corporate pension funds. *Financial Analysts Journal*, **28**, 80–84.

Black, F. (1980) The tax consequences of long run pension policy. *Financial Analysts Journal*, **36**, 1–28.

Black, F. (1989) Should you use stocks to hedge your pension liabilities? *Financial Analysts Journal*, **45**, 10–12.

Black, F. and Scholes, M. (1973) The pricing of options and corporate liabilities. *Journal of Political Economy*, **81**, 637–654.

Blake, D. (2000) *Financial Market Analysis*, John Wiley & Sons, Ltd, Chichester.

Bodie, Z., Light, J., Mørck, R. and Taggart, R. (1985) Corporate pension policy: an empirical investigation. *Financial Analysts Journal*, **41**, 10–16.

Bodie, Z., Light, J., Mørck, R. and Taggart, R. (1987) Funding and asset allocation in corporate pension plans: an empirical investigation, in Bodie, Z., Shoven, J. and Wise, D. (Eds) *Issues in Pension Economics*, University of Chicago Press, Chicago.

Brealey, R. and Myers, S. (1991) *Principles of Corporate Finance*, McGraw-Hill, New York.

Carroll, T. and Niehaus, G. (1998) Pension plan funding and corporate debt ratings. *Journal of Risk and Insurance*, **65**, 427–441.

Chen, K. and D'Arcy, S. (1986) Market sensitivity to interest rate assumptions in corporate pension plans. *Journal of Risk and Insurance*, **53**, 209–225.

Feldstein, M. and Mørck, R. (1983) Pension funding decisions, interest rate assumptions and share prices, in Bodie, Z. and Shoven, J. (Eds) *Financial Aspects of the United States Pension System*, University of Chicago Press, Chicago.

Feldstein, M. and Seligman, S. (1981) Pension funding, share prices and national savings. *Journal of Finance*, **36**, 801–824.

Godwin, J., Goldberg, S., and Duchac, J. (1997) An empirical analysis of factors associated with changes in pension plan interest rate assumptions. *Journal of Accounting, Auditing and Finance*, **11**, 305–322.

Gupta, F., Stubbs, E., and Thambiah, Y. (2000) US corporate pension plans: a value at risk analysis. *Journal of Portfolio Management*, Summer, 65–72.

Harrison, J., and Sharpe, W. (1983) Optimal funding and asset allocation rules for defined benefit pension plans, in Bodie, Z. and Shoven J. (Eds) *Financial*

Aspects of the United States Pension System, University of Chicago Press, Chicago.

Ippolito, R. (1986) *Pensions, Economics and Public Policy*, Dow Jones-Irwin, Homewood, Illinois.

Jin, L., Merton, R. and Bodie, Z. (2006) Do a firm's equity returns reflect the risk of its pension plan? *Journal of Financial Economics*, **81**, 1–26.

Klumpes, P. and Whittington, M. (2003) Determinants of actuarial valuation method changes for pension funding and reporting: evidence from the UK. *Journal of Business Finance and Accounting*, **25**, 781–783.

Modigliani, F. and Miller, M. (1958) The cost of capital, corporate finance and the theory of investment. *American Economic Review*, **48**, 261–297.

Petersen, M. (1996) Allocating assets and discounting cash flows, in *Pensions, Savings and Capital Markets*, Pension and Welfare Benefits Administration, US Department of Labor, 1–26.

Sharpe, W. (1976) Corporate pension funding policy. *Journal of Financial Economics*, **3**, 183–193

Tepper, I. (1981) Taxation and corporate pension policy. *Journal of Finance*, **36**, 1–13.

Tepper, I. and Affleck, A. (1974) Pension plan liabilities and corporate financial strategies. *Journal of Finance*, **29**, 1549–1564.

Treynor, J. (1977) The principles of corporate pension policy. *Journal of Finance*, **32**, 627–638.

4
Defined Contribution Pension Schemes – The Accumulation Phase

The simplest type of funded pension scheme is a defined contribution (DC) pension scheme. Most DC schemes were traditionally arranged on an individual basis, but increasingly employers are switching away from defined benefit schemes[1] towards DC schemes. The pension in a DC scheme is based on the value of the lump sum accumulated during the accumulation phase (i.e. during the member's working life) from the contributions going into the scheme and from the investment returns on these. These contributions can be paid by the member only, the member's employer only or by a combination of the two. If the employer agrees to pay part of the contributions, then once these have been paid, the employer has no further obligation to the employee in respect of the pension. DC schemes therefore have good portability, making them easily transferable between jobs. However, there are key design issues that need to be discussed carefully. Also, DC schemes tend to suffer from high charges and low persistency, both of which lead to significant consumer detriment. In this chapter we examine DC schemes during the accumulation phase. The distribution phase (which starts when the member retires) is considered in the following chapter.

4.1 THE OPTIMAL DESIGN OF DC SCHEMES DURING THE ACCUMULATION PHASE[2]

Although they do not suffer from portability problems, DC schemes impose a range of risks and other problems on the scheme member. The scheme member bears the risk that inadequate contributions might be made into his scheme (for example, due to spells of unemployment, child care or ill-health, or simply because the contracted contribution

---

[1] Defined benefit (DB) schemes are discussed in Chapter 6.
[2] This section draws heavily on Blake, Cairns and Dowd (2001).

rate was not high enough). He also bears asset price risk – the risk of losses in the value of his pension fund due to falls in asset values, especially in the period just prior to retirement. As he retires, he bears interest-rate risk, the risk of retiring when interest rates are low, so that the retirement annuity is permanently low. After he retires, he bears, if he purchases a level annuity, inflation risk – the risk of losses in the real value of his pension due to subsequent unanticipated inflation – and, if he purchases an investment-linked annuity, income risk – the risk that the payments made on the annuity will fluctuate. Throughout, he bears the risks of unfavourable changes in regulatory regimes, for example, the imposition of onerous pension fund investment restrictions.

4.1.1   Stochastic pension scheme design

Despite these problems, DC schemes can be designed to target a particular *benchmark pension* (e.g. a pension relative to final salary) with a specified degree of probability, and in so doing quantify the degree of pension risk – the potential difference between the DC pension and the benchmark pension – inherent in a DC scheme. The appropriate vehicle for designing and stress testing any pension scheme is *stochastic* (or *Monte Carlo*) *simulation* (Blake, Cairns and Dowd, 2001; Blake, 2003). This approach generates a large range of outcomes (that is, a probability distribution function) for the value of the pension fund at any given future date, conditional on various assumptions about pension fund contributions, asset returns, mortality and other relevant factors. We then estimate *values-at-risk* (VaRs) of the pension funds implied by alternative DC scheme designs and use these VaR estimates to make a formal comparison between the two types of scheme. Value-at-risk is now a well-established risk measure, and has been applied successfully in other fields such as banking and risk management (Dowd, 1998).[3] In using VaR here, we need to take a view on the confidence level(s) used to make the comparison.

Suppose we wish to achieve a specified target *replacement ratio* (i.e. ratio of initial pension to final-year salary), for example, two-thirds of final salary, as in a typical defined benefit (DB) scheme. Our simulations will produce an empirical distribution of possible *pension ratios* (i.e. ratios of the DC pension to the benchmark pension) for our DC scheme, and the values of this histogram will typically vary from substantially

---

[3] VaR is discussed in the appendix at the end of Chapter 1.

less than unity at the lower end to well above unity at the upper end. To make our comparison, we need to specify one or more percentiles from our histogram and then compare these values with our target pension ratio of unity. We would take the ith percentile, which is the VaR at the $100 - i$th % confidence level. If this percentile is greater than or equal to unity, we would conclude that the DC scheme successfully replicates the benchmark scheme; if the percentile is less than unity, we would conclude that the DC scheme does not successfully replicate the benchmark scheme. For example, we might make our comparisons with respect to three different percentiles or VaR-confidence levels: the 50th, 20th and 5th percentiles, corresponding to the VaR at the 50%, 80% and 95% confidence levels.

This simulation methodology has some attractive features:

- The model is extremely flexible and can accommodate almost any any set of assumptions or features relating to existing types of pension arrangements.
- The methodology allows the pension scheme designer to carry out 'what if?' experiments and stress tests by changing key assumptions and observing how these changes affect our results. These exercises are very useful because they enable the designer to identify the driving forces behind the results and gauge the sensitivity of the results to particular assumptions.

Stochastic simulation involves the following steps:

- Begin with the parameters defining both the DC pension scheme and the stochastic processes driving asset returns, earnings growth, unemployment, mortality, etc.
- Choose an investment strategy – a set of contribution rates and an asset-allocation strategy – for the relevant investment horizon. Contribution rates may be constant, age-dependent or dependent on the value of the DC assets; similarly, the asset-allocation strategy may be static (that is, 'buy and hold') or dynamic (that is, involve periodic portfolio rebalancing); in the latter case, the asset-allocation strategy may be backward-looking (for example, the portfolio may be re-balanced in response to realised gains or losses) or forward-looking (for example, the outcome of a stochastic dynamic programming exercise).
- Given these various assumptions, the programme will generate an empirical distribution of possible pension ratios at any specified future

date, a key date being the nominated retirement date of the scheme member. This distribution in turn gives us VaR estimates for any chosen confidence level.

- If the VaR estimates are unsatisfactory, we increase the contribution rate and repeat the exercise, and keep doing so until an acceptable proportion of the projected outcomes exceed the target.
- At this point, we have a DC scheme that adequately matches the DB scheme by our selected standard of comparison, and we can then consider the relative costs of the two schemes.

No DC pension scheme can achieve a target pension outcome (for example, the same pension as a DB scheme) with 100% probability; however, it is possible to use stochastic simulation to determine the contribution rate, asset-allocation strategies and other factors (for example, the contingency reserves required for possible mortality improvements) to achieve the target at a chosen degree of probability (such as 50%, 80% or 95%). Naturally, the higher the required probability, the higher the contribution rate, the more conservative the investment strategy, the higher the necessary contingency reserves, and so on.

We will illustrate the stochastic simulation program using the simple case of a typical UK male employee who starts a DC pension scheme on his 25th birthday, lives at least until his 65th birthday when he retires, and makes contributions to his pension scheme throughout his working life; he has no dependants. He faces asset-return risk, interest-rate risk and unemployment risk. Asset-return risk (or price risk) affects the value of his pension fund, given his contributions; interest-rate risk affects the value of his pension when he retires, through its impact on the value of the annuity from which his pension is paid; and unemployment risk affects his income and, hence, his ability to make contributions to his pension fund. We must also make assumptions about the risk factors and the various control variables and assign values to the parameters of the model.

4.1.2   Risk factors

Asset returns

The first risk factor relates to asset returns. A body of evidence appears to support two important hypotheses concerning the returns on long-term assets such as equities, bonds and property. The first is that they exhibit some degree of long-term *mean reversion*.[4] The second is that there exists a positive long-term equity risk premium: the long-term return on equities exceeds that on 'safer' assets, such as bonds.[5] These properties are crucial for fund managers because they help to justify the fund management strategy known as *lifestyling* or *age phasing*. Samuelson (1989, 1991, 1992) argues that when asset returns are mean-reverting, it is rational for long-horizon investors, such as pension funds, to invest more heavily in 'high-risk' equities than in 'low-risk' bonds during the early years of a pension scheme (thereby benefiting from the equity risk premium) and then to switch into bonds as the horizon shortens.

A further justification for a heavy investment in equities in pension scheme portfolios rests on the long-term stability of factor shares in national income and on the requirement of finding suitable matching assets for the accruing pension liabilities. Since there are no financial assets in existence that are linked directly to the growth rate in labour income (because no government or, indeed, corporation has yet issued wage-indexed bonds), pension fund managers must look elsewhere for matching assets. If factor shares do not trend significantly over time, equities (which reflect the return on capital) and property become natural long-term matching assets for these liabilities. Nevertheless, the short-term correlation between equity returns and earnings growth is very low and so any short-term justification for equities will rely more on their high relative returns than on their contribution to reducing portfolio risk. However, wage increases are known to be highly correlated with price inflation.[6] This suggests that index-linked bonds should provide a lower-risk, although also lower-return, match for earnings-linked liabilities than equities.

If it turns out that asset returns are generated by pure *random walks*,[7] the optimal asset allocation may (for certain objective functions) not

---

[4] For example, Lo and MacKinlay (1988) found that the weekly returns on US shares are positively correlated over short periods, while Poterba and Summers (1988) found the returns on US shares were negatively correlated over long periods, indicating that although share prices can deviate from long-term trends in the short term, they do eventually return to trend. Similar evidence of mean reversion for UK assets is found in Blake (1996).

[5] Siegel (1997) shows that US equities generated higher average returns than US Treasury bonds and bills in 97% of all 30-year investment horizons since 1802. Barclays Capital (2006) shows that similar results hold for the UK.

[6] Thornton and Wilson (1992).

[7] If an asset's return follows a random walk, the best guess of the next period's return is the current return, however far this is away from a long-run trend. In other words, the asset's price can drift away indefinitely from the initial price and the variance of the price increases linearly with time (and the standard deviation increases linearly with the square root of time).

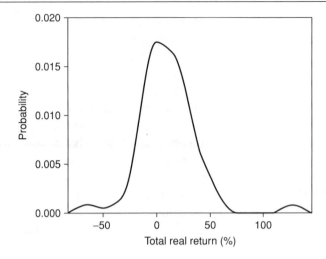

Figure 4.1   Distribution of real returns on UK equities 1950–2005

depend on the length of the investment horizon, and *time diversification* will not be effective.[8] It may also be the case that the size of the equity risk premium is not very precisely determined, even in economies with long and continuous histories of financial market data. Recent evidence further suggests that the equity risk premium may be fairly low in most of the world's financial markets.[9]

There are two other important properties of equity returns that fund managers must take into account, namely leptokurtosis and skewness. The fat tails in the distribution of equity returns (see Figure 4.1) and the skewness in the distribution of returns in some other asset classes, such as property (see Figure 4.2) raise the likelihood of extreme outcomes, both positive and negative. Over the long life of a pension scheme, a number of large positive and negative shocks to equity returns may

---

[8] Time diversification implies that the total risk on a portfolio falls as the length of the investment horizon increases and is a direct consequence of mean-reverting asset returns (Samuelson, 1963 and Merton and Samuelson, 1974).

[9] Brown, Goetzmann and Ross's (1995) analysis of all the world's stock markets that have been in operation since 1900 indicates that, globally, equities outperformed bonds by a negligible amount on average. Goetzmann and Jorion (1999) argue that the high real return of 5.98% on US equities between 1921 and 1995 can be explained by the high level of political stability in the US, as evidenced by an absence of revolution, nationalisation or financial collapse. The average equity return in other parts of the world was just over half that of the US at 3.29%. Fama and French (2002) suggest a risk premium of 3.5% going forward.

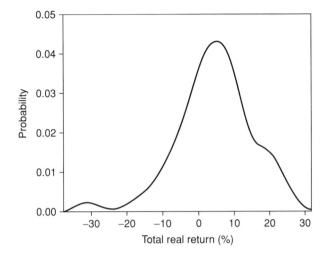

Figure 4.2   Distribution of real returns on UK property 1950–2005

be experienced. Of particular concern to DC pension scheme members will be large negative shocks. But, as Miles and Timmermann (1999) point out, the timing of the shocks is also important. If a large negative shock occurs just after a scheme is implemented, this will have a negligible impact on the fund value, but if the shock occurs just prior to retirement, the outcome could be disastrous. Lifestyling (the investment strategy that gradually switches out of equities into bonds in the period leading up to retirement) is, of course, designed to reduce the impact of such an event, but the implementation of a lifestyle strategy depends, to some extent, crucially on the nature of the leptokurtosis.

In the simulation exercise, we assume that the pension fund is invested across six risky assets: UK equities, UK bonds, UK property, UK T-bills, US equities and US bonds. Using post-war data, we can confirm the above stylised facts about real asset returns: namely that long-term assets appear to exhibit mean reversion, that there appears to be a positive long-run equity risk premium, that most assets exhibit leptokurtosis and skewness and that the contemporaneous correlation beween financial asset returns and real earnings growth is not strong.

The true model generating asset returns is, of course, unknowable. However, we have experimented with a number of well-known asset return models (for more details, see Blake, Cairns and Dowd, 2001):

- Stationary-moment models:
  - multivariate normal model (the standard benchmark asset returns model);
  - mixed multivariate normal model with regime-independent transition probabilities (to account for the observation that the financial markets exhibit both periods of tranquillity and periods of excess volatility);
  - multivariate t model (to allow for fatter tails than the multivariate normal model);
  - multivariate noncentral t (NCT) model (to allow for skewness as well as fatter tails);
  - bootstrap model (a nonparametric distribution model that draws randomly from the historical distribution of returns without imposing a particular distribution of returns such as multivariate normal, see Efron, 1979; Politis and Romano, 1994).
- Regime-switching model: a two-state Markov switching model with transition probabilities that depend on which state or regime the financial markets are in (i.e. the tranquil or the excess volatility state); this contrasts with the mixed multivariate normal model in which the transition probabilities are independent of the state the system is currently in.
- Fundamentals model: Wilkie's (1995) model (a model commonly used by actuaries), which depends on projecting fundamental economic variables, such as the dividend yield.

Interest rates

We need to model the evolution of interest rates over time in order to establish the prevailing *annuity factor* at the scheme member's retirement date. This is the present value, at the time of retirement, of one unit of an annuity for the remaining life of the annuitant. We divide the pension fund on the retirement date by the annuity factor to derive the pension annuity. The discount rate used to derive the annuity factor will typically equal the yield on long-term bonds. We therefore need a model of long-term bond yields that is consistent with the above asset returns model.

Suppose that the gross real return on long-term bonds is given by $R_{Bt} = (1 + r_{Bt})$, while the gross real return on Treasury bills (TBs) (assumed to be the risk-free asset) is given by $R_{ft} = (1 + r_{ft})$, where r_{Bt} and r_{ft} are the total real return on long-term bonds and TBs, respectively.

The logarithmic risk premium on bonds is defined as $\pi_{Bt} = \ln R_{Bt} - \ln R_{ft}$.

Suppose that the nominal yield on bonds (y_{Bt}) is determined by the following equation:[10]

$$\ln y_{Bt} = \overline{\ln y_B} + f_1(\ln y_{Bt-1} - \overline{\ln y_B}) + f_2\pi_{Bt}$$
$$= (1 - f_1)\overline{\ln y_B} + f_1 \ln y_{Bt-1} + f_2\pi_{Bt}$$
$$= f_0 + f_1 \ln y_{Bt-1} + f_2\pi_{Bt} \tag{4.1}$$

where $\overline{\ln y_B}$ is the (natural log of the) long-term yield on bonds. Equation (4.1) incorporates long-term mean reversion as well as a short-term responsiveness to the excess return on bonds. If bond prices rise by more than anticipated, then bond yields will fall by more than anticipated: we therefore expect to find $f_2 < 0$. Using least squares estimation on UK data over the post-war period, we derive the following estimates: $f_1 = 0.90$ and $f_2 = -1.097$.

We need to simulate the bond yield for the year in which the pension scheme member retires at age 65. This is necessary to derive the annuity factor. Suppose this yield is denoted $y_{B,65}$, then the annuity factor is given by:

$$\ddot{a}_{65} = \sum_{t=0}^{\infty}(1 + y_{B,65})^{-t}\,\text{Pr (survive from age 65 to age 65} + t). \tag{4.2}$$

Earnings

While the starting salary affects the monetary value of the retirement pension fund, and therefore the scheme member's pension, it does not affect our key variable of interest, namely the pension ratio. We do, however, need to make assumptions concerning both the particular *lifetime earnings profile* of the member[11] and the distribution of real earnings growth.[12]

Lifetime earnings profiles are typically concave in shape to reflect the fact that the greatest earnings growth usually takes place early in

---

[10] This is consistent with Vasicek's (1977) model.

[11] This is the earnings-age schedule that determines how the member's earnings change relative to average earnings as he progressively ages. They are sometimes also called wage profiles or salary scales.

[12] We also need to make a subsidiary assumption about the impact, if any, of unemployment on subsequent earnings. We make the simple assumption that unemployment has no effect on subsequent earnings, so when the individual is re-employed after a spell of unemployment, he receives the same earnings he would have done had he worked all along.

the career (as a consequence of rapid early promotion or frequent job changes, both of which are associated with the receipt of substantial earnings increments), while earnings growth tends to slow down from mid-life onwards, as individual careers stabilise and workers come to rely more on cost-of-living increases than experience and promotional awards.

In some industries (for example, coal mining), lifetime earnings reach a peak well before retirement age (for example, as miners move from coal-face to surface jobs). Similarly, in some professions (for example, management), the highest paid members often take early retirement[13] or are made redundant in their late 50s and early 60s and this reduces median earnings in the pre-retirement age group. However, sometimes the apparent peaking of wage profiles is the result of a cohort effect: for example, managers in their 50s could be more productive and therefore have higher earnings than managers in their 60s because they are better educated and more of them went to university, yet information on both cohorts is used to construct the wage profile.

It is important to model wage profiles accurately, since their shape will influence both the timing of contributions into the scheme (if contributions are earnings related) and forecasts of final salary. The earlier in a worker's career that pension contributions are received, the longer they benefit from compounded returns and therefore the higher the pension. Wage profiles for men and women in different professions in the UK can be found in the New Earnings Survey (or other sources such as OECD studies). The wage profile used in this chapter belongs to a 'typical' UK worker as reported in Adams (1999). It is shown in Figure 4.3, with median earnings at different ages expressed as a ratio of national average earnings. Given the preceding discussion, it is clear that the 'typical' UK worker is different at different ages due to cohort effects and the relationship between early retirement and salary.

We will assume that the wage profile remains constant over time, but is subject to annual uprating in line with the real growth rate in national average earnings, thereby preserving industry relativities. Real earnings are assumed to have a mean growth rate of 2% p.a. (equal to the average real growth rate over the past 50 years), but subject to some volatility (a standard deviation of 2% p.a.).

---

[13] Such individuals are likely to have built up above-average pension entitlements for their age group, both on account of their high salaries (which gives them a high pension fraction) and their long service (which gives them a high pension multiple and is implied by their above-average salaries for their age).

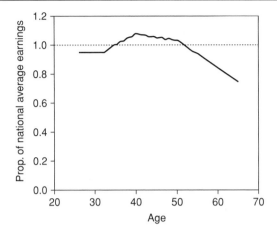

Figure 4.3 Lifetime earnings profile

Unemployment

Unemployment is modelled as a binary variable (1 = employed, 0 = unemployed) for each period, with the age-dependent probability of unemployment taken as equal to the 1998–9 UK national average unemployment rate for men of that age.[14] We also allowed for some stochastic variation around these mean rates to reflect the fact that unemployment varies over the business cycle.

4.1.3 Control variables

The model also incorporates three control variables – variables that must be set by either the pension scheme member or the provider for each period in the model.

Contribution rate

The first of these is the pension fund contribution rate. We have assumed a constant contribution rate of 10% of earnings, which is typical of DC schemes in the UK. A more general analysis could consider the

---

[14] To be precise, we took ONS data for the unemployment rates of men of various age ranges over the period December 1998 to February 1999. Interpolations were then taken to approximate the unemployment rates of men of specific ages, and the resulting unemployment rates were taken as proxies for the likely unemployment probabilities of our member as he ages over time.

possibility that the contribution rate might vary over time in response to changes in salary levels and to the performance of the scheme assets.

Asset allocation

The key control variable in the model is the asset allocation: that is, the asset composition of the pension fund portfolio. We consider the following five asset-allocation strategies:

- a *50/50* low-risk strategy that is 50% in T-bills and 50% in bonds (for most asset-return models this was found to be the minimum-risk static strategy);
- a *pension-fund-average* (PFA) strategy equal to the average allocation of UK pension funds in 1998 (namely 5% in T-bills, 51% in UK equities, 15% in UK bonds, 5% in UK property, 20% in international equities and 4% in international bonds):[15] this might be considered a high-risk strategy on account of its high equity weighting;
- a *lifestyle* strategy with a 100% weighting in the PFA portfolio for the first 20 years, followed by a 5% p.a. switch into the 50/50 portfolio during the remaining 20 years of the accumulation scheme (for a stochastic version of this strategy, see Cairns, Blake and Dowd, 2006);
- a *threshold* (or *funded status*) strategy (for example, see Derbyshire, 1999), which is:
  - 100% invested in the PFA portfolio if the current pension ratio[16] is below a lower threshold (T_L),
  - 100% in the 50/50 portfolio if the current pension ratio is above an upper threshold (T_U), and
  - linearly increases in the 50/50 portfolio as the current pension ratio rises from T_L to T_U. We set $T_L = 0.4$ and $T_U = 0.8$.
- a *portfolio insurance* strategy, based on the *constant proportion portfolio insurance* (CPPI) framework of Perold and Sharpe (1988), Black and Jones (1988) and Black and Perold (1992), in which the weight in the high-risk portfolio is given by:

$$\text{Weight in the PFA portfolio} = C_M(1 - C_F \text{ (Floor/Fund))}$$
$$= C_M(1 - C_F \text{ (Liabilities/Fund))}$$

$$(4.3)$$

---

[15] Source: the CAPS performance measurement service.

[16] Here we take the 'current pension ratio' at time t to be an approximate immediate pension $(F(t)/\bar{a})$ divided by 2/3 of the member's current salary, where $F(t)$ is the current fund size and $\bar{a}$ is an *average* annuity factor for retirees at age 65.

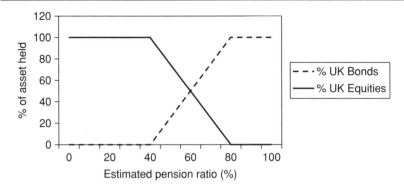

Figure 4.4   The threshold strategy

where C_F is a parameter measuring the significance attached to the fund being above a floor (where, in this example, the floor is set at the level of the liabilities in a comparable DB scheme[17]) and C_M is the multiplier attached to the quasi-surplus ratio: CPPI strategies have values of C_M exceeding unity. The remaining proportion of the fund is invested in the low-risk 50/50 portfolio.[18] We set $C_F = 0.5$ and $C_M = 2$.

The first two asset allocations are static. The third strategy is dynamic, but without any feedback. The fourth strategy incorporates a simple form of feedback control. If investment performance has been poor, so that the current value of the fund is less than 40% of that needed for the member to retire immediately, the fund is fully invested in the PFA portfolio in order to benefit from the higher expected returns. If, on the other hand, investment performance has been good, so that the value of the fund is above 80% of the current pension ratio, the fund should be fully invested in the 50/50 portfolio to protect its value. If the current pension ratio is 50%, the fund should be 25% invested in the 50/50 portfolio (that is, $(0.5 - T_L)/(T_U - T_L)$), etc (see Figure 4.4). The fifth strategy also involves feedback control, but the weight in the PFA portfolio moves in the opposite direction to that of

---

[17] Recall that the ratio of the liabilities to the fund value at retirement is equal to the inverse of the pension ratio.

[18] Short selling was not allowed and the portfolio weights were restricted to lie in the range 0–100%.

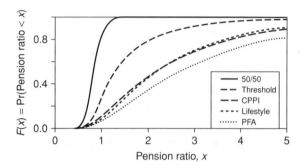

Figure 4.5   Multivariate normal model

the threshold strategy and rises in line with the quasi-surplus ratio in the fund.[19,20]

Retirement age

Finally, we assume in this version of the model that the retirement age is fixed at 65. A more sophisticated model could allow for the retirement age to depend on, say, the size of the pension fund accumulated or the health of the member.

4.1.4   Simulation output

Basis of the simulations

The model generates simulated pension ratios corresponding to each of the asset-return models and each of the asset-allocation strategies. Each of these outputs consists of an empirical distribution function plus associated statistics, with the complete set of outputs being generated by 5000 Monte Carlo simulations.

Value-at-risk statistics have been used to plot the empirical cumulative distribution function of the pension ratio for each model and for each asset-allocation strategy. Selected results are plotted in Figures 4.5 to 4.11:

---

[19] These two strategies are consistent with different investor attitudes to risk and return. The threshold strategy gives no credit for pensions exceeding the upper threshold, but does not penalise underperformance strongly. In contrast, CPPI does give credit for outperformance above the adjusted floor and penalises underperformance severely.

[20] All these strategies are simple both to explain and to implement. Optimal dynamic asset-allocation strategies can, of course, be used, but are much less straightforward to explain (see, for example, Cairns, Blake and Dowd, 2006).

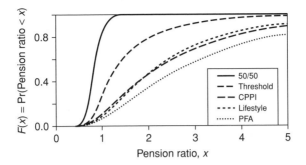

Figure 4.6 Mixed multivariate normal model

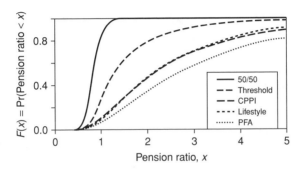

Figure 4.7 Multivariate t model

- In each of Figures 4.5 to 4.11 we have plotted the results for one particular asset-return model.
- Each figure contains five curves: one for each asset allocation strategy considered.

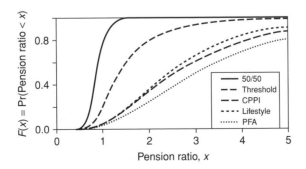

Figure 4.8 Multivariate noncentral t model

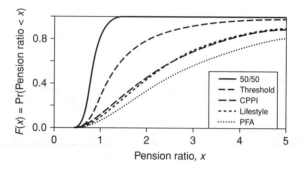

Figure 4.9   Bootstrap model

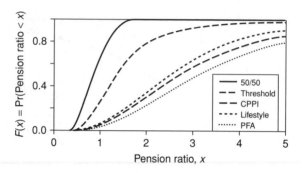

Figure 4.10   Markov switching model

- Each point on a given curve shows the probability that the pension ratio will fall below a particular level. For example, consider the PFA strategy plotted in Figure 4.5 (dotted line). We can see that the probability that the pension ratio is less than 2 is approximately 0.35, or 35%. Similarly, the probability that the pension ratio will fall below

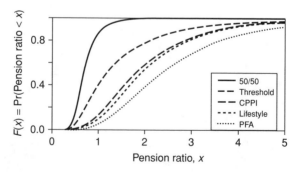

Figure 4.11   Wilkie model

1.5 is about 20%. Alternatively, we can say that we are 80% confident that the pension ratio will exceed the level 1.5.

- In each figure we can compare the five curves in a qualitative sense:
  - If one curve lies more to the right than the other curves then a particular strategy is likely to deliver higher pensions at retirement than the other strategies.
  - If a particular curve rises more steeply from 0 to 1 than the others then the strategy is less variable than the others (that is, the pension ratio at retirement is more predictable).

General comments on the results

These output graphs are all characteristic of distributions with a single peak. Furthermore, almost all have long tails going off to the right. Perhaps their most striking features are the following.

They show very considerable dispersion. Consider the very first case (that is, multivariate normal returns and the PFA asset-allocation strategy – Figure 4.5, dotted line). The simulated pension ratios vary from 0.25 at one extreme to 40 at the other (out of 5000 simulations). If one wants an alternative (and more reliable) indicator of their dispersion, the lower 5% quantile is 0.95 and the upper 5% quantile is 8.8. These indicate a 5% chance that the pension ratio will be less than 0.95, and a 5% chance that it will be greater than 8.8. Each of the empirical distributions shows a very considerable degree of dispersion, however this is measured. These results tell us in no uncertain terms that DC schemes can be very risky indeed for members relative to a benchmark linked to final salary.

They show very striking asymmetry and kurtosis. For example, in the case just considered, we have a skewness coefficient of 2.4 (that is, a long right-hand tail) and a kurtosis of 8.9 (very fat tails), both of which are very high relative to the normal distribution (0 and 3 respectively). Many of the other combinations have even bigger skewness and kurtosis coefficients. There are also very large differences between the mean and the median, another indication of asymmetry. For the particular case under consideration, which is not untypical, the mean is 3.41 while the median is 2.63.

Model risk can be assessed by examining the differences between the asset-return models. For example, the mean pension ratio across the seven asset-return models for the PFA strategy ranges from 2.70 to 3.73, while for the threshold strategy the range is 1.52 to 1.66 (see Table 4.1).

Table 4.1   Model risk for the PFA and threshold strategies

| | Pension ratios for | | | | | |
| | PFA strategy | | | Threshold strategy | | |
	Mean	SD	95% VaR	Mean	SD	95% VaR
Multivariate normal	3.41	2.65	0.95	1.61	1.10	0.74
Mixed multivariate normal	3.56	2.75	1.01	1.63	1.05	0.75
Multivariate t	3.49	3.02	0.95	1.64	1.14	0.74
Noncentral t	3.73	3.21	1.16	1.66	0.98	0.82
Stationary bootstrap	3.51	2.85	0.92	1.64	1.10	0.74
Markov	3.69	2.65	1.11	1.61	1.20	0.64
Wilkie	2.70	1.53	1.04	1.52	1.14	0.51

Standard deviations (SDs) for the same two strategies range from 1.53 to 3.21 and from 0.98 to 1.20, respectively. The differences between models become more significant when we consider tail events. For example, the 95% values-at-risk for the same two strategies range from 0.92 to 1.16 and from 0.51 to 0.82, respectively: we can be 95% confident of doing better than these ratios.

Figure 4.12 shows these differences graphically for the same two investment strategies (PFA and threshold). Differences in the parameterisation of the models show up in the way that, for example, the Markov model always lies a bit to the right of the other curves, while always having roughly the same shape as most of the other curves. The Wilkie model typically stands out of line. This is principally a consequence of the calibration of the model to a longer run of data (which had both lower average real returns and lower volatility). Some differences will, however, also be due to the autoregressive structure of the model. Apart from the Wilkie model, the results for different models look reasonably consistent with one another. Larger differences show up primarily in the tails, which are difficult to see in these graphs. It is in the tails where structural differences between, for example, the multivariate normal and NCT will show up.

These observations justify our consideration of different asset-return models: that is, we wish to choose asset-allocation strategies that are generally good under most models but, equally well, not especially bad

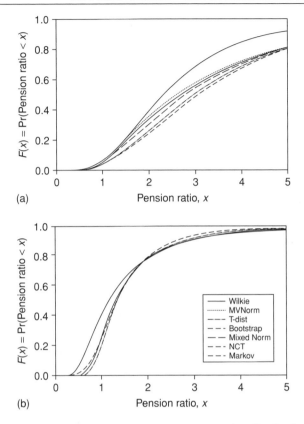

Figure 4.12   The effect of model risk on the cumulative distribution function of the pension ratio for two asset-allocation strategies: (a) pension-fund-average (PFA) strategy; (b) threshold strategy ($T_L = 0.4$, $T_U = 0.8$)

in the remainder of the models. In particular, we should avoid recommending strategies that are very good when we consider one asset-return model, but very bad under another. This is because any model is only an approximation to reality and because the limited amount of historical data we have available still leaves us with a range of plausible models.

A much more important issue is parameter uncertainty. Even if we know the true model (say, it happens to be the multivariate normal model), we still cannot be sure that our estimates of the parameters of the model are suitable. We have estimated these models using data for the last half-century; we cannot be sure that these estimates will be suitable for conducting simulations over the next 40 years. For example, the average real return on UK equities exceeded 10% over the last

Table 4.2   Asset-allocation strategies with the multivariate normal model

	Pension ratios			
	Median	SD	95% VaR	80% VaR
50/50	0.84	0.18	0.61	0.71
PFA	2.63	2.65	0.95	1.53
Lifestyle	2.13	1.86	0.90	1.34
Threshold	1.30	1.10	0.74	0.93
CPPI	2.10	2.06	0.83	1.27

half-century; it is probably overly optimistic to assume that this real return is sustainable over the next 40 years.

Figure 4.12 gives an indication of the possible effects of parameter uncertainty. In particular, considerations of the differences between the Wilkie model and the other models suggests that parameter uncertainty is rather more significant than model risk.

Most striking of all, perhaps, the simulated pension ratios vary enormously across the different asset-allocation strategies. The effect of the choice of asset allocation strategy is much more significant than the effect of parameter uncertainty. Consider the multivariate normal model (Figure 4.5), for example. Table 4.2 shows that the median pension ratio varies from 0.84 (50/50), through 1.30 (threshold) to 2.63 (PFA). The standard deviation of the pension ratio ranges from 0.18 (50/50), through 1.10 (threshold) to 2.65 (PFA). The asset-allocation strategy is thus obviously extremely important. The huge discrepancy between the two sets of outcomes is also reflected in their percentiles: the 80% VaR, for example, ranges from 0.71 (50/50), through 0.93 (threshold) to 1.53 (PFA).

One tentative conclusion we might draw from Figures 4.5 to 4.11 is that the most appropriate investment vehicle for a 40-year DC pension scheme is, overall, a well-diversified, relatively high-return, relatively high-risk portfolio (for example, the PFA portfolio). None of these figures suggests that a switch into lower-risk assets near retirement is appropriate, except possibly as a means of avoiding the most extreme, bad outcomes. For example, the lifestyle strategy can be justified on the grounds that policyholders like the certainty of a reliable estimate of the ultimate pension a few years early, even though they may be sacrificing substantial upside potential. Furthermore, all of the asset models considered here have relatively high mean equity returns. More conservative

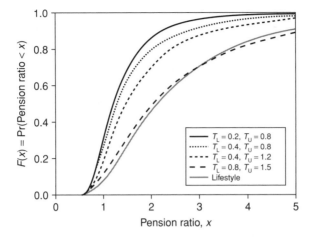

Figure 4.13 Sensitivity of the distribution of the pension ratio to changes in the threshold strategy. The lifestyle strategy is plotted for comparison

parameter values would change the results to some extent: for example, by introducing more obvious cross-over points in the left-hand tails.

It is useful to investigate how sensitive the threshold and CPPI strategies are to changes in T_L, T_U, C_F and C_M. Sample results are plotted in Figures 4.13 and 4.14. In both cases, appropriate choices for the control

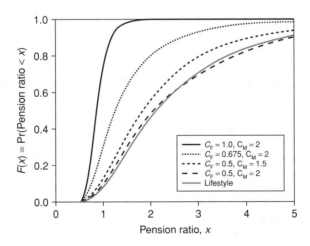

Figure 4.14 Sensitivity of the distribution of the pension ratio to changes in the constant proportion portfolio insurance strategy. The lifestyle strategy is plotted for comparison

Table 4.3   VaRs for the threshold strategy

	VaR confidence level			Critical VaR-CL
	50%	80%	95%	
Multivariate normal	1.30	0.93	0.74	73%
Mixed multivariate normal	1.31	0.95	0.75	74%
Multivariate t	1.30	0.93	0.74	73%
Noncentral t	1.39	1.03	0.82	81%
Stationary bootstrap	1.31	0.94	0.74	74%
Markov	1.37	0.92	0.64	74%
Wilkie	1.17	0.73	0.51	60%

parameters can ensure that the fund is always invested 100% in the PFA portfolio or 100% in the 50/50 portfolio. The graphs show that a wide range of outcomes in between are all possible. This includes results similar to that of the lifestyle strategy.

4.1.5   Choosing the optimal asset-allocation strategy

Recall that the pension ratio is defined as the ratio of the DC pension to a benchmark pension that is equal to two-thirds of final salary. We now select some particular portfolio-allocation strategy, say, the threshold strategy with $T_L = 0.4$ and $T_U = 0.8$, and one or more percentiles, or VaR-confidence levels, on which we will make our comparison. Suppose we take these confidence levels to be 50%, 80% and 95%.

We then get the results reported in Table 4.3. If we take the 50% confidence level, then our multivariate normal VaR is 1.30, so we would accept that this DC scheme does achieve our target pension ratio of 1. However, if we take the 80% confidence level, our VaR drops to 0.93 and we would reject the DC scheme. At the 95% confidence level, the VaR drops further to 0.74. If we want to, we can also look at the critical VaR-confidence level – that confidence level at which we would just accept the DC scheme. In this particular case, this critical confidence level is 73%, so we would accept the DC scheme (as achieving our target) if we have a confidence level less than 73%, but reject it if we required a confidence level greater than 73%. The table also lists the comparable results for the other asset-return processes. One can see that these figures do not vary substantially, except at the 95% confidence level and for the Wilkie and NCT models.

Table 4.4   Required contribution rates for the multivariate normal model

VaR confidence level for the PFA	99%	95%	50%	5%
VaR for the PFA	0.62	0.95	2.63	8.47
	Required contribution rate (%)			
50/50	11.5	15.6	31.3	72.2
Lifestyle	9.0	10.6	12.3	19.3
Threshold	10.0	12.8	20.2	23.7
CPPI	10.3	11.4	12.5	12.9

We can derive similar tables for other asset-allocation strategies and asset-return models. In most cases the final answer – whether or not the DC scheme is an adequate substitute for the benchmark – will depend on the precise criterion used (that is, the choice of VaR confidence level) and will also often vary with the asset-return models and the asset-allocation strategy. However, for reasonable VaR confidence levels, say in the range 50–80%, the evidence in Table 4.3 indicates that the asset-returns model is less important than the asset-allocation strategy.

4.1.6   The trade-off between risk and contribution rates

Finally, we can also follow the procedure in Section 4.1.1 and adjust the contribution rate into the scheme until we achieve the desired VaR confidence level. Table 4.4 shows the contribution rates required by the other asset-allocation strategies to have the same VaRs as the PFA strategy[21] at the 99, 95, 50 and 5% confidence levels, assuming the multivariate normal model for asset returns. For the lifestyle and threshold strategies, the contribution rate needed to achieve the 99% VaR for the PFA strategy is actually less than 10%, since the 99% VaR of the PFA is very low, just 0.62. In all other cases, the required contribution rate to match the PFA is higher, often considerably higher. For the 50/50 strategy, a contribution rate of 31.3% is needed to match the PFA median. With the lifestyle strategy, the downside protection achieved by systematically switching into bonds during the last 20 years of the scheme requires the contribution rate to rise to 12.3% if the same median pension ratio as the PFA strategy is desired by the scheme member. Of the two strategies involving feedback, the threshold strategy looks distinctly more expensive than CPPI, except for the most extreme poor outcomes.

---

[21] Recall that the contribution rate for the PFA is 10%.

4.2 CHARGES[22]

The providers of defined contribution pension schemes, such as life offices, extract charges from both the contributions they receive from policyholders and from the value of the fund accumulated from investing these contributions. These charges pay for scheme administration, profit and key services (such as fund management). However, the complex and often disguised charging structures used by providers are a potential source of consumer confusion. In spite of attempts by the regulatory authority[23] to improve their transparency, the suspicion remains that the structure and scale of pension scheme charges is not well understood by consumers.[24] This section outlines some of the key charge categories and explains their impact on the final value of the pension fund.

4.2.1 Types of charges

Pension scheme charges can be levied on a number of bases, which can be categorised broadly as:

- Charges imposed on contributions:
  - entry charges, either related to or independent of the size of contributions;
  - regular (periodic) charges, either related to or independent of the size of contributions.
- Charges imposed on the fund value:
  - regular charges based on interim value;
  - exit charges based on redemption (i.e. terminal, transfer or paid-up) value.[25]

If charges are extracted prior to the delivery of the service to which they relate, they are said to be *front-loaded*, while if they are extracted afterwards, they are said to be *back-loaded*. Front-loaded charges do not tend to provide the best incentive to deliver good service.

The appendix at the end of this chapter provides a detailed analysis of the impact of all these charges. It shows that it is very difficult to

---

[22] This section draws heavily on Blake and Board (2000).

[23] The Financial Services Authority (FSA) in the UK. Prior to 2000, UK retail financial services were regulated by a combination of the Securities and Investments Board (SIB) and the Personal Investment Authority (PIA).

[24] See, for example, Office of Fair Trading (1997, 1999).

[25] The terminal value referred to here is the value of the accumulated fund on the retirement date of the policyholder. On that date, the accumulated fund is usually used to buy a life annuity from an insurance company in return for a single fixed charge.

determine the total charge that will be levied on a particular fund, principally because of the complex interactions between the components of the total charge, as we now discuss.

4.2.2   Reduction in yield

The complexity of the charging structures listed above and considered in more detail in Section A.1 of the appendix indicates the need for a summary measure of the impact of charges. The conventional approach is to calculate the *reduction in yield* (*RiY*) resulting from the charges. This, broadly, measures the difference between an *assumed yield* (which is set by the regulator[26]) and the *effective yield* (which is defined as the yield at which the compounded gross contributions into the scheme equal the net value of the fund). It should be stressed that, to ensure comparability between funds, the calculation is based on a standard *assumed* or *projected* growth rate (i.e. for the purpose of the *RiY* calculation, providers are required by the regulator to assume a growth rate which is constant both over time and across funds).

The higher the charges, the lower the net contributions invested, and therefore the lower the fund's maturity value and the larger the reduction in yield. While the *RiY* is a mathematically well-defined measure of the fund charge, few retail customers appear to understand it. In the next subsection, a simple alternative to this measure is proposed, one that retains the mathematical rigour of the *RiY*, but that offers a more straightforward interpretation.

Two effects of the use of the *RiY* can be noted. First, because the *RiY* assumes a particular growth rate for the fund, it will generally reflect neither the yield that different funds expect to achieve on the basis of their investment strategy nor the yield they will actually realise. For example, even if some funds were able to levy higher charges on the grounds of superior investment performance, the *RiY* calculation would reflect the fund's higher charges but not its higher expected investment performance. Second, when performance-related charging is used, the link between realised investment performance and charges means that the simple assumption of a single, common growth rate is likely to produce misleading cost estimates. This suggests that the *RiY* approach

---

[26] Before 1999, the assumed yield was set by the PIA/FSA at 9% p.a.; however, as a result of lower inflation, the assumed yield was reduced to 7% p.a. in 1999. The PIA/FSA also revised its other assumptions as follows: 6% p.a. investment returns after retirement, 2.5% p.a. retail price inflation and 4% p.a. average earnings growth.

Table 4.5 Percentage of pension fund value represented by charges and reductions in yield in October 1998

	Regular-premium scheme (£200/month)					Single-premium scheme (£10 000)				
	5 years	10 years	15 years	20 years	25 years	5 years	10 years	15 years	20 years	25 years
Costs as percentage of fund value										
Best overall	3.1	4.1	7.2	8.5	9.8	3.8	7.1	9.2	10.6	10.4
Best commission-loaded	4.0	4.1	7.4	8.9	10.6	3.8	7.1	9.2	10.6	10.4
Industry average	11.6	13.0	14.8	17.7	19.0	9.6	13.3	16.3	19.1	21.9
Worst fund	19.2	22.0	24.6	28.2	27.8	17.4	20.5	27.0	32.9	38.2
Reduction in yield										
Best overall	1.26	0.79	0.90	0.76	0.68	0.84	0.80	0.70	0.61	0.48
Best commission-loaded	1.63	0.79	0.92	0.80	0.73	0.84	0.80	0.70	0.61	0.48
Industry average	4.91	2.65	1.93	1.68	1.39	2.18	1.54	1.29	1.15	1.07
Worst fund	8.47	4.76	3.43	2.88	2.16	4.09	2.47	2.26	2.15	2.08

Source: Money Management (October 1998)

Table 4.6   Reductions in yield, 1994–1999 (%)

	1994	1995	1998	1999
10 years	5.0	4.6	3.6	2.5
25 years	1.6	1.5	1.3	1.2

Source: Chapman (2000)

may become less useful if providers switch to charging structures based more heavily on performance.

Table 4.5 illustrates the charges for regular premium schemes in the UK in October 1998. It shows that, for a 5-year scheme, the best fund had total charges amounting to 3.1% of the terminal fund value, while the worst fund charged 19.2%. For 25-year schemes, the difference between highest and lowest charges amounted to 18.0% of terminal fund value. The table also reports the charges for single-premium schemes,[27] which, despite their simplicity, can also involve high charges. However, Table 4.6 shows that RiYs have fallen over time, especially for shorter-term schemes.[28]

4.2.3   Reduction in contributions

The principal difficulty with the RiY approach is that it can be difficult to explain to a non-specialist. This section outlines a simple alternative to the RiY, the *reduction in contributions* (RiC).[29] This measure, which is presented in detail in Section A.2, expresses the loss in value arising from a fund's charges as the difference between the *gross contribution* and the *effective contribution* applied to the fund, where effective contributions are defined as the contributions that would have to be paid into a

---

[27] These schemes are often used by the self-employed with irregular income patterns, who only become aware of their full year's income towards the end of the financial year and then buy a single-premium policy on the basis of that income before the new financial year to avoid the loss of tax relief.

[28] Note that the figures in Table 4.5 relate to October 1998, whereas the figures for 1998 in Table 4.6 are the averages for the year.

[29] The reduction in contributions is not a new measure. It is also known as a *percentage rate of premium* and it was the measure of reporting charges originally recommended by the SIB for the new disclosure regime for life assurance and unit trusts that came into operation in January 1990 (see Securities and Investment Board, 1988). However, following industry representations, the SIB adopted the reduction in yield measure of reporting charges on the grounds that this 'is a more appropriate approach for a product intended to be a long-term investment vehicle' and that 'the short-term impact of charges is broadly reflected in the discontinuance values which have to be disclosed' (Securities and Investment Board, 1989, p. 15).

Table 4.7 Reduction in yield and reduction in contributions for a typical pension scheme in 1998 (percentages).

	5 years	10 years	15 years	20 years	25 years
Ignoring policy lapses					
Effective yield (g')	3.4	5.8	6.7	7.1	7.3
Reduction in yield (RiY)	5.6	3.2	2.3	1.9	1.7
Reduction in contributions (RiC)	13.1	15.2	17.6	20.2	22.9
Adjusting for policy lapses					
Effective yield (g')	−9.2	−3.7	−0.9	1.0	2.3
Reduction in yield ($LARiY$)	18.2	12.7	9.9	8.0	6.7
Reduction in contributions ($LARiC$)	37.1	47.8	54.4	58.8	62.0

Note: The table illustrates a regular-premium scheme with contributions of £200 per month, and makes the assumptions set out in Table 4.8.

hypothetical zero-load scheme so as to generate the same terminal value as the scheme in question. The RiC has been described as the measure of reporting charges 'most likely to be understood and most useful for the purposes of making comparisons' (Securities and Investment Board, 1988, p. 11).

Table 4.7 shows illustrative calculations of the RiY and RiC for a scheme with regular contributions and a typical charging structure (see Table 4.8). The first panel of the table shows that, as a result of a combination of the front-loading of charges and the effects of compounding, the effective yield on the fund rises with term to maturity and, as a consequence, the RiY falls with term from 5.6% for a 5-year policy to 1.7% for a 25-year policy. However, although the effective yield rises with term, this is not sufficient to compensate fully for the effect of compounding, which results in the RiC rising with term to maturity.[30] The RiC is 13.1% for a 5-year policy and 22.9% for a 25-year policy, exactly equal to the tax break on pension schemes available to a basic rate taxpayer at the time.

It is important to understand that the RiC and RiY are summary methods of reporting and comparing the effect of charges.[31] They have no

---

[30] As a rule of thumb, the following relationship holds between RiC and RiY: $RiC \approx (t/2)RiY$, where t is the term of the policy in years. RiC will rise with term, unless RiY falls sufficiently rapidly.

[31] We can interpret RiC as an *input* measure of reporting charges, while RiY can be interpreted as an *output* measure of reporting charges expressed in terms of reduced future growth.

Table 4.8   Assumptions made in Table 4.7

	Symbol	Value
Charging structure:		
Allocation	a	95%
Bid-offer spread	s	5%
Fund management fee	f	0.75%
Paid-up policy (PUP) fee	x	0%
Policy fee (continues after lapse)	M	£3 p.m.
Uprating factor for policy fee	i	4.5% p.a.
Other assumptions:		
Yield	g	9.0% p.a.
Lapse rate in year 1	q_1	16.20%
Lapse rate in year 2	q_2	13.25%
Lapse rate in year 3	q_3	11.55%
Lapse rate in year 4	q_4	11.04%
Lapse rate from year 5	q_{5+}	6.5% p.a.

Note: The symbols are used in the appendix.

implications for the levels of charges actually levied by firms or for the structure of those charges. For example, the use of the *RiC* does not necessarily imply that an optimal charging structure should be based on contributions. Although it would be easy for consumers to understand, an important implication of a charging structure based solely on contributions is that the total charge will be independent of the realised return on investments. In contrast, a scheme with the bulk of its charges based on the fund value (and so performance-related), provides a strong statement about the scheme provider's own perception of his ability to deliver investment performance in excess of the assumed or projected rate. A scheme with charges levied principally on contributions offers the fund manager little incentive to achieve good performance, and places all of the risk of underperformance on the client.[32]

---

[32] To illustrate, in the case of the 25-year policy just discussed, and either a fund-based charge of 1.7% of the annual fund value or a contribution-based charge of 22.9% of each contribution, the percentage take varies with the realised investment return as follows:

Realised return (%)	5	6	7	8	9	10	11	12	13
Fund-based charges	20.6	21.2	21.8	22.4	22.9	23.4	23.9	24.3	24.7
Contribution-based charges	22.9	22.9	22.9	22.9	22.9	22.9	22.9	22.9	22.9

4.2.4   Changing charging structures and the impact of hidden charges

Funds change their charging structures on a regular basis,[33] which makes it difficult to compare funds over time and raises the question as to whether particular charging structures, and changes to them, are used to conceal the true impact of charges or whether the changes are actually in the clients' best interests.

A different issue relates to hidden charges. The 1998 Towers Perrin survey of European fund management fees shows that some fund managers do not report their full sets of charges. The three key charges are for asset management, broking (i.e. transaction execution) and custody. There are also charges for reporting, accounting and performance measurement. The survey reveals that some fund managers report the asset management fee (as some proportion of the value of the net assets under management) only *after* deducting broking and custody fees.[34] This lack of transparency can lead to incentive problems. Broking fees are related to turnover, which provides an incentive to churn (i.e. overtrade) the portfolio; this is especially so if the transactions are executed by an in-house broker and the broking fee is hidden from the client. Some fund managers, in contrast, use discount brokers to reduce the cost to the client. Some clients impose turnover limits to reduce costs.

Retail fund managers in the UK are subject to a public disclosure regime in a way that UK institutional fund managers are not. Retail schemes are required to report 'all explicit charges and expenses . . . and all other deductions and expenses which may or will bear upon the fund' (Financial Services Authority, 2000, Section 6.6.19). However, while these expenses include the 'costs of investment management', they explicitly exclude 'dealing costs and costs associated with the routine management and servicing of existing property investments' (see, for example, Institute and Faculty of Actuaries, 1999, Section 9.2.6). There is also no disclosure requirement for retail funds to report turnover

---

[33] For example, see *Money Management*'s annual *Personal Pensions* publications.

[34] Some fund managers justify this on the grounds that both the portfolio transactions and the safe keeping are conducted by a third party independent of the fund manager, typically the global custodian. The survey also showed that other fund managers operate full 'clean fees' (i.e. report full charges, including third-party fees, which are merely passed through to the client). Yet other fund managers add a commission to third-party fees before passing them through. In some cases, however, the broker or custodian is related to the fund manager (e.g. is part of the same investment banking group) and, in such cases, it is more difficult to assess charges appropriately.

figures.[35] So, even with retail funds, there is no real disincentive to churn the portfolio.

There are also indirect hidden charges, for example, those imposed on consumers when they deviate from the planned payment schedule. One illustration of this relates to the treatment of paid-up policies (or PUPs), highlighted in an internal report commissioned by AXA Sun Life in 1999.[36] As pension scheme investments cannot be liquidated prior to retirement, policyholders who move to a new pension scheme have the choice of transferring their existing fund to the new scheme or leaving their assets in the original scheme, which is then converted into a PUP by the provider. Policies are also converted into PUPs when policyholders cease making contributions to their schemes. The report finds that only 15% of policyholders who terminate a policy early take transfer values, the rest leave paid-up policies with the original provider. While existing regulations require pension providers to disclose transfer values, there is no obligation to quote PUP maturity values; and few providers do so voluntarily.

Different providers compete on the basis of the transfer and full maturity values that they quote. However, PUP maturity values, which, in principle, should be related to transfer values, can turn out to be poor value for money, because the original providers can continue to extract similar charges to those that they would have done had the policy remained active.[37] For example, the report discusses the case of one company which quotes the highest transfer value amongst twelve leading providers, but ranks twelfth for its PUP maturity value quote.

It seems anomalous that schemes are required only to quote transfer values, when it is known that only 15% of those policyholders not going to full term are likely to obtain this transfer value, while the remaining 85% will receive the different, and unpublicised, PUP value. This means that investors who terminate a scheme early can face significantly higher costs (i.e. the losses arising from the transfer to PUP status) than would be expected from the published transfer values.

---

[35] While life offices and other pension scheme providers present turnover figures in their annual reports, there is no centralised collection and dissemination of this data, and it would therefore be very expensive (at least in terms of time) for potential customers to compare turnover figures across providers.

[36] The report itself was not published, but key results relating to PUPs were made accessible to the media (see, for example, O'Neill, 1999 and Slade, 1999).

[37] See, for example, the paid-up notes for the various personal pension scheme providers listed in *Savings Market* (1997).

The current complex and often disguised charging structures used by providers are a potential source of consumer confusion and detriment.

4.3 PERSISTENCY[38]

The DC personal pensions industry in the UK suffers from very high lapse rates by policyholders. A regular-premium pension scheme involves a substantial commitment of time and resources by both the scheme's sponsor and its members if the desired objectives are to be achieved. Any significant front-loading of charges in schemes means that members suffer a substantial detriment if their contributions lapse prematurely. As the financial regulator argues: *'if investors buy policies on the basis of good advice, . . . they would not normally be expected to cancel premiums to their policies unless forced to do so by unexpected changes in their personal circumstances. This means that persistency can be a powerful indicator of the quality of the selling process.'* (PIA, 1999, p. 3). The financial regulator defines persistency as *'the proportion of investors who continue to pay regular contributions to their personal policies, or who do not surrender their single-premium policy'* (p. 3).

4.3.1 Persistency rates

Table 4.9 shows that persistency rates (i.e. the percentage of policies that have not lapsed) after four years of membership are between 57% and 67%. Although only data for the first four years of a pension scheme are available, the table suggests that very few personal pension scheme members are likely to maintain their membership of the scheme for long enough to build up an adequate pension.

The persistency rate is higher for schemes arranged by independent financial advisers than by company representatives, suggesting that the clients of the former are generally more satisfied with their policies than those of the latter. However, the one-year rates indicate a small improvement in the persistency rates for schemes arranged by company representatives since 1993, and a small decline in that for schemes arranged by independent financial advisers (IFAs). The effect of these two modest changes is that the difference in lapse rates fell by over 40% between 1993 and 1997, with only a 4.3 percentage point difference

---

[38] This section draws heavily on Blake and Board (2000).

Table 4.9   Persistency rates for regular-premium personal pension schemes, 1993–1997 (percentages)

	Company representatives: after				Independent financial advisers: after			
	1 year	2 years	3 years	4 years	1 year	2 years	3 years	4 years
1993	84.1	72.3	63.6	56.7	91.5	83.3	76.6	70.5
1994	83.8	72.7	64.3	57.2	90.9	81.2	73.5	66.9
1995	85.5	74.9	65.5		90.2	80.7	72.2	
1996	86.6	74.6			89.8	79.7		
1997	85.7				90.0			

Source: PIA (1999, Table 1)

in the lapse rates for one-year schemes between the two groups in 1997.

The financial regulator regards these persistency rates as '*disturbing*' (PIA, 1998, p. 10) and offers a number of explanations: members were mis-sold pensions which were either unsuitable or too expensive; regular-premium policies might be unsuitable for those with irregular earnings or uncertain long-term employment; a change of employment may lead to a member joining an occupational scheme and abandoning their personal one; adverse general economic conditions could worsen persistency rates. The financial regulator also offers suggestions as to why the IFAs are more successful than company representatives. First, IFAs tend to advise clients on higher incomes, who are more likely to continue contributing; second, policies chosen by an IFA are likely to be from a wider range of policies than those offered by representatives of any single company, leading to a greater likelihood of the policy matching more closely the particular needs of the client.

4.3.2   Adjusting reported charges for policy lapses

It is possible to incorporate the effect of policy lapses in the calculations of the *RiY* and *RiC*. Details of the calculations appear in Section A.3, but the principal result is that the *lapse-adjusted reduction in yield (LARiY)* rises with higher average takes (i.e. charges) and falls with higher persistency. The latter result follows because the take at maturity is much higher than in earlier years, since the terminal value awarded in the final year (and therefore the corresponding charge) is a very high proportion of the total value of the fund. So, strong persistency means that lower *LARiY*s are needed to achieve the same average take.

According to Chapman (1998),[39] the average *LARiY* in October 1998 was 2.5% for a 25-year scheme, and ranged from 0.9% for Equitable (which had the highest assumed persistency rate over 25 years of 30%) to 5% for Guardian (which had the lowest assumed persistency rate of just 7%). These persistency rates were based on the companies' own persistency experience for the first three years based on PIA November 1997 data and then projected forward from year 4 at the industry average annual lapse rate of 6.5%. The industry average persistency rate over 25 years was assumed to be 16%.

Section A.3 also shows how the *lapse-adjusted reduction in contributions (LARiC)* is calculated. The second panel of Table 4.7 presents both the *LARiY* and *LARiC* on the basis of the most recent annual lapse rates of company representatives' policyholders (see Table 4.9), namely 16.20%, 13.25%, 11.55% and 11.04% for the first four years, and thereafter at 6.5% per annum. It shows that lapses have a remarkable impact on the levels of charges reported. Because the likelihood of maintaining contributions for 25 years is so low, the effective contribution made by a typical policyholder over this period is expected to be just 38p for every £1 of gross contribution.

4.4 CONCLUSIONS

In this chapter we used stochastic simulation to determine the likely distribution of the pensions available from DC pension schemes, for given contribution rates and asset-allocation strategies. We draw four conclusions from this exercise. First, we find that DC schemes can be extremely risky relative to benchmark pensions linked to final salary (far more so than most pension scheme professionals would be likely to admit). Second, the VaR estimates are sensitive both to the asset-return model used and its parameterisation, although the choice of asset-return model is less important than the asset-allocation strategy selected, except when considering extreme tail events in asset returns. Third, a static asset-allocation strategy delivers substantially better results than any

---

[39] Chapman's discussion is in terms of the *annual charge equivalent (ACE)* of a particular charging structure. Section A.3 shows that this always takes the same value as the *LARiY*.

of the dynamic strategies investigated over the long term (40 years) of the sample policy. This is important given that lifestyle strategies are the cornerstone of many DC schemes. Fourth, conservative bond-based asset-allocation strategies require substantially higher contribution rates than more risky equity-based strategies if the same retirement pension is to be achieved.

We found that charging structures tend to be complex, disguised and front-loaded in DC pension schemes. As surveys by the Office of Fair Trading and others confirm, such charging structures can have the effect of confusing consumers to such an extent that they are unable to assess whether the scheme they are being invited to participate in, for a substantial period of time and with a substantial commitment of resources, offers value for money.

Despite the penalties for early exit, very high lapse rates are observed in many DC pension, schemes. However, there is no requirement for financial institutions offering DC schemes to disclose their lapse rates, to disclose their PUP terms or to disclose their charges for policies which are not carried to maturity. It is also important for consumers to understand the consequences, in terms of a reduced fund value, of a policy lapsing, especially if charges are front-loaded. For this reason, the *lapse-adjusted RiC* (*LARiC*) might be a powerful indicator summarising both the impact of charges and the level of consumer satisfaction with a particular provider.[40]

With many companies moving away from defined benefit pension provision towards DC pensions, and with workers in companies without a pension scheme having no alternative but to buy a DC pension scheme from a life office or bank, it is essential that these schemes are well designed and deliver an adequate pension in retirement with a high degree of probability. Our analysis above shows how short of meeting this objective many DC pension schemes still are.

QUESTIONS

1. What is a defined contribution pension scheme?
2. What is meant by the accumulation phase of a DC scheme?

---

[40] *LARiY* and *LARiC* are not the only ways of reporting charges in the case where policies are transferred or become paid-up.

3. What are the key risks in the accumulation phase of a DC scheme?
4. What is stochastic simulation?
5. What is the replacement ratio?
6. What is the pension ratio?
7. What is meant by an 80% VaR confidence level?
8. How does stochastic pension scheme design operate?
9. Explain the trade-off between a high required VaR confidence level and the investment strategy followed by the scheme.
10. What risk factors need to be taken into account when modelling asset returns?
11. Explain the principal models used to generate asset returns.
12. How does the level of interest rates influence the DC pension?
13. How does the lifetime earnings profile influence the size of the DC pension?
14. What are the key control variables in a DC pension plan?
15. Explain the key asset-allocation strategies suitable for a DC pension plan.
16. How critical is the choice of asset-returns model in the distribution of pension ratios on the retirement date?
17. How critical is the asset-allocation strategy in the distribution of pension ratios on the retirement date?
18. Discuss one method of choosing the optimal asset-allocation strategy for a DC scheme.
19. Explain the trade-off between risk and the contribution rate into a DC scheme.
20. What do DC pension scheme charges pay for?
21. What are the main types of charges that pension schemes impose?
22. Explain reduction in yield as a measure of pension scheme charges. How is it defined?
23. Explain reduction in contributions as a measure of pension scheme charges. How is it defined?
24. What is the simple formula linking reduction in contributions and reduction in yield?
25. How can charges be hidden? Provide an example.
26. In what way is persistency a powerful indicator of the quality of the selling process?
27. How can charges be adjusted for the policy lapses?

APPENDIX: CHARGES

This appendix analyses the charging elements of typical personal pension schemes. To illustrate the effects of charges, we define the following terms:

V_T Maturity value of the fund at the end of period T.

V_t Value of the fund at the end of period t; t will have the value 0 at the start of the scheme and T at the end of the last period of contribution (if the scheme goes to maturity).

g_t Growth rate in the fund's value in period t.

C_t Contribution made in period t. We assume that contributions are made at the beginning of each period and that contributions grow at an annual rate of $e\%$ (for example, the rate of growth might reflect the growth rate in national average earnings). Thus: $C_t = C_{t-1} \times (1 + e_{t-1})$, where $e_0 = 0$ and $C_0 = C$.

M_t Policy fee in period t. This is assumed to be uprated at the rate of $i\%$ per annum (for example, i might be related to the rate of change in the retail price index). Thus: $M_t = M_{t-1} \times (1 + i_{t-1})$, where $i_0 = 0$ and $M_0 = M$.

f Fund management fee (expressed as a proportion). This is assumed to be paid annually on the fee date and to be proportional to the value of the fund at that date.

a Allocation of contributions to units, including the levies on any capital units and any loyalty bonuses (expressed as a proportion).

s Bid-offer spread on contributions (expressed as a proportion).

x_t Redemption fee payable at maturity (when $t = T$), transfer fee payable when the policy is transferred (where $t < T$) or fee associated with conversion of the policy to paid-up status (also where $t < T$, but may continue to be paid up to T); prior to any of these events, $x_t = 0$.

F_0 Policy set-up fee (e.g. the independent financial adviser's (IFA's) fee), paid at the start of the policy.

The value of the fund in period t is then given by the following iterative equation:

$$V_t = \{V_{t-1} + a(1 - s)C_{t-1}(1 + e_{t-1}) - M_{t-1}(1 + i_{t-1})\} \quad (4.4)$$
$$\times (1 - f)(1 + g_t)(1 - x_t)$$

where, in the case of $t = 1$, V_0 is replaced by $-F_0$. This can also be expressed as:

$$V_t = -F_0(1 - f)^t \prod_{k=1}^{t} [(1 + g_k)(1 - x_k)]$$

$$+ \sum_{m=1}^{t} \left\{ a(1 - s)C \prod_{k=0}^{m-1} (1 + e_k) - M \prod_{k=0}^{m-1} (1 + i_k) \right\}$$

$$\times (1 - f)^{t+1-m} \prod_{k=m}^{t} [(1 + g_k)(1 - x_k)] \qquad (4.5)$$

In Equation (4.5), C represents the contribution by the policyholder (which is uprated annually by e_t), while the g_t terms measure the returns on the fund. All other terms are related to charges.

A.1   Reduction in yield

The complexity of Equation (4.5) means that there is no simple summary measure for the impact of charges. The conventional approach is to calculate the *reduction in yield* (*RiY*) resulting from the charges.

Suppose that g is the constant growth rate for the fund assumed by the regulator. Equation (4.5) can be used to project the value of the fund in period t based on this assumed growth rate:

$$V_t = -F_0 [(1 - f)(1 + g)]^t \prod_{k=1}^{t} (1 - x_k)$$

$$+ \sum_{m=1}^{t} \left\{ a(1 - s)C \prod_{k=0}^{m-1} (1 + e_k) - M \prod_{k=0}^{m-1} (1 + i_k) \right\}$$

$$\times [(1 - f)(1 + g)]^{t+1-m} \prod_{k=m}^{t} (1 - x_k) \qquad (4.6)$$

The *RiY* is defined as the difference between the assumed return (g) on the fund and the fund's internal rate of return or *effective yield* (g'), which is equal to the yield on a hypothetical zero-load or charge-free scheme[41] with the same gross contributions and having the same terminal value as the scheme in question. Hence, g' is the solution to the following

_____

[41] That is, a scheme in which $a = 1$, $s = 0$, $M = 0$, $f = 0$, $x = 0$, $F_0 = 0$ in Equations (4.4)–(4.6).

equation:

$$V_t = \sum_{m=1}^{t} \left\{ C \prod_{k=0}^{m-1} (1 + e_k) \right\} (1 + g')^{t+1-m} \qquad (4.7)$$

where V_t is defined in (4.6). The reduction in yield is defined as:

$$RiY = g - g' \qquad (4.8)$$

The higher the charges, the lower will be the net contributions invested; hence, the lower will be g' and the larger will be the reduction in yield.

A.2   Reduction in contributions

Reduction in yield is not the only method for reporting charges. There is an alternative method based on contributions: the *reduction in contributions (RiC)*. This is defined as the difference between the gross contributions (C) into a scheme and the scheme's *effective contributions (C')*, as a proportion of gross contributions. Effective contributions are equal to the contributions into a hypothetical zero-load scheme with the same assumed return and having the same terminal value as the scheme in question. The effective contribution is, therefore, the value of C' which solves the following equation:

$$V_t = \sum_{m=1}^{t} \left\{ C' \prod_{k=0}^{m-1} (1 + e_k) \right\} (1 + g)^{t+1-m} \qquad (4.9)$$

where V_t is defined in (4.6). The reduction in contributions is defined as:[42]

$$RiC = (C - C')/C \qquad (4.10)$$

Since the left-hand sides of Equations (4.7) and (4.9) are identical, the right-hand sides must equal each other, which implies that the RiC is

---

[42] It is easy to show that the reduction in contributions is equal to the total compounded charges as a proportion of gross terminal fund value:

$$\frac{\text{Total compounded charges}}{\text{Gross terminal fund value}} = \frac{\sum\limits_{m=1}^{t} \left\{ (C - C') \prod\limits_{k=0}^{m-1} (1 + e_k) \right\} (1 + g)^{t+1-m}}{\sum\limits_{m=1}^{t} \left\{ C \prod\limits_{k=0}^{m-1} (1 + e_k) \right\} (1 + g)^{t+1-m}}$$

$$= \frac{C - C'}{C}$$

$$= RiC$$

related to the gross and effective yields as follows:

$$RiC = 1 - \left[\sum_{m=1}^{t} \left\{ \prod_{k=0}^{m-1} (1 + e_k) \right\} (1 + g')^{t+1-m} \right]$$

$$\div \left[\sum_{m=1}^{t} \left\{ \prod_{k=0}^{m-1} (1 + e_k) \right\} (1 + g)^{t+1-m} \right] \qquad (4.11)$$

A.3   Adjusting for lapse rates

Suppose a lapse occurs in period L (where $0 < L < T$). The value of the fund when the policy is converted to a PUP is:

$$V_L = -F_0(1 - f)^L \prod_{k=1}^{L} [(1 + g_k)(1 - x_k)]$$

$$+ \sum_{m=1}^{L} \left\{ a(1 - s)C \prod_{k=0}^{m-1} (1 + e_k) - M \prod_{k=0}^{m-1} (1 + i_k) \right\}$$

$$\times (1 - f)^{L+1-m} \prod_{k=m}^{L} [(1 + g_k)(1 - x_k)] \qquad (4.12)$$

The value of the PUP in any subsequent period t (where $L < t < T$) is:

$$V_{Lt} = V_L(1 - f)^{t-L} \prod_{k=L+1}^{t} [(1 + g_k)(1 - x_k)] - \sum_{m=L+1}^{t} \left\{ M \prod_{k=0}^{m-1} (1 + i_k) \right\}$$

$$\times (1 - f)^{t+1-m} \prod_{k=m}^{t} [(1 + g_k)(1 - x_k)] \qquad (4.13)$$

where, depending on the policy, M and x_k may be positive for each period between L and t.[43]

If we define q_t as the lapse rate in period t by policyholders from a particular provider, the expected value of a fund from that provider in

---

[43] Estimates by Shuttleworth (1997) indicate that pension providers extract similar charges on PUPs as for active accounts. They are required to apply the same growth rate on PUPs as on active accounts.

period t is:

$$V_t^* = \sum_{L=1}^{t} \text{Pr(lapse in period } L \,|\, \text{no lapses before } L)$$
$$\times \text{ Value of fund at } t \text{ if lapsed at } L$$
$$+ \text{ Pr(no lapses before } t) \times \text{ Value of unlapsed fund at } t$$
$$= \sum_{L=1}^{t} \prod_{k=0}^{L-1} (1 - q_k) q_L V_{Lt} + \prod_{k=0}^{t} (1 - q_k) V_t \qquad (4.14)$$

where $q_0 = 0$ and the product of the $L - 1$ terms $(1 - q_k)$ measures the persistency rate over $L - 1$ periods.

The *lapse-adjusted reduction in yield* (*LARiY*) experienced by the provider's policyholders will depend on the effective yield (g^*) that solves:

$$V_t^* = \sum_{m=1}^{t} \left\{ C \prod_{k=0}^{m-1} (1 + e_k) \right\} (1 + g^*)^{t+1-m} \qquad (4.15)$$

where V_t^* is defined in (4.14). The lapse-adjusted reduction in yield is given by:

$$LARiY = g - g^* \qquad (4.16)$$

An alternative method of accounting for lapse rates has recently been proposed by Chapman (1998). He defines the *annual charge equivalent* (*ACE*) as the single annual charge (as a proportion of fund value) that gives the same average annual take as a company's current range of charges when the company's lapse rates are taken into account.

The *ACE*, denoted h below, is calculated as the solution to:

$$V_t^* = \sum_{m=1}^{t} \left\{ C \prod_{k=0}^{m-1} (1 + e_k) \right\} [(1 + g)(1 - h)]^{t+1-m} \qquad (4.17)$$

However, the *ACE* always takes the same value as the *LARiY*, as can be seen by comparing Equations (4.15) and (4.17). Since the left-hand sides of these equations are identical (and defined by Equation (4.14)), the right-hand sides must equal each other, which implies that:

$$(1 - h)(1 + g) = (1 + g^*) \qquad (4.18)$$

and, hence, that:

$$LARiY = g - g^* = h - hg \approx h \qquad (4.19)$$

since hg is negligible. Thus the ACE and $LARiY$ are equivalent measures.

Finally, the *lapse-adjusted reduction in contributions* (*LARiC*) is found by substituting the effective yield (g^*) from Equation (4.15) for (g') in Equation (4.11).

REFERENCES

Adams, C. (1999) Older people find employers put youth before experience. *The Financial Times*, January 17th.

Barclays Capital (2006) *Equity Gilt Study*. Barclays Capital, London.

Black, F. and Jones, R. (1988) Simplifying portfolio insurance for corporate pension plans. *Journal of Portfolio Management*, **14**(4), 33–37.

Black, F. and Perold, A. (1992) Theory of constant proportion portfolio insurance. *Journal of Economic Dynamics and Control*, **16**, 403–426.

Blake, D. (1996) Efficiency, risk aversion and portfolio insurance: an analysis of financial asset portfolios held by investors in the UK. *Economic Journal*, **106**, 1175–1192.

Blake, D. (2003) Take (smoothed) risks when you are young, not when you are old: how to get the best from your pension plan. *IMA Journal of Management Mathematics*, **14**, 145–161.

Blake, D. and Board, J. (2000), Measuring value added in the pension industry. *Geneva Papers on Risk and Insurance*, **25**, 539–567.

Blake, D., Cairns, A. and Dowd, K. (2001) PensionMetrics: stochastic pension plan design and value-at-risk during the accumulation phase. *Insurance: Mathematics & Economics*, **29**, 187–215.

Brown, S., Goetzmann, W. and Ross, S. (1995) Survival. *Journal of Finance*, **50**, 853–873.

Cairns, A., Blake, D. and Dowd, K. (2006) Stochastic lifestyling: optimal dynamic asset allocation for defined contribution pension plans. *Journal of Economic Dynamics & Control*, **30**, 843–877.

Chapman, J. (1998) Pension plans made easy. *Money Management*, November, 88–91.

Chapman, J. (2000) Pension plans: charges halved and more to come?' *Money Management*, February, 52–60.

Derbyshire, G. (1999) Strategic decisions for DC. *Pensions Management*, October, 56–57.

Dowd, K. (1998) *Beyond Value at Risk: The New Science of Risk Management*. John Wiley & Sons, Ltd, Chichester.

Efron, B. (1979) Bootstrap methods: another look at the jackknife. *Annals of Statistics*, **7**, 1–26.

Fama, E. and French, K. (2002) The equity premium. *Journal of Finance*, **57**, 637–659.

Financial Services Authority (2000) *Conduct of Business Sourcebook*, February, London.

Goetzmann, W. and Jorion, P. (1999) Global stock markets in the twentieth century. *Journal of Finance*, **54**, 953–980.

Institute and Faculty of Actuaries (1999) *Disclosure – PIA Rules*, Guidance Note 22, Version 2.1, February, London and Edinburgh.

Lo, A. and MacKinlay, A. (1988) Stock market prices do not follow random walks: evidence from a simple specification test. *Review of Financial Studies*, **1**, 41–66.

Merton, R.C. and Samuelson, P.A. (1974) Fallacy of the log-normal approximation to optimal portfolio decision making over many periods. *Journal of Financial Economics*, **1**, 67–94.

Miles, D. and Timmermann, A. (1999) Risk sharing and transition costs in the reform of pension systems in Europe. *Economic Policy*, **29**, 253–288.

New Earnings Surveys, Office for National Statistics. Stationary Office, London.

Office of Fair Trading (1997) *Consumer Detriment under Conditions of Imperfect Information*, Research Paper 11, London.

Office of Fair Trading (1999), *Vulnerable Consumers and Financial Services*, Report 255, London.

O'Neill, M. (1999) Sun Life in attack on 'manipulated' pension claims. *Money Marketing*, January 14th.

Perold, A. and Sharpe, W. (1988) Dynamic strategies for asset allocation. *Financial Analysts Journal*, January/February, 16–27.

Personal Investment Authority (1998) *Fourth Survey of Persistency of Life and Pension Policies*, October, London.

Personal Investment Authority (1999) *Fifth Survey of Persistency of Life and Pension Policies*, October, London.

Politis, D. and Romano, J. (1994) The stationary bootstrap. *Journal of the American Statistical Association*, **89**, 1303–1313.

Poterba, J. and Summers, L. (1988) Mean reversion in stock prices: evidence and implications. *Journal of Financial Economics*, **22**, 27–59.

Samuelson, P.A. (1963) Risk and uncertainty: a fallacy of large numbers. *Scientia*, **57**, 1–6.

Samuelson, P.A. (1989) A case at last for age-phased reduction in equity. *Proceedings of the National Academy of Science*, **86**, 9048–9051, Washington, DC.

Samuelson, P.A. (1991) Long-run risk tolerance when equity returns are mean regressing: pseudoparadoxes and vindication of 'businessman's risk', in Brainard, W., Nordhaus, W. and Watts, H. (Eds) *Macroeconomics, Finance and Economic Policy: Essays in Honour of James Tobin*, MIT Press, Cambridge, MA.

Samuelson, P.A. (1992) At last a case for long-horizon risk tolerance and for asset allocation timing, in Arnott, R.D. and Fabozzi, F.J. (Eds) *Active Asset Allocation*, McGraw-Hill, Maidenhead.

Savings Market: An Investment Intelligence Publication (1997), Waterlow Information Services, London.

Securities and Investment Board (1988) *Life Assurance and Unit Trust Disclosure: The Regime for 1990*, December, London.

Securities and Investment Board (1989) *Life Assurance and Unit Trust Disclosure*, Consultative Paper No. 23, May, London.

Shuttleworth, J. (1997) *Operating Costs of Different Forms of Pension Provision in the UK*, Coopers & Lybrand, June, London.

Siegel, J. (1997) *Stocks for the Long Term*. Richard D. Irwin, New York.

Slade, P. (1999) Quote manipulation claims, *The Independent*, January 30th.

Thornton, P.N. and Wilson, A.F. (1992) A realistic approach to pension funding. *Journal of the Institute of Actuaries*, **119**, 229–312.

Towers Perrin (1998) *European Active Investment Management Charges*, August, London.

Vasicek, O.E. (1977) An equilibrium characterisation of the term structure. *Journal of Financial Economics*, **5**, 177–188.

Wilkie, A.D. (1995) More on a stochastic asset model for actuarial use. *British Actuarial Journal*, **1**, 777–964.

5
Defined Contribution Pension Schemes – The Distribution Phase

In the last chapter we examined key issues associated with the accumulation phase of defined contribution (DC) pension schemes. In this chapter we look at various aspects of the distribution phase of DC schemes. We begin by analysing an important component of the distribution phase, namely annuities. We then consider the optimal design of the distribution phase and the role that annuities play in it.

5.1 ANNUITIES

A *life annuity* is a financial contract that provides regular income to the annuity purchaser for his or her remaining life (Blake, 1999).

The primary objectives of a pension scheme are to:

• provide adequate retirement income security for the remaining life of the pensioner and his or her dependants; and
• eliminate the risk that the pensioner outlives his or her resources.

This implies that the primary purpose of a pension scheme is to fund for income rather than capital, since *only* an income stream satisfying certain conditions (in particular that it is lifelong and protected from inflation) can guarantee to meet these objectives. An annuity is, therefore, an essential feature of the distribution phase of a defined contribution pension scheme.

Annuities are sold by life offices. Large occupational DC schemes provide annuities themselves to their retired members, although small DC schemes tend to buy annuities from life offices.

There are many different types of annuities and we consider the key examples.

5.1.1   Purchase arrangements

- *Single-premium annuity*: the cost of the annuity is paid in a single lump sum.
- *Regular-premium* (or *instalment*) *annuity*: the cost of the annuity (which, by definition, will be a deferred annuity) is paid by regular instalments (either in the form of *fixed premiums* or *flexible premiums*). It is rather like an integrated defined contribution pension scheme. During the accumulation stage, there is both an accumulation value and a surrender value. The accumulation value equals the premiums paid plus investment returns less expenses. The surrender value is equal to the accumulation value less a surrender charge, which typically reduces to zero at the end of the surrender charge period. Should the policyholder die during the accumulation stage, the surrender value of the policy goes to the policyholder's estate; similarly, the policyholder can make a withdrawal up to the surrender value during the accumulation period. A variation on this is the:
- *Two-tier annuity*: the accumulation value will be received only if the policy is subsequently annuitised for a minimum period (e.g. five years), and the surrender value is always less than the accumulation value to discourage early withdrawal.

5.1.2   Coverage

- *Single-life annuity*: payments cease on the death of the annuitant (without refund of the balance of capital).
- *Joint-life annuity*: payments cease when the first of the lives covered dies; the second life receives no further payments after this date.
- *Joint-and-last-survivor annuity* (or simply a *joint-survivor annuity*): payments continue until the death of the second life (usually the surviving spouse). Typically, after the death of the first annuitant, the annuity continues at a lower rate, e.g. one-half or two-thirds. The size of the annuity depends on the age difference between the two lives and on gender.
- *Survivor* (or *reversionary*) *annuity*: payments begin on the death of the nominator (the covered life) and continue until the death of the beneficiary of the policy (called the annuitant), unless the beneficiary dies first, in which case the policy expires worthless.
- *Group annuity*: covers a group of individuals, such as the employees of a company, not necessarily by name, rather by characteristics (such as age and sex).

5.1.3   Variations

- *Temporary annuity*: payments are made for a fixed period or until the annuitant dies, whichever is sooner.
- *Certain annuity*: payments are made for a fixed period, whether or not the annuitant dies.
- *Whole annuity*: payments continue until the annuitant dies.
- *Annuity with minimum guarantee* (*period-certain annuity*): payments are made for a minimum period (e.g., five or ten years), however long the annuitant lives.
- *Annuity with minimum guarantee and overlap*: the spouse's income and income during the guarantee period are paid simultaneously.
- *Annuity with proportion*: on the death of the annuitant, the proportion owing since the last payment is paid (important feature if the annuity is paid annually).
- *Annuity with capital protection*: the balance of the capital is paid to the annuitant's estate when s/he dies. Variations on this include:
- *Cash-refund* (or *money back*) *annuity*: the balance of the capital is paid as a lump sum.
- *Instalment-refund annuity*: the balance of the capital is paid in instalments.

5.1.4   Other features

- *Health – impaired life annuities*: where the prospective annuitant is expected to experience heavier mortality than the average annuitant (say as a result of a fatal illness or, indeed, as a result of lifestyle, such as being a smoker), higher than standard annuity rates apply.
- *Long-term care – long-term care annuities* have a long-term care insurance policy attached to them to provide for potential future nursing fees.
- *Gender – unisex annuities*: the annuity rate is the same for males and females. With conventional annuities, for a given purchase price, the annuity payable to a male exceeds that to a female on account of the generally heavier mortality experienced by males. Unisex annuities therefore involve a cross-subsidy from men to women.
- *Tax – compulsory purchase annuities* (CPAs): the full amount of the annuity is subject to income tax. In countries such as the UK, which operate an EET tax system for their pension arrangements (i.e. contributions into the pension scheme are *Exempted* from tax, investment returns are *Exempted* from tax, but the pension in payment is *Taxed*),

it is usually mandatory in DC schemes to use the lump sum on the retirement date to purchase a life annuity; because of the tax subsidy involved in generating this lump sum, the full amount of the annuity is taxed as income. In contrast, the voluntary purchase of a life annuity is typically made from post-tax resources. Such annuities are known as *purchased life annuities* (PLAs). Recognising that an annuity payment involves both an income element and a return of capital element, the tax authorities only tax the income element in the case of PLAs.

5.1.5   Payment terms

Timing of payments

- *Immediate annuity* (*annuity in arrears*): payments commence at the end of the first period.
- *Annuity-due* (*annuity in advance*): payments commence at the beginning of the first period.
- *Deferred annuity*: first payment is delayed for a number of periods.
- *Phased annuities* (*phased* or *staggered vesting*): a series of annuities is purchased at regular intervals.

Payment frequency

- monthly;
- quarterly;
- semi-annual;
- annual.

Currency of denomination

- domestic currency;
- key foreign currencies.

Payment types

- *Level annuity*: pays a fixed amount in nominal terms for the duration of the annuity. All other types of annuity pay variable amounts.
- *Step-down annuity*: an annuity that reduces to specified levels at particular dates in the future.
- *Adjustable annuity*: an annuity that rebases rates periodically (say every three years).

- *Escalating annuity*: an example is a *constant-growth annuity,* where the annuity increases annually at a fixed rate of, say, 5%. The starting payment is much lower than with a level annuity costing the same amount.

- *Index-linked annuity*: an example of an escalating annuity where the payments are increased in line with increases in the consumer price index.

- *Limited price indexed (LPI) annuity*: this compensates for inflation up to a stated limit (e.g. 2.5% per annum).

- *Investment-linked annuities*: The best-known example of these in the US are known as 'variable annuities'. They were first issued in 1952 in the US by the TIAA–CREF (Teachers' Insurance and Annuity Association of America – College Retirement Equity Fund). A lump sum is used to buy units in a diversified fund of assets (mainly equities) and the units are sold on a regular basis to provide the annuity. The size of the annuity, depends on the income and growth rate of assets in the fund. The annuity can fall if the value of the assets falls substantially, so there is some volatility to the annuity, in contrast with a level annuity. But since the pension from a level annuity is based on the return on government bonds, it is possible that the pension from a investment-linked annuity, based on the return on equities, will generate a higher overall income (assuming that the duration of the annuity is sufficiently great and that the charges on the investment-linked annuity are not excessive). Examples of investment-linked annuities in the UK are with-profit and unit-linked annuities. They allow a wider range of investments, including equities, and produce an income related to the performance of the underlying assets. This can either be via a with-profit fund or a conventional unit-linked fund.

- *With-profit annuity*: the capital sum is invested in an insurance company's with-profit fund and the annuity is based on an assumed or anticipated annual bonus (or crediting) rate (e.g. 8%). The initial payment is lower than with an equivalent level annuity, but is higher the higher the assumed bonus, although, as a consequence, the subsequent rate of increase in the annuity is lower. However, the annuity could fall in value if the assumed bonus rate turns out to exceed the actual declared bonus rate. Some providers offer a two-tier bonus system: an annual reversionary bonus, which, once declared, cannot be removed, and an annual terminal bonus, which applies only for the year in question and can be raised or reduced in subsequent years. Although the annuity can

Table 5.1   Example of a with-profit annuity

Year	Reversionary bonus declared (%)	Annuity payments (£)
1	0	11 449
2	0	10 601
3	0	9816
4	0	9089
5	10	9257
6	10	9428
7	10	9603
8	10	9781
9	10	9962
10	9	10 054
11	8	10 054
12	8	10 054
13	6	9868
14	5	9594
15	7.5	9594
16	9.5	9682
17	11	9951
18	12.5	10 366
19	14	10 941
20	15	11 651

Note: Male aged 65 uses £100 000 to purchase a single-life with-profit immediate annuity with an anticipated bonus of 8%: the starting level for the annuity is £11 449. No bonus is declared in the first four years, so the annuity payments must fall. In years 5–10, the actual bonus exceeds the anticipated bonus, and this allows the annuity payments to rise. In years 11–12, the anticipated and declared bonuses are the same and so the annuity payments remain unchanged. From year 13 on, the bonuses vary year by year and the annuity rises or falls accordingly. Source: March (1996).

fluctuate, with-profit annuities normally provide a guaranteed minimum annuity. They are considered less risky than unit-linked annuities due to the 'smoothing' effect of a with-profit fund. Funds are subject to other charges such as an annual management fee, a policy fee and, in some cases, a set-up fee. A recent innovation is the *guaranteed with-profit annuity*, which provides a minimum annual income whatever the underlying investment performance. An example of a with-profit annuity is shown in Table 5.1.

- *Unit-linked annuity*: the capital sum is invested in unit-linked funds (unit trusts or mutual funds) and each year a fixed number of units are sold to provide the annuity. The initial payment is lower than with an equivalent level annuity. The annuity either fluctuates in line with unit trust (or mutual fund) prices, or is assumed to grow at a constant rate, e.g. 10% p.a.; in the latter case, if investment performance is lower than this, the income from the annuity falls and vice versa, in a similar manner to the with-profit annuity. If a unit-linked annuity is selected, the purchase price is exchanged for a number of units in an investment fund at retirement. Some unit-linked funds guarantee a minimum performance in line with a particular index. Such a guarantee would improve the attractiveness of unit-linked annuities.

- *Income draw down* or *managed annuity* (also known as *managed pension* or *income withdrawal*): the capital sum remains invested in a fund and individuals are permitted to draw an income from the fund for a specified period, before purchasing a standard annuity. They were first introduced in the UK as a result of the 1995 Finance Act, following an unprecedented fall in government bond yields, and hence annuity rates, during the early 1990s: individuals retiring during this period found themselves locked into very low level annuities. Until 2006, individuals in the UK could delay drawing an annuity until age 75, during which time they could draw an income from the fund that was between 35% and 100% of that available from a single-life level annuity. Tables for doing this were supplied by the Government Actuary, and the arrangements had to be reviewed triennially. The 2004 Pensions Act in the UK ended the requirement to purchase an annuity at age 75, allowing instead the continuation of a variation of draw down in the form of an *alternatively secured pension* (ASP). Following the 2004 Pensions Act, draw down prior to age 75 is known as an *unsecured pension*. There are various costs or risks associated with draw down. First, the individual might eventually decide to buy an annuity, but annuity rates might actually be lower than at the time of retirement. Second, investment performance during the deferral period might be poor, with the result that the fund falls in value. Third, by not buying an annuity, individuals forego a *mortality cross-subsidy* (a cross-subsidy allowed for in annuity rates which arises because some annuitants will die shortly after taking out an annuity, thereby releasing a *mortality profit*, which insurance companies share with longer-surviving annuitants). The mortality cross-subsidy is cumulative over time, and by delaying the purchase of an annuity, individuals experience a so-called

Table 5.2 Typical charges for a draw-down policy

Set-up charge	£50
Bid-offer spread	5%
Minimum allocation rates	98% on funds between £10 000 and £49 999; 98.5% on funds exceeding £50 000
Draw-down charge	£5.00 per month. Additional £2.50 per month if Protected Rights is part of a larger transfer value received
Investment management charge	between 0.39% and 0.96% of the fund value per annum depending on the unit trust chosen by the individual
Additional charge made by cancellation of units	up to 1% per annum
Charge for changing the level of income drawn	£50 (the first change in any one year is free).

Note: 'Protected Rights' is the name given in the UK to the accumulated value of tax reliefs in DC pension plans.
Source: National Mutual Life (1996)

mortality drag (see Section 5.1.7 below). Fourth, any improvements in mortality will be reflected in even lower annuity rates when the individual eventually does convert to an annuity. Finally, the charges with income draw down are higher and more complex than for annuities, as Table 5.2 shows.

- *Market-value-adjusted (MVA) annuity*: a hybrid arrangement for a deferred annuity lying between a fixed and variable annuity. The annuity rate is fixed for a specified period, but the surrender value of the policy adjusts in line with the market value of the underlying investments if it is surrendered before the end of this period. At regular intervals (e.g. every five years), a window opens enabling a withdrawal to be made without an MVA.

5.1.6 Decomposition of annuity charges

It is possible to decompose the charges (or loads) on annuities extracted by life companies into the following components using estimates derived by Finkelstein and Poterba (2002; hereafter FP): a component arising from the *selection risk* associated with the type of people who purchase annuities, a component arising from the additional risk associated with the type of people who purchase annuities in the voluntary market (*volunteer risk*), a component arising from *escalation risk* (i.e. *inflation risk*) and a component that covers administration costs and profit to the insurance company. It is also possible to identify a size effect, an age effect and a sex effect.

The basis for FP's analysis is the *money's worth* of an annuity (see Mitchell *et al.*, 1999), which is defined as the ratio of the expected present value (*EPV*) to the premium, where the *EPV* is defined as:

$$EPV = \sum_{t=1}^{T} \frac{A(1 + \pi)^t {}_t p_x}{\Pi_{k=1}^t (1 + r_k)} \times 100 \qquad (5.1)$$

where:

A = nominal initial annuity payment

π = escalation factor (zero for level annuity)

r_k = nominal spot yield for year k derived from the government bond spot yield curve

T = maximum length of pension, based on the assumption that no one lives beyond age 112

${}_t p_x$ = probability that an annuitant aged x survives t years.

FP derive estimates of (5.1) based on three different sets of single-life mortality tables: the population mortality tables provided by the Government Actuary's Department and the mortality tables for voluntary and compulsory annuitants provided by the Institute of Actuaries' Continuous Mortality Investigation Bureau. The latter two sets of tables are the IMA80 and IFA80 tables for voluntary purchase male and female life annuities and the PMA92 and PFA92 tables for the compulsory purchase male and female life annuities that must be bought when someone retires from a personal pension scheme. These tables are based on the mortality experience of these two select groups around 1980 and 1992 respectively, and have been adjusted to account for mortality improvements since that period.

If an annuity is fairly priced, its money's worth would be 100%. In practice though, it will be less than this because of the charge components outlined above. FP analyse the money's worth of an immediate single-life annuity with monthly payments and a premium of £10 000. Their decomposition is presented in Table 5.3.

Take, for example, the case of a 65-year-old male and a level annuity. This pays £879.70 in the compulsory purchase market and £844.40 in the voluntary open market, the difference reflecting the greater life

Table 5.3 Decomposition of charges on annuities with £10 000 purchase price

	Level		Escalating at 5%	
	Compulsory	Voluntary	Compulsory	Voluntary
Male aged 65				
Initial annuity payment (£)	879.70	844.40	550.20	522.90
Total implied charge (%)[a]	10.3	13.5	14.2	19.6
composed of:				
Volunteer premium (%)[b]	—	4.2	—	6.5
Escalation premium (%)[c]	—	—	2.2	2.3
Selection premium (%)[d]	4.7	4.6	6.4	6.1
Administration cost and profit[e]	5.6	4.7	5.6	4.7
Size premium[g]:				
£10 000 to £50 000	−1.3	NA	NA	NA
£50 000 to £100 000	0.2	NA	NA	NA
Male aged 70				
Initial annuity payment (£)	1036.10	992.80	703.70	670.40
Total implied charge (%)[a]	13.1	16.3	17.1	21.4
composed of:				
Volunteer premium (%)[b]	—	6.6	—	8.9
Escalation premium (%)[c]	—	—	2.6	1.6
Selection premium (%)[d]	4.7	4.6	6.1	5.8
Administration cost and profit[e]	8.4	5.1	8.4	5.1
Age premium[f]	0.0	2.4	0.1	1.4
Size premium[g]:				
£10 000 to £50 000	−0.6	NA	NA	NA
£50 000 to £100 000	0.3	NA	NA	NA
Female aged 65				
Initial annuity payment (£)	768.50	727.60	445.40	420.30
Total implied charge (%)[a]	9.9	14.7	14.1	20.7
composed of:				
Volunteer premium (%)[b]	—	3.2	—	4.7
Escalation premium (%)[c]	—	—	3.1	3.5
Selection premium (%)[d]	1.9	1.9	3.0	2.9
Administration cost and profit[e]	8.0	9.6	8.0	9.6
Size premium[g]:				
£10 000 to £50 000	−1.4	NA	NA	NA
£50 000 to £100 000	0.5	NA	NA	NA

Table 5.3 (*Continued*)

	Level		Escalating at 5%	
	Compulsory	Voluntary	Compulsory	Voluntary
Female aged 70				
Initial annuity payment (£)	885.20	843.50	560.80	532.10
Total implied charge (%)[a]	12.7	16.7	17.2	22.4
composed of:				
Volunteer premium (%)[b]	—	4.5	—	5.9
Escalation premium (%)[c]	—	—	3.4	3.4
Selection premium (%)[d]	1.8	1.8	2.9	2.7
Administration cost and profit[e]	10.9	10.4	10.9	10.4
Age premium[f]	−0.1	1.2	0.2	0.9
Size premium[g]:				
£10 000 to £50 000	−1.0	NA	NA	NA
£50 000 to £100 000	0.6	NA	NA	NA

Notes:
[a]*The difference between an actuarially fair annuity (100%) and the money's worth of the annuity using the population mortality table (e.g. 100 − 89.7 for the level compulsory annuity for a 65-year-old male).*
[b]*For voluntary annuities only, the difference between the money's worth of the annuity using the voluntary mortality table and the money's worth using the compulsory mortality table (e.g. 95.3 − 91.1 for the level voluntary annuity for a 65-year-old male).*
[c]*For escalating annuities only, the difference between the money's worths of the level and escalating annuities, both evaluated using the own-market mortality table (e.g. 94.4 − 92.2 for the compulsory annuity for a 65-year-old male).*
[d]*The difference between the money's worth of the annuity using the own-market mortality table and the money's worth using the population mortality table (e.g. 94.4 − 89.7 for the level compulsory annuity for a 65-year-old male).*
[e]*The difference between the total implied charge and the sum of the volunteer, escalation and selection premiums.*
[f]*The difference between the sums of the volunteer, escalation and selection premiums at ages 70 and 65.*
[g]*The difference in money's worth between the lower and higher valued annuities, both evaluated using population mortality tables (e.g. 89.7 − 91.0 for the £10 000 and £50 000 annuities for a 65-year-old male).*
Source: Calculations based on the averages from a sample of nine insurance companies reported in Finkelstein and Poterba (2002). Original data provided by Annuity Direct and Moneyfacts for August and November 1998.

expectancy of those who purchase annuities on a voluntary basis over those who are required to do so as part of their pension scheme (we denote this component of charges the *volunteer premium*). The total implied charge is 10.3% of the purchase price in the compulsory market and 13.5% in the voluntary market. This is found as follows: calculate

(5.1) using the population mortality table with $A = £879.70$ for the compulsory annuity and £844.40 for the voluntary annuity, divide this by the purchase price (£10 000) to give the money's worth, which is then subtracted from 100%. Using population mortality to calculate (5.1) is equivalent to assuming the longevity experience of a typical member of the population as a whole.

If, using population mortality, the money's worth is below 100%, this implies that there are additional longevity risks associated with the select group of the population who purchase annuities; we must also make an allowance for the insurance company's administration costs and profit. We quantify these additional risks and costs as follows.

The *selection premium* covers the additional longevity risk of someone who purchases an annuity in comparison with a typical member of the population at large of the same sex and age. The selection premium associated with compulsory annuities is 4.7%: it is measured as the difference in money's worths calculated using (5.1) based on compulsory mortality tables and (5.1) based on population mortality tables. So, even though members of personal pension schemes have no choice about whether or not to buy an annuity, they as a group experience sufficiently lighter mortality than the population as a whole that insurance companies need to charge 65-year-old men a premium of 4.7% to cover this additional risk. The selection premium with voluntary annuities is, at 4.6%, of a similar order of magnitude.

Since those who buy annuities voluntarily experience even lighter mortality than personal pension scheme members, insurance companies charge such purchasers an additional volunteer premium. This is calculated as the difference between the money's worth in the voluntary market using the voluntary mortality table and the money's worth in the voluntary market using the compulsory mortality table. For a 65-year-old male, the volunteer premium is 4.2%.

Table 5.3 also reports evidence of a size effect in annuity provision, and two countervailing influences are apparent. The first is a scale effect: the cost of administering an annuity is independent of its size, so that insurance companies should be willing to pass scale economies onto high-valued policyholders. The table shows that this happens, although evidence is only available on compulsory level annuities: the charge is 1.3 percentage points lower for a 65-year-old man when the purchase price is £50 000 than when it is £10 000. The second effect is a wealth effect: richer people tend to live longer than poorer people, and this should be reflected in a higher *longevity premium*. This effect begins to dominate the scale effect on annuities over £50 000: there is a small increase in charges of 0.2 percentage points as the policy size rises from £50 000 to £100 000.

We can assess the importance of the age effect by comparing these results with those relating to a male aged 70. There are two factors to consider: an older man has, on average, fewer remaining years of life than a younger man, but, because he has survived to a greater age than the younger man and so has greater total life expectancy, the difference in remaining years will be greater than their age difference. The first factor will result in a higher annuity for the older man than for the younger man, but this will be partly counteracted by the second factor: the risk that an annuitant will live a very long time increases with the age at which he purchases the annuity (see, for example, Brugiavini, 1993). The second panel of the table shows that a 70-year-old man receives an annuity that is 18% higher than that for a 65-year-old man in both the compulsory and voluntary level markets. However, the total charges for the 70-year-old are nearly 3 percentage points higher in each market. The selection premium remains the same in both markets, but the volunteer premium is 2.4 percentage points higher. We can interpret the figure of 2.4% as the *age premium* and note that, in the case of 65-year-old men, the age premium is present only in the voluntary market, not the compulsory market. A size effect is also present, although the orders of magnitude differ slightly in comparison with the 65-year-old male.

The final effect that we can identify is a sex effect: women tend to live longer than men and this is reflected in the size of the annuity they are offered for a given premium. A 65-year-old woman receives a level annuity that is 13–14% lower than that of a 65-year-old man, while a 70-year-old woman receives broadly the same annuity as a 65-year-old man. The level and pattern of charges differ, however. The total charge for men is generally higher than for women in the compulsory market, but lower in the voluntary market. Both the selection and volunteer premiums are lower for women than for men. There is a positive age premium in the voluntary market, but at 1.2% it is only half that for men, while in the compulsory market, the age premium is negative (-0.1%): the age premium is the difference between the sums of the volunteer, selection and escalation premiums at age 70 and 65 years, respectively. The wealth component of the size effect is larger for women than for men (0.5 compared with 0.2 at age 65 and 0.6 compared with 0.3 at age 70 as the policy size rises from £50 000 to £100 000).

The initial annuity payment with a 5% escalating annuity is 37% lower than for a level annuity for a 65-year-old man in the compulsory market and 38% lower in the voluntary market. It takes ten years for the escalating annuity to catch up with the level annuity and 19 years before the total cash payments under the two policies are equalised. In the case of a 65-year-old woman, the initial payment from the escalating annuity is 42% lower for both the compulsory and voluntary markets. It takes around 12 years for the two cash amounts to equalise and a further ten years before the total cash payments equalise.

The total implied charge is higher for escalating annuities than for level annuities. This is because both the volunteer and selection premiums are higher and there is an additional escalation premium to take into account. The *escalation premium* covers a type of longevity risk that arises from the backloading of payments with escalating annuities: if the annuitant lives longer than anticipated, the additional payments will be rising with the escalating annuity but remain constant with the level annuity. It is calculated as the difference between the money's worths of the level and escalating annuities, each evaluated using own-market mortality tables. The escalation premium varies between 1.6 and 2.6% for men and between 3.1 and 3.5% for women.

To illustrate, in the case of a 65-year-old man, the volunteer premium is 6.5% with the escalating annuity and 4.2% with the level annuity. The selection premium is 6.4% compared with 4.7% in the compulsory market and 6.1% compared with 4.6% in the voluntary market. In comparison, with a 65-year-old woman, the volunteer premium is 4.7% with the escalating annuity and 3.2% with the level annuity. The selection premium is 3.0% compared with 1.9% in the compulsory market and 2.9% compared with 1.9% in the voluntary market. The age premium is smaller for both men and women in the compulsory market (at 0.1% and 0.2%, respectively) than in the voluntary market (at 1.4% and 0.9%, respectively).

The allowance for administration costs and profit is calculated as the difference between the total implied charge and the sum of the volunteer, escalation and selection premiums. In the level market, this is also equal to the difference between an actuarially fair annuity and the money's worth of an annuity using the own-market mortality table (e.g. 100 − 94.4 for the compulsory level annuity for a 65-year-old male). With escalating annuities, the escalation premium must be subtracted from this figure. The consequence of calculating the administration costs and profit in this way is that the profit margin (assuming identical administration costs across products) is the same in the level and escalating markets for each class of product (compulsory or voluntary) and for each class of annuitant. An alternative definition of administration costs and profit in the case of escalating annuities would be the same as that for level annuities: the difference between an actuarially fair annuity and the money's worth of an annuity using the own-market mortality table. The profit margin would be higher than with the first definition, but would also now contain an allowance for escalation risk.

Apart from this, we find that: compulsory annuities are generally more profitable than voluntary annuities, reflecting the fact that the compulsory market is a captive one; female annuities are more profitable than male annuities; and the profit margin rises with age, especially in the compulsory market.

5.1.7 Mortality drag

The size of an annuity depends on the following factors: the return on the assets purchased with the capital sum (principally government bonds), life office expenses, the degree of escalation, the benefits payable on death and the assumption made about the mortality experience of annuitants, both concerning the average life expectancy of annuitants and the anticipated distribution of life expectancies (i.e. the proportion of annuitants expected to die after one year, after two years, etc.). If the assumptions made about these factors are realised in full, the insurance company will have exactly enough resources to meet every annuity payment due. On the death of an annuitant, the balance of the original capital fund, together with investment returns (collectively called the *mortality profits*), is used to make payments to surviving annuitants. Each annuity instalment has three components: a proportion of the original purchase price, a proportion of the investment return and a proportion of the assumed mortality profit released by the early deaths of annuitants.

In contrast, with draw down, there is no mortality cross-subsidy from those with below-average mortality to those with above-average mortality: every user of a draw down facility bears his or her own longevity risk. The absence of the mortality cross-subsidy is known as *mortality drag*. Mortality drag is equal to the proportion of the surviving cohort of annuitants who will die during the current year. For draw down to be worthwhile, the returns on the invested funds must exceed the annuity yield by a sufficient margin to cover both the mortality drag and the higher charges of draw down (Table 5.4). The mortality drag will be higher for older than for younger people: older people are more likely to die than younger people and also there will be fewer of them, so that

Table 5.4 Example of additional return needed to cover mortality drag and draw-down charges

Age at retirement	Mortality drag (%)	Charges (%)	Additional total return required (%)
60	1.4	1.8	3.2
61	1.5	1.8	3.3
62	1.6	1.8	3.4
63	1.7	1.9	3.6
64	1.9	1.9	3.8
65	2.0	2.0	4.0
66	2.3	2.0	4.3
67	2.5	2.1	4.6
68	2.8	2.2	5.0
69	3.2	2.3	5.5
70	3.5	2.5	6.0
71	3.6	3.0	6.6
72	3.7	3.5	7.2
73	3.9	4.6	8.5
74	4.1	8.4	12.5

Note: *Figures based on a male retiring between 60 and 74, assuming an initial draw-down charge of 3%, an annual charge of 0.5%, an annuity yield of 7.5% and an annuity purchased at age 75.*
Source: National Mutual Life (1996).

the cross-subsidy will be larger and received sooner than for younger people. Since mortality drag rises every year, it becomes increasingly unlikely that alternative investments will be able to do this, and after a certain age it becomes optimal to switch to an annuity.[1] It will also be higher for men than for women for a similar reason: men tend to die younger than women and there are relatively fewer of them at each given age. However, the benefit of draw down is its greater flexibility over the timing of the purchase of the annuity and the higher value of the fund if the annuitant dies early.

If the man in Table 5.4 retires aged 60, and makes use of the draw down facility until age 75, when he purchases an annuity, he will require an additional return on his investments of 1.8% p.a. to compensate for the higher charges of draw down and 1.4% p.a. to compensate for mortality drag. Given that the annuity yield is assumed to be 7.5% p.a., this implies that the total return on investments must exceed an average of 10.7% p.a. between ages 60 and 75 for the benefits of draw down to exceed

---

[1] See Milevsky (1998).

those of purchasing the annuity. If this return is not achieved, either the fund will be depleted more rapidly than anticipated or the income withdrawn would have to be lower than that available from the purchase of an annuity at age 60. The additional total return required increases with age of retirement.

5.2   THE OPTIMAL DESIGN OF DC SCHEMES DURING THE DISTRIBUTION PHASE

In a number of countries, such as Sweden, there is a legal requirement to convert the fund accumulated in a defined contribution pension scheme into a life annuity by a certain age. In the UK, until April 2006, a life annuity had to be purchased some time between the retirement age and 75.[2] Most defined contribution (DC) scheme members will take the annuity immediately on retirement, since they do not have adequate alternative income sources; however, some may be in a position to delay the purchase.

Historically, most annuities sold provide a fixed nominal income for the remaining life of the purchaser (level annuities). The yield on level annuities is related to the yield on long-term fixed-income (mainly government) bonds. This is because annuity providers (principally insurance companies) purchase long-dated government and corporate bonds and use the coupons and principal repayments on these to make the annuity payments. More recently, it has become possible for insurers to sell index-linked annuities (which make payments linked to increases in the retail prices index) as a result of the introduction of long-term index-linked government bonds; again, these bonds provide the essential matching assets for insurance companies.[3] So, in countries where annuitisation is mandatory, members of DC schemes switch quite suddenly from an accumulation programme that typically has a very heavy weight in equities to a distribution programme that is almost entirely invested in bonds.

Given the substantial improvements in longevity over the last century, retirees can expect to live for 15 years or more. Recently, people have begun to question whether it is a sensible strategy to have such a

---

[2] Since April 2006 it has been possible to use an alternatively secured pension, rather than a life annuity, after the age of 75. However, this possibility is available only for those with a religious objection to the pooling of mortality risk. In most cases, it is still mandatory to purchase an annuity by age 75 in the UK.

[3] The UK Government was the first in the developed world to issue long-term index-linked bonds in 1981. Indexed annuities were not available in the UK before this date.

substantial bond-linked investment for such a long period. The question has become more pressing in the UK following the substantial fall in bond yields since the early 1990s. This is explained by the rising demand from insurance companies for bonds to match the annuity purchases of an increasing number of people entering retirement.

The perceived poor value of traditional annuities motivated a search for new *investment-linked retirement-income programmes* (ILRIPs), the principal examples being income draw down and investment-linked annuities. These are discussed in the next section, but in essence they involve the provision of retirement income from a fund with a substantial equity component. There are very few periods in the history of countries with advanced financial systems where equities do not outperform bonds over extended periods.[4] However, equity prices tend to be much more volatile than bond prices, so the higher expected returns from equities are purchased at the cost of greater risk.

Can we quantify the benefits and risks from ILRIPs in comparison with those from bond-based annuities? As in the case of the accumulation phase discussed in the last chapter, we use stochastic simulation to answer this question (see Blake, Cairns and Dowd, 2003).

5.2.1   Alternative distribution programmes

The benchmark against which the ILRIPs will be compared is a life annuity purchased from a life office. This is because a life annuity is the *only* financial instrument that protects the annuitant from outliving his resources: no other distribution programme will guarantee to make payments for however long an individual lives.

The size of the annuity will depend, as we saw in the previous section, on the following factors: the size of the fund, the long-term bond yield on the purchase date, the type of annuity (i.e. level or index-linked), the age, sex and (occasionally) state of health of the annuitant and a margin to cover the life office's profit and costs of marketing, administration and investment management.

There are, however, risks with annuities. When the DC scheme member retires, he bears interest-rate risk: the risk of retiring when interest rates are low, so that the retirement annuity is permanently low. After he

---

[4] Siegel (1997) shows that US equities generated higher average returns than US Treasury bonds and bills in 97% of all 30-year investment horizons since 1802. Barclays Global (2006) show that similar results hold for the UK.

retires, he bears, if he purchases a level annuity, inflation risk: the risk of losses in the real value of his pension due to subsequent, unanticipated inflation. The insurance companies selling annuities face reinvestment risk (the risk of failing to match asset cash flows with expected liability outgo) and longevity risk (the risk that their pool of annuitants has lighter mortality than allowed for, e.g., because of an underestimate of mortality improvements).

The alternatives to annuities that we now discuss involve a substantial investment exposure to equities. A higher level of equity exposure will give rise to a higher expected investment return and, *inter alia*, a higher expected income than a conventional annuity, the income from which is based on the return on bonds. However, there is also an increase in risk as well as higher charges. In addition, some of these alternatives do not, by themselves, hedge longevity risk and so do not satisfy the basic requirement of a pension scheme to provide an income in retirement for however long the scheme member lives. In such cases, we impose the requirement that eventually an annuity is purchased: we will assume that the annuity is purchased at the age of 75.

We have investigated the following distribution programmes for a male policyholder retiring at age 65. With the exception of the first programme, we consider two possibilities for the allocation of the residual fund if the policyholder dies before age 75. In the first, the residual fund is paid as a *bequest* to the policyholder's estate: programmes with this feature are classified as income draw down programmes. In the second, the residual fund reverts to the insurer, in return for which the insurer agrees to pay a *mortality bonus* (also known as a *survival bonus*) at the start of each year while the policyholder is still alive: programmes with this feature are classified as annuity programmes. We assume that the bonus fairly reflects the probability of death during the year and therefore the profit at the end of the year to the insurer if the policyholder dies. This bonus acts to offset the mortality drag that would otherwise be experienced.

For each of the cases described below, a precise mathematical formulation is given in Section 5.2.2:

- *Purchased life annuity*: The policyholder transfers his retirement fund immediately on retirement at age 65 to the insurer in return for a fully index-linked pension. No bequest is payable at the time of death of the policyholder. Instead, a mortality bonus is implicitly payable throughout the duration of the policy. This is the benchmark programme against which all the ILRIPs listed below are compared.

- *Fixed-income programme* with a life annuity purchased at age 75: In this case the policyholder transfers his retirement fund to a managed fund (which invests in a mixture of equities and bonds) when he retires at age 65. He then withdraws a fixed income each year equal to that which he would have obtained had he purchased an annuity at age 65 (if there are sufficient monies in his fund). At age 75, assuming he lives that long, he uses whatever fund remains to purchase a life annuity. There is a possibility that the fund will be exhausted before 75. This follows because when investment performance is disastrous and the value of the fund falls by a significant amount and assets still have to be sold to pay the pension, the remaining fund can become so depleted that even with good subsequent performance it might not recover sufficiently to maintain the pension in future years. This means that high returns can never fully compensate for poor returns if the fund also has to pay a fixed income stream regardless of realised investment performance.

- *Flexible-income programme* with a life annuity purchased at age 75: In this case it is not possible to run out of money before age 75, because if the fund falls in value, the income received has to fall in tandem. The outcome will be similar to that of the flexible unit-linked programme described below, and identical in the case where a mortality bonus is payable. We have investigated four cases with different levels of equity exposure in the managed fund: 25%, 50%, 75% and 100%.

- *Flexible-income programme with a deferred annuity* purchased at retirement age and payable at age 75: In this case the policyholder purchases a deferred annuity at age 65 which will provide an income from age 75 equal to that which would be payable at that age from an immediate annuity bought at age 65. He invests the remaining monies at age 65 in a managed fund. He then draws an income from the fund on the same basis as the flexible-income programme above up to age 75, when the deferred annuity comes into payment. On death before age 75, the value of the deferred annuity policy is lost.

- *Unit-linked programme* with a life annuity purchased at age 75: In this case the policyholder uses his retirement fund to purchase a fixed number of units in a managed fund at age 65. The number of units received will depend on the forecasts for mortality made at age 65. Each year a number of units are sold and the policyholder's income will change in line with changes in the price of these units. At age 75, assuming he lives that long, he uses the residual fund to purchase a life annuity.

- *Flexible unit-linked programme* with a life annuity purchased at age 75: In this case the income received from the programme adjusts in line with changes in mortality. Each year the policyholder receives a payment from the fund equal to that which he would have obtained had he used whatever fund remains to purchase an annuity at that time, with the annuity amount being calculated at a yield in line with the returns expected to be obtained on the managed fund and on the basis of the prospects for mortality at the time. Improvements in mortality result in lower income.

- *Collared-income programme* with a life annuity purchased at age 75: This programme is similar to the flexible-income programme, but involves a smoothing out of investment returns. Instead of investing solely in a managed portfolio, the fund invests in a mixed portfolio of equites and put and call options, with the aim of achieving significant protection against downside equity risk. For each equity unit held, the portfolio is long one at-the-money put option and short one call option. The strike price of the call option is chosen so that the prices of the put and call options are equal. This means that the net cost of the resulting *collar* is zero.[5] As a result, we have 100% participation in equity returns subject to the cap and floor. This is one way of selling some of the upside potential to pay for downside protection. The resulting smoothing of investment returns is similar in some respects to a with-profits policy, although in the present case the smoothing method is much more explicit.

- *Floored-income programme* with a life annuity purchased at age 75: Like the collared-income programme, this programme involves fore-going some upside potential to pay for downside protection. The policyholder is guaranteed to get a minimum return of zero (i.e. holds an implicit at-the-money put option), and pays for this by selling off a proportion of the equity performance above 0%. He will get some proportion (say, k_2) of the rise in the value of equities, with the difference of $(1 - k_2)$ being used to 'pay for' the put. In effect, we sell a fraction of an at-the-money call option $(1 - k_2)$ to pay for the put option. This annual return structure can also be achieved in a more simple way by investing in cash plus k_2 at-the-money call options. This programme is also sometimes known as a participating-equity or guaranteed-equity programme.

---

[5] See Blake (2000, Figure 9.25).

5.2.2   Stochastic pension scheme design

We will illustrate the distribution model using the example of a typical 65-year-old UK male policyholder who started a DC pension scheme on his 25th birthday and made contributions to the scheme throughout his working life; he has no dependants. During his working life, he faced asset-return risk and unemployment risk. Asset-return risk affected the value of his pension fund, given his contributions, and unemployment risk affected his income and, hence, his ability to make contributions to his pension fund.

On the retirement date (denoted time 0), we assume the policyholder has accumulated a personal pension fund of $F(0) = £100\,000$ and has to choose between an index-linked annuity and one of the ILRIPs. Each of the ILRIPs has two options. On death between time t and $t + 1$:

- in the case of income draw down, the residual fund, $F(t + 1)$, at the end of the year of death will be paid to the estate of the policyholder in the form of a *bequest*.
- in the case of an annuity, no bequest is paid to the policyholder's estate. Instead, the insurer (who will, in effect, receive the bequest of $F(t + 1)$) pays a *mortality bonus*, $B(t)$, into the policyholder's fund at the start of every year, conditional on the policyholder still being alive. That is, the fund is increased from $F(t)$ to $F(t) + B(t)$ at time t if the policyholder is still alive at that time. The fair bonus, for all policy types, at time t is $B(t) = [F(t) - P(t)]q_{x+t}/p_{x+t}$, where $P(t)$ is the pension payable at time t, x is the age at retirement, q_y is the probability of death before age $y + 1$ given the policyholder is alive at age y and $p_y = 1 - q_y$ is the corresponding *survival probability*.

In the models discussed below, $\delta = 1$ if a bequest is payable and $\delta = 0$ if mortality bonuses are payable. $D(t + 1)$ represents the bequest payable at $t + 1$ if the policyholder dies between times t and $t + 1$.

Asset-returns model

We will use the following simple model for returns on assets. There are two assets: risk-free bonds and equity. The bond fund, $M(t)$, grows at the constant risk-free real rate of interest of r (continuously compounding) per annum, so that at time t, $M(t) = M(0)\exp(rt)$, where $M(0)$ is the opening balance. Equity units, $S(t)$, constitute a risky investment that follows the log-normal or geometric Brownian motion model, so that at time t, $S(t) = S(0)\exp(\mu t + \sigma Z(t))$, where $S(0)$ is the opening balance,

μ is the expected log real return on equities, σ is the standard deviation of the log real return on equities, and $Z(t)$ is a standard Brownian motion.[6] We work on an annual basis throughout.

Charges

We assume that the charges for all distribution programmes are constant at 1% of fund value, implying a reduction in yield of 1%. As shown above, income draw down is a very expensive product, with charges currently much higher than the 1% we have allowed for. Nevertheless, we adopt a 1% charge for income draw down as well to preserve comparability.

In our simulations we used the following parameters, which are derived from UK data over the last half-century:

Parameter	Symbol	Value (proportion)
Real risk-free return	r	0.01
Expected log real return on equities	μ	0.056
Standard deviation of the log real return on equities	σ	0.244

We assume that the gross returns on equities are independent and identically distributed log-normal random variables with mean $\exp(\mu + \sigma^2/2)$ and variance $\exp(2\mu + \sigma^2)[\exp(\sigma^2) - 1]$. This implies that the expected gross return on equities is 1.09 and the standard deviation of the total return is 0.27. These parameter values are based on the historical distribution of returns on UK Treasury bills and equities and include a 1% reduction in yield on equity returns (for additional expenses associated with equity investment only).

Mortality and financial functions

We will make use of the following mortality and financial functions:

- q_x and p_x are the year-on-year mortality and survival probabilities respectively. Values are the same as those used in the UK mortality table appropriate for male pensioner annuitants, PMA92Base-Ultimate (McCutcheon et al., 1998, 1999).[7]

---

[6] This means that $Z(t)$ is normally distributed with a zero mean and unit variance and is serially uncorrelated.

[7] We have not included the effect of mortality improvements in our analysis. This form of mortality risk is less important for the policyholder than for the underwriting insurer.

- $_tp_x = p_x \times \ldots \times p_{x+t-1}$ is the probability that the pensioner survives from age x to $x + t$.
- $_t|q_x = {_tp_x} - {_{t+1}p_x}$ is the probability that the pensioner will die between ages $x + t$ and $x + t + 1$ given that he is alive at age x.
- $\ddot{a}_y = \sum_{t=0}^{\infty} {_tp_y} e^{-rt}$ is the price at age y for a single-life annuity of 1 unit per annum, payable annually in advance.
- $_s|\ddot{a}_y = \sum_{t=s}^{\infty} {_tp_y} e^{-rt}$ is the price at age y for a (deferred) annuity paying 1 unit per annum from age $y + s$.
- $\ddot{a}_{y:\overline{n}} = \sum_{t=0}^{n-1} {_tp_y} e^{-rt}$ is the price at age y for a temporary annuity of n years of 1 unit per annum payable annually in advance.

Analysing the distribution programmes

In what follows, the quantities $P(t)$, $F(t)$, $B(t)$ and $D(t)$ are all assumed to be expressed using the retail prices index as the unit of currency, i.e. the payments are in real terms. This avoids the need, for example, to scale the pension in line with the RPI in the formulae below.

Programme 1: Purchased life annuity (PLA)

$F(0)$ is used immediately to purchase an index-linked life annuity at a price of $\ddot{a}_x$ per unit of pension (where the rate of interest applied to $\ddot{a}_x$ is the real risk-free rate of interest, r, available in the market). It follows that the pension is $P(t) = F(0)/\ddot{a}_x$ for $t = 0, 1, 2, \ldots$. This is payable until death. No bequest is payable. Instead, mortality bonuses are paid implicitly.

Programme 2: Fixed-income programme (FXD)

Programme 2 assumes that the initial retirement fund $F(0)$ is invested 100% in equities until age 75 with the same fixed pension for $t = 0, 1, 2, \ldots$ paid as in Programme 1. Hence, for $t = 0, 1, \ldots, 9$:

$$P(t) = \frac{F(0)}{\ddot{a}_x} \tag{5.2}$$

$$B(t) = (1 - \delta)\frac{q_{x+t}}{p_{x+t}}(F(t) - P(t)) \tag{5.3}$$

$$F(t + 1) = \frac{S(t + 1)}{S(t)}(F(t) - P(t) + B(t)) \tag{5.4}$$

$$D(t + 1) = \delta F(t + 1) \tag{5.5}$$

Programme 2A ($\Rightarrow \delta = 1$) is the income draw down variant, which pays a bequest of the residual fund to the policyholder's estate if death occurs before age 75. Programme 2B ($\Rightarrow \delta = 0$) is the annuity variant, which pays mortality bonuses at times 0 to 9. If the policyholder is still alive at time $t = 10$ (age 75), the residual fund, $F(10)$, will be used to purchase an index-linked life annuity. Thus, for $t = 10, 11, \ldots,$ $P(t) = F(10)/\ddot{a}_{x+10}$. No bequests are payable after time 10, although, as in Programme 1, mortality bonuses are paid implicitly from that time.

If investment performance is poor, it is possible, in the case of the income draw down variant, for $F(t)$ (and, therefore, $P(t)$) to fall to zero before time 10: this occurred in about 20% of our simulations. In practice, government regulations on income draw down generally prohibit such an eventuality by requiring the amount of pension payable to be reduced if there is a catastrophic fall in the value of the fund.

Programme 3: Flexible-income programme (FLX)

Programme 3 is designed to rectify the principal shortcoming of Programme 2 – namely the possibility of running out of funds before age 75. Again, there is an income draw-down variant that allows for bequests (Programme 3A $\Rightarrow \delta = 1$) and an annuity variant that awards mortality bonuses (Programme 3B $\Rightarrow \delta = 0$) to be paid. We also allow for greater flexibility in the investment strategy by varying the weighting (θ) of the managed fund in equities and the corresponding weighting ($1 - \theta$) in bonds.

Each year the pension adjusts to reflect both the fund size available at the beginning of the year and the prospects for mortality of the policyholder, who is now a year older. This procedure for calculating each year's pension payment ensures that $P(t)$ and $F(t)$ are always positive.

For $t = 0, 1, \ldots, 9$:

$$P(t) = \frac{F(t)}{\ddot{a}_{x+t}} \tag{5.6}$$

$$B(t) = (1 - \delta)\frac{q_{x+t}}{p_{x+t}}(F(t) - P(t)) \tag{5.7}$$

$$F(t + 1) = \left(\theta\frac{S(t + 1)}{S(t)} + (1 - \theta)e^r\right)(F(t) - P(t) + B(t)) \tag{5.8}$$

$$D(t + 1) = \delta F(t + 1) \tag{5.9}$$

At time $t = 10$ (age 75), if the policyholder is still alive, the residual fund, $F(10)$, will be used to purchase an index-linked life annuity. Thus, for $t = 10, 11, \ldots, P(t) = F(10)/\ddot{a}_{x+10}$. No bequests are payable after time 10, although, as in Programme 1, mortality bonuses are paid implicitly from that time.

Programme 4: Flexible-income programme with a deferred annuity (DEF)

Programme 4 allows for either bequests (Programme 4A $\Rightarrow \delta = 1$) or mortality bonuses (Programme 4B $\Rightarrow \delta = 0$). With this programme, part of the fund at time 0 is used to purchase a deferred index-linked life annuity from age 75, with the deferred pension being equal to the Programme 1 pension. Thus, $P(t) = P(0)$ (in real terms) for $t = 10, 11, \ldots$. The cost of the deferred annuity is $P(0)\ _{10|}\ddot{a}_x = F(0)\ _{10|}\ddot{a}_x/\ddot{a}_x$.

This cost is immediately deducted from the initial fund, so that:

$$P(0) = \frac{F(0) - F(0)\ _{10|}\ddot{a}_x/\ddot{a}_x}{\ddot{a}_{x:\overline{10}}} \tag{5.10}$$

$$B(0) = (1 - \delta)\frac{q_x}{p_x}(F(0) - F(0)_{10|}\ddot{a}_x/\ddot{a}_x - P(0)) \tag{5.11}$$

$$F(1) = \frac{S(1)}{S(0)}(F(0) - F(0)\ _{10|}\ddot{a}_x/\ddot{a}_x - P(0) + B(0)) \tag{5.12}$$

$$D(1) = \delta F(1) \tag{5.13}$$

For $t = 1, 2, \ldots, 9$:

$$P(t) = \frac{F(t)}{\ddot{a}_{x+t:\overline{10-t}}} \tag{5.14}$$

$$B(t) = (1 - \delta)\frac{q_x}{p_x}(F(t) - P(t)) \tag{5.15}$$

$$F(t + 1) = \frac{S(t + 1)}{S(t)}(F(t) - P(t) + B(t)) \tag{5.16}$$

$$D(t + 1) = \delta F(t + 1) \tag{5.17}$$

Equation (5.10) indicates that the pension drawn at time t is the level of pension we would get if $F(t)$ were used to purchase an index-linked annuity payable from t for $10 - t$ years. Since $\ddot{a}_{x+9:\overline{1}} = 1$ we have $P(9) = F(9)$ and $F(10) = 0$. In this case, there is no residual fund at time 10 to top up the deferred pension purchased at time 0.

Programme 5: Unit-linked programme (UNI)

With this programme, the policyholder is allocated a set of units $u_0, u_1, \ldots, u_{10}$. For $t = 0, 1, \ldots, 9$, u_t units are cashed in to provide the pension at that time: that is, $P(t) = u_t S(t)$, where the price of one equity unit at time t is $S(t)$ and we assume that $S(0) = 1$. At time 10, the remaining u_{10} units are used to purchase an index-linked life annuity. Thus, $P(t) = u_{10}S(10)/\ddot{a}_{x+10}$ for $t = 10, 11, \ldots$.

Programme 5A ($\Rightarrow \delta = 1$) is the income draw down variant that involves bequests: uncashed units become a bequest on death, so that $D(t) = S(t) \sum_{s=t}^{10} u_s$. Since the insurer will not receive any windfall on death, the total value of the units at time 0 must match the value of the fund. Thus, $\sum_{s=0}^{10} u_s = F(0)$. Furthermore, we assume that the u_t are chosen in such a way that the policyholder will receive the same pension as the index-linked pension throughout retirement if the equity units grow in line with the risk-free rate of interest. Thus:

$$u_t = e^{-rt} u_0 \quad \text{for } t = 1, 2, \ldots, 9$$

and $u_{10} = e^{-10r} \ddot{a}_{x+10} u_0$

$$\Rightarrow u_t = \frac{F(0)e^{-rt}}{\sum_{s=0}^{9} e^{-rs} + e^{-10r} \ddot{a}_{x+10}} \quad \text{for } t = 0, 1, \ldots, 9$$

$$u_{10} = \frac{F(0)e^{-10r} \ddot{a}_{x+10}}{\sum_{s=0}^{9} e^{-rs} + e^{-10r} \ddot{a}_{x+10}} \tag{5.18}$$

Programme 5B ($\Rightarrow \delta = 0$) is the annuity variant that involves mortality bonuses, with uncashed units on death reverting to the insurer. In addition, we will include the same relationship between the u_t: that is,

$$u_t = e^{-rt} u_0 \quad \text{for } t = 1, 2, \ldots, 9$$

and $u_{10} = e^{-10r} \ddot{a}_{x+10} u_0$ \hfill (5.19)

The mortality bonus appears in the form of bonus units allocated at time 0. Alternatively, we can calculate the fair value of the pension payments to establish the u_t directly. Thus:

$$\text{Fair value} = \sum_{t=0}^{9} (u_t \, e^{rt}) e^{-rt} \,_t p_x + \left(\frac{u_{10} e^{10r}}{\ddot{a}_{x+10}} \right) \sum_{t=10}^{\infty} e^{-rt} \,_t p_x$$

$$= u_0 \left(\sum_{t=0}^{9} e^{-rt} \,_t p_x + e^{-10r} \,_{10} p_x \, \ddot{a}_{x+10} \right)$$

$$= u_0 \, \ddot{a}_x$$

$$\Rightarrow u_0 = \frac{F(0)}{\ddot{a}_x}$$

$$u_t = \frac{F(0) \, e^{-rt}}{\ddot{a}_x} \quad \text{for } t = 1, \ldots, 9$$

$$u_{10} = \frac{F(0) e^{-10r} \, \ddot{a}_{x+10}}{\ddot{a}_x} \tag{5.20}$$

It can be shown that Programme 5B produces identical pension payments to those produced by Programme 3B under stochastic simulation
of the price of the equity units $S(t)$ (assuming the same equity weights
in the managed fund). Programmes 5A and 3A produce similar results.

Programme 6: Collared-income programme (COL)

This programme (again involving either bequests – Programme 6A $\Rightarrow$
$\delta = 1$ – or mortality bonuses – Programme 6B $\Rightarrow \delta = 0$) is identical to
Programme 3, except that the investment returns are subject to a floor
and a ceiling implemented using a simple combination of put and call
options on the assets in the underlying fund. To illustrate, we will assume
that the managed fund is 100% equity-invested. We denote the collared
unit value of the fund by $\tilde{S}(t)$ with $\tilde{S}(0) = 1$ and, for $t = 1, \ldots, 10$:

$$\frac{\tilde{S}(t)}{\tilde{S}(t-1)} = \begin{cases} k_0 & \text{if } S(t)/S(t-1) < k_0 \\ k_1 & \text{if } S(t)/S(t-1) > k_1 \\ \dfrac{S(t)}{S(t-1)} & \text{otherwise} \end{cases} \tag{5.21}$$

where $k_0 < k_1$.

For each investment of £1 at time $t - 1$ this return can be synthesised
by the purchase of $1/S(t - 1)$ units of the underlying equity, the purchase
of $1/S(t - 1)$ 1-year put options with a strike price of k_0, and the sale
of $1/S(t - 1)$ 1-year call options with a strike price of k_1. Given k_0, k_1

is chosen to ensure that the prices of the put and call options are equal, so that the total cost of this portfolio at time $t - 1$ is equal to £1. In this exercise we have chosen $k_0 = 1$.

The price of the relevant put option is:

$$P^P(k_0) = S(t - 1)k_0 e^{-r} N(-d_2(k_0)) - S(t - 1)N(-d_1(k_0))$$
$$\text{where } d_1(k_0) = \frac{-\log k_0 + (r + \frac{1}{2}\sigma^2)}{\sigma}$$
$$d_2(k_0) = d_1(k_0) - \sigma. \tag{5.22}$$

where $N(.)$ is the cumulative probability distribution for a standard normal variate. The price of the relevant call option is:

$$P^C(k_1) = S(t - 1)N(d_1(k_1)) - S(t - 1)k_1 e^{-r} N(d_2(k_1))$$
$$\text{where } d_1(k_1) = \frac{-\log k_1 + (r + \frac{1}{2}\sigma^2)}{\sigma}$$
$$d_2(k_0) = d_1(k_1) - \sigma. \tag{5.23}$$

We choose k_1 so that $P^C(k_1) = P^P(k_0)$.

Programme 7: Floored-income programme (FLR)

This programme (again involving either bequests – Programme 7A $\Rightarrow \delta = 1$ – or mortality bonuses – Programme 7B $\Rightarrow \delta = 0$) is identical to Programme 3, except that allocated investment returns are subject to a floor using a put option on the assets in the underlying fund, financed by the policyholder foregoing a proportion of equity returns above the minimum set by the strike price on the put. Again, for illustrative purposes, we will assume that the managed fund is 100% equity-invested.

The allocated investment returns are determined as follows for $t = 1, \ldots, 10$ (where we define the unit value of the fund by $\tilde{S}(t)$ with $\tilde{S}(0) = 1$):

$$\frac{\tilde{S}(t)}{\tilde{S}(t - 1)} = \begin{cases} k_0 & \text{if } S(t)/S(t - 1) < k_0 \\ k_0 + k_1 \left(\dfrac{S(t)}{S(t - 1)} - k_0 \right) & \text{if } S(t)/S(t - 1) \geqslant k_0 \end{cases}$$
$$\tag{5.24}$$

For each investment of £1 at time $t - 1$, this return can be achieved by investing $k_0 e^{-r}$ in bonds and by purchasing $k_1/S(t - 1)$ 1-year put options with a strike price of k_0. In this example we have chosen $k_0 = 1$.

Given k_0, k_1 is chosen to ensure that the cost of this portfolio at time $t - 1$ is equal to 1 (this also requires $k_0 < e^r$). The payoff at t for each unit invested at time $t - 1$ is:

$$k_0 + k_1 \max \left(\frac{S(t)}{S(t-1)} - k_0, k_0 \right) \qquad (5.25)$$

This means that $k_1 = (1 - k_0 e^{-r})/P^P(k_0)$ where $P^P(k_0)$ is evaluated using (5.22).

5.2.3 Simulation output

We use stochastic simulation to design and stress test the various ILRIPs. This involves generating a large number of stochastic scenarios and deriving an empirical distribution function for the variables of interest, conditional on a given set of deterministic factors. We discussed this in some detail in Chapter 4, where we used value-at-risk (VaR) as the relevant risk measure. VaR is a suitable risk measure when the risk exposure is for a single date. However, it is not a suitable risk measure when the risk exposure embraces a range of dates, as it does in the present case. We wish to value the benefits received by the policyholder between the ages of 65 and 75, recognising that there is a possibility that he might die before 75. If this happens with one of the income draw-down programmes, his estate will benefit from a bequest of the residual fund, whereas, with any of the annuities, there is no residual fund to bequest, although the policyholder will have benefited from mortality bonuses while he was still alive. There is, therefore, a value-at-risk at each possible date between retirement and 75, and we need a summary measure for this. We have chosen to use a value function similar to that employed by Merton (1990) and others. This combines utility applied to the different cash flows and corresponding discount factors. We analyse this value function both as a random variable and in expectation, a procedure we call *utility-at-risk* (UtaR) analysis.

The value function

For each ILRIP, there will be a value function of the following discounted-utility form (for example, see Merton, 1990):

$$\Lambda = \sum_{t=0}^{K+\delta} e^{-\beta t} U(P(t), D(t)) \qquad (5.26)$$

with expected value, $\bar{\Lambda} = E[\Lambda]$, where $P(t)$ is non-zero only while the policyholder is still alive, $D(t)$ is only non-zero if a bequest is payable ($\delta = 1$) under the terms of the programme and if the policyholder dies between times $t - 1$ and t, and $65 + K$ is the age of the policyholder at death (rounded down).

The particular preferences of the policyholder are taken into account in three ways. The discount rate β allows him to place more or less weight on cash flows at different times and the form of the utility function allows him to express both his appetite for risk at different levels of income and his preference for different sources of benefit.

We will use the negative exponential utility function:

$$U(P(t), D(t)) = 1 - \exp\left[-\gamma\left(P(t) - P_0 + \alpha D(t)\right)\right] \qquad (5.27)$$

where γ is the absolute risk-aversion parameter, α measures the relative preference for death benefits (if there are any) and $P_0 = F(0)/\ddot{a}_{65}$ is the *benchmark* pension provided by the purchased life annuity (Programme 1). This choice of utility function ensures that the random value function is constant and equal to 0 for the benchmark pension, regardless of the date of death. It also has the effect of reducing the impact of longevity risk (which is a factor that cannot be controlled for) on Λ when considering the other programmes. This allows us to focus more clearly on the effects of the choice of programme and on the investment strategy. The ranking of expected values of Λ under different programmes is not affected by the removal of the effects of mortality risk. However, the distribution of Λ and the perceived riskiness of each programme are affected by the inclusion of P_0.

The relative risk-aversion parameter is defined in the following way. Assume that $P(t) = P$ and $D(t) = 0$ for all t. Then, the relative risk-aversion parameter is $-P.\Lambda''(P)/\Lambda'(P)$ evaluated at P_0, which gives γP_0. For a risk-free real rate of interest of $r = 0.01$ and an initial fund $F(0) = £100\,000$, we find that $P_0 = £8775.564$ using PMA92Base-Ultimate.

General comments on the results

We conducted the stochastic simulations across the following range of values for the risk-aversion parameter, γ : 10^{-5} to 3×10^{-3}, a range that embraces both very risk-averse and risk-loving behaviour by policyholders.[8] However, we fixed the other parameters of the utility function

---

[8] Note that the small size of γ is dictated by the large size of the cash sums being considered.

Table 5.5 Properties of the discounted utility functions for the different ILRIPs when $\gamma = 0.0001$

Programme		Equity %	E(Λ)	St.Dev.(Λ)	UtaR percentiles 20%	UtaR percentiles 50%
1	PLA	0	0	0	0	0
2A	FXD	100	−70	550	−435	73
3A	FLX	25	−76	165	−211	−59
3A	FLX	50	−23	279	−238	10
3A	FLX	75	9	393	−287	44
3A	FLX	100	25	495	−354	59
4A	DEF	100	22	217	−170	38
5A	UNI	100	25	493	−344	45
6A	COL	collar	−90	166	−226	−71
7A	FLR	floor	−64	213	−241	−40
2B	FXD	100	43	524	−218	0
3B	FLX	25	70	149	−29	44
3B	FLX	50	119	282	−70	74
3B	FLX	75	145	396	−126	91
3B	FLX	100	149	495	−197	96
4B	DEF	100	50	213	−118	49
5B	UNI	100	149	495	−197	96
6B	COL	collar	56	145	−40	36
7B	FLR	floor	81	205	−50	39

at the following values: $\beta = 0.03$ (which corresponds to the rate of time preference for a typical UK investor)[9] and $\alpha = 1$ (which gives death benefits the same value in the utility function as pensions in payment).

The properties of the discounted utility functions for the different ILRIPs when $\gamma = 0.0001$ (which corresponds to a relatively low relative risk-aversion parameter) are presented in Table 5.5.

The values in Table 5.5 were determined by carrying out 2000 independent simulations of the equity return process. For each simulation, the levels of pension and death benefit were calculated. Each of these 2000 investment scenarios was then divided into 45 mortality scenarios, corresponding to the death of the policyholder at ages last birthday of 65, 66, ..., 109: we assume that no policyholder survives beyond age 110. Mortality is assumed to be independent of the investment scenario. The probability of death between ages $65 + t$ and $65 + t + 1$, given

---

[9] See Blake (2004).

that the policyholder is alive at age 65, is $_tp_{65} - _{t+1}p_{65}$. The probability of each combined investment/mortality scenario is, therefore, $(_tp_{65} - _{t+1}p_{65})/2000$. Each of these 90 000 scenarios has its own discounted utility and this allows us to calculate the expected discounted utility, its standard deviation and the 20% and 50% UtaRs.

On the basis that we choose the policy with the highest expected discounted utility, we would therefore choose Programme 3B (with 100% equities) or Programme 5B (which, as we have commented earlier, are, in fact, identical). These are the flexible-income and unit-linked annuities paying mortality bonuses.

In Figure 5.1 we have plotted the expected discounted utility, $\bar{\Lambda} = E[\Lambda]$, for each programme for a range of values for the relative risk-aversion parameter. The figure is divided into two parts, corresponding to the income draw down and annuity variants, respectively.

Where a curve coincides with the bold and uppermost line in the graph, we know that this programme is then the best possible programme out of those being considered for a particular level of relative risk aversion. Thus, Programmes 3B (with 100% equities) and 5B are optimal if relative risk-aversion $\gamma P_0 < 1$ (approximately). Programme 3B remains optimal for relative risk-aversion parameters up to about 9, although the optimal equity proportion within Programme 3B gradually shifts from 100% down to 0%. For more risk-averse policyholders, the purchased life annuity (Programme 1) is optimal.

Figure 5.1 reveals the following key results:

- all the optimal policies use mortality bonuses rather than bequests, despite the fact that bequests have the same value in the utility function as pensions in payment;[10]
- all the optimal policies employ simple mixes of equities and bonds rather than more sophisticated strategies involving derivatives (that give downside protection) or deferred annuities.

Figure 5.1 can, for a specific value of γP_0, be used to rank the programmes in order of preference; Table 5.5 does this for $\gamma = 0.0001$. However, the differences in discounted expected utility do not give us any feel for how much worse Programme 6A, say, is compared with Programme 3B when $\gamma P_0 = 0.9$. It would, therefore, be useful to know the answer to the following question: how much extra cash would the policyholder need at time 0 in order for Programme 6A to

---

[10] Raising α sufficiently will change this result of course.

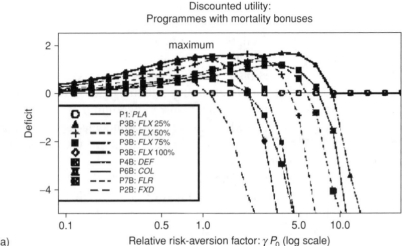

(a)

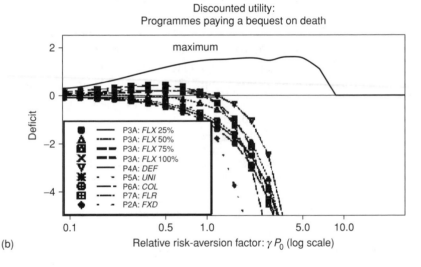

(b)

Figure 5.1 Expected discounted utility, $E[\Lambda]$, for a range of investment-linked retirement income programmes against relative risk aversion: (a) annuity programmes paying mortality bonuses; (b) income draw down programmes paying bequests

have the same discounted expected utility as the optimal Programme 3B with $F(0) = £100\,000$ and $\gamma P_0 = 0.9$? This question is answered in Figure 5.2: we would require an extra 20% approximately, or £20 000 for Programme 6A to match Programme 3B.

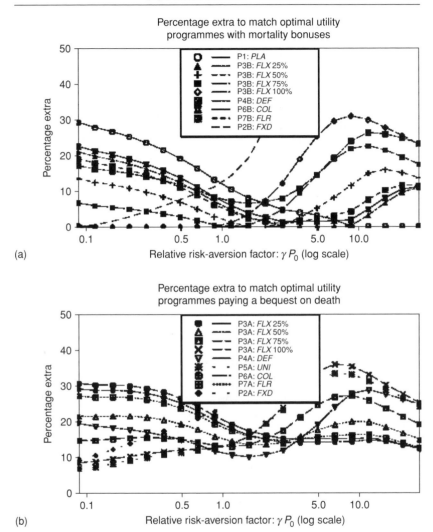

Figure 5.2 Extra cash required at time 0 to match the optimal expected discounted utility as a function of the relative risk-aversion parameter: (a) annuity programmes paying mortality bonuses; (b) income draw down programmes paying bequests

Figure 5.2 is much more informative than Figure 5.1, because it gives a much better impression of the relative quality of each programme. For example, we can now see that for policyholders with a relatively high appetite for risk (low values of γ) some programmes would require as much as 30% extra cash (Programmes 1 and 6A) to match the optimal Programme 3B. Programmes that use lower proportions of equities or use derivatives have lower risk but also lower expected returns, so it is not surprising that they come out relatively poorly in the eyes of a policyholder with a low degree of risk aversion.

At the other end of the spectrum, the figure shows that a very risk-averse policyholder must opt for Programme 1, as all other programmes require significant additional amounts of cash at time 0. However, the differences are not as large as at the left-hand end of the figure, except for Programmes 2A and 2B, which go off the scale. This outcome for Programme 2 reflects the severe penalty attached to programmes that can run out of money before the policyholder dies, especially if he is highly risk averse.

In Figures 5.3 and 5.4, we plot (for $\gamma = 0.0001$) the empirical cumulative distribution functions (CDFs) of the discounted utilities for a selection of different programmes. Each of the 90 000 scenarios contributing to this CDF carries a weight which is equal to $1/2000$ times the relevant probability of death.

We note the following:

- Programme 1 has a degenerate distribution because the choice of utility function removes the effect of mortality risk.
- Figure 5.3(a) shows, using Programme 3 for illustration, that greater equity investment results in a wider spread of values for Λ. While the 100% equity investment strategy generates the highest expected value of Λ, it also has the highest 20% UtaR amongst the Programme 3 investment strategies considered in Table 5.5: the 20% UtaR[11] is, respectively, 0.29, 0.70, 1.26 and 1.97 for the 25%, 50%, 75% and 100% equity-investment strategies. This confirms that the 100% equity-investment strategy has the highest expected utility, but also the greatest chance of poor utility outcomes. UtaR provides us with a way of measuring these poor utility outcomes.
- Figure 5.3(b) demonstrates, again using Programme 3 to illustrate, that programmes offering mortality bonuses have clear stochastic dominance[12] over those involving bequests. The gap is quite large, although it would be lower for higher values of α.

---

[11] The 20% UtaR is the negative of the 20% point of the expected discounted utility.

[12] Investment programme A stochastically dominates investment programme B if the return on A is no worse than the return on B in all states of the world and exceeds it in at least one state of the world.

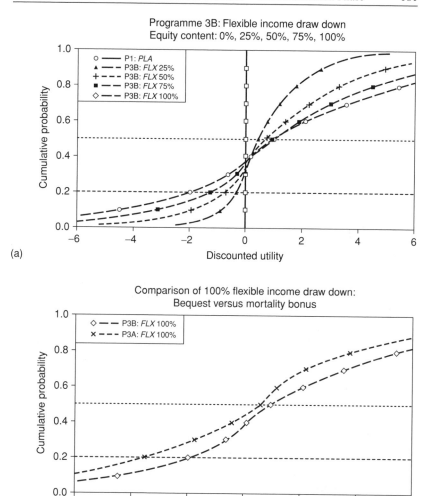

Figure 5.3 Properties of the optimal programme: (a) comparison of equity weightings; (b) comparison of bequests and mortality bonuses

• Figure 5.4(a) compares the fixed- and flexible-income annuity Programmes 2B and 3B (both 100% equity invested). It is clear that the restraint on the amount of pension drawn under 3B is very beneficial for policyholders with this type of utility function. The jump in 2B at 0 corresponds to death during the first ten years.

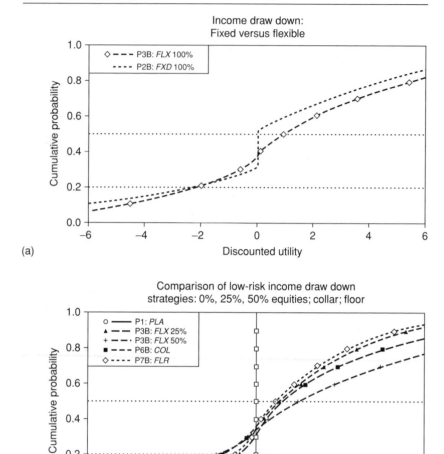

(a)

(b)

Figure 5.4 Selected comparisons: (a) fixed- and flexible-income programmes; (b) low-risk income programmes

- Figure 5.4(b) compares some low-risk annuity programmes. Of particular interest is the closeness between 3B (flexible-income annuity with 25% equity invested), 6B (collared-income annuity) and
  7B (floored-income annuity), although 3B consistently dominates
  6B.

5.2.4   Impact of poor health

The calculations above assumed that the scheme member's mortality probabilities equal those used by the life office to calculate annuity prices. However, a typical group of scheme members will include some in good health and others in poor health. For the latter group, the purchase of a life annuity at retirement at standard rates represents poor value relative to other scheme members in better health. It is often suggested, therefore, that those in poor health should defer annuitisation for as long as possible.

Consider an individual for whom mortality rates are approximately four times those assumed by the life office.[13] This degree of impairment is consistent with, for example, an individual who has just been diagnosed as suffering from Alzheimer's Disease (Macdonald and Pritchard, 2000). Blake, Cairns and Dowd (2003) have shown that it is still optimal for this individual to choose a distribution programme involving a mortality bonus rather than a bequest. However, as the degree of impairment increases much above this, the scheme member is more likely to prefer the programme with the bequest. It is also possible that an impaired life would benefit more from programmes that allow for the accelerated payment of pension. The most beneficial improvement from the point of view of the scheme member would be the payment of higher (i.e. fairer) mortality bonuses from the life office to reflect the higher mortality rates (as is the case with impaired life annuities) rather than from a programme with bequests.

5.2.5   The annuitisation decision

In the discussion above on mortality drag, it was clear that, at some age, it becomes optimal for the scheme member to purchase an annuity. This is because the implied return on the annuity (which is linked to the size of the mortality drag) exceeds any return likely to be available on financial assets.

The optimal age to annuitise depends on the fund size, the scheme member's degree of risk aversion and the intensity of the desire to make

---

[13] Strictly, we assume that, $p_x^{impaired} = (p_x^{PLA})^4$, that is, the force of mortality is 4 times the standard force used by the life office in its annuity pricing. For small q_x^{PLA}, this implies that $q_x^{impaired} = 4(q_x^{PLA})$.

a bequest (the bequest intensity). Suppose that at the end of each year any pre-annuitised scheme member reconsiders annuitisation, taking into account the information available at that time. This means that the decision at time t will depend on the current fund size, $F(t)$, and the current age of the scheme member, $65 + t$. Since $F(t)$ is random, the scheme member does not necessarily know in advance the optimal age at which to annuitise. Suppose it is mandatory to annuitise by age 85 at the latest. The optimisation process (which is an application of dynamic programming) then proceeds as follows:

- Let the optimal value function at time t be denoted $\Lambda^*(t, F(t))$.
- Start at the age $x = 65 + T$, by which annuitisation is compulsory. For each possible fund size at that time calculate the value function $\Lambda(T, F(T)) = \Lambda^*(T, F(T))$.
- Next, work backwards recursively:
  - Assume that the optimal value function $\Lambda^*(t + 1, F(t + 1))$ is known for all $F(t + 1)$. Now consider the decision at time t when the fund size is $F(t)$. We need to compare the value function (a) assuming that the scheme member annuitises immediately with the value function, (b) assuming that the scheme member defers annuitisation until at least time $t + 1$ and then acts optimally thereafter. Under (b) we have several factors to take into account: the probability of survival, the pension payment at time t and the possible bequest if the scheme member dies before time $t + 1$. The scheme member chooses the option that maximises the value function, thus producing an optimal value function $\Lambda^*(t, F(t))$.
  - This procedure is repeated over the full range of possible values for $F(t)$.
- Once this has been done, we can step backwards by one year, repeat the previous step and continue in this way until we reach the age of 65, at which point we stop.

Our results indicate that a scheme member is more likely to prefer to delay (bring forward) annuitisation if his investments have been performing well (badly) and his fund is large (small). To illustrate this, suppose the fund size is almost zero and a scheme member is considering a switch from a draw down programme to the PLA programme. On the one hand, the small fund size means there is very little to bequest. On the other hand, the payment of mortality bonuses through the PLA will have a strong beneficial impact on the utility of consumption, because the marginal utility of consumption gets large as the fund size gets small. So, both bequest and marginal utility of consumption considerations make the scheme member keener to annuitise, relative to a scheme member with more wealth.

The dependence of the annuitisation decision on fund size is illustrated in Figure 5.5, which shows the outcome of the above optimisation process at selected levels of risk aversion (RRA). If the fund–age trajectory enters the shaded area, then the scheme member should annuitise immediately. The graphs are for different levels of RRA. Each graph assumes that before annuitisation, the indicated optimal equity mix has been used. Consider a scheme member with an RRA of 3.15 who is now aged 75 and who has not previously annuitised. If his current fund size is below about £90 000, he should annuitise immediately. But if his current fund is above this level, then it is optimal for him to defer annuitisation. We can also see that the annuitisation region varies considerably with the RRA. We also observe from these graphs that, for any given age and RRA, annuitisation will:

- not be optimal for any fund size;
- be optimal for all fund sizes; or
- be optimal for low fund sizes but not for fund sizes above some threshold.

In each graph the dots show how the scheme member's fund value would change over time if he had opted at age 65 for the PLA. This gives a useful reference point for projecting the stochastic fund size under the draw down programme at different ages. Thus, with an RRA of 1.58, we can see that annuitisation is likely to occur some time between the ages of 72 (if equities perform poorly) and 80 (if equities perform moderately well). However, if equities perform sufficiently well, then the fund–age trajectory will lie above the shaded region and annuitisation might only take place when it is compulsory at age 85. In the plot below, where the RRA is 3.15, the shaded annuitisation 'hill' is somewhat lower, implying that a relatively large proportion of the stochastic trajectories of $F(t)$ will avoid hitting the hill (and so avoid annuitisation) at ages below 85. On the other hand, if $F(t)$ is going to hit the hill, it will probably do so within the first three or four years. We can infer from these observations that in some (i.e. low RRA) cases, the dynamic stochastic element in the annuitisation decision will not add much value (the scheme member will choose to annuitise at around age 80 regardless). However, in other (high RRA) cases, the shape and height of the annuitisation hill are such that the majority of stochastic fund–age trajectories cross over the hill

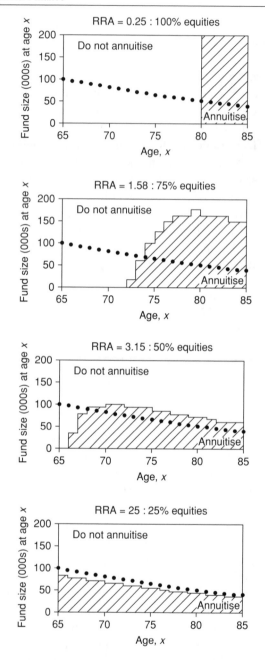

Figure 5.5   Relationship between the annuitisation decision and the scheme member's age and fund size

without hitting it, suggesting that the extra timing choice captured by the dynamic stochastic element is a valuable feature.

It is also interesting to note that at very low levels of RRA, the optimal annuitisation age of 80 is close to the age we would get (namely, 81) by applying Milevsky's (1998) rule, which specifies that we switch at the point where the mortality drag matches the expected excess return on equities over bonds. However, our analysis shows that this decision rule matches the one presented here only for a scheme member who is near to risk neutrality. Our more general analysis demonstrates that decision making is much more complex than the Milevsky rule suggests, with the equity mix and the optimal annuitisation age critically dependent on both the level of risk aversion and the bequest motive.

Finally, Blake, Cairns and Dowd (2003) calculate that the cost of compulsory annuitisation at age 75 (rather than at the optimal age) turns out to lie between 0% and 15% of the initial fund value depending on the level of risk aversion, it being 15% for a risk-neutral scheme member. In other words, a DC scheme member would be prepared to pay up to 15% of the initial fund value to escape the requirement to annuitise at age 75.

5.3   CONCLUSIONS

A crucial component of the distribution phase is the life annuity, which protects individuals from outliving their resources. Annuities can be provided by DC pension schemes themselves and are also sold by life companies. The charges extracted by life companies can be decomposed into a component arising from the selection risk associated with the type of people who purchase annuities, a component arising from the additional risk associated with the type of people who purchase annuities in the voluntary market, a component arising from escalation risk and a component that covers administration costs and profit to the insurance company. It is also possible to identify a size effect, an age effect and a sex effect.

Evaluating the design of a DC pension scheme is as critical for the distribution phase as it is for the accumulation phase. We have shown, in particular, that the best distribution programme:

- pays a mortality bonus to the policyholder in return for the payment of the residual fund on death to the pension provider (i.e. is an annuity programme) rather than one that leaves a bequest to the survivors of the policyholder on death (i.e. is an income draw down programme). In particular, it is important to note that income draw down programmes that do not reduce the pension payout in response to disastrous investment performance can result in the fund becoming exhausted before the policyholder dies;

• if the policyholder is highly risk averse, is a conventional life annuity;
• if the policyholder is more risk-loving, invests in a mixture of bonds and equities, with the optimal mix depending on the policyholder's degree of risk aversion, rather than one that invests in derivatives designed to provide some downside protection or in a deferred level annuity.

QUESTIONS

1. What is a life annuity?
2. Explain the difference between a single-premium and a regular-premium annuity.
3. Explain the difference between a joint-life annuity and a joint-survivor annuity.
4. What is a period-certain annuity?
5. What is a deferred annuity?
6. What is an annuity with capital protection? Give some examples.
7. What is the difference between a compulsory purchase annuity and a purchased life annuity?
8. Give examples of annuities whose payments change over time.
9. Explain the difference between a with-profit annuity and a unit-linked annuity.
10. What is income draw down?
11. What is a mortality cross-subsidy?
12. What are mortality profits?
13. Define the money's worth of an annuity.
14. Define volunteer premium, selection premium and escalation premium.
15. What is meant by the size effect, age effect and sex effect in an annuity rate?
16. What is mortality drag?
17. What is a bequest?
18. What is a mortality bonus?
19. What is a collared-income programme?
20. What is a floored-income programme?
21. How significant in practice does the bequest intensity appear to be?
22. How useful in practice are investment strategies involving derivatives?

23. How useful in practice are investment strategies involving deferred annuities?
24. Upon what factors does the optimal age to annuitise depend?
25. What is Milevsky's rule for deciding when to annuitise? Comment upon its suitability for this purpose.

REFERENCES

Barclays Global (2006) *Equity Gilt Study*. Barclays Global, London.
Blake, D. (1999) Annuity markets: problems and solutions. *Geneva Papers on Risk and Insurance*, **24**, 358–375
Blake, D. (2000) *Financial Market Analysis*. John Wiley & Sons, Ltd, Chichester.
Blake, D. (2004) The impact of wealth on consumption and retirement behaviour in the UK. *Applied Financial Economics*, **14**, 555–576.
Blake, D., Cairns, A. and Dowd, K. (2003) PensionMetrics 2: stochastic pension plan design during the distribution phase. *Insurance: Mathematics & Economics*, **33**, 29–47.
Brugiavini, A. (1993) Uncertainty resolution and the timing of annuity purchases. *Journal of Public Economics*, **50**, 31–62.
Finkelstein, A. and Poterba, J. (2002) Selection effects in the United Kingdom annuities market. *Economic Journal*, **112**, 28–50.
Macdonald, A.S. and Pritchard, D. (2000) A mathematical model of Alzheimer's Disease and the Apoe gene. *ASTIN Bulletin*, **30**, 69–110.
March, H. (1996) The changing world of annuities. *Journal of the Society of Fellows*, **12**, 2–18.
McCutcheon, J.J., Barnett, H.A.R., Berman, C., Daykin, C.D., Forfar, D.O., Grimshaw, D.L., Kirkwood, C.G., Leigh, T.S. and Lockyer, J. (1998) The mortality of immediate annuitants and holders of retirement annuity policies and personal pension plans. *Continuous Mortality Investigation Reports*, **16**, 45–64.
McCutcheon, J.J., Forfar, D.O., Wilkie, A.D. and Leandro, P.A. (1999) Standard tables of mortality based on the 1991–1994 experiences: immediate annuitants. *Continuous Mortality Investigation Reports*, **17**, 27–43.
Merton, R.C. (1990) *Continuous-Time Finance*. Blackwell, Cambridge, Massachusetts.
Milevsky, M. (1998) Optimal asset allocation towards the end of the life cycle: to annuitise or not to annuitise? *Journal of Risk and Insurance*, **65**, 401–426.
Mitchell, O., Poterba, J., Warshawsky, M. and Brown, J. (1999) New evidence on the money's worth of individual annuities. *American Economic Review*, **89**, 1299–1318.
Siegel, J. (1997) *Stocks for the Long Term*. Richard D. Irwin, New York.

6

Defined Benefit Pension
Schemes

In the last two chapters we examined defined contribution (DC) schemes during their accumulation and distribution phases, respectively. In this chapter we investigate the different types of defined benefit (DB) scheme. DB schemes are usually only offered by companies to their employees: these companies are said to sponsor such schemes. They are almost never offered by financial service companies, such as insurance companies, to members of the general public. However, small companies might arrange for an insurance company to operate a DB scheme on their behalf: these are known as insurance-managed DB schemes. Some schemes have a combination of DB and DC features. Such schemes are known as hybrid schemes and we consider these here too. We then consider how the actuarial value of the liabilities in a DB scheme is determined. Following this, we examine the relationship between the three types of scheme in terms of the differing sets of options implicit in their structure,[1] and also how these options are valued. Finally, we investigate the rewards and risks faced by members, sponsors and fund managers from their participation in the different types of scheme.

6.1 TYPES OF DEFINED BENEFIT SCHEME

In a defined benefit scheme, it is the benefit from the scheme, rather than the contributions into the scheme, that is defined. The scheme promises to pay a pension, based on this defined benefit, whatever the size of the fund backing this promise.

The simplest DB scheme offers a fixed monetary pension at retirement, irrespective of earnings or subsequent inflation. Such schemes are common in Germany and the US (where they are known as *fixed amount schemes*).

---

[1] The original treatment of pension fund liabilities as options is contained in Bagehot (1972), Sharpe (1976) and Treynor *et al.* (1976).

Table 6.1 Value of pension benefits as a proportion of salary

Year of employment	Present value of new benefits earned (%)	Value of accrued benefits (%)
1	0.32	0.32
10	0.98	6.88
20	3.10	32.58
30	9.18	115.68
40	26.08	365.14

Assumptions: The scheme pays a benefit equal to 1% of final salary per year of service. Scheme participants enter the scheme at age 25, retire at age 65 and live until age 85. The employee's salary grows at the rate of inflation, which is 5% per year. The interest rate used for discounting nominal annuities is 9% per year.
Source: Bodie (1990, Table 1)

However, the most common type of DB scheme is *a salary-related scheme*. The most common of these is the *final-salary scheme*, in which the pension paid is related to the salary earned in the final year of employment (or the average of the final three or five years of employment) of the scheme member. The actual pension is some fraction of the final salary, where the fraction is calculated as the product of the accrual rate (e.g. 1%) and the number of years of service.

Table 6.1 shows the value of pension benefits as a proportion of final salary. The table shows that benefits are *backloaded*: the present value of benefits earned in each year is greater in later years than earlier years. For example, the present value of benefits earned in the 10th year of membership is 0.98% of final salary, while that earned in the 40th year is equal to 26.08%. The backloading is caused by two factors: the time value of money and inflation. An older worker is closer to retirement than a younger worker and so the present value of an additional unit of pension benefit is higher for the older worker.

Inflation increases backloading for two reasons. First, by increasing the nominal interest rate, it magnifies the time value effect. Second, by increasing nominal wages, it will magnify the uprating component of the benefit earned each year. With each additional year of employment, an additional year of service is earned and the nominal salary is higher.

More recently, *average-salary schemes* have been introduced: the pension is based on the average salary earned during the member's career (usually the average salary calculation adjusts for general price or wage inflation that occurred over the member's career[2]). A number of industry-wide schemes in Holland have switched from using final salaries to career averages.

Another type of DB scheme is the *retirement balance scheme*. The benefit is defined in terms of a lump sum rather than a pension and it is typically measured as the multiple of a specified percentage of career average salary and years of service. If final, rather than average, salary is used, such schemes are known as *pension equity schemes*. They are common in Japan and Australia. They are not proper pension schemes however, unless the lump sum is used to buy an annuity and hence provide lifetime income security.

A DB scheme will show a *surplus* if the value of the assets in the pension fund exceeds the value of the liabilities, namely the present value of the future promised pension payments. A DB scheme will show a *deficit* if the value of the liabilities exceeds the assets. Pension regulators or supervisors (appointed by the government) generally impose strict rules on the elimination of both surpluses and deficits. Surpluses are typically eliminated through *sponsor contribution holidays*, i.e. the sponsor stops making contributions to the fund until the deficit has been eliminated. Deficits are eliminated through a series of deficiency payments, i.e. additional contributions from the sponsor, that extinguish the deficit within a specified period, such as ten years or the average remaining service life of the company's workforce (typically around 15 years).

Hybrid schemes have a mixture of DB and DC components. The main examples are as follows:

- *Sequential hybrid schemes*. These schemes might have a DC element for those below a certain age (e.g. 45) and a DB element for those above it. Such a scheme offers good portability for younger workers, who tend to be more mobile, and a more predictable pension for older workers.
- *Combination hybrid schemes*. These schemes offers a DB pension in relation to salary up to a limit (which might be the basic salary) and a DC pension in respect of salary above this limit (which might be the variable element of salary).

---

[2] Typically, each year's salary is uprated by the increase in retail prices or national average earnings over the period until retirement.

- *Underpinning arrangements.* A variation on the previous scheme type, namely a DC scheme with a DB underpin. Such a scheme provides a minimum pension in case the investment performance is very poor.
- *Cash balance schemes.* These are defined benefit schemes in which the benefit is defined as an individual account within the scheme. The scheme specifies the rate of contribution and the rate of investment return (independent of the performance of the underlying assets in the scheme, but typically linked to the return on bonds) that will be credited to the member's account. The accumulated lump sum at retirement is used to buy an annuity. To the member, a cash balance scheme resembles a DC scheme. It is common in the US (see Rappaport *et al.* 1997).
- *Targeted money purchase* or *targeted benefit schemes.* These are DC schemes but the aim is to deliver a DB pension, so the contributions will have to be adjusted over time if the fund falls short of, or exceeds, the target.

6.2 DEFINED BENEFIT LIABILITIES

Defined benefit liabilities are generally calculated using the *projected unit method*. In the case of a final salary scheme we have:

$$\text{Liabilities} = \phi(t) \times W(t) \times G(t, T) \times \Pi(t, T) \times \ddot{a}(T) \times D(t, T) \tag{6.1}$$

where:

$\phi(t) = $ *Accrual factor* for service by age t (e.g. 5/60 if the member has five years' service and the 60th scale is used to determine the value of benefits).

$W(t) = $ Pensionable salary at age t (e.g. £10 000).

$G(t,T) = $ *Revaluation factor* for earnings between age t and retirement age T ($= 1$ if there is no revaluation of earnings up until the retirement age (this is known as the *current unit method* of valuing liabilities), $= (1 + g)^{(T-t)}$ if the *revaluation rate g* is constant).

$\Pi(t,T) = $ *Retention factor* = probability of remaining in the scheme between age t and retirement age T: the two main reasons for a member not remaining in the scheme until retirement are death-in-service and leaving a scheme early as a result of changing jobs.

$\ddot{a}(T) =$ Expected *annuity factor* (the present value of a life annuity of £1 per annum) at retirement age, $T: \ddot{a}(T) = {}_1p_T/(1+r) + {}_2p_T/(1+r)^2 + {}_3p_T/(1+r)^3 \ldots$, where terms such as ${}_1p_T$ are known as *survival probabilities* and indicate the probability of someone aged T surviving to age $T+1$, etc., and r is the real yield on the long-term bonds that are purchased by the insurance company and from which the pension payments are paid.

$D(t, T) =$ *Discount factor* between age t and retirement age T (= $1/(1+r)^{(T-t)}$ if the discount rate r is constant).

To illustrate, suppose that we assume the following for a single male pension scheme member currently aged 35 and due to retire when he is 65:

$\phi(t) = 5/60$

$W(t) = £10\,000$

$G(t, T) = 1.81$ (assuming earnings growth of 2% p.a. in real terms over the next 30 years to retirement)

$\Pi(t, T) = 0.7$

$\ddot{a}(T) = 13.48$ (assuming mortality experience based on the PMA92 mortality table and a real yield of 2.5% on long-term government bonds)

$D(t, T) = 0.4767426$ (assuming a real discount rate of 2.5% and 30 years to retirement).

Then, the actuarial value of the liabilities is £6784 in respect of this member.

This is explained as follows. The member's projected final salary is £18 100 (£10 000 × 1.81) in real terms, and the member is expecting a pension of 5/60 of his final salary or £1508 (based on current service). This pension is payable for life. Based on the PMA92 mortality table, the pension fund will need to have accumulated £13.48 for each £1 of pension payable or £20 328 (£1508 × 13.48) by the time the member retires. The present value of this sum is £9691. In other words, if we had £9691 today and we invested it for 30 years at a real return of 2.5% p.a. (i.e. the same as the discount rate), we would have exactly the sum of money needed in 30 years' time to purchase a life annuity for the member paying £1508 p.a. in real terms for life. However, suppose that, based on the past experience of the pension scheme, there is only a 70% chance that the member will still be in service by his normal retirement age (i.e. there is a 30% chance that the member dies or leaves service between 35 and 65). If we multiply £9691 by 70% we get £6784. The pension scheme is fully funded if it has assets with a market value of £6784 for this active member.

A pension fund *surplus* is defined as the difference between the market value of the assets in the pension fund and the actuarial value of the liabilities:

$$\text{Surplus}\,(S) = \text{Assets}\,(A) - \text{Liabilities}\,(L) \qquad (6.2)$$

6.3   THE OPTION COMPOSITION OF PENSION SCHEMES

The structure of a DB scheme looks very complicated, but it can be explained very simply using option theory (Blake, 1998). Option theory can also be used to explain the differences between DB schemes, DC schemes and targeted money purchase (TMP) schemes. The relationships between these schemes on the retirement date of the member are shown in Figures 6.1–6.3.

Figure 6.1 shows that the present value of the DC pension on the retirement date depends entirely on the value of the fund assets on that date. Figure 6.2 shows that the present value of the DB pension (L) is independent of the value of the fund assets, while Figure 6.3 shows that the TMP pension has a minimum present value of L, but is higher if asset values exceed L.

Figure 6.4 shows that the DB pension can be replicated using a long put option (P) and a short call option $(-C)$ on the underlying assets of the fund (A), both with the same exercise price (L). The put option is held by the scheme member and written by the scheme sponsor, while the call option is written by the member and held by the sponsor. On the retirement date of the member, which coincides with the expiry date of the options, one of the options is (almost) certain to be 'exercised', while the other will expire worthless. If the value of the assets is less than the exercise price, so that the scheme is showing an actuarial deficit, the member will exercise his or her put option against the sponsor, who will then be required to make a *deficiency payment* $(L - A)$.[3] If, on the other hand, the value of the assets exceeds the exercise price, so that the

---

[3] This is the case in which the pension fund has legal recourse to the sponsoring company in the event of a deficiency. This contrasts with the case in Section 3.2 and Figure 3.4 in which there was no recourse. In that case, the members still had a put option against the sponsor, but the sponsor had a put option on this put option. If the first put option was exercised (i.e. in the event of a deficiency), the second option was immediately exercised, and the deficiency was handed straight back to the members.

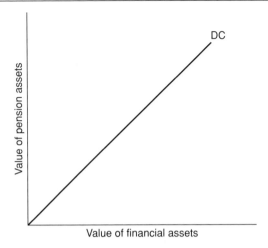

Figure 6.1   A defined contribution pension scheme

scheme is showing an actuarial surplus, the sponsor will exercise his or her call option against the member and recover the surplus $(A - L)$. A member of a DB scheme, therefore, bears no asset-market risk.

It is clear from this how DB and DC schemes are related. A DC scheme is invested only in the underlying assets. A DB scheme is invested in a portfolio containing the underlying assets (and so is, in part, a DC scheme) *plus* a put option *minus* a call option on these assets:

$$\text{DB} = L = A + P - C = \text{DC} + P - C \tag{6.3}$$

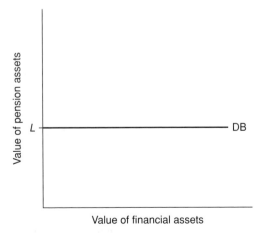

Figure 6.2   A defined benefit pension scheme

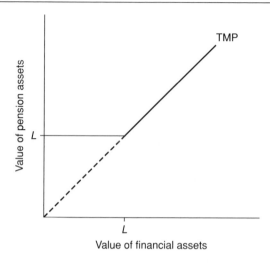

Figure 6.3 A targeted money purchase scheme

Figure 6.5 shows that the TMP pension can be replaced using a long (protective) put option (P) on the underlying assets of the fund (A) with an exercise price (L). The put option is held by the scheme member and written by the scheme sponsor. On the retirement date of the member,

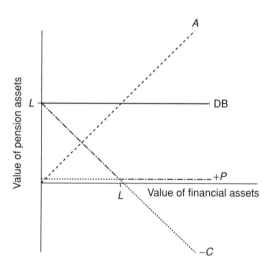

Figure 6.4 The option composition of a defined benefit pension scheme

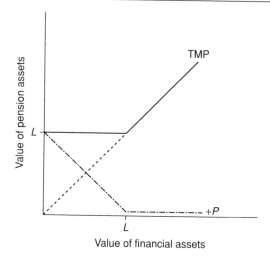

Figure 6.5   The option composition of a TMP pension scheme

which again coincides with the expiry date of the option, the option will be exercised if the value of the assets is less than the exercise price. The effect of the option is to place a floor on the value of the pension received by the member. The present value of the TMP pension on the retirement date is the larger of the two present values provided by the DC and DB schemes, whatever the value of the underlying assets:

$$\text{TMP} = A + P = \text{MAX}(A, L) = \text{MAX}(\text{DC}, \text{DB}) = C + L \quad (6.4)$$

This implies that a TMP scheme is equivalent to a call option (or floor) held by the member on the underlying pension fund assets with an exercise price L *plus* a riskless pure discount bond with a maturity value of L.[4] The call option will only be exercised if, on maturity, A exceeds L.

6.4   VALUING THE OPTIONS

We can now examine in more detail the structure of the pension schemes, and, in particular, show how the options are valued. We will concentrate on a DB scheme and assume throughout that the conditioning date is the

---

[4] We assume here that the target pension with the TMP scheme is the same as that with the DB scheme, but this need not be the case in general. It is also clear that the TMP scheme is equivalent to an *endowment insurance scheme* (see, for example, Gemmill, 1993, Section 10.3). In the US it is known as a *floor-offset scheme*.

start-up date of the scheme ($t = 0$), so that all values dated ahead of $t = 0$ will be expected values conditioned on information available at $t = 0$.

We will assume that the expected value of a scheme member's pension assets at any date t will equal the expected value of the accumulated financial assets (F_t) *plus* the expected discounted value of the remaining contributions until the retirement date (X_t).[5] These, in turn, will depend on the member's starting income (W_0), the contribution rate as a proportion of income into the scheme (α), the expected future growth rate in income (g_W) (which, for simplicity, we assume to be constant for the whole period), the expected returns on the investments in financial assets purchased with the contributions (r_{Ft}), the rate of tax relief on contributions (τ),[6] the total number of years of pensionable service (T) and the survival probabilities from date $t = 0$ ($_k p_0, k = 1, t$). Assuming that the appropriate discount rates used to discount the remaining contributions are the expected returns on financial assets held during the relevant period[7] (which will depend on the fund management strategy pursued by the scheme), the expected value of a member's pension assets at any date t (A_t) is given by:

$$
A_t = F_t + X_t = \sum_{k=1}^{t} \frac{(_k p_0)\alpha W_0 (1 + g_W)^{k-1}}{1 - \tau} \prod_{j=k+1}^{t} \left(1 + r_{Fj}\right)
$$
$$
+ \sum_{k=t+1}^{T} \frac{_k p_0 \alpha W_0 (1 + g_W)^{k-1}}{(1 - \tau)\prod_{j=t+1}^{k}(1 + r_{Fj})} \qquad t = 1, T. \qquad (6.5)
$$

where the symbol Π represents the product of the terms immediately to the right (except for terms associated with $j > t$, which are set to unity since we assume that all cash flows arise at the end of the relevant period).

With a DB scheme, the liabilities at retirement depend on the expected pension at retirement (P), the expected growth rate in the pension (g_P)

---

[5] In this section we use the *implicit lifetime contract method* or *prospective benefits funding method* of determining pension liabilities and assets (see, for example, Disney and Whitehouse, 1996; Haberman and Sung, 1994). This method assumes that the member will work until normal retirement age and then draw a pension until death. This contrasts with the *accrued benefits funding method*, which determines pension liabilities and assets only up to the date of accrual and disregards likely future service (see, for example, Institute and Faculty of Actuaries, 1984). The projected unit method and the current unit method examined in Section 6.2 are examples of the accrued benefits funding method.

[6] We assume for simplicity that the tax rates are the same for the member and the sponsor.

[7] This is consistent with conventional practice by the actuarial profession (e.g., Tepper, 1981). However, financial economists prefer to use the after-tax rate of return on corporate bonds, e.g. Copeland (1984). This is more in line with the practice of the accountancy profession, which recommends using the yield on long-term AA corporate bonds (see, for example, Federal Accounting Standard 87 and International Accounting Standard 19).

and the survival probabilities in retirement ($_{T+k}p_0$, $k = 1, \infty$). Suppose that the retirement pension, P, is equal to some proportion (ω, e.g., two-thirds) of the expected income at retirement $\left(W_0(1 + g_W)^{T-1}\right)$. Therefore, the expected value of the liabilities at any date t is given by:[8]

$$L_t = \sum_{k=1}^{\infty} (_{T+k}p_0)P \left[\frac{1 + g_P}{1 + r_B}\right]^k \left[\frac{1}{\prod_{j=t+1}^{T}(1 + r_{Fj})}\right], \quad t = 1, T. \quad (6.6)$$

The expected actuarial surplus with a DB scheme is defined as the difference between (6.5) and (6.6):

$$S_t = A_t - L_t, \quad t = 1, T. \quad (6.7)$$

With a DC scheme, Equation (6.5) equals the present value of both the assets and liabilities, so that there is no actuarial surplus. With a TMP scheme, the liabilities are the larger of Equations (6.5) and (6.6), but, as with a DC scheme, there is no surplus.

The options embodied in the DB and TMP schemes have the following characteristics. They are European options, since they cannot be exercised before the retirement date.[9] In addition, the underlying asset does not make payouts prior to the expiry date of the option. However, the most important feature of the options is that the exercise price is not constant, as in the standard Black–Scholes model (Black and Scholes, 1973), but is equal to the value of the liabilities. The appropriate option-valuation model is based on a modification to the Black–Scholes framework, which recognises that the options in Equation (6.3) or Equation (6.4) are known as *exchange options*, i.e. options to exchange risky assets at an exercise price that is indexed to the uncertain value of the liabilities (see Fischer, 1978; Margrabe, 1978).

The value of the call option in Equation (6.3) is given by:

$$P^C = N(d_{1t})A_t - N(d_{2t})L_t, \quad (6.8)$$

where:

$$d_{1t} = \frac{\ln(A_t/L_t) + 0.5\sigma_{St}^2(T - t)}{\sigma_{St}\sqrt{T - t}}, \quad (6.9)$$

---

[8] We assume that the discount rates from the retirement date onwards are the discount rates (r_B) on risk-free government bonds with a maturity of around 15 years (on the grounds that such bonds are used to make the pension payments). The discount rates from the retirement date back to date t are the same as those used for discounting projected contributions, namely the expected returns on the financial assets in the pension fund. Again this accords with conventional actuarial practice.

[9] More sophisticated versions of the model could contain options which allow for earlier termination of the pension scheme on the grounds of redundancy (exercised by the sponsor) or ill-health (exercised by the member), etc.

$$d_{2t} = d_{1t} - \sigma_{St}\sqrt{T - t}, \tag{6.10}$$

$$\sigma_{St}^2 = \sigma_{At}^2 + \sigma_{Lt}^2 - 2\sigma_{ALt}, t = 1, T. \tag{6.11}$$

$N(d_{1t})$ and $N(d_{2t})$ are the cumulative normal distribution functions evaluated at d_{1t} and d_{2t}, respectively. Equation (6.11) is the variance (σ_{St}^2) of the surplus (6.7) (i.e. (square of) *surplus risk*) which depends on the standard deviations of the rates of return on assets (σ_{At}) and liabilities (σ_{Lt}), and the covariance between returns on the assets and liabilities (σ_{ALt}).[10]

We need to consider the most appropriate way of modelling the components of (6.11). This involves identifying sources of variability (hopefully small in number) common to both assets and liabilities. What follows is the simplest possible stylised framework for achieving this. Inevitably, substantial simplifying assumptions are involved. Where these assumptions do not correspond well with reality, a more realistic, but also a more complex, framework would be needed. We will suppose that the key sources of volatility facing both assets and liabilities are the volatilities attached to interest rates and growth rates, and that these volatilities will be scaled by the different *durations*[11] of the assets and liabilities (see Macaulay, 1938). We also allow for there to be specific components to the asset and liability volatilities.

From Equation (6.5) we can see that the volatility of the rate of change in the value of pension assets depends on their duration, which equals the weighted sum of the durations of the existing financial assets (D_{Ft}) and of the remaining contributions (D_{Xt}):[12]

$$D_{At} = \theta_t D_{Ft} + (1 - \theta_t)D_{Xt} = \theta_t D_{Ft} + (1 - \theta_t)$$
$$\times \left(\sum_{k=t+1}^{T} \frac{(k - t)(_k p_0)\alpha W_0(1 + g_W)^{k-1}}{(1 - \tau)X_t \prod_{j=t+1}^{k}(1 + r_{Fj})} \right) \quad t = 1, T \tag{6.12}$$

---

[10] See also Leibowitz (1986), who argues that liabilities can be treated as short positions in assets, and liability returns can be treated in a commensurate way.

[11] Duration is defined as the weighted average maturity of a set of cash flows and is a measure of the interest risk attached to that set of cash flows. It is discussed in detail in Appendix C of this book.

[12] The duration of the financial assets is equal to the value-weighted sum of the durations of the individual assets in the portfolio. The duration measure is highly sensitive to the underlying model of the term structure of interest rates used, as shown by Boyle (1978). For example, models with parallel yield curve shifts result in long-term assets having substantially greater durations than models with mean reversion. Nevertheless, Reitano (1991) has shown that there is an 'equivalent parallel yield curve shift' corresponding to any underlying yield curve shift, and this enables conventional Macaulay-type measures of duration to be used.

(where $\theta_t = F_t/(F_t + X_t)$) is the weight of the existing financial assets in total pension assets at time t), and on the standard deviations of the rates of change in the yields on financial assets (σ_r) and in the growth rate in earnings (σ_g). As a first-order approximation, the variance of pension asset returns is given by:

$$\sigma_{At}^2 = D_{At}^2(\sigma_r^2 + \sigma_g^2) + \eta_A^2, \quad t = 1, T \tag{6.13}$$

where η_A is the specific risk on pension asset returns.[13] We assume, for simplicity, that: financial asset returns and growth rates are uncorrelated; the standard deviation of the rate of change in financial asset returns is constant over time; and the standard deviations of earnings growth (g_W), pensions growth (g_P), and later inflation (g_I) and dividend growth (g_E) are all constant over time and equal to each other (which implies that the four growth rates differ, if at all, by constant amounts). These are clearly very strong assumptions and are unlikely to hold exactly in the

---

[13] Equation (6.13) is derived as follows. Assume that in (6.5) the r_{Fj} are expected to be constant over time and the $_k p_0$ are fixed at p, and define $d \equiv p\alpha W_0/(1-\tau)$. For $t = 0$, A_0 in (6.5) can be written:

$$A_0 = X_0 = \sum_{k=1}^{T} \frac{d(1 + g_W)^k}{(1 + r_F)^k}$$

The elasticity of A_0 with respect to $(1 + r_F)$ is given by

$$\frac{\partial A_0}{\partial (1 + r_F)} \frac{(1 + r_F)}{A_0} = -\frac{1}{A_0} \sum_{k=1}^{T} \frac{kd(1 + g_W)^k}{(1 + r_F)^k} \equiv -D_{A_0}$$

The elasticity of A_0 with respect to $(1 + g_W)$ is given by

$$\frac{\partial A_0}{\partial (1 + g_W)} \frac{(1 + g_W)}{A_0} = \frac{1}{A_0} \sum_{k=1}^{T} \frac{kd(1 + g_W)^k}{(1 + r_F)^k} \equiv D_{A_0}$$

The total differential of A_0 can be written:

$$\frac{dA_0}{A_0} = \frac{\partial A_0}{\partial (1 + r_F)} \frac{(1 + r_F)}{A_0} \frac{dr_F}{(1 + r_F)} + \frac{\partial A_0}{\partial (1 + g_W)} \frac{(1 + g_W)}{A_0} \frac{dg_W}{(1 + g_W)} + \varepsilon_A$$

$$= -D_{A_0} \left[\frac{dr_F}{(1 + r_F)} - \frac{dg_W}{(1 + g_W)} \right] + \varepsilon_A$$

where we include a serially and contemporaneously uncorrelated specific risk component (ε_A) to the rate of return on pension assets. The volatility of the rate of return on pension assets is given by (assuming that r_F and g_W are uncorrelated)

$$\sigma_{A_0}^2 = D_{A_0}^2(\sigma_r^2 + \sigma_g^2) + \eta_A^2.$$

Note that σ_r^2 and σ_g^2 are the volatilities of the rates of change in interest rates and growth rates, rather than the volatilities of their levels, so that these will take relatively low values. Similar derivations apply for σ_{At}^2, $t > 0$, and for σ_{Lt}^2 and σ_{ALt} in (6.15) and (6.16) below.

real world. Nevertheless, they are useful assumptions to make if we wish to derive a tractable model.

In a similar way, the volatility of the rate of change in the value of the pension liabilities depends, from Equation (6.6) on their duration (see, for example, Langetieg *et al.*, 1986):

$$D_{Lt} = \sum_{k=1}^{\infty} \frac{k(T_{+k}p_0)P}{L_T} \left(\frac{1 + g_P}{1 + r_F}\right)^k + (T - t), \quad t = 1, T \quad (6.14)$$

As a first-order approximation, the variance of the liability returns is given by

$$\sigma_{Lt}^2 = D_{Lt}^2 \left(\sigma_r^2 + \sigma_g^2\right) + \eta_L^2, \quad t = 1, T \quad (6.15)$$

where the standard deviation of the growth rate in the pension is σ_g and η_L is the specific risk on liability returns. The covariance between asset and liability returns is given by:

$$\sigma_{ALt} = D_{At}D_{Lt} \left(\sigma_r^2 + \sigma_g^2\right) + \eta_{AL}, \quad t = 1, T \quad (6.16)$$

where η_{AL} is the covariance between the specific risks on asset and liability returns.

The value of the put options in Equations (6.3) and (6.4) is derived from put–call parity as (using Equations (6.7) and (6.8)):

$$\begin{aligned} P_t^P &= P_t^C + L_t - A_t = P_t^C - S_t \\ &= (1 - N(d_{2t})) L_t - (1 - N(d_{1t})) A_t, \quad t = 1, T. \quad (6.17) \end{aligned}$$

Two important features of Equations (6.8) and (6.17) are that the option values do not depend explicitly on the riskless rate of interest as in the standard Black–Scholes model, and that the appropriate definition of risk is not the risk, given by (6.13), attached to the *pension assets* (6.5), but the risk, given by (6.11), attached to the *pension surplus* (6.7). Both these features follow because the pension liabilities provide a natural hedge for the pension assets against both interest-rate and growth-rate risks.

The rationale for the first feature comes from the Black–Scholes innovation of constructing a riskless hedge portfolio. In order to do this, it is necessary to hedge against changes in both the value of the underlying assets and the exercise price. Changes in asset values are hedged by holding the assets. The cost of this hedge is equal to the rate of return on the assets. However, because the assets themselves are held in the portfolio, the return from the portfolio exactly offsets the cost of the hedge against changes in asset values. Therefore, the rate of return on assets does not appear in the option pricing formula. Because the hedge portfolio is riskless and generates the riskless rate of return, only the riskless rate of interest appears in the standard Black–Scholes formula. Changes in the exercise price are hedged by holding in the portfolio assets whose returns are perfectly correlated with changes in the exercise price, i.e. with changes in the value of the liabilities. This is achieved by holding, as part of the main portfolio, a portfolio of assets that exactly tracks any changes in the value of the liabilities. We will denote this portfolio the *liability-immunising portfolio*[14] (LIP) and we will assume that it is possible for us to construct such a portfolio. While the LIP will be a risky component of the total portfolio, it will be riskless relative to the liabilities that it is immunising, and so it, too, will generate the riskless rate of return. Therefore, the rate of return on the hedge portfolio is zero, since the return on the liability hedge exactly offsets the return on the asset hedge.

The rationale for the second feature comes from the fact that pension asset and liability values respond to shocks in a similar way. In Equations (6.5) and (6.6), we assume that the main sources of shocks are unexpected changes in yields and growth rates (in earnings or pensions, say). So, for example, an unexpected increase in yields reduces the present values of both assets and liabilities, while an unexpected increase in growth rates has the opposite effect. The volatilities of yields and growth rates are common to both assets and liabilities. The differential effects of these volatilities on the variances of asset and liability returns come from the differing durations of assets and liabilities (see (6.12) and (6.14)), as seen in Equations (6.13), (6.15) and (6.16). Substituting these into Equation (6.11), we get:

$$\sigma_{St}^2 = (D_{At} - D_{Lt})^2 \left(\sigma_r^2 + \sigma_g^2 \right) + \eta_A^2 + \eta_L^2 - 2\eta_{AL}, \quad t = 1, T. \quad (6.18)$$

This shows that the volatility of the surplus depends on the squared *duration gap* between assets and liabilities, the variances of the rate of change in yields and growth rates, and the relationship between the specific risks on assets and liabilities. If the financial asset portfolio is constructed to have returns that are perfectly correlated with changes in the value of the liabilities, then $\eta_A^2 = \eta_L^2 = \eta_{AL}$, and the terms involving η in (6.18) vanish; such a portfolio would be a LIP. If, in addition, the duration of the assets is kept equal to that of the liabilities, then surplus risk can be eliminated altogether. It is the convenient structure

---

[14] It is also known as the liability-matching portfolio.

of Equation (6.18) that justifies the simplifying assumptions that we have made above. A more complex version of (6.18) would be needed if these assumptions were not valid, but it is unlikely that surplus risk could be eliminated completely in this more general framework.

6.5 THE PENSION SCHEME PREFERENCES OF MEMBERS, SPONSORS AND FUND MANAGERS

We are now in a position to examine the preferences for the three types of pension scheme by members, sponsors and fund managers.

From the member's viewpoint, the schemes have different costs, different expected returns and different risks. Suppose that a typical member's reward–risk preferences can be represented by an isoelastic utility function with a constant relative risk-aversion parameter β (see, for example, Merton, 1969).[15] This suggests that the risk–reward indifference curves for the three types of scheme are given as follows:

$$U_{\text{DB}} = g_W - \frac{1}{2}\beta\sigma_g^2 \tag{6.19}$$

for the DB scheme,

$$U_{\text{DC}} = r_{Ft} - \frac{1}{2}\beta\left[D_{At}^2\left(\sigma_r^2 + \sigma_g^2\right) + \eta_A^2\right] \tag{6.20}$$

for the DC scheme, and

$$U_{\text{TMP}} = r_{Ft} - \left(P_t^{\text{P}}/L_t(T - t)\right) - \frac{1}{2}\beta$$
$$\times \left[(D_{At} - D_{Lt})^2\left(\sigma_r^2 + \sigma_g^2\right) + \eta_A^2 + \eta_L^2 - 2\eta_{AL}\right] \tag{6.21}$$

for the TMP scheme, using Equation (6.4).

The DB scheme offers the lowest expected return equal to the anticipated growth rate in the member's earnings, with risk measured by the volatility of those earnings. The DC scheme offers the highest expected return equal to the expected return on financial assets (which for the dynamic efficiency of the economy as a whole, must exceed g_W), but also has the highest risk. The TMP scheme has a lower expected return

---

[15] While the original Black–Scholes model and its offshoots such as the Fischer–Margrabe model being used here, were derived under the assumption that investors are risk-neutral, it is possible to show that a risk-neutral valuation of the option is still valid if, as we are assuming, the average scheme member exhibits constant relative risk aversion (see, for example Rubinstein, 1976; Breeden and Litzenberger, 1978; Brennan, 1979).

than the DC scheme because of the cost of buying the protective put option, but as a consequence has lower risk.

The ranking of preferences depends on the degree of risk aversion as follows:

$$-\infty < \beta \le \beta_{1t} \Rightarrow U_{DC} > U_{TMP} > U_{DB},$$
$$\beta_{1t} < \beta \le \beta_{2t} \Rightarrow U_{TMP} > U_{DC} > U_{DB},$$
$$\beta_{2t} < \beta \le \beta_{3t} \Rightarrow U_{TMP} > U_{DB} > U_{DC},$$
$$\beta_{3t} < \beta \le \infty \Rightarrow U_{DB} > U_{TMP} > U_{DC}, \qquad (6.22)$$

where:

$$\beta_{1t} = \frac{2P_t^P/L_t(T-t)}{\left(2D_{At}D_{Lt} - D_{Lt}^2\right)\left(\sigma_r^2 + \sigma_g^2\right) + 2\eta_{AL} - \eta_L^2} \qquad (6.23)$$

$$\beta_{2t} = \frac{2(r_{Ft} - g_W)}{D_{At}^2\left(\sigma_{At}^2 + \sigma_g^2\right) + \eta_A^2 - \sigma_g^2} \qquad (6.24)$$

$$\beta_{3t} = \frac{2\left(r_{Ft} - \left(P_t^P/L_t(T-t)\right) - g_W\right)}{(D_{At} - D_{Lt})^2\left(\sigma_r^2 + \sigma_g^2\right) + \left(\eta_A^2 + \eta_L^2 - 2\eta_{AL}\right) - \sigma_g^2} \qquad (6.25)$$
$$t = 1, T.$$

Both β_{2t} and β_{3t} will be positive and it is likely that β_{1t} is also positive, although if the duration of the assets is less than half that of the liabilities, β_{1t} will be negative. Individuals who are highly risk averse will prefer the DB scheme, those who are substantial risk takers will prefer the DC scheme, while those who are moderately risk averse and possibly even moderately risk taking will choose the TMP scheme. However, if the durations of assets and liabilities are continuously equalised, Equation (6.25) shows that the TMP scheme will always be preferred to the DB scheme. This is demonstrated in Figure 6.6.

Given these preferences by members for the different schemes, how are the risks shared between members, sponsors and fund managers? With a DC scheme, the position is straightforward: all the risk attached to the pension fund assets is borne directly by the member and none by the sponsor or fund manager, although in the long term the latter two will go out of business if they systematically deliver poor performance. With a DB scheme, the member bears no financial risk (so long as the sponsor remains solvent): he or she receives a pension that is based on

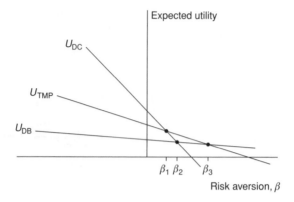

Figure 6.6   Members' preferences over different pension schemes

some pre-set formula, regardless of the value of the financial assets at retirement. All the downside risk is borne by the scheme sponsor, but the sponsor retains the upside potential if asset performance is better than expected.[16] The fortunes of the fund manager will be highly correlated with the extent to which deficits or surpluses are created. With a TMP scheme, all the downside risk is borne by the sponsor, while all the upside potential is retained by the member.

6.6   CONCLUSIONS

Defined benefit schemes are much more complicated than defined contribution schemes, since specific pension liabilities accrue. The benefits can be independent of salary or salary related in some way, the most common examples of the latter are pensions based on final salary or pensions based on average salary. We have shown that different pension schemes can be treated as different combinations of put and call options on the underlying assets in the scheme, with exercise prices related to the value of the liabilities. A defined benefit scheme is equivalent to a defined contribution scheme *plus* a put option (issued by the sponsor) *minus* a call option (issued by the member). This has important implications for the management of pension fund assets, as we shall see in the next chapter.

---

[16] However, members might demand a share of any resulting surplus.

QUESTIONS

1. What are the main types of DB scheme?
2. What is meant by the backloading of benefits? What type of schemes are most prone to this phenomenon?
3. Define pension scheme surplus and pension scheme deficit.
4. What is the purpose of a sponsor contribution holiday?
5. What is meant by a hybrid scheme?
6. What are the main types of hybrid scheme?
7. What is the projected unit method?
8. Explain how pension liabilities are calculated (i.e. explain the formula: Liabilities $= \phi(t) \times W(t) \times G(t, T) \times \Pi(t, T) \times \ddot{a}(T) \times D(t, T)$)
9. Explain the difference between the accrued benefits funding method and the prospective benefits funding method.
10. Explain the option composition of a DB scheme.
11. Explain the option composition of a TMP scheme.
12. What is an exchange option?
13. What is surplus risk?
14. What is a liability-immunising portfolio? What properties does it have?
15. What is the duration gap and how does it influence surplus risk?
16. What effect does risk aversion have on a scheme member's choice of pension scheme? What type of people are likely to prefer DB pensions?

REFERENCES

Bagehot, W. (1972) Risk and reward in corporate pension funds. *Financial Analysts Journal*, **28**, 80–84.

Black, F. and Scholes, M. (1973) The pricing of options and corporate liabilities. *Journal of Political Economy*, **81**, 637–664.

Blake, D. (1998) Pension schemes as options on pension fund assets: implications for pension fund management. *Insurance: Mathematics and Economics*, **23**, 263–286.

Bodie, Z. (1990) Pensions as retirement income insurance. *Journal of Economic Literature*, **28**, 28–49.

Boyle, P.P. (1978) Immunisation under stochastic models of the term structure. *Journal of the Institute of Actuaries*, **105**, 177–187.

Breeden, D. and Litzenberger, R. (1978) Prices of state contingent claims implicit in option prices. *Journal of Business*, **51**, 621–652.

Brennan, M. (1979) The pricing of contingent claims in discrete time models. *Journal of Finance*, **34**, 53–68.

Copeland, T.E. (1984) An economic approach to pension fund management. *Midland Corporate Finance Journal*, **2**, 26–39.

Disney, R. and Whitehouse, E. (1996) What are pension plan entitlements worth in Britain?, *Economica*, **63**, 213–238.

Fischer, S. (1978) Call option pricing when the exercise price is uncertain, and the valuation of index bonds. *Journal of Finance*, **33**, 169–176.

Gemmill, G. (1993) *Options Pricing: An International Perspective*, McGraw-Hill, London.

Haberman, S. and Sung, J.-H. (1994) Dynamic approaches to pension funding. *Insurance: Mathematics and Economics*, **15**, 151–162.

Institute and Faculty of Actuaries (1984) *Terminology of Pension Funding Methods*. Institute and Faculty of Actuaries, London.

Langetieg, T.C., Bader, L.N., Leibowitz, M.L. and Weinberger, A. (1986) *Measuring the Effective Duration of Pension Liabilities*, Salomon Brothers Inc., New York.

Leibowitz, M.L. (1986) *Liability Returns*, Salomon Brothers Inc., New York.

Macaulay, F.R. (1938) *Some Theoretical Problems Suggested by the Movement of Interest Rates, Bond Yields and Stock Prices in the US since 1856*, National Bureau of Economic Research, New York.

Margrabe, W. (1978) The value of an option to exchange one asset for another. *Journal of Finance*, **33**, 177–186.

Merton, R.C. (1969) Lifetime portfolio selection under uncertainty: the continuous time case. *Review of Economics and Statistics*, **51**, 247–257.

Rappaport, A., Young, M., Levell, C., and Blalock, B. (1997) Cash balance pension plans, in Gordon, M., Mitchell, O. and Twinney, M. (Eds) *Positioning Pensions for the Twenty-First Century*, University of Pennsylvania Press, Philadelphia.

Reitano, R.R. (1991) Multivariate duration analysis. *Transactions of the Society of Actuaries*, **43**, 335–376.

Rubinstein, M. (1976) The valuation of uncertain income streams and the pricing of options. *Bell Journal of Economics*, **7**, 407–425.

Sharpe, W.F. (1976) Corporate pension funding policy. *Journal of Financial Economics*, **3**, 183–193.

Tepper, I. (1981) Taxation and corporate pension policy. *Journal of Finance*, **36**, 1–13.

Treynor, J., Priest, W. and Regan, P. (1976) *The Financial Reality of Pension Funding under ERISA*, Dow Jones-Irwin, Homewood, Illinois.

7

Pension Fund Management

This chapter discusses the functions of pension fund managers. It examines the ways in which the fund managers of occupational defined benefit (DB) schemes assess and implement the trustees' portfolio preferences as expressed in the *statement of investment principles* (SIP).[1] It also examines how the assets in defined contribution (DC) schemes are managed (see also Chapter 4). It then discusses the three main types of fund management strategies: passive, active and asset–liability management. We begin by asking what is the purpose of a pension fund. We end with a discussion of the 2001 Myners Review of Institutional Investment in the UK.

7.1 THE ROLE OF A PENSION FUND

Pensions may be financed from a reserve or fund that has been built up over a period of years by investing accumulated contributions in earning assets. This is called *accumulation of funds* or *funded financing*. Alternatively, the pension costs of retired employees may be met solely from the current contributions of the employer and of existing employees or from other revenues on a year-to-year basis. This is known as *pay-as-you-go* (PAYG) *financing* or *assessmentism*. Most occupational pension schemes in the UK are now funded (at least partially), and most of those that are not funded are in the public sector. For example, central-government civil servants, teachers and hospital workers are in unfunded schemes which are financed directly by the Exchequer. Most of the remainder of the public sector (e.g. local authorities and public corporations) are in funded schemes. By definition, defined contribution schemes (e.g. personal and stakeholder pension schemes) are fully funded. This is because they are money-purchase schemes and the size of the pension depends solely on the size of the fund accumulated at the point of retirement.

---

[1] The preparation of a SIP is a legal requirement for UK pension funds under the 1995 Pensions Act.

The objective of a funded scheme is to build up a fund of investment assets from the contributions of both employer and employees, so that the income from, and the capital value of, those assets are available to finance the pension obligations of the employer when the employees retire. For a wholly funded scheme, the value of the fund must eventually be sufficient to pay for the total pension liability without additional financing from the employer (apart from normal employer contributions). When this stage is reached, the fund is said to be *mature*. Before this stage is reached, the fund is said to be *immature*. The required size of the fund, and also the maturity structure of the fund's assets, necessary to match the maturity structure of its liabilities, are determined actuarially. They will depend on such factors as: the sex-and-age composition of the membership of the scheme prior to and after retirement; the prospective longevity of scheme members after they retire; changes in the membership as a result of transfers, withdrawals, normal and premature retirement and death; the levels of contributions and retirement benefits; the rates of return on the assets; and the rate of inflation.

The trustees of a pension fund must consult an *actuary* on the valuation of the fund's assets and liabilities, although they do not actually need to appoint an actuary. If an actuary is not appointed directly, he or she will typically be employed as a consulting actuary by the firm of actuarial or investment consultants that has been appointed as the professional adviser to the trustees. The actuary has the following responsibilities. The actuary has to decide on the rate of interest (i.e. discount rate) and the rate of wage and price inflation that he will use in his actuarial calculations; the rate of interest will typically be related to the average return expected on the investments held in the fund. Using this interest rate, the actuary then determines the contribution rate from employees and the employer necessary to finance the projected pension benefits, bearing in mind any minimum or maximum contribution limits that might be operating. The actuary also has to advise on related benefits, such as widow/er's benefit and disability benefit. Finally, and most importantly, the actuary has to conduct regular *actuarial valuations* (usually on a 3-yearly basis) to ensure that the scheme is being adequately funded and that it is not producing either an *actuarial deficit* or an *actuarial surplus*. If the fund is showing a deficit, the actuary will recommend higher contribution rates for employers and/or employees. If, on the other hand, the fund is showing a surplus, the actuary will recommend ways in which the surplus can be reduced.

In principle, for the scheme to be self-contained and self-financing, it is necessary for the members of the scheme not to begin to receive pensions until the value of assets underlying their accumulated contributions at least equals the expected present value of their future pensions. This means that an employee who joined the scheme half-way through his working life (bringing no transfer value from any previous scheme with him) would have to pay a higher rate of contributions than an employee in the scheme for all his working life if he is to receive the same pension when he retires. In practice, however, most schemes are ongoing schemes, with both contributions into and pensions received from the funds from the beginning. If new contributions and investment income exceed the current value of pensions being paid, then there will be a net increase in the revenues available for investment, the fund will grow and a surplus will develop. If, on the other hand, the reverse holds and a deficit develops, the employer will be forced to make *deficiency payments* in order to keep the fund solvent, since the employer finances the pension scheme on a *balance-of-costs* basis.

Under a PAYG scheme, no substantial fund is built up to meet contingent liabilities. Rather, current contributions are used to finance current pensions directly. Thus, the current workforce finances the pensions of the preceding workforce and relies on the succeeding workforce in turn to pay for its pensions.

The two types of scheme have different costs and benefits. The main advantage of a PAYG scheme is that the initial set-up costs are low, since the high cost of setting up the initial fund of investment assets does not have to be met. Further, the running costs of a new PAYG scheme are lower than those for a new funded scheme. In particular, it is less costly to give past-service rights, or to grant pensions based on final salaries, or to increase pensions after retirement when the rate of inflation is high. Also, the administrative cost is lower and the structure of pension finance is simpler with a PAYG scheme.

Eventually, however, as the schemes mature, the advantages of the funded scheme dominate. Tangible assets are created against the real pension liability and these assets provide an investment income which supplements the contributions made by employees and employers, and this ultimately outweighs the lower administrative costs of the PAYG scheme. When a funded scheme is first introduced, all current pensions are financed from current contributions and any surplus of contributions is devoted to purchasing earning assets for the fund. As the fund grows, the share of pensions financed from the income of the fund also grows.

The fund will continue to grow so long as contributions plus investment income exceed the value of current pensions, since the balance accumulates in the fund.

In addition, even if the employing firm becomes insolvent, the pension fund assets are legally fully protected, whereas if a firm operating a PAYG scheme becomes insolvent, the scheme merely has an unsecured claim on the assets of the firm and comes behind the secured creditors. However, if a funded pension scheme is underfunded, the amount of underfunding (measured as the difference between the actuarial value of the liabilities and the value of the assets) also constitutes an unsecured claim on the assets of the sponsoring company.[2] The legal protection of pension fund assets is likely to give a greater sense of security to employees in a funded scheme compared with those in a PAYG scheme who, while nevertheless paying contributions, have no explicit entitlement to receive pensions and must rely on future generations to finance their retirement. Funding thereby relieves (or at least reduces) the burden on future generations.

This is particularly important in the case of a declining industry, where the ratio of pensioners to employees (the *dependency ratio*) increases sharply, causing severe problems for a PAYG scheme. In this respect, funding can be a more stable method of financing pensions than assessmentism. This is because the size of the fund depends on the previous history of employment in the firm and of contributions made into the fund. So, a firm or industry (e.g. coal mining) that is declining may still have a relatively large fund to finance its large number of pensioners, and it can therefore use this fund as a buffer to protect the smaller number of current employees from being asked to make an unacceptable increase in their rate of contributions; such pension funds are said to be *overmature*. Nevertheless, some pension funds in declining firms or industries can still face very serious problems.

There are various types of pension fund operating in the UK. There are *provident funds* and *pooled funds*. With a provident fund, a separate account is kept for each employee, in which all contributions made by and for him are accumulated and interest added. When the employee retires, he can have the accumulated value of his account converted into an annuity by actuarial calculations based on his life expectancy. Provident funds are therefore rather like group personal pension schemes.[3]

---

[2] The order of priority of pension-scheme members is: first existing pensioners, then early leavers with deferred benefits, followed by current employees.

[3] Provident funds are common in the Far East; for example, Singapore has a Central Provident Fund for the whole population.

But most contributory schemes are based on pooled funds, in which all contributions are pooled and invested as a single sum. Some individuals will, therefore, receive more than is directly proportionate to their contributions, while others will correspondingly receive less. However, the greater diversification of asset holdings that is possible with pooled funds means that for the same contributions it is likely that they will yield higher average pensions than those from provident funds. The distinction between provident funds and pooled funds is clearly more important for defined contribution schemes, such as personal or stakeholder pension schemes, than for defined benefit schemes, such as final-salary occupational schemes, where the pension does not depend on the investment performance of the fund.

There are *internally funded schemes* and *externally funded schemes*. An internally funded scheme is one in which the fund invests in its own parent company's assets (i.e. *self-investment*). This is accomplished by the firm making an appropriate internal balance-sheet allowance for financing future pensions (a procedure known as *booking* or creating *book reserves*). This procedure is widely used in, for example, Germany, and is permissible in the UK, although the 1990 Social Security Act placed a 5% upper limit on the proportion of internal funding. Some of the disadvantages that apply to PAYG are also valid for internal funding: in particular, if the firm becomes insolvent, then the employee's pension is at risk as well as his job. Also, where there is self-investment in the sponsoring company, there may be a conflict of interest between the best interests of the firm and those of the future pensioners, in the sense that such internal funds may not be allocated as efficiently as funds acquired from sources external to the firm. On the other hand, some degree of self-investment may well be beneficial. Employees have a tangible stake in the firm and in its future success, and this may help discourage disruptive or inefficient practices by the workforce. In addition, self-investment is a fairly cheap way of providing funds for investment in the company, and the cost is likely to be much lower than direct access to the capital markets, where there is less reliable information available concerning the particular enterprise than there is internally.

However, most private-sector occupational schemes in the UK are externally funded. This means that a *trust fund* is established and *trustees*, who are independent of the employer, are appointed to supervise the assets of the fund solely in the interests of current and contingent pensioners. In the UK, the trustees' powers are derived from the Trustee Act of 1925, although they may be modified by the particular *trust deed* or instrument establishing the pension fund trust. In most cases, the investment powers of the trustees are mentioned in the deed. Otherwise, these powers are specified in the Trustee Investments Act 1961, the Pensions Act 1995 and the Trustee Act 2000.

The Trustee Investments Act 1961 limited both the type of investment and the proportion of the fund held in different assets, and, in particular, placed strict limits on the amount of self-investment; the limits on self-investment were reinforced by the 1990 Social Security Act.

The Pensions Act 1995 (Section 34(1)) gives wide statutory powers of investment to pension fund trustees who did not have specific powers of investment under their existing trust deeds. The powers of a trustee are defined by the trust deeds or by legislation. Most modern trust deeds expressly confer wide investment powers. However, older trust deeds frequently did not. In the absence of express powers under the trust deeds, trustees have to look to legislation to define their powers. Prior to the 1995 act, trustees were restricted to the powers contained in the Trustee Investments Act 1961. These powers, although generous when originally enacted, eventually became considered to be too narrow. The 1961 act, for example, divides the investments that trustees may make into narrower and wider range investments. Typically, *narrower range investments* are fixed-interest securities and *wider range investments* are shares. Under the 1995 act, trustees are no longer restricted to specified *authorised investments* and can invest in the same range of investments as an absolute owner.

The Trustee Act 2000 radically overhauled trust law in the UK. Existing trust law had failed to keep pace with changes in the conduct of investment business since the 1961 act to such an extent that it was felt that trustees acting under the terms of trust instruments that made no specific provisions as to investment powers would find it impossible to satisfy their primary duty of acting in the best interests of the beneficiaries of the trust. The most relevant part of the act for pension fund trustees is Part I.[4] Part I creates a new, precisely defined statutory duty of care applicable to trustees when carrying out their functions. A *duty of care* signifies a duty to take care to avoid causing injury or loss. The new duty is designed to bring certainty and consistency to the standard of competence and behaviour expected of trustees. It will be a safeguard for beneficiaries and thereby balance the wider powers given to trustees in the act. The duty will be in addition to the existing fundamental duties

---

[4] The following passages draw heavily on the *Explanatory Notes to Trustee Act 2000* prepared by the Lord Chancellor's Department.

of trustees (e.g. to act in the best interests of the beneficiaries and to comply with the terms of the trust). The duty is a default provision and may be excluded or modified by the terms of the trust. This new duty will apply to the manner of the exercise by trustees of a discretionary power. It will not apply to a decision by the trustees as to whether to exercise that discretionary power in the first place.

In relation to the investment of trust funds, the new duty makes statutorily explicit the present common law duty which measures the behaviour of the trustees against that expected of the ordinary prudent man of business. This test includes a subjective element to allow for the particular skills and experience of the trustee in question. Thus, in relation to the purchase of stocks and shares, a higher standard may be expected of a trustee who is an investment banker, specialising in equities, than of a trustee who is a beekeeper, particularly if the investment banker is acting as a trustee in the course of his or her investment banking business. The new duty will apply to any exercise by a trustee of a power to invest trust property or to acquire land, to appoint agents, nominees and custodians, or to insure trust property. Trustees now have the widest possible investment powers, but at the same time have a duty to ensure that they act prudently in safeguarding the capital of the trust.

The trustees also have a legal obligation to keep accounts and have them audited periodically. In addition, they are required to have 3-yearly actuarial reports prepared.

There are pension schemes that are *insured* (all of them in the private sector) and others that are non-insured or, more strictly, *self-insured* (sometimes known as *self-administered*). Most small schemes are arranged through a life-assurance company, which undertakes the investments of the fund. Typically, the life company invests the pension contributions in its own with-profit or managed fund. Most large schemes are self-administered or self-insured, which means that they undertake their own investing – that is, employ their own investment managers who deal with stockbrokers, investment banks or other specialist pension consultants. These schemes are usually either self-trusteed or bank-trusteed. Some small schemes are self-administered, especially those established for partnerships or directors of companies.

7.2 THE FUNCTIONS OF A PENSION FUND MANAGER

A *pension fund manager* is an individual who, or company which, manages the assets in a pension fund on behalf of the trustees of a pension scheme. The fund manager can be employed directly by the pension scheme or can be an independent organisation under contract to the scheme.

The functions of the fund manager are:

- portfolio structuring and analysis – using the trustees' objectives and constraints (in particular, the constraints imposed by the pension fund's liabilities) to structure an optimal portfolio, and then analysing the portfolio's expected return and risk;
- portfolio adjustment – selecting the set of asset purchases and sales as circumstances change;
- portfolio-performance measurement and attribution – ensuring the actual performance of the portfolio, identifying the sources of the performance and comparing the performance against that of a predetermined benchmark portfolio. This function is usually undertaken by an organisation independent of the manager running the pension fund and is discussed in Chapter 8;
- risk management – using hedging instruments (in particular, futures, options and swap contracts) to hedge the interest-rate stock-market and currency risks involved in both domestic and international investment, so as to manage the investment-risk budget set by the trustees; this is discussed in Chapter 9.

7.3   FUND MANAGEMENT STYLES

There are a number of different investment management styles that a fund manager can follow. Which one is appropriate depends on the size of the fund and the preferences of the trustees, and also the size and preferences of the fund management group itself.

As mentioned above, small pension funds may decide to have their portfolios managed by insurance companies (these are called *insurance-managed portfolios*). Sometimes the funds are *pooled*. This increases the degree of *diversification*, but there is no individual attention given to any particular portfolio: every member of the pool has the same set of investments and gets the same return. Pooled funds typically operate through two types of legal entity: *exempt unit trusts*, which are established under a trust deed, and *managed pension funds*, which are a particular type of insurance contract. Each entity is designed to share the same exemptions from income and capital gains tax as fully approved pension funds.[5] The same advantages that apply to pooling in general also apply to this particular type of investment pooling, namely, that trading can take place more economically at lower unit cost because of the larger volumes traded and, in principle, the portfolio can be diversified more effectively since a wider spectrum of assets can be held in the pool than could be held by a small pension fund operating alone. Alternatively, the funds are *segregated* and different funds will have different investments. Large pension funds will either have their investments managed directly through an appointed fund manager or indirectly through a single or group of external financial intermediaries, such as an investment bank.

The most common management style is known as *balanced management*. With this style, the fund manager is responsible for deciding on both the general asset categories that are invested in (such as shares, bonds or money-market securities) and the individual securities within each asset category that are invested in (e.g. BP shares or medium-term gilts). The first decision is known as the *strategic asset allocation* (SAA) decision and the second is known as the *security selection* decision. The balanced-management approach can apply whether the pension fund is small and part of an insurance-managed pool or whether it is large and employs its own fund management group.

The problem with balanced managers is that they cannot be experts in all markets, especially on a global basis. One solution is to have *specialist managers* in each sector who take the security selection decisions. Sitting above the specialists will be an *asset-allocation manager* and possibly an *overlay manager*, whose role is to make temporary changes to asset allocation using futures and options contracts. Another solution is to have *split funding*. This means that a number of balanced managers are appointed. While this does not solve the problem of insufficient expertise in all markets, it forces managers to compete against each other. However, the danger of this is that they may be induced to over-trade the portfolio (this is known as *churning*), so that transaction costs might be excessive. In addition, a *risk manager* has to sit above the individual managers to ensure overall risk control.

There are three main types of portfolio-management strategies: passive, active and asset–liability management.

---

[5] UK pension funds are exempt from taxation on the income and capital gains on their investments with the exception of the tax paid on UK dividends, which, since 1997, has been unrecoverable.

Passive portfolio management involves a *buy-and-hold strategy*; that is, buying a portfolio of securities and holding them for a long period of time, with only minor and infrequent adjustment to the portfolio over time. Passive portfolio management is consistent with two conditions being satisfied in the securities market: *efficiency* and *homogeneity of expectations*. If securities markets are efficient, then securities will be fairly priced at all times. There will be no misvalued securities and hence no incentive to trade actively in securities. Similarly, if securities markets are characterised by investors who have homogeneous (i.e. identical) expectations of the risks and returns on securities, then again there is no incentive to trade actively in securities.

Active portfolio management involves frequent and sometimes substantial adjustments to the portfolio. Active managers do not believe that securities markets are continuously efficient. Instead, they believe that securities can be misvalued, so that trading in them can lead to excess returns (even after adjusting for risk and transaction costs). Alternatively, active managers believe that there are *heterogeneous* (i.e. divergent) *expectations* of risks and returns on securities and that they have better estimates than the rest of the market of the true risks and returns on securities. Again, they attempt to use their better estimates to generate excess returns. In short, the objective of active managers is to 'beat the market'.

Asset–liability management (ALM) is a quantitative technique used by increasing numbers of DB pension funds to structure their asset portfolios by paying due regard to the structure of their liabilities. It is a relatively new modelling technique, beginning in earnest in the late 1980s.

These three strategies are discussed in detail below.

7.4 DIFFERENT FUND MANAGEMENT STRATEGIES FOR DEFINED BENEFIT AND DEFINED CONTRIBUTION SCHEMES

We can expect to see the fund managers of DC schemes pursuing rather different investment strategies from those of the fund managers of DB (e.g. final salary) schemes.

Managers of DB schemes are *net investors*. They have contingent liabilities, in the sense that they have pension liabilities related to final salary. They must, therefore, construct and manage an asset portfolio that has the greatest chance of meeting these liabilities (this is the objective of ALM). They are partially insulated from this commitment as a consequence of the employer's obligation to make deficiency payments in the event that the assets are insufficient to meet liabilities. However, the protection is only partial, since the employer is likely to change the fund manager if he or she underperforms to this extent.

Managers of DC schemes, in contrast, face no such constraints. They are, in effect, *gross investors*. They do not have specific contingent liabilities to take into account. Their objective is to generate the highest return they can on the contributions they receive, consistent with the degree of risk tolerance indicated by the trustees or plan members. The pension depends entirely on the sum of money accumulated at the time of retirement. The fund never shows a deficit and never shows a surplus (unless the projected pension breaches the government's rules on the maximum payout). If the fund manager has made poor investment decisions, the size of the fund will be low and the resulting pension will be small. But by the time this is known, it is too late to do anything about it.

This does not, of course, mean that fund managers will necessarily prefer to manage DC schemes over DB schemes. If their performance figures are published and are consistently poor, they will lose business and ultimately go out of business. But the point remains that DC scheme managers face fewer constraints and are likely to be monitored less intensively and possibly less critically (because their clients are geographically dispersed and collectively unorganised) than managers of occupational schemes.

The Mercer 2000 survey of defined contribution (DC) pension schemes showed that lifestyle was the most common fund management style and also the most common default option, covering 55% of funds. *Lifestyle funds* reduce the level of investment risk in the fund as the retirement date approaches by systematically switching from equities into bonds (see Chapter 4). The most common switchover period is five years prior to the member's normal retirement date (60% of schemes), followed by ten years (25% of schemes). Around 35% of funds offered no investment choice, and where an investment choice was offered, the average number of funds offered was five. Around 25% of funds are passively managed. Global equity funds are also used by 43% of schemes.

It is often questioned whether pension funds should invest abroad when their liabilities are denominated in sterling. Yet there are a number of reasons that can be put forward to support the case for international investment.

The first and most important reason deals with the benefits of diversification. Pension fund managers, in spite of the nature of their liabilities, will generally be interested in achieving a high level of return for a given level of risk. Risks can be reduced by diversification of the port-folio across a range of assets. Diversification within one country can eliminate the *unsystematic risk* that results from the differential perfor-mance of individual firms and sectors. But diversification within one country cannot reduce the *systematic risk* that results from the common effect that the performance of the economy as a whole has on all firms in that economy. However, to the extent that the performances of different national economies are not perfectly correlated, each country's system-atic risk becomes a diversifiable risk in a global context. Such risk can be reduced by holding a global-market portfolio.

Not only can international investment reduce risk, it can also enhance returns in a number of ways. For example, some countries (such as China and the US) might be more successful economically than the home econ-omy of the fund and hence offer higher investment returns. Similarly, if the share of profits in national income changes differentially across countries, then international investment provides a hedge against any fall in the domestic profit share and therefore in equity values. Further-more, there are certain high-value economic activities (e.g. gold and oil extraction) which might not be undertaken in the home economy.

These examples apply mainly to equity investments, rather than to investments in the other main asset categories – bonds and property. Bond markets tend to be much more globally integrated than equity markets, so the benefits from international diversification are reduced, although not entirely eliminated. Property investment, on the other hand, might actually be more risky abroad than it is domestically. This is because it is less liquid and more dependent on local knowledge than either equity or bonds.

While there are undoubted benefits with international investment, there are also additional risks. The most important of these is *currency* (or *exchange-rate) risk*, the risk that the domestic currency might ap-preciate relative to the currency in which the overseas investment is held and so reduce the return on that investment when measured in the domestic currency. (This risk can be hedged with forward, futures or options contracts.) There are other types of risk. *Settlement risk* is the risk that either payment or securities may not be delivered following a transaction; this risk could be high in less-developed financial markets. *Liquidity risk* is the risk that an investor might find himself locked into a particular foreign investment because of the narrowness of the market for that investment, which makes it difficult to liquidate the investment. *Transfer risk* (sometimes called *political risk*) is the risk of being locked into a particular overseas market as a result of an unanticipated imposition of exchange controls. The last three risks can be avoided altogether by disregarding certain markets (such as those in the Third World or even middle-income countries such as Turkey or Korea), while currency risk is unlikely to outweigh the benefits from international diversification.

Davies (1991) reports the responses to a questionnaire on attitudes to international investment by a group of London fund managers. Most of them emphasised the benefits of risk reduction from international investment rather than the prospects of higher returns. Most fund managers felt that the global markets had become much more efficient during the 1980s, partly as a result of their own activities helping to equalise returns across national economies. Nevertheless, the fund managers recognised that anomalies existed and often persisted, especially in the *emerging markets* of the Far East and Latin America, but also in an advanced economy such as Japan.

Although most fund managers believed that the global markets were efficient, they did not take this to its logical conclusion and invest their assets in a *global portfolio*. A number of candidates have been put forward as global portfolios. One candidate uses portfolio weightings based on relative market capitalisations; this would lead to an allocation in UK assets well below 10%. Another uses portfolio weightings based on the share of imports in the consumption basket purchased by pensioners; given that UK pensioners consume a relatively high proportion of UK goods, this implies a much larger weighting in UK assets.

So, if UK fund managers do not invest in a global portfolio, what determines their international asset allocation? In the case of pension funds, the nature of the liabilities remains the most important factor. Pension fund managers are aware of the risks of asset–liability mismatch, since the size of the 'final salary' depends on UK growth and inflation. This led many pension fund managers to invest heavily in UK equities. However, not all pension fund managers felt this way. Some held the view that the efficiency of markets and the convergence of different national economies were now so great that so long as a pension fund held 'real assets,' some currency mismatching was acceptable. Further, overseas equity holdings have increased (relative to domestic equity holdings) since 1997, as a consequence of the change in the taxation relief rules for domestic equities in that year.

Other influences on international asset allocation were the behaviour of other fund managers and the pressure from trustees not to underperform the median fund. This tended to encourage a *herding* approach to portfolio structuring, as opposed to a *contrarian* approach. However, some fund managers pointed out that through an 'education process,' trustees could be led by successive steps to accept the level of international exposure desired all along by the fund managers.

7.5   THE FUND MANAGER'S RELATIONSHIP WITH THE TRUSTEES

7.5.1   Determining the trustees' objectives and constraints

One of the first tasks of the DB pension fund manager (once he or she has been awarded the *mandate* from the pension fund trustees) is to determine the trustees' objectives and constraints. It is important to do this for at least three reasons. First, it is a prerequisite for the initial structuring of the portfolio. Second, it will influence the kinds of portfolio adjustments that can be made. Third, because it affects the initial portfolio structure, it will also influence the portfolio's subsequent performance.

The trustees' objectives and constraints can usually be expressed as follows. While these objectives and constraints apply mainly to DB schemes, they are also relevant for DC schemes, although personal pension scheme members do not typically express their objectives and constraints in this form. An example of a questionnaire designed to identify the objectives and constraints of trustees is given in Appendix 7A at the end of this chapter.

- *Risk–reward profile* – the risk–reward profile of the fund (or the required rate of return on the fund's assets consistent with an acceptable degree of variability in asset values) can only be determined once the liabilities of the fund have been specified. The fund's actuary determines the value of the long-term pension liabilities and the acceptable level of risk, sometimes expressed in terms of a minimum acceptable value to the fund or minimum return on fund assets. The fund manager must then determine a level of portfolio risk consistent with the degree of risk tolerance specified by the trustees. This is part of the process of investment-risk budgeting (discussed in Section 7.5.3). The principal aim of a pension fund has been stated to be 'to achieve the maximum investment return which is consistent with the security of the fund'

(Wolanski, 1980, p. 18). A similar aim holds for DC schemes, although with such schemes there are no formal liabilities.

- *Time horizon* – while the time horizon for pension funds themselves is extremely long (in excess of 30 years for immature funds), the time horizon relevant for trustees, and therefore for pension fund management groups, is much shorter: usually between five and seven years. This is because this is the typical duration of an investment mandate.
- *Mandate restrictions* – the mandate also specifies other aspects of the trustees' preferences. Further, there is often a requirement for trustees to produce a statement on socially responsible investment (SRI) and this may result in certain mandate restrictions being made. For example, it can state the countries or companies whose securities cannot be invested in, such as the shares of defence, tobacco, alcoholic beverage, animal testing, or, indeed, rival companies. It can also state the class or quality of securities that cannot be invested in, for example, options, warrants, preference stock or unsecured debt.
- *Pension-scheme resources* – the fund manager also has to take into account the resources made available by the trustees, both in terms of the initial value of the fund and in terms of the flow of contribution payments (net of pension payments) that are expected to be received. The size of the fund limits the type of investments that may be suitable. For example, a small fund is unlikely to invest directly in commercial property, while the trustees of a large fund are less likely to want large holdings in unit trusts. In addition, the time made available by the trustees to liaise with and monitor the fund manager is important. This is called the *governance budget*.

All the above factors will affect the initial portfolio, adjustments to the portfolio and subsequent performance. It is important for both the trustees and the fund manager to be aware of this from the outset. It is important to isolate the performance of the fund manager from, say, the restrictions placed on him or her by the trustees.

7.5.2 Determining the trustees' benchmark portfolio

The first key task of the fund manager is to determine the trustees' benchmark portfolio (i.e. their optimal strategic asset allocation), against which the fund manager's performance will be assessed.

The first case to consider is that of the trustees of an *immature* pension fund (so that employee and employer contributions and investment income are more than sufficient to meet pension payouts). The trustees are likely to have a fairly high degree of risk tolerance. The benchmark portfolio will depend on the following three factors:

- the expected (or mean) return on a portfolio ($\bar{r}_P$);
- the variance of return on a portfolio (σ_P^2), which is the most common measure of risk in *modern portfolio theory* (MPT);
- the trustees' attitude to risk, which, in MPT, is expressed in terms of either a *degree of risk tolerance* (R_T) or a *degree of risk aversion* (= 1/degree of risk tolerance).

These three factors are the components of the *expected utility* of a portfolio:

$$\bar{U} = \bar{r}_P - \frac{1}{R_T}\sigma_P^2 \qquad (7.1)$$

or

$$\text{Expected utility} = \text{Expected return} - \text{Risk penalty}. \qquad (7.2)$$

The expected utility of a portfolio is equivalent to the *risk-adjusted expected return* on the portfolio. It is derived by subtracting a *risk penalty* from the *expected return*, where the risk penalty depends on the portfolio risk and the trustees' risk tolerance. The higher the degree of risk tolerance (the lower the degree of risk aversion), the greater the degree of risk (and expected return) that can be sustained in the pension fund. For example, if $\bar{r}_P = 0.17(17\%)$, $\sigma_P = 0.30(30\%)$, and $R_T = 3$, then:

$$\bar{U} = 0.17 - \frac{1}{3}(0.30)^2 = 0.14 \ (14\%).$$

Note that $R_T = 3$ implies that $1/R_T = 1/3$; in other words, the trustees have to be compensated with one-third of a point increase in expected return for taking on a one-point increase in variance in order for them to remain indifferent and have the same expected utility.

Suppose the trustees wish to choose a benchmark portfolio containing shares and bonds. In this case, the fund manager's objective is to select the portfolio that maximises:

$$\bar{U} = \bar{r}_P - \frac{1}{R_T} \times \sigma_P^2,$$

subject to:

$$\bar{r}_P = \theta_S\bar{r}_S + \theta_B\bar{r}_B,$$
$$\sigma_P^2 = \theta_S^2\sigma_S^2 + 2\theta_S\theta_B\sigma_{SB} + \theta_B^2\sigma_B^2,$$
$$\theta_S + \theta_B = 1,$$

where

$\bar{r}_S, \bar{r}_B$ = expected returns on shares and bonds;
σ_S^2, σ_B^2 = variance of returns on shares and bonds;
σ_{SB} = covariance between returns on shares and bonds;
θ_S, θ_B = proportion of portfolio in shares and bonds.

Substituting the constraints into the objective function gives:

$$\max_{\theta_S} \ \bar{U} = \theta_S \bar{r}_S + (1 - \theta_S)\bar{r}_B$$

$$- \frac{1}{R_T} \left[\theta_S^2 \sigma_S^2 + 2\theta_S(1 - \theta_S)\sigma_{SB} + (1 - \theta_S)^2 \sigma_B^2 \right]. \quad (7.3)$$

Differentiating with respect to θ_S, setting the result equal to zero and solving for θ_S, we get:

$$\theta_S^* = \frac{\sigma_B^2 - \sigma_{SB}}{(\sigma_S^2 - 2\sigma_{SB} + \sigma_B^2)} + \frac{(\bar{r}_S - \bar{r}_B)}{2(\sigma_S^2 - 2\sigma_{SB} + \sigma_B^2)} \times R_T \quad (7.4)$$

as the optimal proportion of the portfolio to be invested in shares. This increases linearly with the degree of risk tolerance, R_T, and with the spread between the expected returns on shares and bonds.

A standard procedure for inferring the trustees' degree of risk tolerance is to use Equation (7.4) in reverse. Trustees are asked to select their preferred combination of shares and bonds. To help the trustees, they could be given the *portfolio opportunity set* derived from holding different combinations of shares and bonds. This is shown in Figure 7.1 as the curved line *BPS*. At *B*, the portfolio is invested 100% in bonds (the least risky portfolio), while at *S* the portfolio is invested 100% in shares (the most risky portfolio). Suppose the trustees pick a particular mix, say 60% shares to 40% bonds. This portfolio is represented by point *P* in Figure 7.1. The fund manager now has some idea of both the benchmark portfolio of shares and bonds and of the trustees' degree of risk tolerance. This is because *P* must be a tangency point between the portfolio opportunity set and the trustees' *indifference curve* in *mean–variance space* (i.e. the trade-off between return and risk that leaves the trustees with the same level of expected utility or welfare). The indifference curve can be represented by the equation:

$$\bar{r}_P = \bar{U} + \frac{1}{R_T}\sigma_P^2, \quad (7.5)$$

where $\bar{U}$ = intercept (measures *expected utility* level from portfolio *P* in units of expected return).

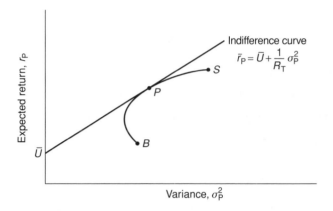

Figure 7.1 Inferring the trustees' risk tolerance

If the degree of risk tolerance is assumed to be constant, then the indifference curve is linear, as shown in (7.5). If we know P, we can calculate the slope of the line tangent at P and, given this, derive the trustees' degree of risk tolerance:

$$R_T = \frac{1}{\text{Slope of line tangent at } P} \qquad (7.6)$$

The higher the degree of risk tolerance, the flatter the indifference curve and the closer portfolio P will be to S. In other words, the higher the degree of risk tolerance, the greater the amount of risk (and hence equities) that can be sustained in the portfolio.

Consider now the case of a *mature* pension fund (so that contributions and investment income are just sufficient to meet pension payouts). In this case, the trustees will be concerned about minimising the mismatch between assets and liabilities. In other words, the trustees will be concerned that the value of the assets (or equivalently the return on the assets) in the portfolio should never be less than the value of the liabilities (or equivalently the payout on the pension liabilities). This type of behaviour is an example of *asset–liability management* (ALM) and is sometimes called *safety-first* portfolio behaviour.[6]

---

[6] The trustees of some mature pension funds (in particular, those with very high degrees of risk tolerance) might still be more interested in expected utility maximisation than in safety-first investment behaviour. This is because any additional investment returns can be used to reduce the employer's contributions into the scheme and at the limit lead to a complete contributions holiday

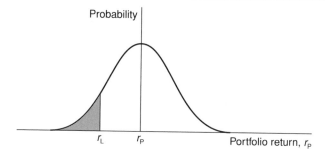

Figure 7.2 The safety-first investment criterion

Of course, in a world with risk it is not possible to guarantee that the return on the assets will never be less than the payout on the liabilities. Instead, the fund manager will attempt to minimise the *probability* that the return on the assets will be less than the payout on the liabilities, that is:

$$\text{min probability } (r_P < r_L) \qquad (7.7)$$

where r_P = rate of return on portfolio of assets; r_L = rate of payout on pension liabilities.

If the portfolio return is generated by the *normal* (or Gaussian) *distribution*, then the optimum portfolio would be the one for which the expected return on the portfolio, $\bar{r}_P$, is the maximum number of standard deviations away from r_L. This is demonstrated in Figure 7.2. The shaded area is the probability of the return on the portfolio being less than r_L. This area is minimised when the number of *standard deviations* between $\bar{r}_P$ and r_L is maximised. Since the number of standard deviations between $\bar{r}_P$ and r_L is given by $(\bar{r}_P - r_L)/\sigma_P$, (7.7) is equivalent to:

$$\max \ k = \frac{\bar{r}_P - r_L}{\sigma_P}. \qquad (7.8)$$

To illustrate, suppose that $r_L = 0.1(10\%)$ and we have the following two portfolios:

---

for the employer. In other words, the pension fund can be used as an investment vehicle for the employer as well as for the provision of pensions for the employees.

	Portfolio A	Portfolio B
$\bar{r}_P$	0.17	0.20
σ_P	0.30	0.35

For portfolio A, we have:

$$\frac{\bar{r}_P - r_L}{\sigma_P} = 0.23$$

while for portfolio B, we have:

$$\frac{r_P - r_L}{\sigma_P} = 0.29$$

therefore, portfolio B is preferred.

All portfolios having the same value k in (7.8) will be equally preferred under the safety-first criterion, and this fact allows us to construct indifference curves in mean–standard-deviation space, under the safety-first criterion. Rearranging the expression in (7.8), we get:

$$\bar{r}_P = r_L + k\sigma_P. \tag{7.9}$$

Figure 7.3 shows how the optimal portfolio is selected. The optimal portfolio P is the tangency portfolio between the indifference curve and the portfolio opportunity set APB.

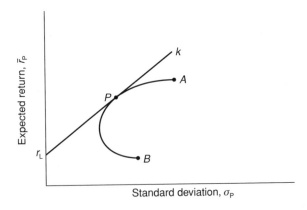

Figure 7.3 The optimal safety-first portfolio

7.5.3   Investment risk budgeting

Risk budgeting allocates resources on a risk basis, rather than on a returns basis. *Investment risk budgeting* involves (e.g. see Boardman, 2001 and Stanyer, 1999):

- determining the liability profile;
- modelling long-term investment returns;
- agreeing with the trustees the benchmark portfolio and the total permissible level of investment risk;
- identifying the investment management activities where the investment risk can be 'spent', such as stock selection and market timing;
- taking corrective action when investment risk has been 'overspent'; and
- evaluating the success of the risk budget process by calculating and analysing the risk-adjusted returns.

The investment risk budget will be higher for pension funds that have more solvent sponsors and lower for pension funds with large deficits and financially weak sponsors. Although the risk budget will be spent by the trustees, it is important that trustees agree the size of the risk budget with the sponsor. If the risk budget is spent successfully, the sponsor will gain through lower contributions. But if the risk budget is spent unwisely, the sponsor will be required to make additional contributions. The trustees should secure the willingness of the sponsor to do this.

Having agreed a benchmark portfolio in the light of the pension scheme's liabilities and the trustees' attitude to risk, the total permissible level of investment risk then has to be agreed. The total risk of the fund is composed of benchmark risk and active risk (or tracking error). *Benchmark risk* is the risk that the benchmark asset allocation fails to match the liabilities. This is because the benchmark asset allocation might be overweight equities compared with the asset–liability matching allocation, or for reasons of diversification, might be overweight international equities. *Active risk* is the degree of deviation of the actual portfolio from the benchmark portfolio.

Investment risk budgeting controls the level of active risk that the fund manager is able to assume in relation to the level of benchmark risk in an attempt to capture excess returns over the benchmark. This depends on the degree of correlation between benchmark risk and active risk. If the two risks are perfectly correlated, total risk is the sum of the two risks (i.e. the sum of their standard deviations). If, as is more likely, the two risks are uncorrelated, total risk is much less than the sum of the two risks. For example, if benchmark risk is 5% and active risk is 2%, total risk is 7% if the two risks are perfectly correlated, but only 5.4% (i.e. the square root of the sum of the two variances) if the two risks are uncorrelated. The active risk can be 'spent' on stock picking or market timing (tactical asset allocation) or both, but only up to the agreed limit. Once the limit has been reached, any increase (i.e. 'overspend') in active risk has to be matched by a corresponding reduction in benchmark risk.

The trade-off between active risk and benchmark risk should take into account the differential returns from assuming active and benchmark risks. To illustrate, suppose the asset–liability matching portfolio is 50% in UK equities and 50% in UK bonds, but that the trustees agree to invest passively 65% in UK equities and 35% in UK bonds. Suppose this gives a total risk of 3%, all of which is benchmark risk. This means that (if asset returns are normally distributed) in two years out of every three, the benchmark portfolio return can be expected to lie within 3% of the matching portfolio return, and in one year in six, it can be expected to be more than 3% below the benchmark return. Suppose that the same total risk of 3% could also be achieved if the fund manager were 60% passively invested in UK equities, 40% passively invested in UK bonds, and was also allowed 2% active risk. If equities outperform bonds by 6%, then the fund manager needs to produce an excess return of 0.5% on the equities in the 60–40 portfolio to match the return on the 65–35 portfolio (i.e. 0.5% extra on 60% of the 60–40 portfolio is the same as 6% on the extra 5% equity in the 65–35 portfolio). If the fund manager delivers more than 0.5% extra, then the active 60–40 portfolio is a more efficient way of allocating the risk budget than the passive 65–35 portfolio.

Assuming active risk also implies the possibility of underperformance, it is important to state the degree of underperformance that is acceptable and the degree that is unacceptable. For example, the trustees might specify that 'underperformance by more than 3% should not happen more frequently than one year in every six' or that 'underperformance by more than 6% is not acceptable'.

Having determined the trustees' objectives and constraints, the fund manager is now in a position to manage the pension fund. However, it is likely that the share portfolio and the bond portfolio will be managed separately. In addition, the fund manager has to decide whether to manage the fund passively, actively or using ALM. We will consider all these factors in turn.

7.6   PASSIVE FUND MANAGEMENT

In this section we will examine the passive management of share and bond portfolios. We will assume that the pension fund is immature, so that the trustees are interested in maximising a risk–return utility function and that their degree of risk tolerance has been assessed.

We will also assume that there is a consensus view of the expected returns and risks associated with different securities. Finally, we will assume that it is possible for investors to borrow and lend at the same riskless interest rate. In short, we have the stylised world of MPT, in which stock markets are efficient. Such a world justifies passive fund management as the appropriate management technique, since investors cannot expect to earn positive (risk-adjusted) excess returns from actively trading securities after adjusting for transaction costs. There are two main types of passive strategy: *buy-and-hold* and *index matching* (or *indexing*).

Buy-and-hold involves the purchase of securities and holding on to them indefinitely or, in the case of fixed-maturity securities (such as money-market securities and bonds), until maturity, and then replacing them with similar securities. The return from a buy-and-hold strategy will be dominated by income flows (i.e. dividend and coupon payments), and in the case of shares, by *long-term* capital growth. Expectations of *short-term* capital gains or losses are ignored; in the case of bonds, capital gains and losses are ignored altogether, because at maturity only the par value of the bond will be received.

Since there is a consensus view that all securities are fairly priced at all times, it does not really matter which securities are bought and held. However, by only buying and holding a few securities, a substantial amount of diversifiable risk might remain in the resulting portfolio. A version of buy-and-hold that eliminates diversifiable risk is index matching.

Index matching involves the construction of an *index fund* that is designed to replicate the performance of the market index. The optimal portfolio is determined (depending on the degree of risk tolerance) as a combination of a riskless asset and the index fund. This is shown in Figure 7.4, which depicts the *capital-market line* (which shows the equilibrium relationship between expected return on the portfolio and portfolio risk as measured by the standard deviation of return on the portfolio), and where M is the consensus view of the *market portfolio* (i.e. the portfolio consisting of all the securities in the economy, weighted

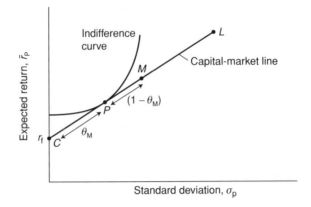

Figure 7.4 Passive portfolio management

according to their relative market values) and C represents the riskless asset. Given the trustees' indifference curve (and degree of risk tolerance), the optimal portfolio P is invested in the following proportions: θ_M in the market portfolio and $(1 - \theta_M)$ in the riskless asset. It can be shown (see Blake 2000, Equation (13.32) on p. 481) that:

$$\theta_M = \frac{1}{2}\left(\frac{\bar{r}_M - r_f}{\sigma_M^2}\right) R_T \qquad (7.10)$$

where $\bar{r}_M$ = consensus expected return on the market; σ_M^2 = consensus variance of the return on the market; r_f = return on the riskless asset (e.g. Treasury bills). For example, if $\bar{r}_M = 0.18(18\%)$, $\sigma_M = 0.35(35\%)$, $r_f = 0.1(10\%)$, and $R_T = 3$, then $\theta_M = 0.98$, that is, 98% of the fund is invested in the market and 2% is invested in the riskless asset.[7]

Several types of indexing are possible.

- *Complete indexing* involves the construction of an index fund which exactly matches the underlying market portfolio. In the case of shares, this could be the FT-A All Share Index; in the case of bonds, it could be the J.P. Morgan Bond Index; in the case of an international portfolio, it could be the Morgan Stanley Capital International Index. Complete indexing is very expensive. For example, the FT-A All Share Index contains more than 800 securities weighted according to their relative

---

[7] Note that, if the indifference curve is linear in expected-return–variance space, as in Figure 7.1, then it will be convex when it is redrawn in expected-return–standard-deviation space, as in Figure 7.4.

market proportions. To construct a portfolio of 800 securities with the same proportions as the index would involve extremely high brokerage commissions (which are ignored by the underlying index). Also, the constituents of the index change quite frequently and so the rebalancing of the index fund (that is, selling the deleted securities and purchasing the added securities) involves dealing spreads as well as brokerage commissions (and these are also ignored by the underlying index). A bond-index fund is even more expensive to construct. Over time, the average maturity of a bond index will decline unless new long-maturing bonds are added to replace those that mature and automatically drop out of the index. Three cheaper alternatives have been suggested: stratified sampling, factor matching and commingling.

- *Stratified sampling* involves the construction of an index fund based on a sample of securities from the total population comprising the index. The idea is to divide the total set of securities into sectors or strata (which are, for example, industry-based for shares or maturity-based for bonds). An overall sample proportion is selected, for example, 5%. Then the top 5% of securities that have the highest correlation with the market index are included in the index fund. This procedure limits initial transaction costs and subsequent rebalancing costs, but increases the risks of *tracking error* – the error in not exactly replicating the market index.

- *Factor matching* (or *risk matching*) is more sophisticated than stratified sampling. Stratified sampling involves selecting securities on the basis of a single factor, for example, industry grouping or maturity range. Factor matching involves the construction of an index fund using securities selected on the basis of a number of factors (or risk indices). The first factor is generally the level of systematic or market risk, so the selected portfolio must be chosen to have the same volatility of return as the market (see below). The other factors (in the case of shares) could be sector breakdown, dividend pattern, firm size and financial structure (i.e. debt/equity ratio). The selected index fund would be a portfolio of, say, fifty securities that matches the market in terms of the above five factors and has the highest correlation with the market.

- *Commingling* involves the use of *commingled funds*, such as *unit trusts* or *investment trusts*, rather than the explicit formation of an index fund. Commingling may be especially suitable for small pension funds and may provide an acceptable compromise between the transaction costs of complete indexing and the tracking error of stratified sampling.

Apart from the transaction costs involved in setting up and rebalancing, there are other problems with running an index fund. The most important one concerns income payments on the securities. The total return on an index includes not only capital gains but also income in the form of dividend or coupon payments. In order to match the performance of the index in terms of income, the index fund would have to have the same pattern of income payments as the index. It would also have to make the same reinvestment assumptions as the index. Since the index fund was constructed to replicate the capital structure of the index, it is unlikely to replicate the income pattern (unless exact matching was used). Similarly, the index assumes that gross income payments are reinvested costlessly back into the index on the day that each security becomes ex-dividend.

In practice, however, these assumptions are violated in four ways. First, the dividend or coupon payment is not made until an average of six weeks after the ex-dividend date. Second, the payment is received net of tax (non-taxpaying investors such as pension funds have to wait even longer before receiving a tax rebate and, since 1997, can no longer do so in the case of UK dividend payments). Third, there are dealing costs of reinvesting income payments. Fourth, the income payments on different securities are going to be trickling in all the time, and no fund manager is going to invest small sums of money on the day they are received. Instead, the small sums are going to be accumulated until a suitable large sum is available for reinvestment. The effect of all these factors is that the index fund will begin to drift away from the index and will eventually have to be rebalanced. Another problem concerns the effect of changing the constituents of the index. When the announcement of the change is made, the price of the security being deleted falls, while the price of the security being added rises. These effects can cause major tracking errors between the index fund and the index.

All these factors lead to the index fund invariably underperforming the index. So it appears that passive fund managers cannot even match the index, let alone beat it. But this appearance is deceptive. The appropriate test is how well an index-fund manager performs on a risk-adjusted and transaction-cost-adjusted basis compared with a fund manager pursuing an active strategy.

Despite these problems, passive fund management is becoming increasingly important as a fund-management strategy. And it is also a sensible strategy if there is a consensus about the market portfolio's expected return and risk. The only occasions on which a passive fund manager

Table 7.1   Illustration of cost averaging

Month	Price per share (£)	Monthly investment (£)	No. of shares purchased
January	2.13	25	11.74
February	2.00	25	12.60
March	1.61	25	15.59
April	1.59	25	15.72
May	1.00	25	25.00
June	1.21	25	20.65
July	2.14	25	11.65
August	2.24	25	11.18
September	1.89	25	13.23
October	1.50	25	16.67
November	2.50	25	10.00
December	2.69	25	9.29
Total	22.50	300	173.18
Average cost paid per share (£)			1.73
Average market price of share (£)			1.88

Source: *Daily Telegraph*, 22 April 2000.

goes into active mode are when either (a) the client's preferences change or (b) the consensus concerning the market portfolio's expected return and risk changes. The first case leads to a new combination of the riskless asset and the index fund. The second case leads to a rebalancing of the existing index fund.

A simple way of implementing buy-and-hold is cost averaging. *Cost averaging* involves making regular payments of the same value into a fund, whatever the price of the security being purchased. By doing this, the average cost of purchasing the security is lower than the average market price of the security, as the example in Table 7.1, involving a £25-a-month savings scheme, shows.

7.7   ACTIVE FUND MANAGEMENT

Active fund management is suitable for immature pension funds whose trustees have a high degree of risk tolerance and are, therefore, interested in maximising expected utility. However, mature pension funds might be actively managed in the expectation of reducing employers' contributions. Personal DC pension scheme members might also wish to have the assets in their fund actively managed. There are different active strategies for share and bond portfolios.

7.7.1   Active share-fund management

A portfolio will be actively managed whenever it is believed that there are misvalued securities around, or when there are heterogeneous expectations of the risks and returns on securities, so that there is no consensus view of the market portfolio. Expectations of price movements are vitally important with active management. This contrasts with passive management, where expectations are less important but where risk aversion dominates behaviour. Active fund management operates around five activities: *country selection, strategic asset allocation, sector selection, security selection* (sometimes called *stock-picking*) and *market timing* (sometimes called *tactical asset allocation*).

To simplify the problem of constructing the portfolio, the fund manager breaks it down into a number of stages. At the first stage, called the *country-selection* stage, the fund manager decides what proportion of the total portfolio to devote to each country: for example, 80% to the UK, 8% to the USA, 6% to Japan, 4% to Germany and 2% to Australia. At the second stage, called the *strategic asset allocation* stage, he or she decides the proportions of each country portfolio devoted to broad asset categories, especially shares and bonds. The optimal strategic asset-allocation decision has been demonstrated before (see Equation (7.4)). It depends on the trustees' degree of risk tolerance and on the fund manager's estimates of the risks and returns on shares and bonds. The strategic asset allocation decision is extremely important since it dominates the performance of most portfolios. This is because returns on securities within each asset category are usually highly correlated; that is, they generally rise or fall together. This implies that selecting the best-performing asset category is more important for performance than selecting the best-performing securities within each asset category. However, restrictions placed on them by trustees may mean that fund managers do not have a completely free hand in making their strategic asset allocation decisions.

The third stage is known as *sector selection* (or group selection). At this stage, funds are allocated to different sectors of each asset category. So, for example, with bonds, the sectors could be short-term, medium-term and long-term bonds. With shares, the sectors could be the components of the Standard Industrial Classification (e.g. banks, breweries, electrical, textiles, pharmaceuticals, and so on). Some fund managers use a different hierarchical ordering: for example, the sector-selection decision might be made before the country-selection decision. This new ordering became more common after the introduction of the euro. With a common currency, sector influences within Europe became more important than country influences.

The fund manager then proceeds to the fourth stage: the *security-selection* stage. At this stage, the fund manager in charge of a particular asset category selects securities from that category. This is done independently of the securities being selected within another category, so that any cross-category correlations between bonds and shares are completely ignored when forming the share and bond portfolios. This common feature of hierarchical or stage-by-stage decision-making is known as *separability*: the bond portfolio is treated as being separable from the share portfolio.

We will assume that the strategic asset-allocation decision (and where appropriate the country- and sector-selection decision) has been made (according to Equation (7.4)). We can therefore concentrate attention on the security-selection decision. Security selection is important whenever fund managers are prepared to accept the overall consensus for the market as a whole but believe that certain individual securities are mis-valued. In other words, most shares are fairly priced but a few are either underpriced or overpriced. A good stock-picker believes he or she knows which securities are misvalued. An overpriced security has an expected return that is less than, or a risk estimate that is more than, the market consensus estimate, while an underpriced security has an expected return that is more than, or a risk estimate that is less than, the market consensus estimate. In MPT, the fair price of a security is determined using the *capital asset pricing model* (CAPM) and the *security-market line* (SML). A security is said to be fairly priced when its *equilibrium expected return* $\bar{r}_i^*$ is given by:

$$\bar{r}_i^* = r_f + (\bar{r}_M - r_f)\beta_i \qquad (7.11)$$

where β_i = beta of the ith security, defined as the ratio of the *covariance* between the return on the security and the return on the market (σ_{iM}) to the *variance* of the return on the market (σ_M^2), that is, $\beta_i = \sigma_{iM}/\sigma_M^2$. Equation (7.11) is the equation of the CAPM. It states that the equilibrium return on a risky security is equal to the risk-free return (r_f) plus a *risk premium*, which equals the product of the *market-risk premium* ($\bar{r}_M - r_f$) and the *beta* of the security (β_i).

The *beta* of a security measures the security's embodiment of *systematic risk* (or *market risk*). The higher the systematic risk, the higher the beta and the greater the expected return on the security has to be in order for the security to be held in equilibrium and to compensate investors for the additional undiversifiable risk they are bearing. The total risk of a security can be decomposed into the security's systematic risk plus its *specific risk* (or squared *active risk* or *tracking error*):

$$\text{Total risk} = \text{Systematic risk} + \text{Specific risk}$$

or

$$\sigma_i^2 = \beta_i^2 \sigma_M^2 + \eta_i^2 \tag{7.12}$$

where σ_i^2 = variance of the return on the ith security; η_i^2 = specific risk of the ith security.

Because the specific risk of a security can be eliminated by low-cost diversification (i.e. it is diversifiable), this component of total risk will not be 'priced' (or compensated for) in equilibrium. Only the component of total risk (namely, the systematic risk) that is correlated with the market and hence undiversifiable, because market risk is undiversifiable, will be priced in equilibrium.

The graphical representation of the CAPM is called the security-market line (see Figure 7.5). Both the CAPM and the SML show that the expected (or required) return on a risky security increases linearly with the security's beta (since the market risk premium is common to all securities). When a security is fairly priced, its expected return will lie along the SML.

The beta for a portfolio of securities (β_P) is the weighted average of the betas of the individual securities:

$$\beta_P = \sum_{i=1}^{N} \theta_i \beta_i \tag{7.13}$$

where θ_i = proportion (by value) of the ith security in the portfolio.

The difference between the return expected by the fund manager, $\bar{r}_i^*$, and the equilibrium expected return (or the average return expected by the marked as a whole), as given by Equation (7.11), is known as the *alpha* of the security:

$$\alpha_i = \bar{r}_i - \bar{r}_i^* \tag{7.14}$$

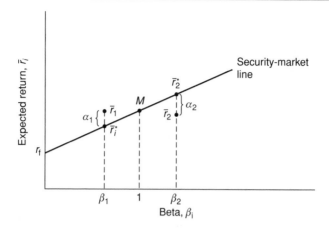

Figure 7.5   Security selection: alpha values for shares

where α_i = alpha of the ith security. For example, suppose that $\bar{r}_M$ = 0.18 (18%), r_f = 0.10(10%), and β_1 = 0.75, then $\bar{r}_1^*$ = 0.16(16%). If $\bar{r}_i$ = 0.17(17%), then α_1 = 0.01 (i.e. 1%). This means that the security offers a 1% higher return than it should have and is therefore underpriced.

When a security's alpha is positive, the security is underpriced. When a security's alpha is negative, the security is overpriced. When a security is fairly priced, its alpha is zero (see Figure 7.5). The alpha for the portfolio (α_P) is the weighted average of the alphas of the individual securities in the portfolio:

$$\alpha_P = \sum_{i=1}^{N} \theta_i \alpha_i \qquad (7.15)$$

where θ_i = proportion (by value) of the ith security in the portfolio.

The objective of a stock-picker is to select portfolios of securities with positive alphas, a procedure which has been called 'the quest for alpha'. In other words, the stock-picker will construct portfolios of securities which, in comparison with the market portfolio, have less-than-proportionate weightings in the overpriced (negative-alpha) securities (since they are expected to fall in price) and more-than-proportionate weightings in the underpriced (positive-alpha) securities (since they are expected to rise in price).

The most sophisticated version of the quest for alpha is called *portable alpha* (or *alpha transfer*). With this strategy, the management of market returns (beta) is separated from attempts to add value (alpha). The aim is to establish a range of alpha-generating strategies, without restriction as to type, in a way that does not alter the underlying asset allocation of the portfolio. It is known as portable because the alpha can be associated with any asset class that offers the most attractive opportunities at the time and the beta can be associated with any benchmark. The most common strategy used to separate alpha from beta is to use derivatives (i.e. futures and options) overlays, often combined with market-neutral (long–short) hedge funds. For example, put options can be used to capture the alpha on securities that are perceived to be overvalued in a passive index fund. Another example might be a UK pension fund that wishes to outperform the French equity market. The pension fund could take a position in CAC40 futures contracts to achieve the passive equity market (beta) exposure and a forward foreign exchange contract to hedge the currency exposure. These contracts generate the French equity market return in sterling, with the outperformance (alpha) coming from, say, a US long–short strategy. In other words, a US long–short hedge fund is attached ('ported') to a French equity market benchmark.

The final activity of the fund manager is market timing. A fund manager engages in security selection when he or she accepts the overall consensus for the market portfolio but believes that individual securities are misvalued. A fund manager engages in *market timing* when he or she does not accept the consensus about the market portfolio. In other words, he or she is more bullish or more bearish than the market. Market timing is equivalent to adjusting the beta of the portfolio over time (see Figure 7.6). If the fund manager is expecting a bull market, he or she wants to increase the beta of the portfolio (i.e. to make it more *aggressive*). If he or she is expecting a bear market, he or she wants to reduce the beta of the portfolio (i.e. to make it more *defensive*). One way of doing this would be to buy high-beta shares in a bull market and sell them in a bear market. However, the transaction costs involved would make this an expensive strategy. A cheaper alternative is to keep the portfolio of risky assets constant and to raise or lower beta by lowering or raising the proportion of the portfolio held in cash. This can be a cheaper alternative, since moving into or out of cash is generally cheaper than moving between different shares. An even cheaper alternative is to use futures or options, buying stock-index futures and call options and selling put options in expectation of a bull market, and selling stock-index futures and call options and buying put options in a bear market.

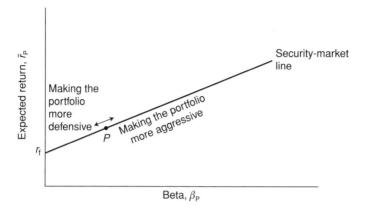

Figure 7.6 Market timing

7.7.2 Active bond-fund management

As with shares, a bond fund will be actively managed whenever there are misvalued bonds around, or when there are heterogeneous expectations about the risks and returns on bonds, so that there is no consensus view of the market portfolio for bonds. Similarly, with the asset-allocation decision having been made, active bond-fund management operates around the activities of security selection and market timing. However, there is a difference between share- and bond-portfolio managers. Most share managers engage in security selection, whereas most bond managers engage in market timing.

A bond-picker will construct a portfolio of bonds which, in comparison with the market portfolio, has less-than-proportionate weightings in the overpriced bonds (since they are expected to fall in price) and more-than-proportionate weightings in the underpriced bonds (since they are expected to rise in price). In other words, the portfolio has relatively low weightings in negative-alpha bonds and relatively high weightings in positive-alpha bonds (see Equation (7.14)), where alpha is defined with respect to the *bond-market line*[8] (see Figure 7.7). For example, suppose that $\bar{r}_M = 0.12(12\%)$ and $r_f = 0.10(10\%)$, then the equation

---

[8] The bond-market line plots bond returns against relative duration. It is more conventional in finance to use yield curves (i.e. plots of bond yields against maturity). Yields and yield curves are examined in Appendix B of the book.

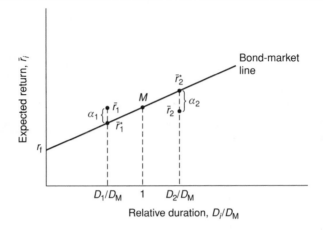

Figure 7.7   Security selection: alpha values for bonds

for the bond-market line is:

$$\bar{r}_i^* = r_f + (\bar{r}_M - r_f)D_i/D_M$$
$$= 0.10 + (0.02)D_i/D_M \qquad (7.16)$$

where $\bar{r}_i^* =$ equilibrium expected return on the ith bond; $D_i/D_M =$ relative duration of the ith bond (where D_M is the duration of the market portfolio of bonds). If, for Bond 1, $D_i/D_M = 0.5$, then $\bar{r}_i^* = 0.11(11\%)$. If $\bar{r}_1 = 0.12(12\%)$, then $\alpha_1 = 0.01$ (i.e. 1%). The bond offers a 1% higher return than it should have and is therefore underpriced.

A market timer engages in active management when he or she does not accept the consensus for the market portfolio, and is either more bullish or more bearish than the market. Expectations of interest-rate changes are, therefore, a crucial input into a successful market timing strategy. A bond-market timer is interested in adjusting the relative duration of his or her portfolio over time (market timing with bonds is sometimes called *duration switching* or *rate-anticipation switching*). If the fund manager is expecting a bull market because he or she is expecting a fall in the general level of interest rates, he or she wants to increase the duration of the portfolio by replacing low-duration bonds with high-duration bonds. If the fund manager is expecting a bear market because he or she is expecting a rise in the general level of interest rates, he or she wants to reduce the duration of the portfolio by replacing high-duration bonds with low-duration bonds.

Active bond-portfolio management is generally not as profitable as active share-portfolio management. There are several reasons for this. First, there are more shares than bonds traded in the UK. The most liquid bonds are UK Government bonds and then only at certain maturities. Because of active trading in these bonds, they are less likely to be mispriced. In addition, the volatility of bond prices is generally much less than that of share prices, so the opportunity for substantial mispricing of bonds is, in any case, much less than that for shares. Further, with only a few bonds suitable for active trading, the portfolio consisting of those bonds will be relatively undiversified and will, therefore, be relatively risky, thereby reducing the risk-adjusted excess returns from active trading.

Bond-portfolio adjustment involves the purchase and sale of bonds; that is, the *switching* or *swapping* of bonds. There are two main classes of bond switches: *anomaly switches* and *policy switches*. An anomaly switch is a switch between two bonds with very *similar* characteristics but whose prices (or yields) are out of line with each other. A policy switch is a switch between two *dissimilar* bonds because of an anticipated change in the structure of the market (e.g. quality ratings are expected to change), which is expected to lead to a change in the relative prices (or yields) of the two bonds. Policy switches involve greater expected returns, but also greater potential risks, than anomaly switches.

The simplest example of an anomaly switch is a *substitution switch*. This involves the exchange of two bonds which are similar in terms of maturity, coupon and quality rating, and every other characteristic, but which differ in terms of price (or yield). Since two similar bonds should trade at the same price and yield, then whenever a price (or yield) difference occurs, an arbitrage opportunity emerges. The 'dear' bond is sold short and the 'cheap' bond is purchased. Later, if and when the anomaly has been eliminated, the reverse sets of transactions are made in order to close out the position. The time taken for the elimination of the anomaly is known as the *work-out period*. The work-out period is important for calculating the rate of return on the switch. The shorter the work-out period, the greater the annualised rate of return. If the position has to be held until maturity before the anomaly is corrected, the annualised return from the switch may be negligible.

Table 7.2 illustrates a typical substitution switch. If, historically, the difference between the prices of two bonds A and B has never been more than £0.50 and the difference between the yields to maturity has

Table 7.2 A substitution switch

		Date 1			Date 2		Profit	
	Action	Price (£)	Yield (%)	Action	Price (£)	Yield (%)	Price (£)	Yield (%)
Bond A	Sell	100	10.00	Buy	100	10.00	0	0.00
Bond B	Buy	99	10.20	Sell	100	10.00	1	0.20
Total							1	0.20

never been more than 0.10% (i.e. ten basis points), then, clearly, at date 1 an anomaly exists and so a substitution switch is made. The cheaper Bond B is purchased and the dearer Bond A is sold short. By date 2 the anomaly has been eliminated. Bond A was correctly priced and its price has not changed between the two dates. Bond B was underpriced and its price rises by £1, while its yield falls by twenty basis points. If dates 1 and 2 are a year apart, the rate of return on capital employed of £100 is only 1%. However, if the two dates are one month apart, the annualised rate of return is 12.68%. It is important to note that this switch involves the short sale of one bond *and* the purchase of another bond: there is a *relative* mispricing between the bonds, but it is impossible to know in advance which bond is *absolutely* mispriced.

If the coupon and maturity of the two bonds are similar, then a substitution swap involves a one-for-one exchange of bonds. However, if there are substantial differences in coupon or maturity, then the duration of the two bonds will differ. This will lead to different responses if the general level of interest rates changes during the life of the switch. It will, therefore, be necessary to weight the switch in such a way that it is hedged from changes in the level of interest rates but still exposed to changes in the anomalous yield-differential between the bonds.

To illustrate, suppose that Bond A in the last example has a duration of ten years, while Bond B has a duration of two years. This means that Bond A is five times more responsive to interest-rate fluctuations than Bond B. To protect against unanticipated shifts in interest rates, the relative investment in the two bonds is determined as follows:

$$\text{Investment in Bond A/Investment in Bond B}$$
$$= \text{Duration of Bond B/Duration of Bond A} \qquad (7.17)$$

Expressing this in terms of nominal amounts:

Nominal of Bond B bought

$= $ Nominal of Bond A sold

$\times \dfrac{\text{Duration of Bond A} \times \text{Price of Bond A}}{\text{Duration of Bond B} \times \text{Price of Bond B}}$

$\approx 5 \times$ Nominal of Bond A sold.   (7.18)

So, for every Bond A sold, five of Bond B have to be bought. Consider what would happen if there was a one-for-one exchange and interest rates fell by 1%. The price of Bond A would rise by 10% (i.e. 1% times its duration of ten), from £100 to £110. The price of Bond B would rise by 2% (i.e. 1% times its duration of two), from £99 to £101. Suppose also that the price of Bond B rose by another £1 to £102 to correct the anomaly. So, although the relative mispricing has been corrected, the substitution switch has made a loss of £8. Similarly, differences in coupon rates between the two bonds will affect the profitability of the switch and this has to be taken into account.

Another type of anomaly switch is a *pure yield-pick-up switch*. This simply involves the sale of a bond with a given yield to maturity and the purchase of a similar bond with a higher yield to maturity. With this switch there is no expectation of any yield or price correction, so no reverse transactions take place at a later date.

Policy switches are designed to take advantage of an anticipated change. The change could be: (a) a shift in interest rates; (b) a change in the structure of the yield curve; (c) a change in a bond's quality rating; or (d) a change in sector relationships. A shift in interest rates is exactly what a market timer is looking out for. So, switching from low-duration to high-duration bonds if interest rates are expected to fall is an example of a policy switch (as we have seen, it is also known as a *duration switch* or *rate-anticipation switch*). The other changes listed above lead to what are known as *inter-market* (or *inter-sector*) *spread switches*. We can give some examples.

Normally, the yield curve is a smooth relationship between yield and maturity. But occasionally there may be humps or dips in the yield curve, as in Figure 7.8. If the humps and dips are expected to disappear, then the prices of bonds (e.g. Bond A) on the hump can be expected to rise (their yields will fall) and the prices of bonds (e.g. Bond B) in the dip can be expected to fall (their yields will rise). So, one example of a switch is the purchase of Bond A and the short sale of Bond B.

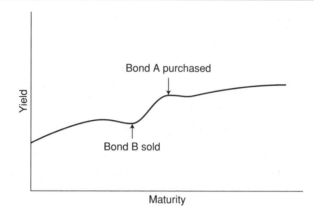

Figure 7.8   Bond switching

A bond whose quality rating is expected to fall will fall in price. To prevent a capital loss, it can be switched for a bond whose quality rating is expected to rise or remain unchanged.

An example of a change in sector relationships is a change in taxes affecting two sectors. For instance, one sector (e.g. the domestic-bond sector) might have withholding taxes on coupon payments, whereas another sector (e.g. the international bond sector) might not. If it is anticipated either that withholding tax will be applied to all sectors or that it will be withdrawn from all sectors, then another switch is possible.

7.7.3   Mixed active–passive fund management

So far we have considered pure passive and pure active strategies, but it is possible for fund managers to use mixtures of the two. For example, the asset-allocation decision can be passive, but the fund manager actively engages in security selection. This is known as a *security-selection style* of management. Alternatively, the fund manager might construct passive portfolios of individual securities, but make active asset-allocation decisions. This is known as an *asset-allocation style* of management.

Another mixed strategy is *core–satellite* portfolio management, also known as *enhanced passive management*. This is a management strategy pursued by very large funds. The fund manager has a large *core portfolio* that is never traded, because doing so would result in adverse market movements. But surrounding the core portfolio are a number of smaller *satellite portfolios*. The satellite portfolios are actively managed and

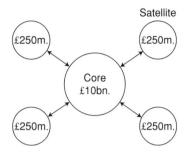

Figure 7.9   Core–satellite portfolios

even have the ability to take short positions, because they can borrow securities from the core portfolio; that is, they can go short against the core (see Figure 7.9).

With bond portfolios, an example of a mixed strategy is *contingent immunisation*. The fund manager begins with an active strategy, and continues in this mode until the end of the investment horizon or until the return on the active strategy falls below a threshold level, at which point the bond portfolio is immunised for the remainder of the investment horizon.

Another type of mixed active–passive strategy involves options and futures. With one version of this strategy, fund managers have passive portfolios of cash-market securities. The portfolio is not traded because of the high transactions costs of trading in the cash market. Instead, the fund managers trade a view on individual securities by buying or selling individual stock options. Similarly, they can engage in market timing and shift the beta of their share portfolio (or the duration of their bond portfolio) by buying or selling stock-index or gilt options and futures. This is because transaction costs are low (at least for institutional investors) and liquidity is generally high in the markets for derivatives.

With another version of this strategy, what are called *equitised cash portfolios* (or *synthetic equity funds* or *guaranteed equity funds*) are constructed. The entire value of the portfolio is held passively in money-market instruments. The active part of the strategy is performed entirely with futures. Yet another version is known as a *90–10 portfolio*. In this case, 90% of the portfolio is held in cash and 10% in options. With money-market interest rates at around 10%, the strategy locks in the initial value of the portfolio (since £90(1 + 0.1) ≈ £100), but gains from the intrinsic value of the options if they expire in-the-money.

7.8   ASSET–LIABILITY MANAGEMENT

Asset–liability management (ALM) is important when it is essential to deliver the liability cash flows (i.e. pensions in payment) with a high degree of probability (Fabozzi and Konishi, 1991; Campbell and Viceira, 2002; Blake, 2003).

The trustees of a mature pension fund will want to ensure that the present value of the fund's assets is at least as great as the present value of the pension liabilities. The stream of future pension liability cash flows needs to be predicted. To do this, the actuary needs to make assumptions about 'demographic' variables, such as the rate at which scheme members retire or leave service or the rate at which pensioners die. These will depend on the age and sex composition of the workforce. The actuary also needs to make assumptions about 'economic' variables, such as the rate of return on assets, interest rates and the rate of wage and price inflation. While some of these variables are easy to predict, others are less so. It is the uncertainties that are attached to projections of these demographic and economic variables that ALM strategies need to hedge if they are going to be successful.

The starting point of ALM is *asset–liability modelling*, which begins by making forecasts (based on the above assumptions) about how a pension fund's liabilities are going to accrue over a particular time horizon, which might be 5, 10 or 15 years ahead. These forecasts and projections are made under different scenarios concerning likely outcomes. Typically, three scenarios are adopted: most likely, best-case and worst-case. This provides a realistic range of possible outcomes, and in the last case spells out the extent of the risks that the pension fund trustees face.

There are two main uses of asset–liability modelling. The first is to indicate the consequences of adopting any particular investment strategy. The second is to discover alternative strategies that increase the probability of meeting the fund's objectives (i.e. ALM). Proponents of asset–liability modelling argue that the strategy allows pension funds to generate higher returns without any consequential increase in risk.

The modelling exercises might indicate, for example, that if current investment returns are sustained, there would be no need to change the employer contribution rate over the next five years. However, the worst-case scenario might indicate that the employer contribution rate might have to rise by 10% over the next five years. The exercise therefore allows the employer to plan for this possibility. As another illustration, the modelling exercise might indicate that, because a pension fund is maturing, it should switch out of equities into fixed-income bonds, which are more likely to meet pension liabilities with lower risk of employer deficiency payments.

While all this seems eminently sensible, the technique is not without its critics. As with many long-term forecasting exercises, the predictions are only as good as the assumptions used to generate them. Some claim that the assumptions made about future investment returns are likely to be so unreliable that the modelling exercise provides very little value. Less sceptical proponents of asset–liability modelling argue that the 'models are to be used and not believed', with the usefulness of the technique being 'to provide a disciplined quantitative framework for qualitative discussions on investment policies' (Roger Urwin, *Financial Times*, 18 April 1991).

Another problem encountered with the technique comes from fund managers who are concerned that it gives an unwarranted role to actuaries in designing investment strategies, in particular, asset-allocation strategies. Actuaries have always played a leading role in determining the value of a pension scheme's liabilities, but with the advent of asset–liability modelling, actuaries have begun to play a role in establishing the long-term asset allocation over, say, a 10-year horizon. Fund managers claim they are being reduced to the subsidiary role of determining short-term (tactical) asset allocation and stock selection relative to this new long-term benchmark. However, not all fund managers are critical of this redefinition of respective roles. Many have positively welcomed the formal separation of long-term policy decisions from short-term tactical decisions that asset–liability modelling allows.

Another potential problem concerns the interpretation of performance measurement in the light of the technique. Asset–liability modelling justifies different pension funds pursuing very different investment policies. For example, small, fast-growing funds might pursue very aggressive investment policies, while large mature funds might adopt passive investment policies. This makes it very difficult to interpret a single performance league table drawn up on the assumption that all funds are pursuing the same objective of maximising returns. Performance-measurement services started to take this into account by constructing peer-group performance league tables, drawn up for subgroups of funds following similar objectives. However, the stock market crash of 2000, combined with falling interest rates, led to a substantial widening of pension fund deficits and to a radical rethink of both fund-management strategies and appropriate performance measures. These are discussed later in the section on liability-driven investment.

Asset–liability modelling begins by calculating the pension liabilities, typically using the projected unit method as previously considered in Equation (6.1):

$$\text{Liabilities} = \phi(t) \times W(t) \times G(t, T) \times \Pi(t, T) \times \ddot{a}(T) \times D(t, T)$$

$$(7.19)$$

where:

$\phi(t) = $ *Accrual factor* for service by age t (e.g. 5/60 if the member has five years' service and the 60th scale is used to determine the value of benefits).

$W(t) = $ Pensionable salary at age t.

$G(t,T) = $ *Revaluation factor* for earnings between age t and retirement age T ($= 1$ if there is no revaluation of earnings up until the retirement age, $= (1 + g)^{(T-t)}$ if the *revaluation rate g* is constant).

$\Pi(t,T) = $ *Retention factor* $=$ probability of remaining in the scheme between age t and retirement age T: the two main reasons for a member not remaining in the scheme until retirement are death-in-service and leaving a scheme early as a result of changing jobs.

$\ddot{a}(T) = $ Expected *annuity factor* (the present value of a life annuity of £1 per annum) at retirement age, T: $\ddot{a}(T) = {}_1 p_T /(1 + r) + {}_2 p_T /(1 + r)^2 + {}_3 p_T /(1 + r)^3 \ldots$, where terms such as ${}_1 p_T$ are known as *survival probabilities* and indicate the probability of someone aged T surviving to age $T + 1$, etc. and r is the real yield on the long-term bonds that are purchased by the insurance company and from which the pension payments are paid.

$D(t,T) = $ *Discount factor* between age t and retirement age T ($= 1/(1 + r)^{(T-t)}$ if the discount rate r is constant).

The *surplus* is defined as the difference between the market value of the assets and the actuarial value of the liabilities:

$$\text{Surplus} = \text{Assets } (A) - \text{Liabilities } (L) \qquad (7.20)$$

Surplus risk (also called *mismatch risk* or *shortfall risk*) is defined as the standard deviation of the surplus and is equal to:

Surplus risk $= \sqrt{}$ [(Standard deviation of the Assets)^2
  $+$ (Standard deviation of the Liabilities)^2
  $- 2 \times$ {(Correlation between the Assets and Liabilities)
  $\times$ (Standard deviation of the Assets)
  $\times$ (Standard deviation of the Liabilities)}]   (7.21)

With ALM, the aim is to select the fund's *contribution rate* and *strategic asset allocation* (SAA) over time in a way that minimises a weighted sum of *surplus risk* (7.21) and *contribution risk* (i.e. volatility of the required contributions into the pension scheme) subject to the constraints that the surplus (7.20) is zero on the retirement date of the scheme member and never falls outside a specified range before retirement (see, for example, Haberman and Sung (1994)):

Choose: Contribution rate and Strategic asset allocation to:

Minimise: Loss function $=$ Surplus risk $+ \lambda \times$ Contribution risk

subject to:

Surplus $= 0$ on the retirement date

Surplus $\geq LB$ and $\leq UB$ before retirement   (7.22)

where *LB* is the lower bound below which the surplus may not go and *UB* is the upper bound. The weight λ shows the relative importance to the sponsoring employer of minimising contribution risk in comparison with minimising surplus risk: the higher the value of λ, the greater the relative importance of contribution risk in determining the optimal strategic asset allocation. It is the trustees' task to choose the value of λ, taking into account the employer's capacity to bear contribution risk.

The ALM exercise (7.22) involves two objectives and two instruments (or controls) for achieving those objectives. Broadly speaking, the contribution rate is set and adjusted to ensure that the surplus always lies within permitted boundaries and the SAA is set and adjusted to minimise a *loss function* (i.e. *surplus risk* $+\lambda\times$ *contribution risk*) that is specific to a particular pension scheme.

7.8.1 Managing surplus risk

To minimise surplus risk, the SAA is selected to match the pension liabilities in two key respects: *size* and *volatility*.

Ensuring full funding

First, if pension schemes are always fully funded, so that assets are always sufficient to meet liabilities in full (implying Assets = Liabilities at all times), then it is clear from (7.20) that the surplus will always be zero. This is achieved by adjusting the contribution rate (especially the employer's contribution rate) into the fund to ensure that the surplus is always zero.

In practice, there are usually some tolerance limits around this equality. In the UK, for example, it is permissible for the value of assets to vary between 90% and 105% of the value of liabilities before remedial action needs to be taken, implying that the surplus cannot exceed 5% of the value of the liabilities ($UB = 0.05 \times$ Liabilities) or fall below -10% of the value of the liabilities ($LB = -0.1 \times$ Liabilities). If the value of assets exceeds the 105% limit, the scheme has up to five years to reduce the value to 100% of liabilities (Social Security Act 1986). The most common means of doing this is the employer's contributions holiday, although other means are available: employee contributions holiday, improved pension benefits (i.e. raising Liabilities) or selling off financial assets (i.e. reducing Assets), the proceeds from which are returned to the sponsor subject to a 35% tax.

If the value of assets falls below 90% of the value of liabilities, the scheme has up to three years to raise the value to 90% of liabilities and a further seven years to raise the value to 100% of liabilities (Pensions Acts 1995 and 2004). The most common means of doing this is additional employer contributions (i.e. deficiency payments).

Matching volatility

Second, if it were possible for the assets in the pension fund to be selected in such a way that their aggregate volatility matches that of the liabilities,[9] then it is clear from (7.21) that surplus risk could be reduced to zero. This requires the assets in the pension fund to have both the same volatility as the pension liabilities (Standard deviation of the Assets = Standard deviation of the Liabilities) and to be perfectly correlated with

---

[9] We called such a portfolio of assets the liability-immunising portfolio (LIP) in Chapter 6.

them (Correlation between the Assets and Liabilities $= 1$). In this case:

Surplus risk $= \sqrt{\ }$ [(Standard deviation of the Liabilities)^2

$+$ (Standard deviation of the Liabilities)^2

$- 2 \times \{(1)$

$\times$ (Standard deviation of the Liabilities)

$\times$ (Standard deviation of the Liabilities)$\}]$

$= \sqrt{\ }$ [2 $\times$ (Standard deviation of the Liabilities)^2

$- 2 \times$ (Standard deviation of the Liabilities)^2]

$= 0$ (7.23)

When surplus risk is zero, the value of the assets and liabilities will always go up and down exactly in line with each other.

The volatility of the liabilities

In reality, however, assets do not exist with these precise characteristics. With existing assets, surplus risk can be reduced but not completely eliminated: the assets and liabilities will go up together and down together, but not exactly in line. We can see why this is the case by examining the standard deviation of the liabilities in (7.19):[10]

Standard deviation of the liabilities $\approx \phi(t) \times W(t)$

$\times \sqrt{[\{\bar{\Pi} \times \bar{a} \times \bar{D} \times \text{Standard deviation of the revaluation factor } G(t,T)\}^2}$

$+ \{\bar{G} \times \bar{a} \times \bar{D} \times \text{Standard deviation of the retention factor } \Pi(t, T)\}^2$

$+ \{\bar{G} \times \bar{\Pi} \times \bar{D} \times \text{Standard deviation of the annuity factor } \ddot{a}(T)\}^2$

$+ \{\bar{G} \times \bar{\Pi} \times \bar{a} \times \text{Standard deviation of the discount factor } D(t, T)\}^2]$

(7.24)

The definition (7.24) assumes that the factors determining the volatility of $G(t,T)$, $\Pi(t,T)$, $\ddot{a}(T)$, and $D(t,T)$ are all independent of each other; mean values of variables are represented by bars over the variables. In (7.24), $\phi(t)$ and $W(t)$ are known at the time the calculation is made, so

---

[10] Equation (7.24) is derived from a first-order Taylor expansion of (7.19) about the sample means of the variables, assuming zero correlation between the variables. We will illustrate this for the following two-variable case: $f(x, y) = x.y$. The first-order expansion is $f(x, y) = f(\bar{x}, \bar{y}) + f_x(\bar{x}, \bar{y})(x - \bar{x}) + f_y(\bar{x}, \bar{y})(y - \bar{y}) = \bar{x}.\bar{y} + \bar{y}.(x - \bar{x}) + \bar{x}.(y - \bar{y})$. The variance of $f(x, y)$ is therefore $\bar{y}^2 . \text{var}(x) + \bar{x}^2 . \text{var}(y)$ under the assumption that x and y are independent.

any volatility in the liabilities arises from volatility in the revaluation, retention, annuity and discount factors.

The volatility of the revaluation factor

The standard deviation of the revaluation factor $G(t,T)$ depends on the volatility of the member's earnings between now and retirement. No financial asset presently exists to match this volatility perfectly. This is because no government or corporation has so far issued wage-indexed bonds; that is, bonds whose coupon and principal value are linked to national average earnings. Such bonds would provide a perfect matching asset for liabilities linked to average earnings growth, although they would provide a less than perfect match if the member's earnings did not grow exactly in line with national average earnings. The nearest financial instrument available for matching liabilities linked to earnings growth is a price index-linked bond. This is because it is known that price inflation and wage inflation are highly correlated (Thornton and Wilson, 1992).

But even if a pension fund held only index-linked bonds in its portfolio, it would still be exposed to *productivity shocks*. This follows from the relationship that determines wage inflation:

$$\text{Wage inflation} = b_1 \times \text{Price inflation} + b_2 \times \text{Productivity growth}$$

(7.25)

On average we would expect both price inflation and productivity improvements to be incorporated fully into earnings growth (i.e. we would expect $b_1 = b_2 = 1$), although in slump conditions we might observe b_1, $b_2 < 1$, while in boom conditions we might observe b_1, $b_2 > 1$. Suppose, we set $b_1 = b_2 = 1$, then it will be the case that (assuming price inflation and productivity growth are independent of each other and therefore uncorrelated):

$$\text{Standard deviation of wage inflation}$$
$$= \text{Standard deviation of price inflation}$$
$$+ \text{Standard deviation of productivity growth} \quad (7.26)$$

This indicates that an index-linked bond will perfectly match the pension scheme's exposure to price inflation, but leave it exposed to productivity shocks (i.e. the standard deviation of productivity growth). An unanticipated increase in the productivity of the workforce (say as result of a technological innovation) will raise their wages and hence the liabilities of the pension scheme, but this will not be matched by an increase in the value of the assets held in the fund.

The volatility of the retention factor

The standard deviation of the retention factor $\Pi(t,T)$ depends on the volatility of both staff turnover and death-in-service rates between now and retirement.

The volatility of the annuity factor

The standard deviation of the annuity factor $\ddot{a}(T)$ depends in a highly complex manner on a combination of mortality risk, inflation risk and interest-rate risk.

Longevity risk

Longevity risk is the uncertainty attached to the survival probabilities, $_1p_T$, $_2p_T$, etc. There has been an enormous improvement in life expectancy over the last 20 years, which pension providers (such as insurance companies and pension schemes) have seriously underestimated. If pension providers underestimate the improvement in life expectancy, then the cost of providing a pension will be higher than was anticipated at the time that the member joined the scheme, which might have been 40 years or more before the pension begins to be drawn.

Inflation risk

When the pension becomes payable it should be matched with an instrument whose payouts replicate as closely as possible the underlying pension payments. Most pensions in payment in the UK are subject to *limited price indexation* or LPI (i.e. retail price inflation up to a maximum of 2.5% p.a.), so the nearest available matching asset for this liability is an index-linked bond. In other words, the *inflation risk* associated with paying LPI pensions is minimised by holding index-linked bonds. (The perfect matching asset, the asset that reduces the inflation risk that faces the pension payer to zero, would be an LPI bond, although such an instrument does not currently trade.)

Interest-rate risk

Interest-rate risk is the uncertainty attached to the yield curve. If there is an unanticipated fall in yields, then the cost of buying index-linked bonds rises. This is precisely what happened in the case of the *guaranteed annuities* offered by the UK life office Equitable Life. Equitable Life sold deferred annuities with guaranteed high yields between 1957 and 1988, but it failed to hedge its exposure to interest-rate risk. If interest rates fell, this would increase the cost of buying the bonds that are used to make the annuity payments. By the late 1990s, when the annuities started to get paid, interest rates had fallen to their lowest level for 40 years and Equitable Life found itself with insufficient reserves to pay the now very high cost of buying the requisite bonds.

The choice of discount rate

The choice of discount factor $D(t,T)$ in (7.19) (and in consequence its standard deviation in (7.24)) has been the subject of increasing disagreement in recent years. The nature of the disagreement can be expressed simply as follows. Should the discount rate reflect the liabilities to be paid, or should it reflect the pension fund's asset allocation? In other words, should the discount rate reflect the growth rate in liabilities, or should it reflect the weighted-average expected return on the assets in the pension fund?

If the discount rate is set to equal the growth rate g in liabilities, then it is clear from (7.19) that:

$$D(t,T) = 1/(1 + g)^{(T-t)} = 1/G(t,T) \qquad (7.27)$$

in which case the value of liabilities in (7.19) reduces to:

$$\text{Liabilities} = \phi(t) \times W(t) \times G(t,T) \times \Pi(t,T) \times \ddot{a}(T) \times (1/G(t,T))$$
$$= \phi(t) \times W(t) \times \Pi(t,T) \times \ddot{a}(T) \qquad (7.28)$$

and the standard deviation of the liabilities in (7.24) reduces to:

$$\text{Standard deviation of the liabilities} \approx \phi(t) \times W(t)$$
$$\times \sqrt{[\{\bar{a} \times \text{Standard deviation of the retention factor } \Pi(t,T)\}^2}$$
$$+ \{\bar{\Pi} \times \text{Standard deviation of the annuity factor } \ddot{a}(T)\}^2]$$
$$\qquad (7.29)$$

So, the only source of volatility that a pension fund need be concerned about is the volatility of the retention and annuity factors. However, as we indicated above, this is only a strictly legitimate procedure if the pension fund is fully invested in wage-indexed bonds (or in price-indexed bonds as the next best asset class). Some argue that pension liabilities should still be discounted in this manner, even though such bonds do not exist. If the retention factor is stable over time, then (7.29) simplifies to:

$$\text{Standard deviation of the liabilities} \approx \phi(t) \times W(t) \times \bar{\Pi}$$
$$\times \text{Standard deviation of the annuity factor } \ddot{a}(T) \qquad (7.30)$$

Others (such as actuaries) argue that the discount factor should reflect the reality of the asset allocation that is actually adopted by the pension fund, in which case r should equal the weighted-average expected return on the N assets in the pension fund:

$$r = \theta_1 \times \bar{r}_1 + \theta_2 \times \bar{r}_2 + \cdots + \theta_N \times \bar{r}_N \qquad (7.31)$$

where

θ_1 = weight in the pension fund of asset 1 (e.g. 50% in UK equities), etc.

$\bar{r}_1$ = expected real return on asset 1 (e.g. 8% for UK equities), etc.

If there is a significant equity component in the asset allocation of the pension fund, then the standard deviation of the discount rate could be quite high (since the volatility of equities is much higher than that of other assets) and could come to dominate the standard deviation of the liabilities itself.

7.8.2   Managing contribution risk

Contribution risk deals with the volatility of contributions into the scheme. If surplus risk is minimised, contributions into the scheme will be higher but more stable over time than if surplus risk is not minimised.

Now employers usually like to have lower contributions than higher contributions. But there is no free lunch. The *only* way to have lower average contributions is to invest more of the fund in equities and to accept greater surplus risk (i.e. a large fall in the value of the equities held in the pension fund that is not matched by a corresponding fall in the value of the liabilities) as a consequence. This, in turn, means that there will be greater contribution risk, i.e. contributions will be more volatile than if surplus risk is minimised. When the equity market is booming, there is likely to be an employer contribution holiday, but when the equity market slumps, there will be a scheme deficit that needs to be removed over a recovery period agreed by the trustees. Furthermore, this call on the employer happens at a time when the employer's own share price is also likely to have fallen, a double whammy to the employer. The employer has to go to the market in an attempt to raise funds to put into his pension fund. If successful, the employer's gearing level might rise to dangerously high levels. If unsuccessful, the company itself could become insolvent.

So, the trustees face a complex trade-off between surplus risk-contribution risk and the expected level of contributions into the fund. A heavy investment in low-volatility assets, such as cash, index-linked bonds and property, will lower surplus risk and contribution risk, but raise average contributions. A heavy investment in equities will raise surplus risk and contribution risk, but lower average contributions. It is this trade-off that turns the selection of the asset allocation of the pension fund from a purely technical exercise into one that *must* take account of the attitude of the employer, as the voluntary sponsor of the pension scheme, to both surplus risk and contribution risk.

The optimal strategic asset allocation for a pension fund is given in Appendix 7B at the end of this chapter.

7.8.3   Key ALM strategies

In this section we will consider the main types of ALM strategy: immunisation, cash-flow matching horizon matching and liability-driven investing (LDI).

Immunisation

Classical immunisation (or *duration matching*) involves the construction of a bond portfolio which has an assured return over a given investment horizon (equal to that of the payout on the fund's liabilities) regardless of changes in the level of interest rates. Equivalently, it involves the construction of a bond portfolio with a present value equal to (or, even better, never less than) the present value of the liabilities regardless of changes in the level of interest rates. In short, the bond portfolio is *immunised* against interest-rate changes.

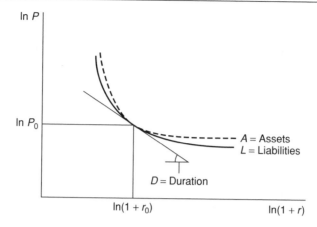

Figure 7.10   Classical immunisation in terms of present values

Figure 7.10 shows the effect of immunisation in terms of the present values of assets and liabilities. *A* is the (logarithm of the) present-value profile for the portfolio of fixed-income bonds and *L* is the (logarithm of the) present-value profile for the liabilities. When the current interest rate is r_0, the values of the bonds and the liabilities are both P_0. When interest rates rise, the present values of both the bonds and liabilities fall. The present value of the bonds falls in order to match the increase in yields when coupon payments are fixed. The present value of the liabilities falls because lower contributions need to be collected as the interest earned on them increases. Similarly, when interest rates fall, the present values of both the bonds and liabilities rise. But the important point to note is that, whatever happens to interest rates, the present value of the bonds is never less than the present value of the liabilities: indeed, except when the interest rate is r_0, the present value of the bonds always exceeds that of the liabilities. This result arises for two reasons: the bond portfolio is constructed to have the same *duration* and (at least) the same *convexity* as the liabilities. Duration measures the slope of the present-value profile at any given interest rate, while convexity measures the curvature.

Duration and convexity are first- and second-order measures of *interest-rate risk* (see Appendix C of the book). This is because they measure the interest-rate sensitivity of the present-value profile: the lower the duration and the greater the convexity, the less sensitive the bonds and liabilities are to interest-rate changes; that is, the lower the degree of interest-rate risk that they contain. As interest rates rise, the present value of the portfolio falls, but the return from reinvesting the portfolio's cash flows (coupon payments and maturing bonds) increases. A perfectly immunised portfolio exactly balances these offsetting effects; that is, exactly offsets interest-rate risk with *reinvestment risk* (i.e. the risk of reinvesting maturing funds on less favourable terms). By constructing the bond portfolio to have a duration equal to the specified investment horizon, both the return on the portfolio and the value of the portfolio will be immunised against interest-rate changes. We can demonstrate these results using a portfolio containing a single bond.

We will consider a bond with five years to maturity, a current value of £114.28, an annual coupon payment of £13.77 and a yield to maturity of 10%. The duration of the bond is given by:

$$\text{Duration} = \frac{d}{P_d} \left(\frac{(1 + rm)^{T+1} - (1 + rm) - (rm)(T)}{(rm)^2 (1 + rm)^T} \right) + \frac{B}{P_d} \frac{T}{(1 + rm)^T}$$

$$= \frac{13.77}{114.28} \left(\frac{(1.1)^6 - (1.1) - (0.1)(5)}{(0.1)^2 (1.1)^5} \right) + \frac{100}{114.28} \frac{5}{(1.1)^5}$$

$$= 4 \text{ years} \tag{7.32}$$

where d = annual coupon payment; P_d = current dirty price of the bond (i.e. clean price plus accrued interest); B = maturity value of the bond; T = years to maturity; rm = yield to maturity. As well as being a measure of a bond's interest-rate risk, duration also measures the average time it takes for a bond to return cash flows (i.e. coupon payments and principal repayment) to investors. Equation (7.32) shows that the five-year bond takes an average of four years to return cash flows to investors. It can be shown that the duration of a bond increases with the bond's maturity and decreases as a bond's coupon and yield to maturity increase.

If this bond is held for exactly the same time as its duration (i.e., four years) and then sold, its value in four years' time will be the same whatever happens to interest rates (i.e. reinvestment rates). This can be seen from Table 7.3.

So, whatever happens to reinvestment rates, the value of the bond in year 4 is always equal to £167.30. This follows because as interest rates change, the change in the income component of the value of the bond is always offset by the change in the capital component of the bond's value, where the bond is valued at its duration date (i.e. year 4). The income component is given by the sum of the first four elements of Table 7.3:

Income component = £13.77$((1 + rm)^3 + (1 + rm)^2 + (1 + rm) + 1)$.

Table 7.3 The value of the bond in year 4 as reinvestment rates change

Year	Cash flow	Reinvestment rates (%)		
		9	10	11
1	13.77	$13.77\,(1.09)^3$	$13.77\,(1.1)^3$	$13.77\,(1.11)^3$
2	13.77	$13.77\,(1.09)^2$	$13.77\,(1.1)^2$	$13.77\,(1.11)^2$
3	13.77	$13.77\,(1.09)$	$13.77\,(1.1)$	$13.77\,(1.11)$
4	13.77	13.77	13.77	13.77
5	113.77	$113.77\,(1.09)^{-1}$	$113.77\,(1.1)^{-1}$	$113.77\,(1.11)^{-1}$
Year 4 value		167.30	167.30	167.30

The capital component is given by the last element of the table:

$$\text{Capital component} = £113.77(1 + rm)^{-1}$$

If the interest rate falls from 10 to 9%, the income component falls by £0.95 and the capital component rises by £0.95. Similarly, if the interest rate rises from 10 to 11%, the income component increases by £0.93 and the capital component falls by £0.93.

If the bond was held for any other period than its duration, the value of the bond would not be independent of the interest rate. For example, had the bond been held to maturity, the year 5 value of the bond would be £182.40 (at 9%), £184.10 (at 10%), and £185.80 (at 11%).

It follows from the fact that the year 4 value of the bond is constant, regardless of interest rates, that the return from holding the bond must also be constant, regardless of interest rates, if the holding period is equal to the bond's duration. The initial cost of the bond is £114.28 and the terminal value is £167.30, therefore the rate of return over four years is:

$$\text{Rate of return} = (167.30/114.28)^{1/4} = 0.10 \ (\text{i.e.}10\%)$$

equal to the original yield to maturity on the bond. By holding a bond for its duration, it is possible to lock in the initial yield to maturity.

Now, if a pension fund has liabilities of £100 000 that arise in four years' time, the fund manager could recommend that the trustees invest in a portfolio of 598 (i.e. £100 000/£167.30) of these bonds.

The same principles apply to portfolios of bonds. The duration of a portfolio of bonds is simply the weighted sum of the durations on the individual bonds:

$$D_P = \sum_{i=1}^{N} \theta_i D_i, \qquad (7.33)$$

where D_P = duration of the portfolio with N bonds; D_i = duration of ith bond; θ_i = proportion (by value) of ith bond in the portfolio.

It is possible to construct a portfolio with a specified duration from a whole range of bonds with different durations. For example, the portfolio could be constructed from bonds with durations close to that of the liability (this is called a *focused* or *bullet portfolio*), or it could be constructed from bonds with durations distant from that of the liability (this is known as a *barbell portfolio*). Consider, for example, a liability with a duration of 10 years and a set of bonds with durations of 4, 9, 11 and 15 years, respectively. A focused portfolio would contain the 9- and 11-year duration bonds with weights of 50% each, giving a duration of:

$$0.50(9) + 0.50(11) = 10 \text{ years}$$

A barbell portfolio would consist of the 4- and 15-year duration bonds with weights of 45.5% and 54.5%, respectively, giving a duration of:

$$0.455(4) + 0.545(15) = 10 \text{ years}$$

The advantage of a barbell strategy is that a much wider range of portfolios with different durations can be constructed compared with a focused strategy. However, the disadvantage of the barbell strategy is that it has greater *immunisation risk* than the focused strategy.

Immunisation risk arises whenever there are nonparallel shifts in the yield curve. As the example illustrated in Table 7.3 showed, the immunisation effect works because there were parallel shifts in the yield curve that is, the reinvestment rate fell from 10 to 9% at each maturity. If this does not happen, then matching the duration to the investment horizon no longer guarantees immunisation. Nonparallel shifts in the yield curve will lead to the income component of the value of the portfolio changing either too much or too little compared with the change in the capital component; that is, there will be immunisation risk. This risk is reduced if the durations of the individual bonds in the immunising portfolio are close to that of the liabilities (i.e. if a focused portfolio is used). In this case, nonparallel yield-curve shifts will affect the individual bonds and the liabilities in a similar way. The effects of nonparallel yield-curve shifts are divergent if the durations of the individual bonds in the immunising

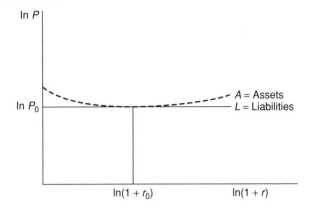

Figure 7.11 Classical immunisation in terms of investment horizon values

portfolio are distant from that of the liabilities (as in a barbell portfolio), even though the duration of the portfolio itself is the same as that of the liabilities.

While immunisation is usually regarded as a passive strategy, the portfolio will have to be periodically rebalanced and therefore an immunisation strategy has certain active elements. There are two main reasons for rebalancing: (a) changes in interest rates and (b) the passage of time. Immunisation is only effective for small changes in interest rates. As the change in interest rates increases, the effectiveness of immunisation decreases. However, the discrepancy always favours the portfolio holder, as shown in Figure 7.11. For example, if the interest rate falls from 10 to 5%, the year 4 value of the portfolio in the last example rises to £167.70, while if the interest rate rises to 20%, the value of the portfolio rises to £168.73. The passage of time will automatically reduce the duration of the portfolio. But the reduction in duration may not occur at the same rate as time decays. For example, after one year, the duration of the portfolio might decline by only 0.8 years. So, periodically, the portfolio has to be rebalanced with respect to both the new reinvestment rate and the remaining investment horizon.

So far we have considered the construction of an immunised portfolio to meet a single liability at a single future date. But a pension fund has to meet a schedule of liabilities over time. This involves the construction of a *dedicated portfolio* which is capable of meeting the schedule of liabilities from both the income and capital components and which declines to zero on the payment of the last liability. There are four ways of

Table 7.4 Cash-flow matching

Number of bonds	Coupon (%)	Maturity (years)	Cash flows (£) Year 1	Year 2	Year 3
9	11.11	3	100	100	1000
8	12.50	2	100	900	—
7	14.29	1	800	—	—
Total			1000	1000	1000

dedicating a portfolio: multi-period immunisation, cash-flow matching, horizon matching and liability-driven investing.

Multi-period immunisation

When there are multiple liabilities, it is no longer sufficient simply to match the duration of the portfolio to the average duration of the liabilities as in classical immunisation. Instead, it is necessary for each liability payment to be immunised (that is, duration-matched) individually by a portfolio payment stream. The procedure for doing this is known as *multi-period immunisation.*

Cash-flow matching

A very simple alternative to multi-period immunisation is *cash-flow matching.* This involves finding the lowest-cost portfolio that generates a pattern of cash flows that exactly matches the pattern of liability payments. The procedure for doing this is as follows. A bond (the lowest-cost if more than one is available) is purchased with the same maturity and value as the last liability payment. The coupon payments on the bond help to finance the earlier liabilities. Taking these coupon payments into account, another bond (again the lowest-cost) is purchased with the same maturity as the penultimate liability payment. Working backwards in this way, all the liabilities can be matched by payments on the bonds in the portfolio. To illustrate, annual liability payments of £1000 for three years could be met by the purchase of nine 11.11% 3-year bonds, eight 12.50% 2-year bonds and seven 14.29% 1-year bonds (see Table 7.4).[11] Where the liability cash flows are indexed to inflation, inflation-linked bonds will be used in place of fixed-income bonds.

---

[11] This is how life offices stack up the bonds they need to make annuity payments.

There are two main advantages of cash-flow matching over immunisation. First, there is no need for duration matching. Second, there is no need to rebalance the portfolio as interest rates change or with the passage of time, as there is with immunisation. Cash-flow matching is therefore a pure passive buy-and-hold strategy. However, in the real world it is unlikely that bonds exist with the appropriate maturity dates and coupon payments. To guarantee that the liabilities are paid when due in the absence of perfect matching, the cash-flow matching strategy would have to be overfunded and there will also be monitoring and rebalancing costs to take into account. An immunisation strategy might well end up meeting the required objectives at lower cost. However, the introduction of a *strips market* in UK gilts has allowed the principal and income components on bonds to be separated, and this has helped to reduce the cost of cash-flow matching.

Horizon matching

Horizon matching is a combination of cash-flow matching and immunisation. For example, a fund manager might construct a portfolio in which cash flow matches the liabilities for the next four quarters, but which is immunised for the remaining investment horizon. At the end of the four quarters the portfolio is rebalanced to cash-flow match over the subsequent four quarters, and again immunised for the remaining period. An alternative to using immunisation is to use a long-dated interest-rate swap.

Liability-driven investing

Liability-driven investing (LDI) is the latest and most sophisticated form of ALM (Scherer, 2005). The aim of LDI is to secure the expected liability cash flows at the lowest cost to the sponsor. LDI will be judged against a liability benchmark, such as 'bonds plus 3%' or 'inflation plus 6%'. However, LDI also allows the 'matching' and 'return-seeking' objectives to be separated, so that if the investment risk budget is large enough, it will allow the trustees to take advantage of additional investment opportunities, once the trustees' degree of risk tolerance has been assessed. Accordingly, two portfolios are involved in the LDI implementation, a *matching portfolio* and a *return-seeking* or *LDI-extra portfolio*. Nevertheless, risk must always be measured against the liability benchmark to ensure that the risk budget is spent in the most effective way.

Further, it should be noted that the software requirements needed to implement and manage an LDI strategy are substantial.

LDI begins with a forecast of the liability cash flows, followed by an analysis of all the sources of volatility attached to the liabilities, as identified in Sections 7.8.1 and 7.8.2 above:

- inflation risk;
- interest-rate risk;
- productivity shocks;
- longevity risk;
- contribution risk of the sponsor.

The liabilities of the pension scheme increase if inflation or productivity increase, if interest rates fall or if life expectancy improves. The liabilities themselves are at risk if the sponsor becomes insolvent. A full LDI implementation therefore seeks to hedge all these risks (unless the cost of doing so is prohibitive) and, having done that and if the risk budget and trustee risk tolerance permit, add value through, say, a market-neutral strategy, such as portable alpha. In hedging these risks, LDI recognises that the key traditional asset classes are either poor short-term hedges for liabilities (equities) or are highly illiquid (property), with the result that the asset portfolio can be volatile and unpredictable in comparison with the liability benchmark.

The key instruments used to hedge these risks are:

- index-linked bonds or inflation swaps;
- fixed-interest bonds or interest-rate or duration swaps;
- longevity bonds or mortality swaps;
- insolvency protection, e.g. letters of credit or credit default swaps.

While index-linked bonds can hedge inflation, the index-linked gilts market is too small to meet demand in full. This led to the development of inflation swaps. In exchange for a fixed annual payment (e.g. 3% p.a.) or in exchange for the return on a bond fund or a cash fund, the buyer receives the RPI inflation rate for periods of up to 40 years. The inflation swap is also frequently a zero-coupon swap, in which the offsetting inflation and interest elements are rolled up and paid at maturity. The swap can also be cash collateralised. So the matching portfolio here will contain index-linked bonds and any gaps will be filled with inflation swaps.

As we saw above, fixed-interest bonds are the classic interest-rate immunisation instrument. More recently, an interest-rate or duration swaps market has developed, in which fixed-interest payments are exchanged for floating-interest payments for periods extending up to 50 years. To reduce the costs of the swap, rather than match every future projected cash flow, the adjacent cash flows can be bucketed together. This, however, introduces an element of duration and convexity mismatch, and when the yield curve changes can lead to rebalancing, which can add to the costs of this strategy.

Longevity bonds are annuity bonds whose coupon payments are linked to a mortality index. They provide a good hedge against longevity risk and are discussed in more detail in Chapter 9. Mortality swaps swap fixed for floating mortality-linked cash flows. The fixed payments might be linked to the mortality projected by the Government Actuary's Department for, say, English and Welsh males who were aged 65 in 2006. The floating payments are linked to the realised mortality experience of this population cohort. Currently, the market in mortality-linked instruments is underdeveloped and so mortality risk is still a risk that is difficult to hedge in size. This issue is discussed in more detail in Chapter 9.

Insolvency of the corporate sponsor is a key risk faced by pension scheme trustees if the scheme is in deficit, as the scheme has, in effect, made an unsecured loan to the sponsor. This risk can be covered by some form of insolvency protection. The sponsor might well agree to this, since it will give comfort to the trustees who might otherwise demand from the sponsor a much higher annual contribution rate in order to remove the deficit more promptly. One way of providing this is a *letter of credit* (LoC) from a bank (in exchange for an annual fee to the bank), which pays out in the event of sponsor insolvency. With the LoC in place, the deficit can be removed over the period of the LoC at a rate preferred by the sponsor.

Another way of achieving this is through a *credit default swap*. The buyer pays the bank a fixed annual payment over the life of the swap. The bank makes no payment unless a specified *credit event* occurs. Credit events include a material default, insolvency or debt restructuring. If such a credit event occurs, the bank makes a payment to the pension fund and the swap terminates. The size of the payment is usually linked to the decline in a reference asset's market value or to (100 − the asset's recovery rate) following the credit event.[12]

Once the swaps or other hedging instruments are in place, there should be a near-perfect matching of future asset and liability cash flows, as in Figure 7.12.

---

[12] Some pension funds combine a long position in government bonds with a short position in a portfolio of credit default swaps. In this way they create a well-diversified portfolio in synthetic corporate bonds.

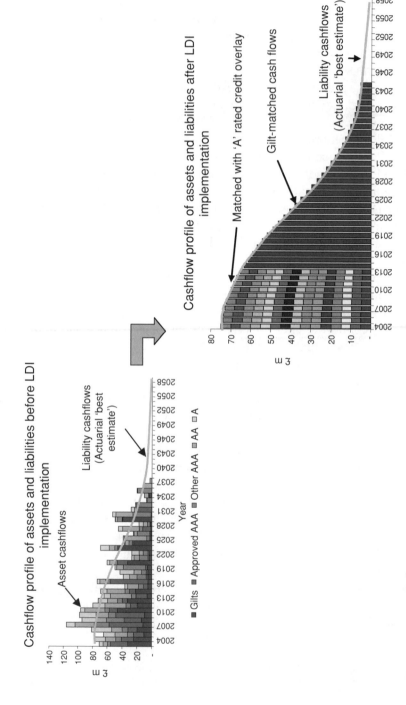

Figure 7.12 Cashflow profile of assets and liabilities before and after LDI implementation. *Source:* J. P. Morgan ALM Advisory Group

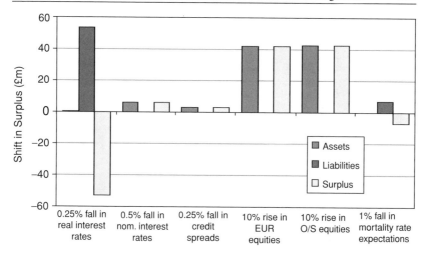

Figure 7.13   Response of the pension fund surplus to changes in key variables.
Source: Barrie and Hibbert from Munro (2005). Reproduced by permission

It is important to recognise that not all risks can be hedged. Inflation swaps, for example, can hedge the inflation risk in (7.25) above, but not the productivity shocks. Currently, wage inflation swaps are not widely available. It is also important to realise that the hedging of one set of risks might lead to other, hopefully smaller, risks having to be assumed. For example, the bonds used to hedge the liabilities might have a different rating to the liabilities and this leads to a credit spread risk. Finally, it is important to understand that some risks (e.g. equity risk) might be willingly assumed in order to generate a higher return.

Munro (2005) points out the dangers of not taking an integrated approach to LDI and attempting to hedge risk exposures in isolation. She uses the illustration of a typical £1.2bn UK pension fund, with an SAA of 69% in equities and 18% in bonds and inflation-linked liabilities with an average life of 20 years. The risks faced by this pension fund are shown in Figure 7.13. The figure shows that: a 25-basis-point fall in real interest rates creates a £50m deficit, while a 10% rise in equity markets induces a surplus of £40m. The responsiveness to nominal interest rates and credit spreads is small, while a 1% fall in mortality rate expectations results in a deficit of £7.5m.

Figure 7.14 shows how these variables influence the volatility (i.e. standard deviation) of the surplus, which stands at £17m. The most significant factor is real interest-rate risk, which accounts for £12m of

Total risk = Factors that increase risk – Factors that reduce risk

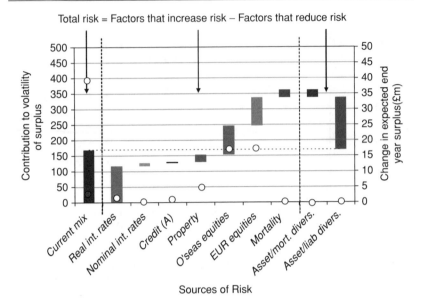

Sources of Risk

Figure 7.14   Response of the volatility of the pension fund surplus to changes in key variables.
Source: Barrie and Hibbert from Munro (2005). Reproduced by permission

the total. The other key source of volatility is equity risk, which adds an additional £8m, but this is more than offset by diversification benefits across the various liability and asset exposures.

So, although interest-rate risk is the key risk faced by this pension fund, Figure 7.15 shows that overlaying a real interest-rate swap in isolation has little effect on the overall volatility of the surplus, even though the swap is doing its proper job of hedging the real interest-rate exposure. The reason for this is that asset–liability diversification (the last element of the figure) has also been reduced by the real interest-rate swap overlay, confirming that managing one risk in isolation can have little impact on total risk in a fund which also has significant interest-rate exposure. In this case, total risk would be reduced if the interest rate swap were combined with a strategy that also dealt with the equity exposure, such as a dynamic asset-allocation strategy or a strategy that increased the overall degree of diversification, such as private equity and high-yield corporate bonds. The dynamic asset-allocation strategy will be designed to change automatically to changes in funding levels, market values of assets and interest rates. In Chapter 4, we considered two such dynamic asset allocation strategies, namely portfolio insurance and threshold (or funded status).

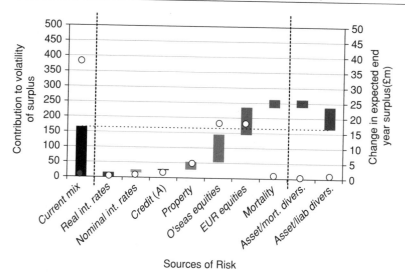

Figure 7.15   Overlaying an interest-rate swap.
Source: Barrie and Hibbert from Munro (2005). Reproduced by permission

There are two types of LDI strategy: narrow LDI and broad LDI (Dyson, 2004). *Narrow LDI* is designed to limit the volatility between assets and liabilities on a day-to-day basis. This is a sensible strategy for pension funds with large deficits. Downside risk is severely contained and this gives time for the trustees to receive gradual funding improvements from the sponsor. *Broad LDI*, while still acknowledging the objective of generating asset returns at least as high as the growth rate in liabilities, is prepared to accept greater day-to-day volatility in the surplus in exchange for increased overall asset performance. Broad LDI will also incorporate:

- a fuller integration of the scheme's objectives, the trustees' risk tolerance and the sponsor's ongoing attitude to funding;
- a more complete analysis of risk, including both surplus risk and asset risk, and also of diversification into a wide range of low-correlation asset classes;
- a more dynamic asset allocation, both strategic and tactical, with stronger profit-taking and loss-limiting disciplines.

Any active element in the LDI will also have its own benchmark. For narrow LDI and trustees with a limited risk budget or with low risk tolerance, the active element might be a portable alpha strategy. This will have a cash benchmark, and the objective will be to outperform cash. This is because the portable alpha strategy will involve holding a portfolio of alternative assets, which will have a low correlation with the market and so will generate the riskless rate as a baseline. Such a portfolio might contain high-yield debt, emerging-market debt, market-neutral hedge funds, leveraged loans and commodities. Some portable alpha strategies will add, in addition, a cash-for-bonds swap to this, and for them the objective will be to outperform bonds.

There will be a larger active element in broad LDI than narrow LDI. For broad LDI and trustees with a large risk budget and high degree of trustee risk tolerance, an *unconstrained equity strategy* with an *absolute return* benchmark (i.e. not linked to an index or peer-group benchmark) might be considered. Unconstrained mandates allow positions in assets to be taken, irrespective of the index or benchmark. Fund managers are free to exploit profit opportunities without taking account of the weighting of any asset in the index or benchmark. Frequently, this will involve taking short positions in assets that are believed to be overvalued (Clarke *et al.*, 2004). Some large pension funds have adopted the strategy of a passively managed core combined with satellite portfolios with unconstrained mandates. Unconstrained portfolios geared up using derivatives are also used as part of portable alpha strategies. Nevertheless, many unconstrained strategies are still *benchmark relative* strategies, in that, although they have no stock or sector limits applied to them, the risk and performance of the strategies are still judged against an index. This is because the index helps to define the broad, although not necessarily exclusive, set of assets used in the strategy and provides some meaningful benchmark against which to measure the fund manager's performance.

Some investment banks are beginning to offer pooled integrated LDI products, suitable for smaller pension funds. Most of the products are based around a portfolio of fixed-income bonds and interest-rate and inflation swaps, which allow a cash-flow matching strategy to be implemented that is hedged against adverse movements in interest rates and inflation. For example, State Street Global Advisers has introduced Pooled Asset Liability Matching Solutions (PALMs), which have embedded LPI (limited price indexation) swaps. PALMs deliver future projected cash flows (i.e. pensions in payment) linked to their projected LPI liabilities at the maturity of each of the LPI swaps. Another example is Barclays Global Investors, which has launched a range of pooled LDI funds in both sterling and euros.

7.9   THE MYNERS REVIEW OF INSTITUTIONAL INVESTMENT

In March 2001, the HM Treasury-sponsored review of institutional investment chaired by Paul Myners, chief executive of Gartmore, was published. Its recommendations were immediately accepted in full by the government. The report called for a new approach to institutional investment, identified a series of current distortions to effective decision-making and suggested ways of tackling them.

In introducing his report, Paul Myners said:

> Our funded pensions system, our highly-developed equity culture and the professionalisation of investment in the UK are an enviable success story. I pay tribute to the commitment and dedication of institutions and their advisers in bringing this about. Nevertheless, the industry and its decision-taking structures face forbidding challenges: an ageing population, unrecognisably different labour markets, shifting employer attitudes. In the world we now face, an ever-higher premium is likely to be placed on efficiency and flexibility. The review finds that savers' money is too often being invested in ways that do not maximize their interests. It is likely to follow too that capital is being inefficiently allocated in the economy. The review sets out a blueprint for change, to drive clearer incentives and tougher customer pressures throughout the savings and investment industry.
>
> [(Myners, 2001)]

The review identified the following main distortions:

- *pension fund trustees*, who are the very centre of the system, are being asked to take crucial investment decisions, yet many lack resources and expertise. They are often unsupported by in-house staff and are rarely paid;
- as a result, they rely heavily on a narrow group of *investment consulting* (mainly actuarial) *firms* for advice. Such firms are small in number, have a narrow range of expertise and little room for specialisation. Furthermore, their performance is not usually assessed or measured;
- a particular consequence of the present structure is that *asset allocation* (the selection of which markets, as opposed to which individual stocks, to invest in) is an under-resourced activity. This is especially unfortunate given the weight of academic evidence suggesting that these decisions can be critical determinants of investment performance;
- a lack of *clarity about objectives* at a number of levels. Fund managers are being set objectives which, taken together, appear to bear little coherent relationship to the ultimate objective of the pension fund, namely to meet its pension obligations;

- fund managers are often set objectives which give them unnecessary and artificial incentives to *herd*. So-called *peer-group* benchmarks, directly incentivising funds to copy other funds, remain common. Risk controls for active managers are increasingly set in ways which give them little choice but to cling closely to stock-market indices, making meaningful active management near-impossible;
- there is also extreme vagueness about the *timescales* over which fund managers' performance is to be judged. This is a real (but wholly unnecessary) cause of *short-termism* in fund managers' approach to investment;
- fund managers remain unnecessarily reluctant to take an *activist* stance in relation to corporate underperformance, in companies where they own substantial shareholdings, even where this would be in their clients' financial interests;
- an important cost to pension funds, namely *broking commission*, is subject to insufficient scrutiny. Clearer and more rigorous disciplines could be applied to these costs, which are substantial;
- in the life insurance industry, competition, though intense, tends not to focus directly on investment performance, and this issue needs to be tackled if stronger incentives to efficient investment decision-making in the industry are to be created.

The review makes a number of proposals to deal with these distortions. The key proposal is the introduction of a *statement of the principles of institutional investment*, incorporating a short set of clear principles of investment decision-making. The idea is modelled on the approach taken on corporate governance by the Cadbury (1992), Greenbury (1995) and Hempel (1998) codes. These principles would apply first to pension funds and subsequently to other institutional investors. As with the Cadbury code, they would not be mandatory. However, where a pension fund chose not to comply with them, it would have to explain to its members why not.

The proposed set of principles for defined benefit pension schemes is as follows:

- *Effective decision-making*. Decisions should be taken only by persons or organisations with the skills, information and resources necessary to take them effectively. Where trustees elect to take investment decisions, they must have sufficient expertise to be able to evaluate critically any advice they take. Trustees should ensure that they have sufficient in-house staff to support them in their investment responsibilities. Trustees should also be paid, unless there are specific reasons to the contrary. It is good practice for trustee boards to have an investment subcommittee to provide appropriate focus. Trustees should assess whether they have the right set of skills, both individually and collectively, and the right structures and processes to carry out their role effectively. They should draw up a forward-looking business plan.

- *Clear objectives.* Trustees should set out an overall investment objective for the fund that: (a) represents their best judgement of what is necessary to meet the fund's liabilities, given their understanding of the contributions likely to be received from employer(s) and employees; and (b) takes account of their attitude to risk, specifically their willingness to accept underperformance due to market conditions. Objectives for the overall fund should not be expressed in terms that have no relationship to the fund's liabilities, such as performance relative to other pension funds, or to a market index.
- *Focus on asset allocation.* Strategic asset allocation decisions should receive a level of attention (and, where relevant, advisory or management fees) that fully reflect the contribution they can make towards achieving the fund's investment objective. Decision-makers should consider a full range of investment opportunities, not excluding from consideration any major asset class, including private equity. Asset allocation should reflect the fund's own characteristics, not the average allocation of other funds.
- *Expert advice.* Contracts for actuarial services and investment advice should be opened to separate competition. The fund should be prepared to pay sufficient fees for each service to attract a broad range of both kinds of potential providers.
- *Explicit mandates.* Trustees should agree with both internal and external investment managers an explicit written mandate covering agreement between trustees and managers on: (a) an objective, benchmark(s) and risk parameters that together with all the other mandates are coherent with the fund's aggregate objective and risk tolerances; (b) the manager's approach in attempting to achieve the objective; and (c) clear timescale(s) of measurement and evaluation, such that the mandate will not be terminated before the expiry of the evaluation timescale other than for clear breach of the conditions of the mandate or because of significant changes in the ownership or personnel of the investment manager. The mandate should not exclude the use of any set of financial instruments without clear justification in the light of the

specific circumstances of the fund. The mandate should incorporate a management fee inclusive of any external research, information or transaction services acquired or used by the fund manager, rather than these being charged to clients.

- *Activism*. Making intervention in companies, where it is in shareholders' interests, a duty for fund managers. The mandate should incorporate the principle of the US Department of Labor Interpretative Bulletin on activism. Managers should have an explicit strategy, elucidating the circumstances in which they will intervene in a company; the approach they will use in doing so; and how they measure the effectiveness of this strategy. The US Department of Labor Interpretative Bulletin 26 on activism is as follows:
  - The fiduciary act of managing plan assets that are shares of corporate stock includes the voting of proxies appurtenant to those shares of stock;
  - The fiduciary obligations of prudence and loyalty to plan participants and beneficiaries require the responsible fiduciary to vote proxies on issues that may affect the value of the plan's investment;
  - An investment policy that contemplates activities intended to monitor or influence the management of corporations in which the plan owns stock is consistent with a fiduciary's obligations under ERISA[13] when the responsible fiduciary concludes that there is a reasonable expectation that activities by the plan alone, or together with other shareholders, are likely to enhance the value of the plan's investment, after taking into account the costs involved. Such a reasonable expectation may exist in various circumstances, for example, where plan investments in corporate stock are held as long-term investments or where a plan may not be able to easily dispose of such an investment;
  - Active monitoring and communication activities would generally concern such issues as the independence and expertise of candidates for the corporation's board of directors and assuring that the board has sufficient information to carry out its responsibility to monitor management. Other issues may include such matters as consideration of the appropriateness of executive compensation, the corporation's policy regarding mergers and acquisitions, the extent of debt financing and capitalisation, the nature of long-term business plans, the corporation's investment in training to develop

---

[13] The 1974 Employee Retirement Income Security Act.

its workforce, other workplace practices and financial and nonfinancial measures of corporate performance. Active monitoring and communication may be carried out through a variety of methods, including by means of correspondence and meetings with corporate management as well as by exercising the legal rights of a shareholder.

- *Appropriate benchmarks.*[14] Trustees should: explicitly consider, in consultation with their investment manager(s), whether the index benchmarks they have selected are appropriate – in particular, whether the construction of the index creates incentives to follow suboptimal investment strategies; if setting limits on divergence from an index, ensure that they reflect the approximations involved in index construction and selection; consider explicitly for each asset class invested, whether active or passive management would be more appropriate given the efficiency, liquidity and level of transaction costs in the market concerned; where they believe active management has the potential to achieve higher returns, set both targets and risk controls that reflect this, giving managers the freedom to pursue genuinely active strategies.

- *Performance measurement.*[15] Trustees should arrange for measurement of the performance of the fund and make formal assessment of their own procedures and decisions as trustees. They should also arrange for a formal assessment of performance and decision-making delegated to advisers and managers.

- *Transparency.* A strengthened statement of investment principles should set out: (a) who is taking which decisions and why this structure has been selected; (b) the fund's investment objective; (c) the fund's planned asset-allocation strategy, including projected investment returns on each asset class, and how the strategy has been arrived at; (d) the mandates given to all advisers and managers; and (e) the nature of the fee structures in place for all advisers and managers, and why this set of structures has been selected.

- *Regular reporting.* Trustees should publish their statement of investment principles and the results of their monitoring of advisers and managers and send them annually to members of the fund. The statement should explain why a fund has decided to depart from any of these principles.

---

[14] These are discussed in more detail in the next chapter.
[15] This is discussed in more detail in the next chapter.

The following principles are proposed for defined contribution schemes:

- when selecting funds to offer as options to scheme members, trustees should consider the investment objectives, expected returns, risks and other relevant characteristics of each such fund;
- where a fund is offering a default option to members through a customised combination of funds, trustees should ensure that an objective is set for the option, including expected risks and returns;
- schemes should, as a matter of best practice, consider a full range of investment opportunities, including less liquid and more volatile assets. In particular, investment trusts should be considered as a means of investing in private equity;
- the Government should keep under close review the levels of employer and employee contributions to defined contribution pensions, and the implications for retirement incomes.

In commenting on the proposed set of principles, Paul Myners said: 'The principles may seem little more than common sense. In a way they are – yet they certainly do not describe the status quo. Following them would require substantial change in decision-making behaviour and structures.'

Fund managers responded to the Myners Report in March 2002 by agreeing to reveal the full costs of managing pension fund assets. The Investment Management Association (IMA) issued a pension fund disclosure code concerning new 6-monthly reports to trustees. The code requires fund managers to provide two types of information: a general statement and a detailed breakdown of the £12bn a year fund management costs into fund manager fees, custody fees, auditing fees, dealing costs, brokerage commissions and stamp duty. The National Association of Pension Funds (NAPF) published new guides for trustees of defined benefit and defined contribution pension schemes in March and May 2002, respectively. They were designed to simplify the complex language surrounding pension scheme investment and provide help for trustees in making sure their investment processes comply with Myners' recommendations.

The 2004 Pensions Act formalised many of the proposals contained in the Myners Report, such as the requirement for trustees to publish a statement of funding principles.

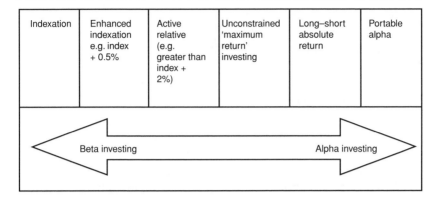

| Indexation | Enhanced indexation e.g. index + 0.5% | Active relative (e.g. greater than index + 2%) | Unconstrained 'maximum return' investing | Long–short absolute return | Portable alpha |

Beta investing   Alpha investing

Figure 7.16   The choices available to trustees. *Source*: Martin Currie Investment Management, *Pensions Week*, 8 May 2006

7.10   CONCLUSIONS

Trustees have a responsibility to both the sponsor of an occupational pension scheme and to its members, especially if the scheme is defined benefit. The members want to know that the pension promise is secure, while the sponsor wants to deliver pensions at the lowest cost. The trustees of young, immature pension schemes might decide to have the pension scheme actively managed; if they are more risk averse, they might choose passive investment. The trustees of mature pension schemes, on the other hand, are more likely to be concerned about the size and volatility of the pension fund surplus (or deficit). In this case, pension fund managers will wish to manage both the surplus and surplus risk using one of the techniques of asset–liability management, such as liability-driven investing. Trustees therefore have the spectrum of choices shown in Figure 7.16.

QUESTIONS

1. What are the advantages and disadvantages of funding over pay-as-you-go?
2. What does a pension actuary do?
3. What is the purpose of an actuarial valuation?
4. What is the difference between an internally and an externally funded scheme?
5. What is the difference between an insured and an uninsured scheme?
6. What is the role of trustees?

7. What are the functions of a fund manager?
8. What is the difference between pooled and segregated funds?
9. What is the difference between balanced and segregated fund management?
10. What is meant by the strategic asset allocation?
11. What is meant by security selection?
12. What is an overlay manager?
13. What is meant by passive portfolio management?
14. What is meant by active portfolio management?
15. What is meant by asset–liability management?
16. What is the difference between gross and net investors?
17. What are lifestyle funds?
18. What is systematic risk?
19. Why might a UK pension fund with liabilities denominated in sterling consider investing abroad?
20. Explain how a gross investor's expected utility depends on the expected return and risk penalty.
21. How is the risk penalty defined?
22. What is a portfolio opportunity set?
23. What are mean–variance indifference curves?
24. What does the degree of risk tolerance measure?
25. What does investment risk budgeting involve?
26. What is benchmark risk?
27. What is tracking error?
28. What is the market portfolio?
29. What is the capital-market line?
30. What are the main types of indexing?
31. What are the five activities of active share-fund management?
32. What is meant by beta?
33. What is the capital asset pricing model?
34. What is the security-market line?
35. What is the market risk premium?
36. What does a security's risk premium depend on?
37. How can total risk be decomposed? Why is this decomposition useful?
38. What is meant by alpha? Why is it useful?
39. What is meant by portable alpha?
40. What do active bond-fund managers attempt to do?
41. What is the bond-market line?

42. What is the difference between anomaly switches and policy switches?
43. What is core–satellite portfolio management? What is another name for it?
44. How does a guaranteed equity fund operate?
45. Pension liabilities depend on six factors. What are they?
46. How is the surplus defined?
47. What is surplus risk? How is it measured?
48. Asset–liability management involves minimising a loss function. What is the loss function and how is it minimised?
49. How is surplus risk managed?
50. How can surplus risk be reduced to zero?
51. What determines the volatility of the liabilities?
52. There is disagreement over the choice of discount rate for pension liabilities. Explain the nature of this disagreement.
53. What is contribution risk? How is it managed?
54. What are the key ALM strategies?
55. What is immunisation? How does it work?
56. What is cash-flow matching?
57. What is horizon matching?
58. What is LDI? How is it implemented?
59. What are the two portfolios needed for an LDI implementation?
60. What are the key instruments in the LDI matching portfolio?
61. What is the difference between narrow and broad LDI?
62. What is meant by an unconstrained equity strategy?
63. What is an absolute return benchmark?
64. In his review of institutional investment in the UK, what were the main distortions that Paul Myners identified?
65. What were the key recommendations of the Myners Report?

APPENDIX 7A: INVESTMENT-OBJECTIVES QUESTIONNAIRE

1. How would you describe your outlook for the economy over the next five years?
   a. Very positive
   b. Somewhat positive
   c. Neither positive nor negative

      d. Somewhat negative

      e. Very negative

      f. I am undecided

2. How do you feel about investing in common stocks in general?

      a. I think stocks are very attractive and should occupy a dominant position in our portfolio.

      b. Common stocks should have a place in our investment portfolio.

      c. I think stocks are relatively risky and their use should be limited.

      d. I think stocks should be used very sparingly, if at all.

3. How would you generally categorise your investment objectives?

      a. Growth – maximum growth of capital with little or no income considerations.

      b. Growth with income – primary emphasis on capital growth of the fund with some focus on income.

      c. Income.

4. Does the portfolio have current income objectives (interest plus dividends)?

      a. No income objective

      b. 3%

      c. 4%

      d. 5%

      e. 6%

      f. 7%

      g. Other. If other, please describe.

5. Some plans have a need for growing investment 'income' (i.e. dividends and interest) over time. Do the plan's assets have a need for growth in 'income'?

      (Yes/No)

6. If your investment manager is very positive on the outlook for common stocks, what is the maximum percentage of your portfolio you would allow to be invested in common stocks?

      a. 0%

      b. 20%

      c. 40%

      d. 60%

      e. 80%

      f. 100%

      In bonds?

      a. 0%

      b. 20%

c. 40%

d. 60%

e. 80%

f. 100%

7. If your investment manager is very negative on the outlook for common stocks, what is the minimum percentage of your portfolio you would allow to be invested in common stocks?

a. 0%

b. 20%

c. 40%

d. 60%

e. 80%

f. 100%

In bonds?

a. 0%

b. 20%

c. 40%

d. 60%

e. 80%

f. 100%

8. (i) What average annual 'absolute' rate of return (as opposed to return 'relative' to a market index) do you consider to be the investment objective for a fund, on a long-term basis?

   a. 12–14% p.a.

   b. 10–11.9% p.a.

   c. 8–9.9% p.a.

   d. 6–7.9% p.a.

   e. Other.

(ii) An increase in investment return is usually associated with an increase in the acceptable level of fluctuation of the portfolio value cycle to market cycle. Would you be willing to accept a wider possible range of fluctuation in an attempt to achieve a higher return?

   (Yes/No)

9. If a target rate of return over and above the inflation rate has been established, please specify.

a. Not determined

b. Keep pace with inflation

c. 1% above inflation

d. 2% above inflation

   e. 3% above inflation

   f. 4–5% above inflation

   g. Other. If other, please describe.

10. Plan 'risk' can be defined in different ways. Please indicate below the single item that best describes how you tend to view risk.

   a. The possibility of not meeting the actuarial assumption (if a pension plan).

   b. The possibility of not achieving an established larger rate of return.

   c. Not at least equalling the rate of inflation.

   d. High degree of fluctuation in the value of the portfolio within a market cycle.

   e. The chance of a great loss in the value of an individual security regardless of how well the overall portfolio might perform.

   f. Other. If other, please specify.

11. The primary emphasis in examining the investment performance for the account should be on:

   a. Comparing actual returns to an 'absolute' percentage return-target.

   b. 'Relative' comparison. That is, comparing the actual account returns to various market indices.

   c. Using both 'absolute' and 'relative' measures.

   d. I have no real preferences.

12. Bond interest varies with quality and length of maturity of the bond. What bond quality do you feel is appropriate for the portfolio?

   a. All AAA rated

   b. None lower than AA

   c. None lower than A

   d. None lower than BAA

13. The time period used in evaluating investment return has a significant impact on the probability of realising the stated return objective. The longer used, the better chance that up and down market cycles will average out to your desired return. What investment time horizon seems most appropriate for the account?

   a. Ten years or more

   b. Five years

   c. Three years

   d. A complete market cycle

   e. I do not know

14. What regularity of direct contact with your adviser is preferable?
Meetings:
a. Annually
b. Semiannually
c. Quarterly
d. When deemed necessary by either the investment manager or client.
Written or oral communication:
a. Quarterly
b. More frequently than quarterly
c. When deemed necessary by investment manager or client.
15. Is geographic location of your manager important to you? (Yes/No) Comment.
16. Would you consider investing a portion of the assets in tangible vehicles?
(Yes/No) If yes, which of the following?
a. Real estate
b. Oil and gas
c. Precious metals
d. Other
17. Would you be inclined to consider the use of put and call option strategies to increase portfolio income and/or reduce volatility?
(Yes/No)

(*Source*: Shearson Lehman Brothers 1990.)

APPENDIX 7B: DERIVATION OF THE OPTIMAL CONTRIBUTION RATE AND ASSET ALLOCATION IN A DEFINED BENEFIT PENSION FUND

The objective is to choose the contribution rate to ensure that the surplus is zero at the end of a T-year control period and to choose the strategic asset allocation to ensure that the loss function (Ψ) is minimised:

$$\min_{q(t)} \Psi = \sigma_A^2(t+1) + \sigma_L^2(t+1) - 2\sigma_{AL}(t+1) + \lambda \left(c(t) - \bar{c}(t)\right)^2$$

$$\text{subject to} \quad E(A(t+1)) + c(t) = L(t+1)$$

where

$A(t) = \iota'q(t) =$ value of assets at time t, where $q(t)$ is a vector of the values of the N assets in the pension fund and ι is the unity (or summation) vector

$E(A(t + 1)) =$ expected value of assets at time $t + 1$

$c(t) = [L(t + 1) - A(t + 1)] =$ required contributions if no control period

$\qquad = \dfrac{[L(t + 1) - A(t + 1)]\,r_P}{1 - (1 + r_P)^{-T}} =$ required contributions on the basis of a T-year control period and a discount rate of r_P which is defined below

$\bar{c}(t) =$ normal contributions

$\lambda =$ weight in the loss function of contribution risk relative to surplus risk

Normal contributions are calculated by the actuary on the basis of a notional portfolio $(\bar{A}(t))$ that fully funds liabilities:

$$\bar{A}(t) = L(t)$$

Suppose the actuarial returns assumed on the assets are $\bar{r}$. The actuarial return assumed on the notional portfolio is therefore:

$$\bar{r}_P = \bar{\theta}'\bar{r}$$

where $\bar{\theta}$ are the portfolio weights assumed by the actuary for the notional fund.

The increase in the value of the notional portfolio over time is:

$$\begin{aligned} \Delta \bar{A}(t) &= \bar{A}(t + 1) - \bar{A}(t) \\ &= \bar{r}_P \bar{A}(t) \\ &= \bar{r}_P L(t) \end{aligned}$$

since this must also equal the increase in the value of the liabilities.

Liabilities are calculated as (assuming a final salary scheme with a sixtieths accrual scale):

$$L(t) = D(t,T)\ddot{a}(T)\left(\frac{t - t_0}{60}\right)W(T)$$

where

$$D(t,T) = \frac{1}{(1+r_{\mathrm{P}})^{T-t}} = \text{discount factor}$$

t_0 = time of joining scheme

T = time of retirement

$W(T)$ = projected final salary

$\ddot{a}(T)$ = annuity factor at retirement.

The increase in the value of the liabilities is:

$$\Delta L(t) = L(t+1) - L(t)$$
$$= \left[\frac{1}{(1+\bar{r}_{\mathrm{P}})^{T-t-1}} \left(\frac{t+1-t_0}{60} \right) - \frac{1}{(1+\bar{r}_{\mathrm{P}})^{T-t}} \left(\frac{t-t_0}{60} \right) \right]$$
$$\times \ddot{a}(T)W(T).$$

This is funded from the increase in assets and normal contributions $\bar{c}(t)$, so normal contributions are given by:

$$\bar{c}(t) = \Delta L(t) - \Delta \bar{A}(t)$$
$$= \kappa W(t), \text{ say, as a proportion } \kappa \text{ of current earnings.}$$

We make the following definitions:

$$E(A(t+1)) = (\iota + \bar{r})'\boldsymbol{q}(t)$$
$$\sigma_{\mathrm{A}}^2(t+1) = \boldsymbol{q}(t)'\Sigma\boldsymbol{q}(t),$$

where Σ = covariance matrix of asset returns

$$L(t+1) = D(t+1, T)\ddot{a}(T) \left(\frac{t+1-t_0}{60} \right) W(T)$$

$$D(t+1,T) = \frac{1}{(1+r_{\mathrm{P}})^{T-(t+1)}}$$

$$\ddot{a}(T) = \frac{_1p_T}{1+r} + \frac{_2p_T}{(1+r)^2} + \cdots$$

where $_jp_T$ = survival probabilities and r is the discount rate for the annuity factor

$$W(T) = (1 + g)^{T-t} W(t)$$
$$\simeq \left[(1 + \bar{g})^{T-t} + (T - t)(1 + \bar{g})^{T-(t+1)}(g - \bar{g}) \right] W(t)$$

where g = actual average growth rate in earnings and
$\bar{g}$ = expected growth rate in earnings

$$\sigma_L^2(t + 1) = D(t + 1, T)^2 \ddot{a}(T)^2 \left(\frac{t + 1 - t_0}{60} \right)^2 (T - t)^2$$
$$\times (1 + \bar{g})^{2(T-(t+1))} \sigma_g^2 W(t)^2$$
$$= H(t)^2 \sigma_g^2 W(t)^2, \text{ say}$$

$$\sigma_{AL}(t + 1) = q(t)' \rho D(t + 1, T) \ddot{a}(T) \left(\frac{t + 1 - t_0}{60} \right) (T - t)$$
$$\times (1 + \bar{g})^{T-(t+1)} W(t)$$
$$= q(t)' \rho H(t) W(t)$$

where ρ = vector of covariances between asset returns and earnings growth

The pension fund's objective now becomes:

$$\operatorname*{Min}_{q(t)} \Psi = \sigma_A^2(t + 1) + \sigma_L^2(t + 1) - 2\sigma_{AL}(t + 1)$$
$$+ \lambda \left(L(t + 1) - (\iota + \bar{r})' q(t) - \kappa W(t) \right)^2$$

where the constraint has been incorporated into the objective function. The first-order conditions for a minimum are:

$$2\Sigma q(t) - 2H(t) W(t) \rho$$
$$- 2\lambda \left(L(t + 1) - (\iota + \bar{r})' q(t) - \kappa W(t) \right) (\iota + \bar{r})$$
$$= \underline{0}$$

$\Rightarrow$

$$\Sigma q(t) + \lambda (\iota + \bar{r})' q(t)(\iota + \bar{r})$$
$$= H(t) W(t) \rho + \lambda \left(L(t + 1) - \kappa W(t) \right)(\iota + \bar{r})$$
$$= z(t), \text{ say}$$

$\Rightarrow \quad [\Sigma + \lambda \Omega(t)] \, q(t) = z(t)$

$\Rightarrow \quad q(t) = [\Sigma + \lambda \Omega(t)]^{-1} z(t)$

where, in the case of three assets:

$$(\iota + \bar{r})' q(t)(\iota + \bar{r})$$

$$= ((1 + \bar{r}_1)(1 + \bar{r}_2)(1 + \bar{r}_3)) \begin{pmatrix} q_1 \\ q_2 \\ q_3 \end{pmatrix} \begin{pmatrix} 1 + \bar{r}_1 \\ 1 + \bar{r}_2 \\ 1 + \bar{r}_3 \end{pmatrix}$$

$$= \begin{bmatrix} (1+\bar{r}_1)^2 q_1 + (1+\bar{r}_1)(1+\bar{r}_2)q_2 + (1+\bar{r}_1)(1+\bar{r}_3)q_3 \\ \vdots \end{bmatrix}$$

$$= \begin{bmatrix} (1+\bar{r}_1)^2 & (1+\bar{r}_1)(1+\bar{r}_2) & (1+\bar{r}_1)(1+\bar{r}_3) \\ \vdots & \vdots & \vdots \end{bmatrix} \begin{pmatrix} q_1 \\ q_2 \\ q_3 \end{pmatrix}$$

$$\equiv \Omega(t)\boldsymbol{q}(t).$$

REFERENCES

Blake, D. (2000) *Financial Market Analysis*, John Wiley & Sons Ltd, Chichester.

Blake, D. (2003) UK pension fund management after Myners: the hunt for correlation begins. *Journal of Asset Management*, **4**, 32–72

Boardman, R. (2001) Budgeting for risk. *Pensions Week*, 27 August.

Cadbury, A. (1992) *Report of the Committee on the Financial Aspects of Corporate Governance*, Gee Publishing, London.

Campbell, J. and Viceira, L. (2002) *Strategic Asset Allocation: Portfolio Choice for Long-term Investors*, Oxford University Press, Oxford.

Clarke, R., de Silva, H. and Sapra, S. (2004) Toward more efficient portfolios: relaxing the long-only constraint. *Journal of Portfolio Management*, **31** (Fall), 54–63.

Davies, E. P. (1991) International diversification of institutional investors. *Journal of International Securities Markets* (Summer), 143–167.

Dyson, A. (2004) A practical framework for liability-led investing, in *Pensions World Supplement – Understanding Liability-Led Investment*, May.

Fabozzi, F. and Konishi, A. (Eds) (1991) *Asset–Liability Management*, Probus, Chicago.

Greenbury, R. (1995) *Directors' Remuneration Report of a Study Group Chaired by Sir Richard Greenbury*, Gee Publishing, London.

Haberman, S. and Sung, J-H. (1994) Dynamic approaches to pension funding. *Insurance: Mathematics and Economics*, **15**, 151–162.

Hempel, R. (1998) *Committee on Corporate Governance – Final Report*, Gee Publishing, London.

Munro, J. (2005) *Making Sense of Liability Driven Investing*, AXA Investment Managers, June 16.

Myners, P. (2001) *Institutional Investment in the United Kingdom: A Review,* HM Treasury, London, March.

Pensions Management Special Supplement (2004), *Liability-Led Investing*, December 2004.

Scherer, B. (2005) *Liability Hedging and Portfolio Choice*, Risk Books, London.

Stanyer, P. (1999) Balancing your budget, *Pensions Management*, September.

Thornton, P.N. and Wilson, A.F. (1992) A realistic approach to pension funding. *Journal of the Institute of Actuaries*, **119**, 229–312.

Wolanski, H. (1980) Management and monitoring of pension funds investment, in Philip, A. (Ed.) *Pension Funds and their Advisers*, AP Financial Registers, London.

8

Pension Fund Performance Measurement and Attribution

At the end of each year (sometimes at the end of each quarter) the pension fund manager's performance is going to be measured. Sometimes this function is performed by the fund manager himself or herself; more generally it is performed by an independent performance measurement service. The questions that are important for assessing how well a fund manager performs are:

- How do we measure the *ex post* returns on his or her portfolio?
- How do we measure the risk-adjusted returns on his or her portfolio?
- How do we assess these risk-adjusted returns in the light of the objectives set for the fund manager?

To answer these questions we need to examine returns, risks and benchmarks of comparison. We can then analyse performance attribution, in both actively managed funds and asset–liability managed funds; passively managed funds ought to replicate closely the return on the set benchmark portfolio. We examine the recent realised investment performance generated by both DC and DB pension funds in the UK. We end with a discussion of performance-related fund management fees and the frequency with which fund managers should have their performance assessed.

8.1 *EX POST* RETURNS

There are two ways in which *ex post* returns on the fund can be measured: *time-weighted rates of return* (or geometric means) and *money-weighted* (or *value-weighted*) *rates of return* (or internal rates of return). The simplest method is the money-weighted rate of return, but the preferred method is the time-weighted rate of return, since this controls for cash inflows and outflows which are beyond the control of the fund manager. However, the time-weighted rate of return has the disadvantage of requiring the fund to be valued every time there is a cash flow.

Consider the following, showing the value of, and cash flow from, a fund over the course of a year:

Time	0	6 months	1 year
Value of fund	V_0	V_1	V_2
Cash flow	—	CF	—

The money-weighted rate of return (r) is the solution to (assuming compound interest):

$$V_2 = V_0(1+r) + CF(1+r)^{\frac{1}{2}} \tag{8.1}$$

or to (assuming simple interest):

$$V_2 = V_0(1+r) + CF\left(1 + \tfrac{1}{2}r\right) \tag{8.2}$$

in the latter case, this implies that:

$$\text{Money-weighted rate of return} = \frac{V_2 - (V_0 + CF)}{V_0 + \tfrac{1}{2}CF} \tag{8.3}$$

The time-weighted rate of return is defined as:

$$\text{Time-weighted rate of return} = \frac{V_1}{V_0}\frac{V_2}{V_1 + CF} - 1. \tag{8.4}$$

If the semi-annual rate of return on the portfolio equals r_1 for the first six months and r_2 for the second six months, then we have:

$$V_1 = V_0(1+r_1) \tag{8.5}$$

and

$$V_2 = (V_1 + CF)(1+r_2) \tag{8.6}$$
$$= (V_0(1+r_1) + CF)(1+r_2)$$

Substituting (8.5) and (8.6) into (8.4) gives:

Time-weighted rate of return
$$= \frac{V_0(1+r_1)}{V_0}\left(\frac{(V_0(1+r_1)+CF)(1+r_2)}{V_0(1+r_1)+CF}\right) - 1$$
$$= (1+r_1)(1+r_2) - 1 \tag{8.7}$$

which is a chain-linking of returns between cash flows.

Table 8.1 Example of time-weighted rate of return

Time	0	6 months	1 year
Share-price index	(1.0)	(0.8)	(1.2)
Cash flow into Fund A	20	—	—
Value of Fund A including cash flow	120	96	144
Cash flow into Fund B	10	10	—
Value of Fund B including cash flow	110	98	147

It is clear that the time-weighted rate of return reflects accurately the rate of return realised on the portfolio. The cash flow could be an inflow (CF > 0) such as a dividend payment or a contribution payment from the employer, or an outflow (CF < 0) such as a pension payout. Both inflows and outflows are beyond the control of the fund manager and their effects should be excluded from influencing the performance of the fund.

We can illustrate this using the example in Table 8.1, where the initial value of two funds is £100. Both funds receive £20 during the year, but the timing of the cash flows is different: Fund B receives cash at a time when shares are relatively cheap.

The money-weighted rate of return can be calculated as follows:

$$\text{Money-weighted rate of return on Fund A} = \frac{V_2 - (V_0 + CF_1)}{(V_0 + CF_1)}$$

$$= \frac{144 - 120}{120}$$

$$= 0.20 \quad (20\%)$$

$$\text{Money-weighted rate of return on Fund B} = \frac{V_2 - (V_0 + CF_1 + CF_2)}{V_0 + CF_1 + \frac{1}{2}CF_2}$$

$$= \frac{147 - 120}{115}$$

$$= 0.2348 \quad (23.48\%).$$

So, the Fund B manager is performing better than the Fund A manager according to the money-weighted rate of return measure.

The time-weighted rate of return is calculated as follows:

$$\text{Time-weighted rate of return on Fund A} = \frac{V_1}{(V_0 + CF_1)} \frac{V_2}{V_1} - 1$$

$$= \frac{96}{120} \frac{144}{96} - 1$$

$$= 0.20 \ (20\%)$$

$$\text{Time-weighted rate of return on Fund B} = \frac{V_1}{(V_0 + CF_1)} \frac{V_2}{(V_1 + CF_2)} - 1$$

$$= \frac{88}{110} \frac{147}{98} - 1$$

$$= 0.20 \ (20\%).$$

The time-weighted rate of return of 20% is the same in both cases. This reflects the true performance of both funds over the period, since they were both invested in the same shares. (Note that the money-weighted and time-weighted rates of return are the same when there is no intermediate cash flow, as in the case of Fund A.)

8.2   BENCHMARKS OF COMPARISON FOR ACTIVELY MANAGED FUNDS

In order to assess how well an active pension fund manager is performing, we need one or more benchmarks of comparison. Once we have determined appropriate benchmarks, we can then compare whether the fund manager outperformed, matched or underperformed the benchmarks on a risk-adjusted basis.

The two main types of benchmarks used in the UK are *external* asset-class benchmarks and *peer-group* benchmarks. When external performance measurement began in the early 1970s, most pension funds selected customised benchmarks (which involved tailoring the weights of the external benchmarks to the specific circumstances of the fund). Shortly after, curiosity about how other funds were performing led to the introduction of peer-group benchmarks. More recently, following the recognition that the objectives of different pension funds differ widely, there has been a return to customised benchmarks. Increasingly, however, a third benchmark–one linked to the growth rate in liabilities–is being used.

Table 8.2   Example of index construction

Day	Share number	Price (£)	Number of shares (millions)	Capitalisation (£m.)
1	1	0.65	50	32.50
	2	0.82	50	41.00
	3	1.15	75	86.25
	4	0.25	100	25.00
Total		**2.87**		**184.75**
2	1	0.70	50	35.00
	2	0.78	50	39.00
	3	1.23	75	92.25
	4	0.21	100	21.00
Total		**2.92**		**187.25**

An appropriate benchmark is one that is consistent with the preferences of the fund's trustees and the fund's tax status. For example, a different benchmark is appropriate if the fund is a *gross fund* (and does not pay income or capital gains tax, as with a pension fund) than if it is a *net fund* (and so does pay income and capital gains tax, such as the fund of a general insurance company). Similarly, the general market index will not be appropriate as a benchmark if the trustees have a preference for high-income securities and an aversion to shares in rival companies or, for moral reasons, the shares in (for example) tobacco companies. Yet again, the FT-A All Share Index would not be an appropriate benchmark if half the securities were held overseas. There will, therefore, be different benchmarks for different funds and for different fund managers. For example, consistent with the asset-allocation decision, there will be a share benchmark for the share-fund manager and a bond benchmark for the bond-fund manager.

So the benchmark will be an index of one kind or another. It is important to understand the structure of the relevant index. We can distinguish between *absolute* and *relative* indices, between *price-weighted* and *value-weighted* indices, and between *arithmetic* and *geometric* indices. These can be explained using Table 8.2, which contains the input data for an index containing four shares.

If day 1 is the base date, then the base price-weighted absolute index is given by:

$$\text{Index} = \frac{2.87}{0.0287} = 100$$

and the base value-weighted absolute index is given by:

$$\text{Index} = \frac{184.75}{1.8475} = 100$$

On day 2, the *price-weighted absolute index* is:

$$\text{Index} = \frac{2.92}{0.0287} = 101.74$$

while the *value-weighted absolute index* is:

$$\text{Index} = \frac{187.25}{1.8475} = 101.35$$

The day 2-to-day 1 price-relatives for the four shares are given by:

Share number	Price-relative
1	1.0769 (0.70/0.65)
2	0.9512 (0.78/0.82)
3	1.0696 (1.23/1.15)
4	0.8400 (0.21/0.25)

The *equal-weight arithmetic relative index* for day 2 is:

$$\text{Index} = \frac{1.0769 + 0.9512 + 1.0696 + 0.8400}{4} \times 100 = 98.44.$$

The *equal-weight geometric relative index* for day 2 is

$$\text{Index} = [(1.0769)(0.9512)(1.0696)(0.8400)]^{1/4} \times 100 = 97.95.$$

So, the four indices give quite different results even across just one day's price movements, with two rising and two actually falling. So it is important that the returns on the portfolio are constructed in the same way as the benchmark index. For example, the FT-A All Share and the FTSE 100 indices are value-weighted arithmetic absolute, whereas the FT30 index and the FT Government Securities index are equal-weight geometric relative. It is also important to recognise that the only type of index that the fund manager would be able to replicate the return on would be a value-weighted arithmetic absolute index, since this is how a real portfolio of assets is constructed. A real portfolio consists of a fixed number of securities, and the value of the portfolio is found by multiplying the number of each security held (e.g. 1000 ABC shares) by the price of the security (e.g. £3.48) and then summing over the total number of securities held. As can be seen, a value-weighted arithmetic absolute index is constructed in the same way and is the only index constructed in this way.

As mentioned above, not only is a pension fund manager's performance compared with the return on a market index, it is also often compared relative to the performance of other pension fund managers. This provides a second benchmark of comparison. Pension fund managers are generally ranked in order of decreasing returns, and the objective of every fund manager is to be in the first *quartile* of performance, and certainly to be above the *median* fund. Of course, only half the funds can beat the median fund!

There is often a third benchmark against which the performance of a pension fund manager is compared. This is an *absolute return* benchmark (i.e. not linked to an index or peer-group benchmark), such as the rate of inflation in the retail price index. So, another test is whether the fund manager can generate a portfolio return sufficient to beat inflation and therefore provide a positive real return to the fund. An even more stringent benchmark is the rate of wage inflation, as measured by increases in the index of national average earnings; this is because wage inflation is typically two percentage points higher than price inflation, reflecting the fact that real wages in the UK grow at about 2% per annum. This performance measure is consistent with a pension fund's liabilities, which, in the case of final-salary schemes, increase on average at the rate of wage inflation.

8.3 RISK-ADJUSTED MEASURES OF PORTFOLIO PERFORMANCE FOR ACTIVELY MANAGED FUNDS

The *ex post* rate of return on a fund has to be adjusted for the fund's exposure to risk. The appropriate measure of risk depends on whether the beneficiaries of the fund's investments have other well-diversified investments or whether this is their only set of investments. In the first case, the *systematic risk* (beta) of the fund is the best measure of risk. In the second case, the *total risk* (standard deviation) of the fund is best. If the portfolio is a bond portfolio, then the appropriate measure of market risk is *relative duration*.

8.3.1   Performance measures based on risk-adjusted excess returns

There are three performance measures based on risk-adjusted excess returns (i.e. returns in excess of the riskless rate of interest), each one distinguished by the risk measure used.

The first is the *excess return* to *volatility measure*, also known as the *Sharpe ratio* (Sharpe, 1966). This uses the total risk measure:

$$\text{Excess return to volatility (Sharpe)} = \frac{r_P - r_f}{\sigma_P} \quad (8.8)$$

where r_P = average return on the portfolio (usually geometric mean) over an interval (typically the last twenty quarters); σ_P = total risk as measured by the standard deviation of the return on the portfolio (calculated over the last twenty quarters): note, the geometric mean is used to construct the average return, but the arithmetic mean must be used to construct the standard deviation; r_f = average risk-free return (usually geometric mean) over the same interval. The Sharpe ratio is illustrated in Figure 8.1. *BM* is the benchmark portfolio (it could be the market portfolio). *A*, *B*, *C* and *D* are four portfolios. Portfolios *A* and *B* beat the benchmark on a risk-adjusted basis, while portfolios *C* and *D* underperform the market. Portfolio *A* is the best (i.e. is ranked highest according to the Sharpe ratio) and Portfolio *D* is the worst. The ranking of the portfolios on a risk-adjusted basis is *A, B, C, D*; but the ranking of the portfolios without adjusting for risk is *B, C, A, D*. This shows the

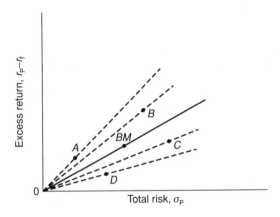

Figure 8.1   Excess return to volatility

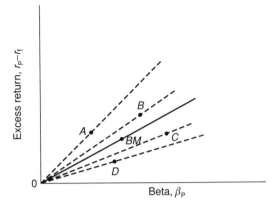

Figure 8.2   Excess return to beta

importance of adjusting for risk. Portfolio C, for example, was exposed to substantial risk during the year, but did not generate sufficient returns to compensate for that exposure.

The second performance measure is the *excess return to beta measure*, also known as the *Treynor ratio* (Treynor, 1965). This uses the systematic risk measure:

$$\text{Excess return to beta (Treynor)} = \frac{r_P - r_f}{\beta_P} \qquad (8.9)$$

where β_P = beta of the portfolio (calculated over the last twenty quarters). This is illustrated in Figure 8.2.

The third is the excess return to relative duration measure, a measure suitable for bond portfolios:

$$\text{Excess return to relative duration} = \frac{r_P - r_f}{D_P/D_M} \qquad (8.10)$$

where D_P/D_M = duration of bond portfolio relative to the duration of the market. This is illustrated in Figure 8.3.

How should these measures be interpreted? Let us compare the Sharpe and Treynor ratios. Suppose that the Sharpe and Treynor ratios for an individual fund and for the market are as follows:

	Individual fund	Market
Sharpe	1.3	1.6
Treynor	5.0	4.0

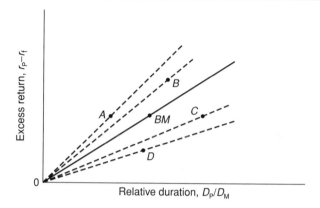

Figure 8.3   Excess return to relative duration

Comparing Treynor ratios, the individual fund manager is good at market timing, but, comparing Sharpe ratios, is less good at security selection: he has taken on a lot of specific risk (which could have been diversified away) and has not been adequately rewarded for doing so.

8.3.2   Performance measures based on alpha

As an alternative to ranking portfolios according to their risk-adjusted returns in excess of the riskless rate, it is possible to rank portfolios according to their alpha values. Again, three different performance measures are available depending on the risk measure used.

If the risk measure is total risk, the appropriate alpha value is defined with respect to the capital-market line:

$$\bar{r}_P = r_f + \left(\frac{\bar{r}_M - r_f}{\sigma_M} \right) \sigma_P \tag{8.11}$$

where $\bar{r}_P$ = expected return on the portfolio; $\bar{r}_M$ = expected return on the market; σ_M = standard deviation of the market. The corresponding alpha is:

$$\alpha_\sigma = r_P - \bar{r}_P \tag{8.12}$$

This is shown in Figure 8.4. The best-performing fund is the one with the largest alpha.

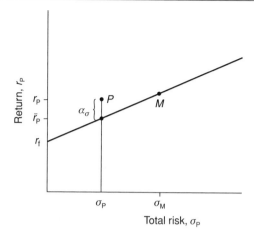

Figure 8.4 Alpha defined on volatility

If the risk measure is systematic risk, the relevant alpha is defined with respect to the security-market line:

$$\bar{r}_P = r_f + \left(\bar{r}_M - r_f\right)\beta_P \tag{8.13}$$

so that

$$\alpha_\beta = r_P - \bar{r}_P \tag{8.14}$$

This is known as the *Jensen differential performance index*, or simply as the *Jensen alpha* (Jensen, 1969). It is illustrated in Figure 8.5.

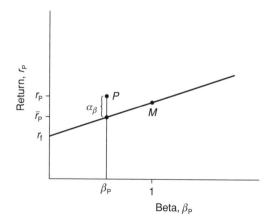

Figure 8.5 Alpha defined on systematic risk

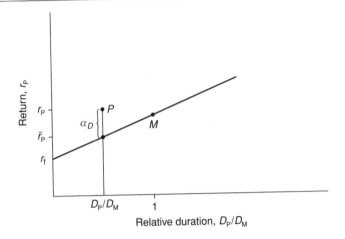

Figure 8.6 Alpha defined on relative duration

If the risk measure is relative duration, the relevant alpha value is defined with respect to the bond-market line:

$$\bar{r}_P = r_f + (\bar{r}_M - r_f)\frac{D_P}{D_M} \tag{8.15}$$

so that:

$$\alpha_D = r_P - \bar{r}_P \tag{8.16}$$

This is illustrated in Figure 8.6.

A performance measure using alpha that is analogous to the Sharpe ratio is the *information ratio* (*IR*):

$$IR = \frac{\alpha_\beta}{\eta_P} \tag{8.17}$$

where α_β is the Jensen alpha (see (8.14)) and η_P is *active risk* or *tracking error* on the portfolio and is derived from the decomposition of total risk (see (7.12)):

$$\text{Total risk} = \text{Systematic risk} + \text{Specific risk}$$

or

$$\sigma_P^2 = \beta_P^2\sigma_M^2 + \eta_P^2 \tag{8.18}$$

where σ_P^2 = variance of the return on the portfolio and η_P^2 = specific risk of the portfolio (i.e. the square of active risk or tracking error). The information ratio corrects the alpha for active risk and penalises measured performance if the active risk assumed by the fund manager (which could be completely eliminated through diversification) is excessive.

8.4 PERFORMANCE ATTRIBUTION FOR ACTIVELY MANAGED FUNDS

Having discussed various measures of the performance of a fund, the next task is to identify the sources of that performance. This involves breaking down the total return into various components. One way of doing this is known as the *Fama decomposition of total return* (after Fama, 1972).

The Fama decomposition is shown in Figure 8.7 in the case where the relevant measure of risk is systematic risk, beta. Suppose that Fund P generates a return r_P and has a beta of β_P. The fund has performed well over the period being considered. Using the Jensen differential performance index, it has a positive alpha value, equal to $(r_P - r_2)$. The total return r_P can be broken down into four components:

$$\text{Return on the portfolio} = \text{Riskless rate}$$
$$+ \text{Return from trustees' risk}$$
$$+ \text{Return from market timing}$$
$$+ \text{Return from security selection.} \quad (8.19)$$

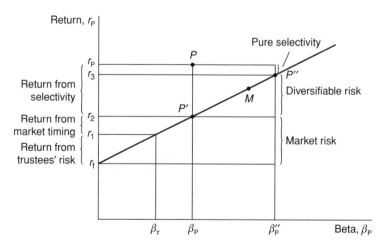

Figure 8.7   Fama decomposition of total return

The first component of the return on the portfolio is the riskless rate, r_f: all fund managers expect to earn at least the riskless rate.

The second component of portfolio return is the return from the trustees' risk. The fund manager will have assessed the trustees' degree of risk tolerance to correspond with a beta measure of β_τ, say. The trustees are therefore expecting a return on the portfolio of at least r_1. The return from the trustees' risk is therefore $(r_1 - r_f)$.

The third component is the return from market timing. This is also known as the return from the fund manager's risk. This is because the pension fund manager has chosen (or at least ended up with) a portfolio with a beta of β_P, which differs from that expected by the trustees. The fund manager has implicitly taken a more bullish view of the market than the trustees. He or she has consequently decided to raise the beta of the portfolio above that expected by the trustees. He or she has done this by selecting a portfolio with a larger proportion invested in the market portfolio and a smaller proportion invested in the riskless asset than the trustees would have selected. In other words, the fund manager has engaged in market timing. With a portfolio beta of β_P, the expected return is r_2, so that the return from market timing is $(r_2 - r_1)$.

The fourth component is the return from selectivity (i.e. the return from security selection). It is equal to $(r_P - r_2)$ and is known as the return from selectivity for the following reason. Consider portfolios P' and P in Figure 8.7. They both have the same amount of market risk, because they both have the same beta, β_P. However, they have different total risks. Portfolio P' contains no diversifiable risk since it lies on the security-market line (SML). Portfolio P, however, lies above the SML. It is, therefore, not a linear combination of the market portfolio and the riskless asset (only portfolios along the SML are). In other words, P differs from P' because P's manager has engaged in active security selection. This has resulted in portfolio P earning an additional return, but the fund manager has had to take on diversifiable risk to do so.

Is the extra return worth the risk? To answer this question we need to compare portfolio P with another portfolio which lies on the SML and which has the same total risk. Suppose that this other portfolio is P''. P'' is found as follows. Suppose that the total risk of P and P'' is $\sigma_P^2 = 30$. Since P'' lies on the SML, we know that all the risk of P'' is undiversifiable and that this is equal to $(\beta_P'')^2 \sigma_M^2$ (see Equation (7.12)). If $\sigma_M^2 = 25$, it follows that:

$$\beta_P'' = \sigma_P / \sigma_M = \left(\frac{30}{25}\right)^{1/2} = 1.1$$

The return on P'' is r_3 (given that the beta of P'' is β_P'') while the return on P is r_P. Since r_P is greater than r_3, it means that the risk from selecting P was worthwhile. The additional return from taking on additional diversifiable risk is $(r_3 - r_2)$. But the portfolio P fund manager has done even better than this, and earned an additional return $(r_P - r_3)$, known as the return from pure selectivity.

Figure 8.7 can also be used to show a different decomposition from that given by Equation (8.19). The return $(r_2 - r_f)$ is the return from taking on market risk: it is equal to the sum of the returns from the trustees' risk and the manager's risk. Similarly, the return from security selection can be broken down into the return from diversifiable risk and the return from pure selectivity. Therefore, an alternative decomposition to Equation (8.19) is:

Return on the portfolio $=$ Riskless rate

$+$ Return from market risk

$+$ Return from diversifiable risk

$+$ Return from pure selectivity.   (8.20)

We can illustrate the Fama decomposition using the following data on a pension fund based on the previous twenty quarters:

$$r_P = 20\%, \quad r_M = 16\%,$$
$$\sigma_P = 15\%, \quad \sigma_M = 12\%,$$
$$\beta_P = 0.9, \quad r_f = 10\%.$$

The trustees' desired beta is given as $\beta_\tau = 0.8$. Using this, we can calculate the expected return on the trustees' desired portfolio. A beta of 0.8 implies a portfolio that is 80% invested in the market and 20% invested in the riskless asset. Therefore:

$$r_1 = 0.2(10) + 0.8(16)$$
$$= 14.8\%.$$

This means a return from trustees' risk of:

$$r_1 - r_f = 14.8 - 10.0$$
$$= 4.8\%.$$

However, the actual beta of the portfolio is 0.9, implying that it is 90% invested in the market and 10% invested in the riskless asset. This, in turn, implies an expected return on the actual portfolio of:

$$r_2 = 0.1(10) + 0.9(16)$$
$$= 15.4\%.$$

This gives a return from market timing of:

$$r_2 - r_1 = 15.4 - 14.8$$
$$= 0.6\%.$$

The next step is to find the portfolio P'' with the same total risk as the pension fund portfolio P. This portfolio has a beta of:

$$\beta_P'' = \sigma_P/\sigma_M$$
$$= 15/12$$
$$= 1.25.$$

Portfolio P'' is invested 125% in the market and –25% in the riskless asset (i.e. with borrowings at the riskless interest rate equal to 25% of the fund's value). The expected return on this portfolio is:

$$r_3 = -0.25(10) + 1.25(16)$$
$$= 17.5\%.$$

Therefore, the return from diversifiable risk is:

$$r_3 - r_2 = 17.5 - 15.4$$
$$= 2.1\%.$$

This leaves the return from pure selectivity as:

$$r_P - r_3 = 20.0 - 17.5$$
$$= 2.5\%.$$

The decomposition of total return can be used to identify the different skills involved in active fund management. For example, one pension fund manager might be good at market timing but poor at stock selection. The evidence for this would be that his $(r_2 - r_1)$ was positive but his $(r_P - r_2)$ was negative. He should therefore be recommended to invest in an index fund but be able to select his own combination of the index fund and the riskless asset. Another pension fund manager might be good at stock selection but poor at market timing. He should be allowed to choose his own securities but someone else should choose the combination of the resulting portfolio of risky securities and the riskless asset.

The Fama decomposition was done in terms of beta and is therefore important for share portfolios. It is possible to perform a similar decomposition in terms of bond portfolios using relative duration (see, for example, Fong *et al.*, 1983).

Another method of decomposing the total return on the portfolio is due to Brinson *et al.* (1986, 1991). Assume that there are N asset categories in the portfolio and define:

θ_{ajt} = actual weight in asset class j at time t,
θ_{sjt} = strategic (or normal) asset allocation in asset class j at time t,
r_{ajt} = actual return on asset class j at time t,
r_{sjt} = strategic return on asset class j at time t.

As an accounting identity:

$$\sum_{j=1}^{N} \theta_{ajt} r_{ajt} = \sum_{j=1}^{N} \theta_{sjt} r_{sjt} + \sum_{j=1}^{N} \theta_{sjt}(r_{ajt} - r_{sjt})$$

$$+ \sum_{j=1}^{N}(\theta_{ajt} - \theta_{sjt})r_{sjt} + \sum_{j=1}^{N}(\theta_{ajt} - \theta_{sjt})(r_{ajt} - r_{sjt}) \quad (8.21)$$

that is:

Total return = Strategic return + Return from security selection

+ Return from market timing + Residual return

$$(8.22)$$

The strategic return is the return on an agreed benchmark, such as a market or peer-group or absolute return index.

The strategic asset allocation is the benchmark portfolio agreed between trustees and fund manager in the light of an asset–liability modelling exercise. Brinson *et al.* (1986) in their study used the average portfolio allocation over the sample period (of length T) as the strategic or normal portfolio weights:

$$\omega_{nijt} = \sum_{t=1}^{T} \omega_{aijt}/T \quad (8.23)$$

for all i and j. This definition seems reasonable if the funds are in a steady state, in the sense that they have achieved their target portfolio composition across major asset groups and that long-run investment opportunities are stationary.

8.5 LIABILITY-DRIVEN PERFORMANCE ATTRIBUTION

Liability-driven performance attribution (LDPA) (see Plantinga and van der Meer, 1995) is a framework for analysing performance measurement and attribution in the case of asset–liability managed (ALM) portfolios; that is, portfolios whose investment strategy is driven by the nature of the investing client's liabilities.

We can illustrate LDPA using the following balance sheet for an ALM pension fund:[1]

Assets		Liabilities	
Liability-driven assets	A	Pension liabilities	L
General assets	E	Surplus	S

Suppose that the *pension liabilities* (L) generate a predetermined set of future cash outflows. The fund manager can meet these cash outflows by investing in fixed-interest bonds (A) with the same pattern of cash flows; these bonds constitute the *liability-driven assets* (LDAs)[2] in the balance sheet above. Suppose that the pension fund *surplus* (S) is invested in *general assets* (E). These can be any assets matching the risk–return preferences expressed by the pension scheme's trustees (e.g. equities). The surplus is defined as assets ($A + E$) *minus* liabilities (L).[3] The return on the surplus is defined as:

$$r_S S = r_E E + r_A A - r_L L \tag{8.24}$$

where r_S = rate of return on the surplus; r_E = rate of return on the general assets; r_A = rate of return on the LDAs; r_L = payout rate on the liabilities.

---

[1] The components of the balance sheet are measured in *present value* terms. Also, for simplicity of exposition, we assume that L relates to accrued past service; thus, future contributions are excluded from the balance sheet. This is the *accrued benefits method* of valuing pension liabilities.

[2] Also known as *liability-matching assets*. If the pension liabilities are indexed to uncertain real wage growth or to future inflation, then the LDAs will be the assets most likely to match the growth rate in earnings or in inflation over the long term (e.g. indexed bonds, equities and property). But to keep the analysis simple, we assume that the cash flows on future pension payments are known.

[3] Following the 1986 Finance Act/1988 Income and Corporation Taxes Act, the surplus on UK pension funds cannot exceed 5% of the value of the liabilities and must be reduced to below this level over a five-year period using a number of methods, the most common of which is the employer contribution holiday. Following the 1995 Pensions Act and subsequent amendments, deficits exceeding 10% must be reduced to the 10% level over a three-year period and full funding must be restored within ten years.

Both the pension liabilities and the LDAs will be sensitive to changes in interest rates. Higher interest rates reduce the present value of pension liabilities. Similarly, higher interest rates reduce the value of fixed-interest bonds, since a given stream of fixed-coupon payments is worth less today when yields on alternative assets are higher.[4]

Assuming that interest-rate risk is the only source of risk to this portfolio, we can use Equation (8.24) to derive a decomposition of portfolio performance as follows. First, we rewrite the equation for the income on the general assets as:

$$r_E E = r_E S + r_E (E - S) \tag{8.25}$$

and the equation for the income on the LDAs as:

$$r_A A = r_A L + r_A (A - L) \tag{8.26}$$

Then, we can divide each side of (8.24) by S and substitute (8.25) and (8.26) to get the LDPA:[5]

$$
\begin{aligned}
r_S &= \frac{r_E S + r_E (E - S)}{S} + \frac{r_A L + r_A (A - L)}{S} - \frac{r_L L}{S} \\
&= r_E + \lambda (r_A - r_L) + \gamma (r_E - r_A) \\
&= r_E + \lambda (r_A - \bar{r}_A) + \lambda (\bar{r}_A - r_L) + \gamma (r_E - r_A)
\end{aligned}
\tag{8.27}
$$

or

Rate of return on the surplus

    = Rate of return on the general assets

      + Rate of return on the LDAs due to security selection

      + Rate of return on the LDAs due to market timing

      + Rate of return from a funding mismatch   (8.28)

where $\lambda = L/S =$ financial leverage ratio; $\gamma = (L - A)/S = (E - S)/S =$ funding mismatch ratio; $\bar{r}_A =$ expected return on bonds when they are correctly priced on the basis of the spot yield curve (i.e.

---

[4] It is theoretically possible to structure the LDAs in such a way that the pension fund is immunised against interest-rate movements. The LDAs are then known as a liability immunising portfolio (LIP); LIPs were discussed in Section 6.4. When this happens, the surplus will not respond at all to interest-rate movements.

[5] In the case where the surplus is exactly zero, the decomposition in (8.27) is not defined. The fund manager has just generated a sufficient return to meet the payout rate on liabilities. The LDPA in this case would be based on $r_L = r_E(E/L) + r_A(A/L)$ where (E/L) is the portfolio weight in general assets and (A/L) is the portfolio weight in LDAs (see (8.24)).

when the future coupon payments are discounted using the appropriate spot yields; see, for example, Section B.2.4 in Appendix B of the book or Blake, 2000: Section 5.5.4).

The four-component LDPA in (8.27) can be explained as follows:

- The *rate of return on general assets* (r_E). This can be analysed using standard techniques, for example, comparing performance against a pre-agreed peer-group or external benchmark as in Section 8.4 above.
- The *rate of return on the LDAs due to stock selection* in terms of, say, credit quality management or sector management. This follows because r_A is the actual return generated by the bonds chosen by the fund manager, whereas $\bar{r}_A$ is the benchmark return on the bonds if they were correctly priced according to the spot yield curve: $(r_A - \bar{r}_A)$ is therefore the excess return arising from the stock-selection skills of the fund manager.
- The *rate of return on the LDAs due to market timing*; that is, from choosing a portfolio of bonds with a maturity structure that differs from that of the underlying liabilities, thereby deliberately leaving the portfolio partially exposed to interest-rate risk.
- The *rate of return from a funding mismatch*; that is, from active management of the LDAs such that part of this category is invested in riskier general assets such as equities.

We can illustrate the LDPA using an example. Suppose that a pension fund has the following balance sheet at the start and end of the year:

	Assets			Liabilities	
	Start year	End year		Start year	End year
LDAs (A)	900	997	Pension liabilities (L)	1000	1107
General assets (E)	150	169	Surplus (S)	50	59
Total	1050	1166	Total	1050	1166

We will assume that the LDAs are bonds, while the general assets are equities (and that equities have no yield curve (or interest rate) effect). The value of the liabilities is calculated as the present value of the liability cash flows using appropriate spot yields as discount rates. We have the following returns on the components of the balance sheet:

Component	Actual rate of return (%)	Benchmark rate of return (%) (assumption)
Bonds	$r_A = 10.78$	$\bar{r}_A = 10.62$
Equities	$r_E = 12.67$	$\bar{r}_E = 13.30$
Liabilities	$r_L = 10.70$	

The actual rates of return are found by taking the difference between the end-of-year and start-of-year values as a ratio of the start-of-year values. The benchmark return on bonds is calculated in a similar way but based on start- and end-year present values of coupon payments using appropriate spot yields. The benchmark return on equities is simply the return on a relevant index, for example, the FT-A All Share Index.

Using Equation (8.27) with $\lambda = L/S = 20$ and $\gamma = (L - A)/S = 2$ (using start-of-year values), the LDPA is determined as follows:

Component	Return (%)
General assets (r_E)	12.67
Security selection ($\lambda(r_A - \bar{r}_A)$)	3.20
Market timing ($\gamma(\bar{r}_A - r_L)$)	−0.16
Funding mismatch ($\gamma(r_E - r_A)$)	3.78
Total	19.49

The total rate of return on the surplus of 19.49% is made up of 12.67% from the performance of the general assets, 3.20% from successful security selection, 3.78% from a successful funding mismatch and a loss of 0.16% from unsuccessful market timing. The security selection and market timing effects are magnified by a high leverage ratio (λ) of 20 (the minimum that is permissible since the surplus may not (in the long term) exceed 5% of liabilities), while the funding mismatch effect is magnified by a smaller funding mismatch ratio (γ) of 2. The positive net return of 3.04% from active fund management (i.e. the sum of the returns from security selection and market timing) and the positive net return from a funding mismatch help to generate a high surplus return. However, this cannot conceal the fact that the fund manager underperformed the benchmark in terms of general assets by 0.63%.

The LDPA therefore tells us a great deal about the investment skills of the pension fund manager when he or she is constrained on the liability side of the balance sheet. The only additional information that is required over the conventional performance measurement framework is as follows: the present value of the pension liabilities (as determined by the pension scheme's actuary), together with the payout rate on these, and the value of LDAs, together with a customised benchmark return on these.

8.6   REALISED INVESTMENT PERFORMANCE

Good or bad investment performance by DB and DC pension funds have very different consequences for scheme members. With DB schemes, the investment performance of the fund's assets is of no direct relevance to the scheme member, since the pension depends on the final salary and years of service only and not on investment performance. The scheme member can rely on the sponsoring company to bail out the fund with a deficiency payment if assets perform very badly (i.e. the member exercises the implicit put option against the sponsor, as discussed in Section 6.3). In extreme circumstances, however, it is possible for a firm and possibly the scheme to become insolvent.[6] Of course, if the assets perform well, the surplus is retained by the sponsor (who exercises the implicit call option against the member in this case, as discussed in Section 6.3).

However, investment performance is critical to the size of the pension in the case of a DC scheme: scheme members bear all the investment risk in such schemes. Scheme members, especially personal pension scheme members, can find themselves locked into a poorly performing fund, facing very high costs of transferring to a better performing fund. In addition, the type of funds in which personal pension scheme members invest can, and do, close down, and then the assets do have to be transferred to a different fund. In this section we examine the investment performance of pension scheme assets, beginning with those of DC schemes.

8.6.1   Investment performance of DC funds

The anticipated return in a high-risk investment vehicle is greater than in a low-risk investment vehicle, but there can be wide differences in

---

[6] To avoid this risk, 74% of companies in the UK had closed their DB schemes to new members by 2006, while 41% had closed their schemes to additional contributions from existing members (Association of Consulting Actuaries' *Smaller Firms Pension Survey 2006*).

Table 8.3   Distribution of returns generated by UK unit trusts, 1972–1995

Sector	Top quartile	Median	Bottom quartile	Ratio of fund sizes
UK Equity Growth	16.0	13.6	11.9	3.2
UK Equity General	14.3	13.4	13.1	1.4
UK Equity Income	15.4	14.0	12.4	2.3
UK Smaller Companies	18.7	15.5	12.8	5.3

Note: The first three columns are averages measured in percentages per annum for the sample period 1972–1995; the last column gives the ratio of fund sizes after 40 years based on the top and bottom quartile returns. The formula is (assuming the same contribution stream):

$$\frac{(1 + g_T)^M - 1}{g_T} \times \frac{(1 + g_B)^M - 1}{g_B}$$

where g_T and g_B represent the top and bottom quartile growth rates from the table and M represents the number of years (here 40).
Source: Blake and Timmermann (1998) and Lunde, Timmermann and Blake (1999).

realised returns, even for schemes in the same risk class. Blake and Timmermann (1998) conducted a study of the investment performance of unit trusts in the UK, one of the key investment vehicles for DC schemes. Table 8.3 shows the distribution of returns generated by unit trusts operating in the four largest sectors. These figures indicate enormous differences in performance, especially over the long life of a pension scheme. For example, the 4.1 percentage point per annum difference between the best- and worst-performing unit trusts in the UK Equity Growth sector leads, over a 40-year investment horizon, to the accumulated fund[7] in the top quartile being a factor of 3.2 times larger than the accumulated fund in the bottom quartile for the same pattern of contributions. The 5.9 percentage point per annum difference between the best- and worst-performing unit trusts in the UK Smaller Companies sector leads to an even larger fund size ratio after 40 years of 5.3.

So, personal pension scheme members can find themselves locked into poorly performing funds. But should it not be the case in an efficient capital market that systematically underperforming funds fail to survive and are taken over by more efficient fund managers? Lunde, Timmermann and Blake (1999) investigated this possibility. They found

---

[7] This comprises regular contributions plus investment returns on these.

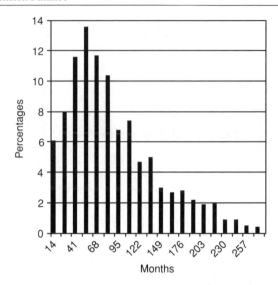

Figure 8.8   Duration of UK unit trusts from inception. Note: The histogram shows the distribution of the lifetimes in months of the 973 unit trusts which were wound up or merged during the sample period 1972–1995. *Source*: Lunde, Timmermann and Blake (1999, Table 1)

that underperforming trusts are eventually merged with more successful trusts, but that on average it takes some time for this to occur. Figure 8.8 shows the distribution of durations across the whole unit trust industry of trusts that were eventually wound up or merged. The modal duration is 4.25 years (51 months), but the average duration is about 16 years. Across the whole unit trust industry, the average return on funds that survived the whole period was 13.7% per annum, while the average return on funds that were wound up or merged during the period was 11.3% per annum. This implies that a typical personal pension scheme member might find him or herself locked into an underperforming trust that is eventually wound up or merged into a more successful fund, experiencing an underperformance of 2.4% p.a. over a 16-year period. This translates into a fund value that is 19% lower after 16 years than a fund that is not wound up or merged. So it seems that, in practice, personal pension scheme members cannot rely on the markets to provide them with a painless way of extricating them from an underperforming fund. They have to do it themselves, paying between 15–18% of the value of their accumulated fund in transfer costs (Blake, 2003).

8.6.2 Investment performance of DB funds

The investment performance of DB pension funds is much more important for the scheme sponsor than for the scheme member. The recent history of the UK pension fund industry embraces a period of substantial deficiency payments in the 1970s (arising from the UK stock market crash in 1974–75), and the build up of huge surpluses during the bull markets of the 1980s and 1990s. These surpluses have enabled sponsors to reduce their contributions into their schemes (i.e. to take employer contribution holidays). In other words, during the 1980s and 1990s, UK pension scheme sponsors benefited enormously from the investment successes of their fund managers. This was followed by the stock market crash of 2000 (caused by the bursting of the dot.com bubble) and the consequential re-emergence of large pension fund deficits, exacerbated by the increasing longevity of pensioners.

The investment performance of DB pension fund managers in the UK between 1986 and 1994 has been investigated by Blake, Lehmann and Timmermann (1999, 2002).[8] The data set used covers the externally appointed fund managers of more than 300 medium-to-large pension funds. The UK pension fund industry is highly concentrated, and most of these managers come from just five groups of professional fund managers (UBS Global Asset Management, Merrill Lynch Investment Management, Aberdeen (formerly Deutsche) Asset Management, Schroder Investment Management and Gartmore Pension Fund Managers).

While the median performance was very good over the sample period, the median return conceals a wide distribution of performance. This can be seen from Table 8.4, which shows the cross-sectional distribution of returns realised by the pension funds in the sample over the period 1986–94 in the most important individual asset classes as well as for the total portfolio. The interquartile range is quite tight, below 2 percentage points for most asset classes and only just over 1 percentage point for the total portfolio return. This suggests evidence of a possible herding effect in the behaviour of pension fund managers, since fund managers do not like their *relative* performance to get too much out of line with each other. Nevertheless, the difference between the best- and worst-performing funds is very large, as the last row of Table 8.4 indicates.

Table 8.5 shows how well UK pension funds have performed in comparison with other participants in the market. The fourth column shows

---

[8] Very similar results have been found for the US , see Lakonishok, Shleifer and Vishny (1992).

Table 8.4 Fractiles of total returns by asset class for UK pension funds, 1986–1994 (Average annualised percentages)

	UK equities	International equities	UK bonds	International bonds	UK Index bonds	Cash/ other	UK property	Total
Min	8.59	4.42	6.59	−0.64	5.59	2.67	3.05	7.22
5%	11.43	8.59	9.44	2.18	7.20	5.46	5.07	10.60
10%	11.85	9.03	9.95	7.56	7.81	7.60	6.58	10.96
25%	12.44	9.64	10.43	8.30	7.91	8.97	8.03	11.47
50%	13.13	10.65	10.79	11.37	8.22	10.25	8.75	12.06
75%	13.93	11.76	11.22	13.37	8.45	11.72	9.99	12.59
90%	14.81	12.52	11.70	14.55	8.80	14.20	10.84	13.13
95%	15.46	13.14	12.05	18.15	8.89	16.13	11.36	13.39
Max	17.39	14.68	17.23	26.34	10.07	19.73	13.53	15.03
Max–Min	8.80	10.26	10.64	26.98	4.48	17.06	10.48	7.81

Note: The table shows the fractiles of the cross-sectional distribution of returns on individual asset classes as well as on the total portfolio.
Source: Blake, Lehmann and Timmermann (1998, Table 1).

that the average UK pension fund underperformed the market average by 0.45% per annum; and this is before the fund manager's fee is taken into account. Further, only 42.8% of funds outperformed the market average. The main explanation for this is the relative underperformance in UK equities, the largest single category with an average portfolio weighting

Table 8.5 Performance of UK pension funds in comparison with the market, 1986–1994 (Percentages)

	Average market return	Average pension fund return	Average out-performance	Average portfolio weight	Percentage out-performers
UK equities	13.30	12.97	−0.33	53.7	44.8
International equities	11.11	11.23	0.12	19.5	39.8
UK bonds	10.35	10.76	0.41	7.6	77.3
International bonds	8.64	10.03	1.39	2.2	68.8
UK index bonds	8.22	8.12	−0.10	2.7	51.7
Cash/other investments	9.90	9.01	−0.89	4.5	59.5
UK property	9.00	9.52	0.52	8.9	39.1
Total	12.18	11.73	−0.45		42.8

Note: International property is excluded since no market index was available.
Source: Blake, Lehmann and Timmermann (1998; 2002, Table 2).

of 54% over the sample period; the average underperformance is –0.33% per annum, and only 44.8% of UK pension funds beat the average return on UK equities. To be sure, relative performance is better in other asset categories, especially UK and international bonds, but the portfolio weights in these asset categories are not large enough to counteract the relative underperformance in UK equities.

Tables 8.4 and 8.5 together indicate how close the majority of the pension funds are to generating the average market return. The median fund generated an average total return of 12.06% per annum, just 12 basis points short of the average market return, and 80% of the funds were within one percentage point of the average market return. Thus, although some funds achieve extremely good (or bad) returns, the bulk of funds cluster very closely together. There are several explanations for this result:

- It is extremely difficult to beat the market (i.e. the average) consistently.
- Given the size of pension fund investments, it is difficult for managers to do anything other than invest the bulk of their funds in large, blue chip stocks. This results in many funds holding rather similar portfolios.
- It is a consequence of the widely reported *herding* effect by which managers, whose reputation is based on their *relative* performance against each other,[9] will tend to select very similar portfolios to avoid the loss of reputation that arises from relative underperformance.[10]
- The growth in popularity of index tracking would, again, tend to result in rather similar portfolios across funds.

All this suggests that, despite their claims to be active fund managers, the vast majority of UK pension fund managers are not only herding together, they are also closet index matchers.

---

[9] Davis (1988) reports a survey of UK and US fund managers in which they acknowledge the existence of a herding effect. More recent studies from the US confirm the importance (in the assessment of fund managers' performance) of their relative performance against a peer-group benchmark (see Brown, Harlow and Starks, 1996 and Chevalier and Ellison, 1997).

[10] While fund managers receive higher fee incomes if they generate higher fund values, earning greater returns usually also involves taking on greater risk, the result of which could be very poor performance relative to other fund managers, and this would be damaging for reputations. Thus, with charges based on fund values, the additional return that could be expected from choosing an active investment strategy that differed substantially from that of the median fund manager is unlikely to compensate for the risk of ending up in the fourth quartile and the resulting loss of reputation. The outcome is herding of both behaviour and performance, not only around the median fund manager, but also around the index.

There are some other features of UK pension fund performance worthy of note (Blake, Lehmann and Timmermann, 1999, 2002). First, there was some evidence of spillover effects in performance, but only between UK and international equities. In other words, the funds that performed well or badly in UK equities also performed well or badly in international equities. This suggests that some fund managers were good at identifying undervalued stocks in different markets. This result is somewhat surprising since the world's equity markets are much less highly integrated than the world's bond markets, yet there was no evidence of spillover effects in performance across bond markets.

Second, there was evidence of a size effect in performance. Large funds tended to underperform smaller funds. The above studies found that 32% of the quartile containing the largest funds were also in the quartile containing the worst-performing funds, whereas only 15% of the quartile containing the smallest funds were also in the quartile of worst-performing funds. These results confirm the often-quoted view that 'size is the anchor of performance': because large pension funds are dominant players in the markets, this severely restricts their abilities to outperform the market.

The third feature concerns the abilities of UK pension fund managers in active fund management; that is, in their attempts to beat the market in comparison with a passive buy-and-hold strategy. A key task of pension fund managers is, as we have seen above, to establish and maintain the strategic asset allocation set by the scheme's actuary or investment consultant. This is essentially a passive management strategy. However, fund managers claim that they can 'add value' through the active management of their fund's assets, i.e. security selection and market timing.

Blake, Lehmann and Timmermann (1999, 2002) decomposed the total return generated by fund managers into the following components (using the modelling framework of Brinson *et al.*, 1986, 1991, see Eqn (8.21)):

Component	Percentage
Strategic asset allocation	99.47%
Security selection	2.68%
Market timing	−1.64%
Other	−0.51%
Total	100.00%

They found that 99.47% of the total return generated by UK fund managers can be explained by the strategic asset allocation, i.e., by the benchmark portfolio. This is the passive component of pension fund performance. The active components are security selection and market timing (or TAA). The average pension fund was unsuccessful at market timing, generating a negative contribution to the total return of -1.64%. The average pension fund was, however, more successful in security selection, making a positive contribution to the total return of 2.68%. But the overall contribution of active fund management was just over 1% of the total return (or about 13 basis points), which is *less than the annual fee that active fund managers charge* (which range between 20 basis points for a £500m fund to 75 basis points for a £10m fund).[11]

Active investment performance is even worse in international markets than in domestic markets according to studies of UK pension funds' active management in international equity markets (Timmermann and Blake, 2005; Blake and Timmermann, 2005). Using the Brinson *et al.* (1986, 1991) decompositions of the investment performance of a large sample of UK pension funds, these studies show that not only do the funds underperform substantially relative to regional benchmarks (i.e. the FT/S&P indices for the four regions considered, namely Japan, North America, Europe (excluding the UK) and Asia-Pacific (excluding Japan)), but this underperformance is much larger than has been found in studies of performance in the domestic market. The results suggest that the pension funds earned negative returns from active management (i.e. from international market timing and from selecting stocks within individual foreign regions). The average fund underperformed a passive global equity benchmark by 70 basis points per annum. This is substantially greater than UK pension funds' underperformance in their domestic equity market (33 basis points per annum, according to Table 8.5). This underperformance is mainly caused by unsuccessful market timing attempts, i.e. by systematic – and *ex post* misjudged – changes in the portfolio weights across international regions. These results help to explain the so-called *home country bias*, namely the above-average weighting of domestic assets in most investors' portfolios, when modern portfolio theory would suggest that a well-diversified portfolio would contain a substantial proportion of international assets. Of course, UK pension funds with liabilities dominated in sterling would still be expected to hold a significant proportion of assets in sterling (i.e. the home country bias is in some sense natural for such investors).

The final feature concerns the consistency of investment performance over time. Modern finance theory and evidence suggests that, in an

---

[11] *Pensions Management*, September 1998.

Table 8.6 Consistency of pension fund performance (percentages)

Years above average	Total fund				UK equities				
	1980– 84	1985– 89	1992– 96	Mean	1980– 84	1985– 89	1992– 96	Mean	Pure chance
5	3	3	5	4	2	5	5	4	3
4	25	18	17	20	14	18	21	18	16
3	26	28	28	27	35	26	28	30	31
2	25	34	35	31	31	27	26	28	31
1	15	14	13	14	15	18	15	16	16
0	6	3	2	4	3	6	5	4	3

Note: The table shows the percentage of funds achieving the stated number of years of above-average performance during each five-year period. The final column shows the percentages that would be expected if fund performance was purely random.
Source: CAPS *General Reports* 1985, 1989, 1996

efficient financial system, it is impossible to achieve consistently superior net investment performance over time.[12] While there may be differences in the academic literature about the degree of financial market efficiency at the margin, there is no academic support for the proposition that a fund manager is able to obtain consistently superior investment performance over extended periods of time, after taking into account risk, research costs and trading costs. Similarly, while in any given period some fund managers will perform better than the average and others will perform worse, there is nothing in the academic literature to suggest that any outperformance will persist over any extended period.

Table 8.6 provides empirical evidence that is consistent with this theoretical view. It shows the consistency of performance for each of three nonoverlapping five-year periods achieved by a large number of UK occupational pension funds. The table reveals that, across all three periods, only 4% of funds managed to achieve above-average performance in each of the five years, while another 4% of funds underperformed in each of the five years. About half the funds had superior performance in three or more years and about half had below-average performance in three or more years. Comparing these figures with those in the final column confirms that this distribution is almost exactly what would be expected if above- (or below-) average performance arose entirely by chance in each year. This pattern is found consistently in each of the three

---

[12] See, for example, Blake (2000, Chapter 11).

five-year periods and is not affected by whether the investments considered are UK equities or more broadly based portfolios. Similar results were found for UK unit trusts for periods in excess of three years.[13]

Other studies have found some evidence that consistency of performance was possible, particularly in the top and bottom quartiles, but only over very short horizons. For example, Blake, Lehmann and Timmermann (2002) found that, in the case of occupational pension funds, UK equity managers in the top quartile of performance in one year had a 37% chance of being in the top quartile the following year, rather than the 25% that would have been expected if relative performance arose purely by chance. Similarly, there was a 32% chance of the UK equity managers in the bottom quartile for one year being in the bottom quartile the following year. There was also evidence of consistency in performance in the top and bottom quartiles for cash/other investments, with probabilities of remaining in these quartiles the following year of 35% in each case. However, there was no evidence of consistency in performance for any other asset category or for the portfolio as a whole. Nor was there evidence of any consistency in performance over longer horizons than one year in any asset category or for the whole portfolio.[14] This evidence is consistent with the suggestion that so-called 'hot hands' in investment performance is a short-term phenomenon which does not persist for the extended periods that would be needed to justify the widespread use of measures that use past performance as an indicator of expected future performance.[15]

---

[13] The (short-term) underperformance in this section refers to funds that continue in existence and temporarily generate below-average performance. In contrast, the (long-term) underperformance analysed in Section 8.6.1 refers to funds that eventually 'die' because of their systematic poor performance.

[14] Lunde, Timmermann and Blake (1999) found similar results for unit trusts: for example, a unit trust specialising in UK equity which was in the top quartile in one year had a 33% chance of remaining in the top quartile the following year, while there was a 36% chance of it remaining in the bottom quartile for two consecutive years.

[15] Again, very similar results have been found in the US (see Grinblatt and Titman, 1992; Hendricks *et al.*, 1993; Brown and Goetzmann, 1995; Carhart, 1997). For example, Carhart (1997) argues that the short-term persistence effect identified by Hendricks *et al.* (1993) is mostly driven by the one-year momentum effect found by Jegadeesh and Titman (1993). However, individual funds do not, on average, earn higher returns from following a momentum strategy, but rather because they happen by chance to hold relatively large positions in the previous year's winning stocks. The only persistence that is significant is concentrated in strong underperformance by the worst-return mutual funds. Carhart's findings do not, therefore, support the existence of skilled or informed mutual fund portfolio managers because: 'hot hands' funds infrequently repeat their abnormal performance; transaction costs consume gains from following a momentum strategy in stocks; and expense ratios, portfolio turnover costs and load fees are significant and negatively related to performance. Tonks (2005) finds some evidence of one-year persistence in UK pension

8.7   PERFORMANCE-RELATED FUND MANAGEMENT FEES

It would be wrong and would also eventually lead to market inefficiencies if fund managers were required to invest only in passive index funds. Active fund managers can help to make markets efficient. One way of rewarding active fund managers is through the use of performance-related fees. However, such fees would have to be designed appropriately to remove any incentive on the part of fund managers to take on excessive risks or to behave in other undesirable ways. Such fees provide an element of common interest between policyholder and provider – as good performance has a direct benefit to both parties and the unavoidable risk of underperformance is also shared.

Performance-related fees typically take one of two forms: a simple proportion of the absolute value of the fund or a proportion of the difference between the fund's realised performance and a benchmark (Starks, 1987).

The first form is less extreme from the viewpoint of the fund manager, since it does not involve refunds and can be specified as:

$$\text{Performance-related fee in period } t = f_i V_t \qquad (8.29)$$

where f_i is the fee rate if the fund manager's return is in the ith quartile and V_t is the value of the fund at time t.

An example of this fee structure is presented in Figure 8.9, which shows the fee rates payable from a sample fund that uses performance-related fees, based on a Monte Carlo simulation.[16] The 90% confidence interval for the fees lies between 0.22 and 0.45% p.a., while there is a 25% chance that the fee will exceed 0.37% p.a. and a similar chance that it will be less than 0.31% per annum. A mean annual charge of 0.34% implies a total take of approximately 8.9% of the terminal fund value over an investment horizon of 25 years.

The second form is likely to provide a stronger incentive to fund managers because it rewards only performance over and above the benchmark and does not offer a reward for simply tracking the benchmark. In this case, the fee is determined as some proportion, f_1, of the difference

---

funds' performance over the period 1983–97 even after allowing for a momentum effect, but this persistence is much weaker over longer investment horizons.

[16] The Monte Carlo simulation assumes the following: a fund with a 25-year investment horizon, a distribution of returns which is normal with a mean of 9% per annum and a standard deviation of 18%, and 1000 replications. Based on long-run returns reported in Barclays Capital (2006), such a portfolio would be invested 35% in equities and 65% in bonds.

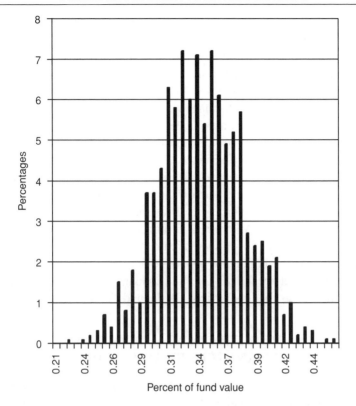

Figure 8.9 Frequency distribution of performance-related fees.
Note: The frequency diagram shows the distribution of performance-related
fees in a fund with fees calculated according to the following performance
scale: 1st quartile, fee is 0.59%; 2nd quartile, fee is 0.44%; median quartile, fee
is 0.34%; 3rd quartile, fee is 0.24%; 4th quartile, fee is 0.09%

between the fund's realised performance, r_{Pt}, and some benchmark, r_{Pt}^{*},
plus a base fee, f_2 (to cover the fund manager's overhead costs), which
depends on the absolute value of the fund:

$$\text{Performance-related fee in period } t = f_1 (r_{Pt} - g^{\#})V_t + f_2V_t \quad (8.30)$$

This rewards good *ex post* performance and penalises poor *ex post* performance. Whatever promises about superior *ex ante* performance had
been made by the fund, the fund would have to accept a reduced fee, or
even pay back the client, if r_{Pt} were sufficiently below r_{Pt} (although the
latter case generally involves credits against future fees rather than cash

refunds). This fee structure also provides a strong incentive against taking excessive risks, since fund managers who do so face the possibility of losing money. In contrast, the fee structure in (8.29) only reduces fees if the fund manager both takes risks and produces very poor performance.

It is particularly important for the fee rate to be symmetric about the target r_{Pt}^*, so that underperformance is penalised in exactly the same way that outperformance is rewarded. The worst possible fee structure from the client's point of view would be one that rewarded outperformance but did not penalise underperformance. Such a fee structure would simply encourage the fund manager to take risks with the client's assets. If the fund manager's risk-taking paid off, he would receive a large fee. If, on the other hand, performance was disastrous, the fund manager would still get the base fee. All the risk of underperformance (at least in the short term) therefore falls on the client.

Benchmarks are important, but so are fee structures. They can either provide the right incentives for fund managers or they can seriously distort their investment behaviour (Blake and Timmermann, 2002).

8.8   HOW FREQUENTLY SHOULD FUND MANAGERS BE ASSESSED?

A final issue of importance concerns the frequency with which fund managers are assessed against the benchmark (Blake and Timmermann, 2002). Despite having very long-term investment objectives, the performance of pension fund managers is typically assessed on a quarterly basis. This is said to provide another disincentive from engaging in active fund management because of the fear of relative underperformance against the peer group and the consequent risk that an underperforming fund manager will be replaced.

The frequency with which fund managers have their performance assessed ought to be related to the speed with which market anomalies are corrected. Suppose the benchmark has been set in relation to the pension fund's strategic asset allocation (SAA). Then it is the fund manager's performance in the two active strategies of stock selection and market timing that should be judged against the benchmark provided by the SAA. So the critical question is how long does it take for undervalued stocks to become correctly priced or for market timing bets to succeed? If financial markets are relatively efficient, then pricing anomalies should be corrected relatively quickly. This appears to suggest that a relatively short evaluation horizon is appropriate. To illustrate using a somewhat extreme example, if a market timing bet that involves, say, a significant underweighting of the US stock market, has not paid off after ten years, then we might be tempted to say that the bet was a bad one.

However, two points speak against the use of relatively short evaluation horizons. The first has to do with time variations in the investment opportunity set, as represented by the relative expected returns and the conditional variances and covariances between the different asset classes (i.e. the first two moments of the distribution of returns). Many studies in the finance literature suggest that the first and second moments of returns on different asset classes vary systematically as a function of the underlying state of the world (see, for example, Timmermann and Blake, 2005). Nevertheless, there is considerable uncertainty about how best to model such variations. But it seems reasonable to expect a successful market-timing strategy to be linked to the ability to anticipate changes in the underlying economic state. This tends to evolve over fairly long periods of time, as exemplified by the ten-year expansion in the US economy up to 2000. If clients, such as pension fund trustees, want fund managers to time swings in the business cycle, a long evaluation horizon would seem more appropriate.

The second justification for using a longer investment horizon is that performance is measured with so much noise that it is, in effect, impossible to assess true fund-management skills based on a short performance horizon. Under reasonable assumptions[17], it is possible to generate the following relationship between the length of the performance record and the power of the test for assessing fund management skills:

Power	Required data record
25%	3.5 years
50%	8 years
90%	22 years

These figures are derived from Figure 8.10. The *power of the test* measures the probability of correctly rejecting the null hypothesis that the fund manager generates no abnormal performance and hence is unskilled. It is clear from the figures that it takes a long time to detect with reasonable confidence that the performance of the fund manager is abnormal and therefore that he/she is genuinely skilled. This result is dependent on unchanging investment opportunity sets, which is in itself an unlikely eventuality over a 22-year time horizon.

---

[17] See the appendix at the end of this chapter.

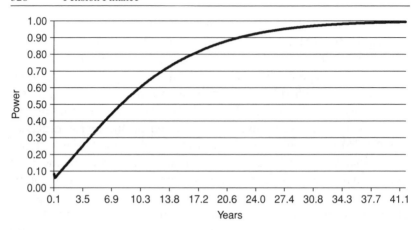

Figure 8.10 Power function – probability of correctly detecting abnormal performance

8.9 CONCLUSIONS

Pension fund performance measurement involves the calculation of risk-adjusted *ex post* returns over an agreed assessment period. This is then compared against an agreed benchmark established to reflect the objectives set for the fund manager by the pension fund trustees. The performance can also be decomposed into constituent components in order to identify the market-timing or stock-selection skills of the fund manager. The impact of liabilities on performance can also be taken into account. The aim is to assess both how and how well the fund manager has been performing.

On the basis of empirical studies of UK pension fund managers, we draw the following conclusions:

- The performance of fund managers seems to be so heavily concentrated around the peer-group median that performance rankings are largely uninformative about fund manager skill, because very small changes in performance of only a few basis points by a particular fund would produce very large changes in its ranking, without indicating any substantive change in the skill of the fund manager. Equally, the small numbers of managers at the extremes of the distribution have such large differences in performance between themselves, that even quite major changes in performance by one of these managers would result in no change in the rankings.

- The benchmark return against which fund managers are to be judged must be interpreted with considerable caution. To illustrate, one of the key benchmarks is the peer-group benchmark, but the peer group does not remain constant over time as some managers will drop out (i.e. fail to survive) while other new ones will join. This makes it difficult to construct a consistent benchmark. In the case of some performance measurement services, the information on nonsurviving funds is actually removed from their database. Since the nonsurviving funds will generally have had poor performance prior to their demise, their deletion from the database will raise the average benchmark performance[18] and make the remaining funds appear to have worse performance relative to the now biased benchmark than was actually the case. Blake and Timmermann (1998) estimated the resulting bias to be approximately 0.8% per annum for UK unit trusts.[19]
- There seems, on average, to have been a rather small return to active fund management on a risk-adjusted basis.
- Superior investment performance does not seem to persist for periods in excess of one year.
- It takes more than 20 years of performance records to distinguish skilful fund managers from lucky ones.
- Genuinely skilled fund managers should be willing to accept suitably designed performance-related fund management fees.
- Unskilled fund managers should run passive funds and accept correspondingly lower fees.
- The maturing of pension funds suggests that customised scheme-specific benchmarks that reflect the maturity of a particular scheme's liabilities should become increasingly used, while, correspondingly, those based on external or peer-group benchmarks should become less so.

QUESTIONS

1. What is meant by performance measurement?
2. What is meant by performance attribution?
3. What are *ex post* returns?
4. What are time-weighted rates of return?

---

[18] This effect is called *survivor bias* or *median drag*.

[19] Using US data, survivor biases of up to 1.4% per annum have been reported, see Malkiel (1995).

5. What are money-weighted rates of return?
6. What are the main types of benchmark for actively managed funds?
7. Explain why a value-weighted absolute index is the only type of index a fund manager could attempt to replicate the return on.
8. Explain the Sharpe ratio.
9. Explain the Treynor ratio.
10. Explain the Jensen alpha.
11. Explain the information ratio.
12. Explain the Fama decomposition.
13. Explain LDPA.
14. What are the main empirical findings relating to the investment performance of DC pension funds?
15. What are the main empirical findings relating to the investment performance of DB pension funds?
16. What are the main types of performance-related fees?
17. How frequently should fund managers be assessed?

APPENDIX: DERIVING THE POWER FUNCTION

Suppose a fund's monthly excess returns are generated by the equation:

$$R_t = \alpha + \beta R_{Mt} + \varepsilon_t$$

where R_t is the excess return on the fund in period t, over and above the risk-free rate of return, β is its beta, R_{Mt} is the excess return on the market portfolio in period t, and ε_t is the residual in period t and is normally distributed with zero mean and standard deviation σ. Suppose α measures the fund's genuine ability to outperform. How long will it take for the trustees to detect with reasonable statistical reliability whether the fund produces abnormal performance? To answer this question, suppose that $\alpha = -0.1$ and it is known that $\beta = 1$ and $\sigma = 0.5$. For continuously compounded monthly returns data, these parameter values correspond to a fund that underperforms the index by 1.2% per year, while the idiosyncratic risk is 6% per year. Assuming that the size of the statistical test for the fund manager's ability to add value, p, is the standard 5%, we can illustrate the difficulty of conducting statistical inference about management skills by calculating the power function for a test of the null hypothesis:

$$H_0 \text{ (no abnormal performance)} : \alpha = 0$$

against the alternative hypothesis:

$$H_1(\text{abnormal performance}) : \alpha \neq 0.$$

We do so by computing how many months of data are needed to ensure a 10, 25 or 50% probability of correctly identifying the fund's abnormal performance. The null hypothesis is rejected if:

$$|Z| \equiv \left| \frac{\bar{\alpha} - \alpha_0}{\sigma/\sqrt{T}} \right| > z_{1-p/2}$$

where $\bar{\alpha} = \sum_{t=1}^{T} (R_t - R_{Mt})/T$ is the estimated mean performance and α_0 is the value of α under the null hypothesis of zero abnormal performance. $z_{1-p/2}$ is the $(1 - p/2)$ quantile of the distribution of the performance test statistic. The null is rejected if:

$$\bar{\alpha} < \alpha_0 - z_{1-p/2}\sigma/\sqrt{T}$$

or

$$\bar{\alpha} > \alpha_0 + z_{1-p/2}\sigma/\sqrt{T}.$$

Otherwise it is accepted. Suppose that, under the alternative hypothesis, the fund manager's performance is α_1, so that $\bar{\alpha}$ has a normal distribution with mean α_1 and standard deviation $\sigma/\sqrt{T}$. Then the rejection probability can be computed from:

$$\Pr(\bar{\alpha} < \alpha_0 - z_{1-p/2}\sigma/\sqrt{T}) = \Pr\left(\frac{\bar{\alpha} - \alpha_1}{\sigma/\sqrt{T}} < \frac{\alpha_0 - \alpha_1 - z_{1-p/2}\sigma/\sqrt{T}}{\sigma/\sqrt{T}} \right)$$

$$= \Pr\left(Z < \frac{\alpha_0 - \alpha_1}{\sigma/\sqrt{T}} - z_{1-p/2} \right)$$

$$= N\left(\frac{\alpha_0 - \alpha_1}{\sigma/\sqrt{T}} - z_{1-p/2} \right),$$

where $N(.)$ is the cumulative density function for a standard normal variate. Likewise, by symmetry of the normal distribution,

$$\Pr(\bar{\alpha} > \alpha_0 + z_{1-p/2}\sigma/\sqrt{T}) = \Pr\left(Z > \frac{\alpha_0 - \alpha_1}{\sigma/\sqrt{T}} + z_{1-p/2} \right)$$

$$= N\left(\frac{\alpha_1 - \alpha_0}{\sigma/\sqrt{T}} + z_{1-p/2} \right)$$

For example, if $p = 0.05$ so that $z_{1-p/2} = 1.96$ and $\alpha_0 = \alpha_1 = 0$, then $\Pr(Z < -2) = \Pr(Z > 2) = 0.025$, so that the power of the test equals the size of the test at 5%.

However, if $\alpha_0 = 0, \alpha_1 = -0.1$ and $\sigma = 0.5$, we get the following relation between power (the probability of correctly rejecting the null) and sample size:

$$\Pr(\text{Reject } H_0 \mid \alpha_1, \alpha_0, \sigma, T)$$
$$= \text{Power}(\alpha_1, \alpha_0, \sigma, T)$$
$$= N\left(\frac{\alpha_0 - \alpha_1}{\sigma/\sqrt{T}} - z_{1-p/2}\right) + N\left(\frac{\alpha_1 - \alpha_0}{\sigma/\sqrt{T}} + z_{1-p/2}\right)$$
$$= \Pr(Z < -1.96 + 0.2\sqrt{T}) + P(Z < -1.96 - 0.2\sqrt{T}).$$

This relationship is used to calculate the results in the main text.

REFERENCES

Barclays Capital (2006) *Equity Gilt Study*. Barclays Capital, London.

Blake, D. (2000) *Financial Market Analysis*, John Wiley & Sons, Ltd, Chichester.

Blake, D. (2003) *Pension Schemes and Pension Funds in the United Kingdom*, second edition, Oxford University Press, Oxford.

Blake, D. and Timmermann, A. (1998) Mutual fund performance: evidence from the UK. *European Finance Review*, **2**, 57–77.

Blake, D. and Timmermann, A. (2002) Performance benchmarks for institutional investors: measuring, monitoring and modifying investment behaviour, in Knight, J. and Satchell, S. (Eds) *Performance Measurement in Finance: Firms, Funds and Managers*, Butterworth Heinemann, Oxford, pp. 108–141.

Blake, D. and Timmermann, A. (2005) Returns from active management in international equity markets: evidence from a panel of UK pension funds. *Journal of Asset Management*, **6**, 5–20.

Blake, D., Lehmann, B. and Timmermann, A. (1999) Asset allocation dynamics and pension fund performance. *Journal of Business*, **72**, 429–462.

Blake, D., Lehmann, B. and Timmermann, A. (2002) Performance clustering and incentives in the UK pension fund industry. *Journal of Asset Management*, **3**, 173–194.

Brinson, G.P., Hood, L.R. and Beebower, G.L. (1986) Determinants of portfolio performance. *Financial Analysts Journal*, July–August, 39–48.

Brinson, G., Singer, B. and Beebower, G. (1991) Determinants of portfolio performance II: an update. *Financial Analysts Journal*, May–June, 40–48.

Brown, K.C., Harlow, W.V. and Starks, L.T. (1996) Of tournaments and temptations: an analysis of managerial incentives in the mutual fund industry. *Journal of Finance*, **51**, 85–110.

Brown, S.J. and Goetzmann, W. (1995) Performance persistence. *Journal of Finance*, **50**, 679–698.

CAPS (various), *General Reports*, Combined Actuarial Performance Services, Leeds.

Carhart, M. (1997) On persistence in mutual fund performance. *Journal of Finance*, **52**, 57–82.

Chevalier, J. and Ellison, G. (1997) Risk taking by mutual funds as a response to incentives. *Journal of Political Economy*, **105**, 1167–200.

Davis, E.P. (1988) *Financial Market Activity of Life Insurance Companies and Pension Funds*, Economic Paper No.21, Bank for International Settlements, Basle.

Fama, E. (1972) Components of investment performance. *Journal of Finance*, **27**, 551–567.

Fong, H.G., Pearson, C., and Vasicek, O. (1983) Bond performance: analysing sources of return. *Journal of Portfolio Management*, Spring, 46–50.

Grinblatt, M. and Titman, S. (1992) The persistence of mutual fund performance. *Journal of Finance*, **47**, 1977–84.

Hendricks, D., Patel, J. and Zeckhauser, R. (1993) Hot hands in mutual funds: short-run persistence of relative performance. *Journal of Finance*, **48**, 93–130.

Jegadeesh, N. and Titman, S. (1993) Returns to buying winners and selling losers: implications for stock market efficiency. *Journal of Finance*, **48**, 65–91.

Jensen, M. (1969) Risk, the pricing of capital assets and the evaluation of investment portfolios. *Journal of Business*, **42**, 167–247.

Lakonishok, J., Shleifer, A. and Vishny, R. (1992) The structure and performance of the money management industry. *Brookings Papers: Microeconomics*, 339–391.

Lunde, A., Timmermann, A. and Blake, D. (1999) The hazards of mutual fund underperformance. *Journal of Empirical Finance*, **6**, 121–152.

Malkiel, B.G. (1995) Returns from investing in equity mutual funds. *Journal of Finance*, **50**, 540–572.

Plantinga, A. and van der Meer, R. (1995) Liability-driven performance attribution, *Geneva Papers on Risk and Insurance*, **20**, 16–29.

Sharpe, W. (1966) Mutual fund performance. *Journal of Business*, **39**, 119–38.

Starks, L. (1987) Performance incentive fees: an agency theoretic approach. *Journal of Financial and Quantitative Analysis*, **22**, 17–32.

Timmermann, A. and Blake, D. (2005) International asset allocation with time-varying investment opportunities. *Journal of Business*, **78** (1, part 2), 71–98.

Tonks, I. (2005) Performance persistence of pension fund managers. *Journal of Business*, **78**, 1917–1942.

Treynor, J. (1965) How to rate management of investment funds. *Harvard Business Review*, January–February, 63–75.

9

Risk Management in Pension Funds

As we have seen in earlier chapters, pension funds, especially those of defined benefit schemes, face a number of risks in both the accumulation and distribution stages. Many of these risks can be managed (or mitigated or hedged), at least partially. In the case of asset–liability management, key risks (such as inflation or interest-rate risk) are managed continuously as an integral part of the overall fund management process (see Section 7.8.3). Sometimes, however, the risk exposure is temporary and the associated risk hedge will also be temporary. In this Chapter we will examine how accumulation stage risks, such as security-price risk, interest-rate risk and currency risk, can be hedged using the key hedging instruments – futures, options and swaps. We will also examine how an important risk facing pension funds and annuity providers during the distribution stage, namely longevity risk, can be hedged using a new class of financial instruments, known as longevity (or survivor) bonds and mortality-linked derivatives.

9.1 THE OBJECTIVE OF HEDGING

The objective of *hedging* (or *risk management* or *risk mitigation*) is to transfer risk from one individual or corporation to another individual or corporation. The counterparty offloading the risk is the *hedger*; the counterparty taking on (or assuming) the risk is the *insurer* or *speculator*.

The hedger might be concerned with, say, adverse movements in security prices or with increases in volatility, which increase the overall riskiness of his position. For example, if a pension fund has a long position (i.e. net asset position) in cash-market securities, the fund manager will be concerned about the prices of those securities falling and will want to protect against this possibility. Alternatively, if the pension fund has a short position (i.e. net liability position) in cash-market securities, the fund manager will be concerned about rising prices and will want to protect against this possibility.

In order to hedge successfully and so transfer all (or at least most) risk, the hedger will have to select a suitable hedging instrument. A good hedging instrument will be one whose price movements mirror closely those of the underlying cash-market securities. Three of the most suitable hedging instruments will therefore be instruments that are derivative upon cash-market securities – namely, financial futures, options and swaps.

These derivatives were first introduced in the 1970s in response to the huge increase in interest- and exchange-rate volatility that resulted from the ending of fixed exchange rates and the increase in world inflation rates that followed the two oil price shocks of the 1970s. The first hedging instruments were therefore designed to hedge against adverse movements in interest rates and exchange rates. Later, the introduction of (exchange-traded) options on individual shares, and options and futures on stock-market indices allowed share-price movements to be hedged as well. Currently, attempts are being made to establish a market in mortality-linked instruments with the aim of allowing longevity risk to be hedged.

Pension funds have been involved in hedging since the early 1980s. However, the UK Government initially treated pension fund activities using futures and options as trading, and hence not exempt from taxation. This severely limited these activities. But the 1990 Social Security Act exempted pension fund profits from futures and options from taxation, and this has significantly increased their use.

9.2   HEDGING WITH FUTURES

Futures contracts can be used to hedge interest-rate risk (both short-term and long-term), stock-market risk and exchange-rate risk. There are some simple rules for hedging with futures:

- if *short cash* (i.e. expecting a cash inflow and worried that prices will rise or interest rates will fall), then *buy futures* (i.e. put on a *long hedge*);
- if *long cash* (i.e. holding cash or securities and worried that prices will fall or interest rates will rise), then *sell futures* (i.e. put on a *short hedge*).

The number of futures contracts required to hedge a cash position is determined as follows. We construct a *hedge portfolio* from a long position in the cash security and a short position in h units of the corresponding futures contract (where h is the *hedge ratio*). If the initial cash position is a short one, then the hedge portfolio involves a long position in h units of the futures contract. In the first case, the value of the hedge portfolio (V^H) is given by:

$$V^H = P^S - hP^F \tag{9.1}$$

where P^S is the value of the cash security and P^F is the value of the futures contract. The optimal hedge ratio is determined to ensure that the hedge portfolio is riskless, or, in other words, has a constant value independent of whether the value of the cash security rises or falls. This requires:

$$\Delta V^H = \Delta P^S - h\Delta P^F \tag{9.2}$$
$$= 0$$

(where Δ denotes a change in the value of), so that the hedge ratio is determined as:

$$h = \frac{\Delta P^S}{\Delta P^F} \tag{9.3}$$

Equation (9.3) says that the hedge ratio is set equal to the ratio of the change in (or volatility of) the price of the underlying cash-market security being hedged to the change in (or volatility of) the futures contract being used to hedge it. If the price of the cash-market security happens to be more volatile than that of the futures contract, then the hedge ratio will exceed unity, so that more futures contracts will be needed to hedge the underlying cash position than the face value of that position. The opposite holds if futures are more volatile than cash.

The number of futures contracts necessary to hedge a cash security is given by:

$$\text{Number of contracts} = \frac{\text{Face value of cash exposure}}{\text{Face value of futures contract}} \times h \tag{9.4}$$

that is, the number of contracts equals the hedge ratio scaled up by the ratio of the face value of the cash exposure to the face value of the futures contracts. With the number of contracts determined in this way, the hedge will be *perfect* (i.e. completely riskless for small changes in security prices). This is depicted in Figure 9.1, which shows the value of a hedged portfolio comprising a long position in cash securities (P^S) and a short position in h futures contracts (P^F). If the hedge is put on when the value of the cash portfolio is P_0^S, then the hedged position locks in a portfolio value P_0^H equal to the futures price P_0^F at the time the hedge is implemented. This value is locked in so long as the hedge

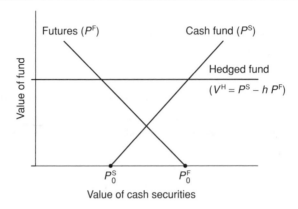

Figure 9.1 Hedging with futures

is maintained until the expiry date of the futures contracts, whatever subsequently happens to the value of the underlying securities.

9.2.1   Hedging with stock-index futures

Stock-index futures contracts (such as the FTSE 100 contract on LIFFE – the London International Financial Futures and Options Exchange) can be used to hedge the systematic risk from holding equity portfolios. We can illustrate the use of such contracts with the following example.

Suppose that on 1 April a pension fund manager is uncertain about where the market is going over the next three months and wishes to hedge £1m of his equity portfolio, which has a beta of 1.15. On 1 April the FTSE 100 index is standing at 2204.0 and the value of the June contract on LIFFE is 2300.0. Because the fund manager is long in the cash market, he will need to be short in the futures market to hedge the portfolio. The fund manager has to calculate the number of futures contracts that have to be sold in order to hedge the portfolio. He has to calculate the cost of putting on the hedge and he also has to calculate the value of the portfolio, that he is locking in.

Since the value of each one-point movement (known as a *tick*) in the LIFFE FTSE 100 contract is worth £10, the fund manager will need to sell futures contracts according to the following formula:

$$\text{Number of contracts} = \frac{\text{Face value of cash exposure}}{\text{Face value of futures contract}} \times \beta_{\text{P}}$$

$$= \frac{\text{Face value of cash exposure}}{\text{Tick value} \times \text{Futures price}} \times \beta_{\text{P}} \quad (9.5)$$

where β_P, the beta of the portfolio, is the hedge ratio. Using the data in the example, this means that the fund manager needs to sell:

$$\text{Number of contracts} = \frac{1\,000\,000}{10 \times 2300.0} \times 1.15$$
$$= 50 \text{ June contracts}$$

to hedge the portfolio exactly. Because the portfolio beta exceeds unity, more contracts will be needed for a perfect hedge than if the portfolio exactly matched the market index and had a beta of unity.

The portfolio value that the fund manager is locking in is based on the index value of the June contract, namely 2300.0 (so long as the futures contract is held to expiry). The fund manager knows that, whatever happens to the cash index between 1 April and 30 June, his hedged portfolio will have a value on 30 June determined by:

Terminal value of hedged fund = Initial value of hedged fund

$$\times \left[1 + \left(\frac{P^F(1 \text{ April}) - P^S(1 \text{ April})}{P^S(1 \text{ April})} \right) \times \beta_P \right] \qquad (9.6)$$

where P^F = futures index or price; P^S = cash index or price; that is,

Terminal value of hedged fund

$$= \pounds 1\,000\,000 \times \left[1 + \left(\frac{2300.0 - 2204.0}{2204.0} \right) \times 1.15 \right]$$
$$= \pounds 1\,050\,091.$$

The fund manager cannot use futures contracts to lock in the current value (as of 1 April) of the cash index; he can only lock in the current value (as of 1 April) of the futures index for 30 June. The reason why the portfolio value is fixed for 30 June is that the cash and futures positions are exactly offsetting. If the cash index rises between 1 April and 30 June, the value of the cash portfolio rises by an amount which exactly offsets the fall in the value of the futures contracts. The opposite holds for a fall in the index over the period.

We have considered the case of a pension fund manager who has a long cash portfolio and is worried that equity prices will fall; he therefore sells futures. Another pension fund manager might be expecting a cash inflow into his fund in the near future and is worried that equity prices will rise before the cash inflow arrives. He is therefore said to be 'short cash' and will want to hedge this position by buying futures contracts.

9.2.2 Hedging with bond futures

Bond futures contracts (such as the long gilt contract on LIFFE) can be used to hedge the systematic risk or the interest-rate risk from holding bond portfolios. Suppose that a fund manager believes that interest rates will rise and that, as a consequence, the value of his bond portfolio will fall. One alternative would be to sell the bonds and repurchase them after interest rates have risen. But this would involve transaction costs, and also there is no guarantee of being able to repurchase the same portfolio of bonds. A much cheaper alternative is for the fund manager to use the long gilt futures contract to temporarily 'step outside' his portfolio.

Bond futures contracts are priced off the *cheapest-to-deliver* (CTD) bond from the range of deliverable bonds. If the price of the CTD bond changes, so does the futures price and in the same direction. The relationship between changes in the futures price and the price of the CTD bond (see, for example, Blake, 2000, Chapter 8) is given by:

$$\Delta P^{\mathrm{F}} = \frac{1}{\mathrm{PF_{CTD}}} \Delta P_{\mathrm{CTD}} \tag{9.7}$$

where $\Delta P^{\mathrm{F}} =$ change in the price of the long gilt future; $\Delta P_{\mathrm{CTD}} =$ change in the price of the CTD bond; $\mathrm{PF_{CTD}} =$ price (or conversion) factor for the CTD bond (which converts the CTD bond into a bond with a yield to maturity of 6% as required by the specification of the LIFFE long gilt futures contract[1]). It follows from Equation (9.7) that the futures price moves by less than the cash bond if the price factor ($\mathrm{PF_{CTD}}$) exceeds unity and by more otherwise. This relationship can be used to hedge CTD bonds.

Suppose that on 1 April a pension fund manager is expecting a cash inflow of about £1.20m in two months' time, which he intends investing in the CTD bond (which we suppose to be Treasury 10.5% 2023–25 with a price factor of 1.3032131 and currently trading at £118 per £100 nominal). He is concerned that yields will fall and gilt prices will rise against him. Because he is short cash, he decides to hedge his exposure by purchasing long gilt futures contracts on LIFFE. To do this he buys

---

[1] The price factor measures the volatility of the bond to be hedged relative to that of the CTD bond. If the price factor exceeds unity, the bond to be hedged is more responsive to a given change in interest rates than the CTD bond, and therefore more futures contracts are needed to hedge this bond than the CTD bond. LIFFE publishes the price factors for the different deliverable bonds for the various gilt futures contracts traded.

June contracts according to the following formula:

$$\text{Number of contracts} = \frac{\text{Face value of cash exposure}}{\text{Face value of futures contract}} \times \text{PF}_{\text{CTD}} \quad (9.8)$$

where $h = \text{PF}_{\text{CTD}}$ is the hedge ratio and where:

$$\text{Face value of cash exposure} = \frac{\text{Market value of cash exposure}}{P_{\text{CTD}}} \quad (9.9)$$

where P_{CTD} is the market price of the CTD bond. That is:

$$\text{Number of contracts} = \frac{£1\,000\,000}{£100\,000} \times 1.3032131 = 13$$

since the long gilt futures contract on LIFFE has a face value of £100 000. Note that the number of contracts depends on the face value of the futures contract *and* the face value of the cash exposure. Since P_{CTD} is £118 per £100 nominal, a market exposure of around £1.2m is equivalent to a nominal exposure of around £1m (i.e. £1m $\approx$ £1.2m/1.18).

When a bond other than the CTD bond is being hedged, the duration of both bonds must be taken into account. This procedure is known as *duration-based hedging*.

Duration is defined as follows:

$$\begin{aligned}
D &= \frac{d}{P_d} \times \sum_{t=1}^{T} \frac{t}{(1+rm)^t} + \frac{B}{P_d} \times \frac{T}{(1+rm)^T} \\
&= \frac{d}{P_d} \left[\frac{(1+rm)^{T+1} - (1+rm) - (rm)(T)}{(rm)^2(1+rm)^T} \right] + \frac{B}{P_d} \times \frac{T}{(1+rm)^T}
\end{aligned}$$
$$(9.10)$$

where:

D = duration (measured in years)
d = annual coupon
B = par value of bond
P_d = dirty price of bond (i.e. clean price plus accrued interest)
t = time in years to tth cash flow
T = time in years to maturity
rm = yield to maturity.

Duration measures the interest-rate sensitivity of the price of a bond (see Appendix C of the book). It is easy to show that the following relationship between a bond's price, its yield to maturity and its duration holds:

$$\Delta P_d = (-D) \times P_d \times \Delta rm/(1 + rm) \qquad (9.11)$$

Equation (9.11) shows that for a given change in yield, the change in the price of a bond is greater, the greater its duration. Therefore, the more price-sensitive the bond to be hedged is compared with the CTD bond, the larger the number of futures contracts that will be needed to hedge that bond.

Suppose that the bond to be hedged is the Treasury 11.5% 2023 (denoted by the subscript H below), then the *duration hedge ratio* is given by:

$$\text{DHR} = \frac{\Delta P_H}{\Delta P_{CTD}} = \frac{D_H \times P_H \times \Delta rm_H \times (1 + rm_{CTD})}{D_{CTD} \times P_{CTD} \times \Delta rm_{CTD} \times (1 + rm_H)} \qquad (9.12)$$

This ratio can be simplified if we assume parallel yield-curve movements (i.e. $\Delta rm_{CTD} = \Delta rm_H$):

$$\text{DHR} = \frac{\Delta P_H}{\Delta P_{CTD}} = \frac{D_H \times P_H \times (1 + rm_{CTD})}{D_{CTD} \times P_{CTD} \times (1 + rm_H)} \qquad (9.13)$$

It can be simplified even further if we assume parallel percentage-yield-curve movements (i.e. $\Delta rm_{CTD}/(1 + rm_{CTD}) = \Delta rm_H/(1 + rm_H)$):

$$\text{DHR} = \frac{\Delta P_H}{\Delta P_{CTD}} = \frac{D_H \times P_H}{D_{CTD} \times P_{CTD}} \qquad (9.14)$$

Using (9.14) and assuming that $P_H = £126.25$, $D_{CTD} = 11.6$ years and $D_H = 13$ years, then:

$$\text{DHR} = \frac{13 \times 126.25}{11.6 \times 118.00} = 1.199.$$

In terms of duration, the Treasury 11.5% 2023 bond is equivalent to 1.2 CTD bonds, in the sense that it is about 20% more volatile than the CTD bond. This suggests that the appropriate number of contracts required to hedge this bond is given by:

$$\text{Number of contracts} = \frac{\text{Face value of cash exposure}}{\text{Face value of futures contract}} \\ \times \text{PF}_{CTD} \times \text{DHR} \qquad (9.15)$$

that is (assuming again a nominal exposure of £1 000 000):

$$\text{Number of contracts} = \frac{£1\,000\,000}{£100\,000} \times 1.3032131 \times 1.199$$

$$= 16 \text{ contracts.}$$

In terms of hedging bond portfolios, again it is possible to use duration-based hedging. Suppose that the duration of the portfolio is 14.2 years and the weighted average price (per £100 nominal) of the bonds in the portfolio is £110.125. Then the appropriate duration hedge ratio for the portfolio is:

$$\text{DHR}_P = \frac{D_P \times P_P}{D_{\text{CTD}} \times P_{\text{CTD}}} \tag{9.16}$$

where D_P = duration of the portfolio; P_P = weighted average price of the bonds in the portfolio; that is:

$$\text{DHR}_P = \frac{14.2 \times 110.125}{11.6 \times 118.00} = 1.142$$

The number of futures contracts necessary to hedge a £10m bond portfolio is given by

$$\text{Number of contracts} = \frac{\text{Face value of cash exposure}}{\text{Face value of futures contract}} \times \text{PF}_{\text{CTD}} \times \text{DHR}_P$$

$$= \frac{£10\,000\,000}{£100\,000} \times 1.3032131 \times 1.142$$

$$= 149.$$

9.2.3 Hedging with currency futures

Exchange-rate risk can be hedged using currency futures contracts. To illustrate, we can consider the case of a UK pension fund manager who is expecting dividend payments on his US investments of $3m. It is now 1 April and the dividend payments are due on 1 June. They will be repatriated immediately, and the fund manager is concerned that sterling will rise against the dollar between 1 April and 1 June. To hedge against this risk the fund manager decides to buy sterling currency futures contracts on the Chicago Mercantile Exchange (CME), which have a contract size of £62 500 traded against the dollar (i.e. the fund manager is short cash sterling and therefore needs to be long sterling contracts to hedge the exposure).

Suppose that on 1 April the spot exchange rate is $1.75 per £, and the June CME futures price is $1.77. At the spot exchange rate, the dividend payments are valued at £1 714 285.71 (i.e. $3 000 000/$1.75) in sterling. The number of sterling contracts necessary to hedge this exposure is determined as follows:

$$\text{Number of contracts} = \frac{\text{Face value of cash exposure (sterling)}}{\text{Face value of futures contract (sterling)}}$$

(9.17)

that is:

$$\text{Number of contracts} = \frac{£1\,714\,285.71}{£62\,500} = 27.$$

So, a short exposure of £1 714 285.71 can be hedged by buying twenty-seven sterling futures contracts. The contracts have a sterling value of £1 687 500 (i.e. 27 × £62 500) and a dollar value of $2 986 875 (i.e. £1 687 500 × $1.77).

9.3   HEDGING WITH OPTIONS

Hedging using options can be a more flexible alternative to hedging using futures. Futures are used when the amount and timing of the exposure are known with certainty: a futures contract locks in the price of a specific amount of an asset at a specific future date. Options can be used when either the amount or the timing of the exposure is not known with certainty. Options can also be used when the hedger wants to protect against adverse price movements but would like to benefit from favourable price movements: with futures, the hedger gains when prices move in one direction but loses when prices move in the opposite direction. In addition to being able to hedge interest-rate risk, stock-market risk and exchange-rate risk, it is also possible to use options contracts to hedge the specific risks of individual securities (a hedging possibility not available using futures in a number of markets).

9.3.1   Hedging with individual stock options

The simplest way for a pension fund manager to hedge a long position in ABC shares is to purchase an at-the-money put option with an *exercise price* equal to the current price of the share. Figure 9.2 shows the profit-and-loss profile for this combination when the share price is trading at

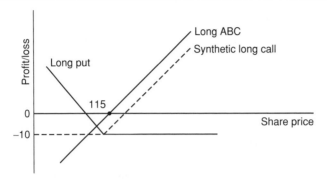

Figure 9.2 A fixed hedge using a long at-the-money put

115p (shown by the dashed line). The fund manager is protected (at the cost of the premium on the put) if the share price falls below 115p and keeps the gains he would make if the share price rises above 115p. But this profit-and-loss profile is exactly the same as that of a long call option. In other words, the combination of a *long share* and a *long put* is equivalent to a *synthetic long call*.

The pension fund manager has a number of alternatives to hedge a portfolio of ABC shares. He could hold on to ABC and buy an at-the-money put. Alternatively, he could sell ABC and buy an at-the-money call. Obviously, he will do whatever is cheaper, taking into account transaction costs. Suppose that on 1 April, with ABC trading at 115p, the June 115p call is trading at 12p and the June 115p put at 10p. The riskless rate of interest is 10% and ABC has annual dividends of 6% (assume quarterly dividends are paid at the end of each quarter). We can consider the two hedging alternatives.

The first alternative involves holding on to ABC, earning the dividends, and buying the put option. The net cash flow per share from this position as of 30 June is as follows (which includes the interest paid on the funds borrowed to buy the put option):

$$\begin{array}{ll}
\text{Purchase of 115p put option on} & \\
\text{1 April} \times \text{interest factor}: & -10 \times 0.1(91/365) \\
\text{Dividends on ABC on 30 June}: & \underline{115 \times 0.06(91/365)} \\
 & -8.53\text{p}
\end{array}$$

The second alternative involves selling ABC and investing the proceeds at 10% and buying the call option. The net cash flow per share from this position as of 30 June is as follows:

Interest earned on ABC sale:	$115 \times 0.1(91/365)$
Purchase of 115p call option on 1 April $\times$ interest factor:	$-12 \times (1 + 0.1(91/365))$
	$\overline{-9.43\text{p}}$

So, the first alternative is less expensive than the second: it is better to hold on to ABC and buy the put. This solution is likely to be reinforced when transaction costs are taken into account. The second alternative involves a sale and a purchase and so incurs two sets of transaction costs involving spreads and commissions. The first alternative involves only one set of transaction costs. A further disadvantage of the second alternative is the risk of not being able to buy back the ABC shares at the end of June, especially if a large block had been sold on 1 April. At the end of June the market for ABC stock might be quite thin and a large block of shares might not be readily available on the market to be repurchased.

To avoid the costs and risks associated with selling the underlying security, there is a hedging alternative to selling the security and buying call options, and this is to retain the security and write call options. This is illustrated in Figure 9.3. The combination is a *synthetic short put* and the hedger is protected from a limited decline in the price of ABC shares because of the premium earned from writing the call option. The premium on the June call option is 12p and this protects the hedger from a 12p fall in the share price.

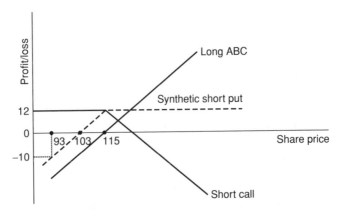

Figure 9.3   A fixed hedge using a short at-the-money call

Comparing Figure 9.2 and 9.3, it is clear that the share price would have to fall to less than 93p (or by more than 19%) before hedging with a short call leads to larger losses than hedging with a long put. Nevertheless, the long put (Figure 9.2) gives complete downside protection whatever the fall in the share price, and has better upside potential in the event of the share price rising rather than falling. We can see that the profit on the short call (Figure 9.3) is limited to 12p whatever the rise in the share price, whereas with the long put (Figure 9.2), the upside potential is unlimited.

So, we have the following simple rules for hedging with options:

- if the cash position is adversely affected by *falling* prices, then *buy puts* or *sell calls*;
- if the cash position is adversely affected by *rising* prices, then *sell puts* or *buy calls*.

But when should options be used in preference to futures? The answer depends (a) on whether the exposure in terms of amount or timing is certain or uncertain, and (b) on whether the exposure is symmetrical or asymmetrical.

The exposure is *certain* (both in amount and timing), for example, for a pension fund manager planning to repatriate dividends denominated in dollars on a given future date and wishing to guarantee the sterling value of the dividends. In this case, a currency futures or forward contract is the appropriate hedging instrument. On the other hand, a pension fund manager wanting to reduce the volatility of his or her fund's value through a partial hedge faces an *uncertain* exposure over an *uncertain* time interval. In this case, an options contract is the appropriate hedging instrument.

The exposure is *symmetrical* when it is equally responsive to a rise or fall in the underlying security price. This means that a price move in one direction benefits the cash position, while a price move in the opposite direction damages the cash position, and the hedger wishes to protect against the second possibility. In this case, a futures contract is the appropriate hedging instrument. The exposure is *asymmetrical* when the cash position is damaged by a price move in one direction but does not benefit from a price move in the opposite direction. An example of this is a bank that has provided an interest-rate cap guarantee to a borrower: the bank loses if interest rates fall but does not benefit if interest rates rise. In this case, an options contract is the appropriate hedging instrument.

Once an options hedge has been chosen, the next step is to decide whether to use a fixed hedge or a ratio hedge. A *fixed hedge* is a one-off options hedge designed to limit the maximum loss on the hedged position, but to benefit from any upside potential. In other words, a fixed options hedge is rather like an insurance policy: in return for a premium, the minimum value of a cash position is guaranteed. A fixed hedge hedges the full amount of the actual or expected exposure and the hedge is maintained until the exposure is eliminated, at which point the options are either sold or exercised. The hedges illustrated in Figures 9.2 and 9.3 were examples of fixed hedges.

A *ratio* (or *delta-neutral*) *hedge* is designed to establish and preserve a combined cash-and-options position that is delta-neutral over time. The *delta* of an option measures the responsiveness of the option price (P^O) to changes in the price of the underlying security (P^S):[2]

$$\text{Delta} = \frac{\Delta P^O}{\Delta P^S} \qquad (9.18)$$

We know from Equation (9.3) that the hedge ratio is determined by (using Equation (9.18)):

$$h = \frac{\Delta P^S}{\Delta P^O} = \frac{1}{\text{Delta}} \qquad (9.19)$$

Since the delta is the inverse of the hedge ratio, a delta-neutral hedge is one in which the ratio between the number of options and the number of securities being hedged is always kept equal to the inverse of the option delta. This implies that a ratio hedge has to be rebalanced whenever the option delta changes.

To illustrate, we will consider a ratio hedge involving a combination of a long position in ABC shares and a long position in put options. The number of put option contracts necessary to hedge the ABC shares is determined as follows:

$$\text{Number of contracts} = \frac{\text{Number of shares}}{\text{Option delta} \times 1000}$$

Since the standard options contract size is for 1000 shares (in the UK), we must divide the number of shares by 1000. In addition, because the delta of an option is always less than unity, more options contracts will be required to construct a ratio hedge than a fixed hedge. For example, if the delta of the put option used to hedge 30 000 ABC shares is 0.75,

---

[2] Delta is equal to the term $N(d_1)$ in Equation (1.27) in the case of both a call and a put option (see Equation (1.28))

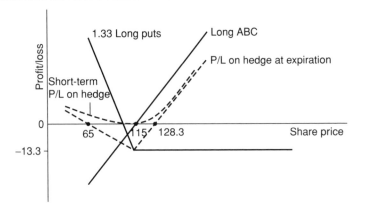

Figure 9.4   A ratio hedge using at-the-money puts

then the number of put options required to construct the ratio hedge is given by:

$$\text{Number of contracts} = \frac{30\,000}{0.75 \times 1000} = 40 \text{ contracts}$$

equivalent to 1.33 (i.e. 1/0.75) contracts per 1000 shares (compared with a fixed hedge, which uses 1 contract per 1000 shares).

Figure 9.4 illustrates a ratio hedge using 1.33 long at-the-money puts per 1000 ABC shares. It shows both the short-term profit-and-loss profile and the profit-and-loss profile at expiration. In the short term, the hedge is both delta-neutral and *gamma-positive*, so that it shows a short-term profit whether the price of ABC shares rises or falls.[3] As the share price changes, the ratio hedge will have to be rebalanced. The process of *ratio-hedge management* is illustrated in Figure 9.5. The initial position is at *A*. Suppose that after several weeks the share price has fallen to 105p, so that the hedger is sitting on a profit. However, this profit is not guaranteed, so the hedger will want to lock in the profit by rebalancing the hedge at *B* with respect to the new option delta. The hedge is again rebalanced at *C* when the share price falls to 95p, and a further profit is locked in.

Because frequent rebalancing will be an expensive process, it is advisable to use a ratio hedge only when a cheaper alternative is not available; that is, when it is desired to hedge a cash position continuously over time

---

[3] *Gamma* measures the change in an option's delta as the price of the underlying security changes. It measures the convexity of the option premium with respect to the price of the underlying security.

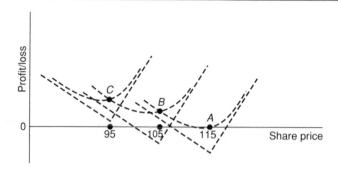

Figure 9.5   Ratio-hedge management

rather than for a specific date. When a specific sum is going to be hedged for a specific date, then a fixed options hedge or even a futures hedge should be used.

9.3.2   Hedging with stock-index options

The aim of hedging with individual stock options is to hedge the specific (or nonsystematic) risks of individual shares. The aim of hedging with stock-index options, on the other hand, is to hedge the systematic (or market) risk of a portfolio of shares. We must, therefore, take into account the beta of the portfolio being hedged. The specific risks attached to the individual shares in the portfolio remain unhedged by this strategy.

The number of contracts needed to hedge a portfolio of shares is determined as follows. For a fixed hedge:

$$\text{Number of contracts} = \frac{\text{Face value of cash exposure}}{\text{Face value of index}} \times \beta_P \quad (9.20)$$

For a ratio hedge:

$$\text{Number of contracts} = \frac{\text{Face value of cash exposure}}{\text{Face value of index}} \times \frac{\beta_P}{\text{Option delta}}$$
$$(9.21)$$

To illustrate, we will suppose that on 15 July a pension fund manager has a £5m portfolio with a beta of 1.15, which he intends to hedge by buying LIFFE November 1850 put options on the FTSE 100 index (which have a tick value of £10). The closing index on 15 July is 1825.00 and the fund manager intends employing a fixed hedge. The number of contracts to hedge the portfolio is found using (9.20):

$$\text{Number of contracts} = \frac{£5\,000\,000}{£10 \times 1825.00} \times 1.15 = 315.$$

Hedging with individual stock options eliminates all risks, while hedging with stock-index options eliminates only systematic risk. A pension fund manager who hedges the systematic risk in his portfolio is therefore taking on a *relative-performance bet* against the market (i.e. he has created a *relative-performance portfolio*). He is eliminating the market risk in his portfolio but leaving it exposed to specific risk, which, if he is good at security selection, he will be very pleased to do. In short, he is hoping to beat the market, having eliminated market risk.

9.3.3   Hedging with bond options

It is possible to hedge long-term interest-rate risk using options on bond futures. The following rules apply:

- calculate the best futures hedge;
- for a fixed hedge, replace the futures hedge with the same number of options contracts;
- for a ratio hedge:

$$\text{Number of contracts} = \frac{\text{Number of contracts in futures hedge}}{\text{Option delta}}$$

$$(9.22)$$

where the number of contracts in the futures hedge is given by Equation (9.15).

In the bond-portfolio example above, 149 futures contracts were needed to hedge the portfolio. As an alternative, the portfolio could be hedged using 149 put options on the futures contracts. If the delta of the put options is 0.82, then 182 put options contracts would be needed for a ratio hedge.

9.3.4   Hedging with currency options

As with other types of options hedges, hedging with currency options is useful when the hedger wants to insure against downside exchange-rate risk, but wants to preserve some of the benefits of favourable exchange-rate movements. For example, the Philadelphia Stock Exchange (PSE) sterling currency option has a contract size of £31 250 traded against the dollar.

To illustrate, we will consider a UK pension fund manager with a US portfolio valued at $1m on 1 April, when the current exchange rate is $1.59 and the three-month forward rate is $1.65 per £. Suppose that he decides to hedge half the portfolio against a rise in sterling over the next three months. The fund manager is short sterling cash and therefore needs to be long call options and/or short put options; if he is both long calls and short puts, he has created *synthetic long futures* or *forwards*. A fixed hedge would involve the purchase of the following number of PSE June 160 sterling call options contracts (i.e. with an exercise price of $1.60 per £1):

$$\text{Number of contracts} = \frac{\text{Face value of cash exposure (sterling)}}{\text{Face value of option contract (sterling)}} \quad (9.23)$$

that is:

$$\text{Number of contracts} = \frac{\$500\,000/\$1.59}{£31\,250}$$
$$= \frac{£314\,465.41}{£31\,250}$$
$$= 10.$$

If the *option premium* is 3.5 cents per £, then the total cost of the contracts is $10 937.50 (i.e. 10 contracts × $0.035 premium × £31 250). If, instead, a ratio hedge is used and the option delta is 0.435, then 23 contracts (i.e. 10/0.435) will have to be purchased and this will raise the cost of the hedge to $25 156.25.

The cost of the options, therefore, lies between 2.2% (i.e. $10 937.50/$500 000) and 5.0% (i.e. $25 156.25/$500 000) of the fund being hedged. Since this is usually much greater than the cost of forward cover (about 0.5% of the value of the exposure), options are generally less favoured than forward cover. Because of the option premium, the effective exchange rate locked in by the option is $1.635 (i.e. exercise price of $1.60 + premium of $0.035).

9.4   HEDGING WITH SWAPS

Swaps provide an alternative to futures and options as hedging instruments. For example, a pension fund manager with fixed coupon bonds in his portfolio who expected a temporary rise in interest rates could execute an *asset swap* and hence earn a return related to market rates.

This can be illustrated as follows. Suppose that the pension fund manager holds £50m nominal of bonds trading at par with a coupon of £10 per £100 nominal. He executes an asset swap with a bank whereby he retains ownership of the bonds but makes fixed-rate payments to the bank of 9.75% on £50m and in return receives floating-rate payments from the bank equal to LIBOR (the London Inter-Bank Offer Rate). The cash flows involved in this transaction from the pension fund's point of view are as follows. The pension fund:

earns from the fixed-coupon bond	10%
pays to the bank	(9.75%)
receives from the bank	LIBOR
	LIBOR + 0.25%

and so receives floating-rate payments on £50m of LIBOR plus 0.25%. In other words, the pension fund has transformed its fixed-coupon bonds into *synthetic floating-rate notes* (FRNs) yielding LIBOR plus 0.25%.

If, at the time of the swap, LIBOR was 9.50%, then the synthetic FRNs would yield 9.75%, which is less than the yield on the fixed-coupon bonds. If, however, immediately after the swap had taken place LIBOR rose to 10.50%, then the synthetic FRNs would yield 10.75%. This is a yield of 0.75% higher than that on the fixed-coupon bonds, equivalent to £375 000 per annum on £50m. The increase in yields would reduce the value of the underlying bonds, of course, but the pension fund manager believes that the increase in interest rates is only temporary, say, because the government has imposed a temporary credit squeeze. If this squeeze is expected to last about eighteen months, at which time interest rates are expected to return to their original levels, the fund manager could unwind the swap. Bond prices would return to their original levels and the fund manager would have saved the costs involved in selling the bonds before rates rise and repurchasing them before rates subsequently fall again; this was the only procedure available to fund managers to protect themselves against rising interest rates before the introduction of swaps, futures and options.

This is an example of a temporary hedge using a swap. Section 7.8.3 showed how swaps can be used on an ongoing basis to hedge continuous risks, such as inflation and interest-rate risk.

9.5   HEDGING LONGEVITY RISK

The life expectancy of people everywhere has increased substantially over the last century, and it is very difficult to forecast these increases accurately. This is what is meant by *aggregate longevity risk*. Under a state-run PAYG system, the government bears aggregate longevity risk. It is one thing for a government to bear such a risk, it is quite another to expect a pension fund or annuity provider to accept this risk unconditionally. Pension funds and annuity providers can hedge the *select* (i.e. specific) *longevity risk* in their pool of pensioners by having a sufficiently large pool, but they are currently unable to hedge the aggregate longevity risk that they face, since mortality-linked hedging instruments are not currently widely available.

9.5.1   Longevity risk

Consider an individual who will live for exactly T additional years. This individual could use a lump sum to purchase an annuity from an insurance company or buy an annuity bond (which pays coupons only and has no principal repayment) directly from the financial markets; both will yield a constant income stream for T periods. In the absence of arbitrage, both investments should cost the same. The market price of a T-year annuity bond is (see Equation (A.18) in Appendix A of the book):

$$P = \frac{d}{(1+r)} + \frac{d}{(1+r)^2} + \cdots + \frac{d}{(1+r)^T}$$
$$= \frac{d}{r}\left(1 - (1+r)^{-T}\right) \tag{9.24}$$

where d is the annual coupon and r is the relevant discount rate. If someone purchases this bond at price P and then lives exactly T years, this is equivalent to someone purchasing a T-year annuity for an amount P, which pays d per year in arrears.

In reality, neither individuals nor insurance companies know exactly how long an individual annuitant will live. In the case of an annuity bond, which continues to pay out coupons for as long as the individual is alive, its price depends on the whole probability distribution of death rates for this individual: in other words, T is a random variable, not a fixed parameter. As a consequence, the market price of such annuity bonds depends on expectations about the random variable T:

$$P = E\left(\frac{d}{r}\left(1 - (1+r)^{-T}\right)\right) \tag{9.25}$$

where E is the expectation operator.

Annuity bonds with random maturities are currently not traded on financial markets, but insurance companies still provide life annuities with uncertain T. Each insurance company will attempt to minimise its exposure to longevity risk by holding a portfolio of fixed-term bonds that matches the anticipated mortality profile of its annuitants and by building up a large enough pool of annuitants to reduce the probability that payouts will be worse than expected.

However, an insurance company cannot predict mortality perfectly. To consider the effects of errors in forecasting longevity increases, we denote the conditional probability of dying at age x having survived to age $x - 1$ (the hazard rate) by q_x. Suppose that the insurance company forecasts longevity increases by adjusting data from an actuarial table q_x^0 by multiplying by an exponential adjustment factor f^{x-x_0}, where x_0 is the current age of the annuitant and f is a scalar (which is less than unity if longevity increases over time and equal to unity in the case of no longevity increases). This is one way in which the UK Institute of Actuaries' Continuous Mortality Investigation Bureau (CMIB) makes mortality adjustments.

In terms of the q_x, the unconditional probability of dying after $T > 0$ periods (conditional on having lived to age x_0) is $q_{T+x_0} \Pi_{x=x_0}^{x_0+T-1}(1 - q_x)$. This unconditional probability is used in computing the expected value in Equation (9.25), so Equation (9.25) is equivalent to (if we also take into account the adjustment factors):[4]

$$P = \sum_{T=1}^{\infty} \left(\frac{d}{r} \left(1 - (1+r)^{-T} \right) \right) q_{T+x_0}^0 f^T \prod_{x=x_0}^{x_0+T-1} (1 - q_x^0 f^{x-x_0}) \quad (9.26)$$

Errors in the adjustment factor f can have a large impact on Equation (9.26). Historical evidence on longevity forecasts suggests that forecast errors of 15–20% in f for intervals of ten or more years ahead are not uncommon (c.f. Table 18.7 in MacDonald, 1996). Another indicator of the difficulty in forecasting longevity increases is that historical values of these adjustment factors are not constants: they differ considerably between men and women, across ages and types of pensioners. For instance, the historical improvement rate for men aged 70 between 1967–70 and 1979–82 was 0.74 for life office pensioners and 0.91 for immediate

---

[4] This expression takes the value of the bond if it pays out for T years and multiplies by the *unconditional* probability of surviving for T years and then sums over all possible values of T. It is equivalent to the following expression using *conditional* probabilities:

$$P = \sum_{T=1}^{\infty} d \, q_{T+x_0}^0 f^T (1+r)^{-T}.$$

annuitants, i.e. those who purchase annuities voluntarily (MacDonald, 1996). The impact of such forecast errors on survival probabilities is significant. For example, assuming a 20-year adjustment factor of 0.80 for a 65-year-old man and forecast errors for mortality rates of up to 10% over a ten-year period, then using the PMA80 mortality tables (constructed to reflect the mortality experiences of males who are obliged to buy pension annuities), the forecast probability of a 65-year-old man living to 85 ranges between 33.7% and 43.8%, while that of him living to 95 ranges between 5.3% and 15.3%.[5]

To determine the effects of these forecast errors on annuity yields, we use Equation (9.25) to solve for the annuity yield d/P:

$$\frac{d}{P} = E\left(\frac{\left(1 - (1+r)^{-T}\right)}{r}\right)^{-1} \tag{9.27}$$

To compute the actuarially fair yield (i.e. with zero cost loading), we substitute survival probabilities determined from standard mortality tables into Equation (9.27). For a male aged 65, a discount rate of $r = 7\%$ and a 20-year adjustment factor of 0.80, the PMA80 tables and Equation (9.27) lead to an actuarially fair annuity yield of 10.6%, but forecast errors suggest it lies between 10.3% and 10.9%. Thus, the percentage difference in yields is about 5%.[6] For a woman, the PFA80 tables lead to an actuarially fair yield of 9.5% in the absence of longevity risk, but forecast errors suggest it lies between 9.2% and 9.7%, again a percentage difference of about 5%.

The effects of longevity forecast errors are more serious for escalating annuities, because payments in the future will be higher than with flat annuities. For escalating annuities, Equation (9.27) becomes:

$$\frac{d}{P} = E\left(\frac{(1+\pi)}{r - \pi}\left(1 - \left(\frac{1+r}{1+\pi}\right)^{-T}\right)\right)^{-1} \tag{9.28}$$

---

[5] The quoted adjustment factors are in units of twenty years and need to be converted to one-year factors. This is done in our case as follows. For a 20-year adjustment factor of 0.8, the one-year adjustment factor is $0.8^{1/20}$. The lower bound on the adjustment factor is the one-year adjustment factor times $0.90^{1/10}$, while the upper bound is the one-year adjustment factor times $1.10^{1/10}$; this converts a 10% forecast error either way over ten years to the appropriate one-year forecast error.

[6] That is $(10.9 - 10.3)/10.6$.

where π is the uprating factor. For example, with an annuity escalating at 4% p.a., the percentage difference between upper and lower bounds[7] rises considerably: to 9.5% for women and to 8.9% for men.

Given the significance of longevity forecasts for insurance company profitability, it is not surprising that cost loadings to cover longevity risk are built into prices, or that some insurers simply offer uncompetitive annuity rates, thereby effectively staying out of the market.[8] Insurance companies cannot at present reduce these loadings without taking on unreasonable risks; indeed, anecdotal evidence for the UK indicates that the failure of some insurance companies to accurately predict improvements in longevity has led to serious problems among suppliers of deferred annuities, which are even more susceptible to longevity risk than immediate annuities.[9] Similar calculations for a 20-year deferred annuity escalating at 4% p.a. to be received by a woman when she reaches the age of 65 suggest a range of about 22% in annuity yields under different longevity forecasts. These business considerations suggest why the market for deferred annuities in the UK is relatively thin.[10] Deferred annuities are particularly important in the case where a defined benefit plan is wound up, say as a result of the insolvency of the sponsoring company, and also, potentially, for early leavers.

Because the private sector is less able to absorb the aggregate risks associated with longevity forecast errors than the government, we will examine whether the government can do anything to help alleviate this problem and reduce costs to annuitants.

---

[7] The term 'bound' is used to represent outcomes with typical historical forecast errors.

[8] The difference between the best and worst annuity quotes can be as much as 30% over all the companies offering annuities in the UK, yet there is almost no variation in the type of policy offered. Even across the top ten providers (which account for the bulk of the market), the differences can be substantial and there is a distinct absence of competition amongst the remaining 200 providers. Since the purchase of retirement annuities is mandatory in the UK and since many thousands of workers retire every week, it is very easy for companies wanting to attract new business to do so by temporarily offering the best annuity yield. However, there must invariably come a point when some of these companies will either have written their quota or make a commercial decision to concentrate on other types of business that are subject to smaller long-term risks.

[9] Anecdotal evidence for the UK also suggests that, currently, life companies are having to make annuity payments for two years longer than originally anticipated.

[10] Only £10 million in single-premium deferred annuities were issued in 1996, about one-eightieth of the level of single-premium immediate annuities sold in that year (Association of British Insurers, 1997, Table 12).

9.5.2   A new hedging instrument: longevity (or survivor) bonds

When insurance companies write annuities, they use the premiums collected to buy appropriate matching assets; that is, assets whose cash payments match as closely as possible the anticipated pattern of payouts on the liabilities that they now face. In the case of level annuities, they invest principally in fixed-income bonds. In the case of index-linked annuities, they hold index-linked bonds: no insurance company would be prepared to write index-linked annuities if it could not lay off the resulting inflation risk through the purchase of an index-linked bond issued by, say, the government or a utility.

Thinking along the same lines, a simple solution to the problem of longevity risk would be for the government to issue *longevity* (or *survivor) bonds*; that is, bonds whose future coupon payments depend on the percentage of the whole population of retirement age (say 65) on the issue date still alive on the future coupon payment dates. This proposal was first made by Blake and Burrows (2001).[11] For a bond issued in 2000, for example, the coupon in 2020 will be proportional to the fraction of 65-year-olds in the population who have lived to age 85. The coupon is, therefore, directly proportional to the amount an insurance company needs to pay out as an annuity to the average individual with an average pension. A new tranche of bonds would be issued at the start of every year. The bonds would be traded on the open market and could be resold. Large occupational plans, which also bear aggregate longevity risk, would similarly be natural purchasers of such bonds.

9.5.3   The implications of longevity bonds

We will examine the implications of introducing longevity bonds, both for annuity providers and for the government.

Longevity bonds aim to lower the costs of retirement provision for the average pensioner. This is because they are designed to hedge aggregate longevity risk. They are not designed to hedge select longevity risks. There are some key select risks to take into account[12]: (a) pensioner annuitants are likely to live longer than the average of the population of

---

[11] However, we should note that this proposal is not new: longevity bonds share similarities with Tontine bonds, especially the 1759 Geneva Tontine Bond (see Cooper, 1972; Jennings and Trout, 1982).

[12] In the UK case, these select risks have been quantified by Finkelstein and Poterba (2002) and were discussed in Chapter 5.

the same age and (b) given that an insurance company is underwriting a finite sample of lives, the characteristics of any particular insurance company's pool of annuitants may differ from that of the pensioner annuitant population as a whole: for example, women and wealthy pensioner annuitants with large lump sums to annuitise tend to live longer than the average pensioner annuitant. Longevity bonds only eliminate the risk associated with aggregate longevity increases for the average of the whole population and do not eliminate select risks such as those associated with gender or wealth.[13] In short, by minimising aggregate risk, insurance companies would have the proper incentives to develop wide mortality pools and do what they do best: provide insurance against specific risks.

For instance, if the longevity of the rich increases more than that of the poor and the insurance company chooses an equally-weighted pool of rich and poor, the payouts by the insurance company will decline less rapidly than the coupon payments from the longevity bonds. The rate at which this happens depends on the differences between terms $q^0_{T+x_0} f^T \prod_{x=x_0}^{x_0+T-1} \left(1 - q^0_x f^{x-x_0}\right)$ in Equation (9.26) for the insurance company's own annuitant pool and those for the population as a whole. The q's and f's will be lower for the insurance company's annuitant pool and the forecast errors higher than for the population as a whole. The implication of this is that insurance companies that choose to have mortality pools different from the population at large continue to bear some select longevity risk, but that is a commercial decision. The insurance companies, therefore, bear what is more generally known as *basis risk*, but this risk will still be lower than aggregate longevity risk.

However, the important point to recognise is that there are no obvious matching assets for the select longevity risks assumed by annuity providers once they hold longevity bonds to hedge aggregate longevity risk. The provider will hedge these select risks by offering *lower* annuity rates to *all* annuitants. This disadvantages the average annuitants who are not members of the select groups. The *only* way of dealing with this problem is to reduce the select longevity risks to zero by the government making pension plans and pension annuities mandatory for

---

[13] It would, of course, be possible for the government to choose the population of pensioner annuitants as 'the population' for which it issues survivor bonds, or to design the bond to meet the more specific circumstances of the pensioners (such as gender- or wealth-adjusted mortality rates). But it is unlikely that any government would agree to do this, since this would involve a substantial cross-subsidy from the general taxpayer.

all members of society. But this leads directly to questions about the role of government in pension provision.

Why should the government (and ultimately taxpayers) issue longevity bonds and absorb the risks associated with mortality fluctuations? One possible justification can be found in the Arrow–Lind Theorem (1970) on social risk-bearing, which shows that, by dispersing an aggregate risk across the population (of taxpayers) as a whole, the associated risk premium can be reduced to zero. The government could, therefore, issue longevity bonds at a lower yield (namely, the risk-free rate) than any private corporation could. The private corporation will have many fewer shareholders than there are taxpayers, and some of the shareholders may hold large blocks of shares which constitute a significant proportion of their net worth. These shareholders will demand a risk premium, whereas the government can act as a risk-neutral insurer. Another justification lies in the government's own public health campaigns, which are aimed directly at improving the life expectancy of the whole population, and this has important implications for annuity provision by the private sector.[14] Similarly, the reform of social security pensions (which are themselves equivalent to non-tradeable longevity bonds) and the transfer of pension provision from the public to the private sector would be eased greatly by the existence of tradeable longevity bonds.

By issuing longevity bonds, the government would be helping to complete markets. But is the government really the best organisation to issue them? In practice, a key assumption underlying the Arrow–Lind Theorem may be violated. Real world tax systems do not give each household an equal share of the tax burden, and some households may be affected directly by the variation in longevity risks. For example, if older households experience an improvement in life expectancy, their resources may be stretched as they try to finance a longer-than-expected retirement period. The longevity bond would require the government to collect more taxes to pay off their now more costly annuity bonds, and when this happens, if the taxes are also levied on older workers, they face a tax burden that is correlated with other shocks to their well-being, thereby violating one of the conditions of the Arrow–Lind Theorem. In contrast, when the risk is borne by an insurance company, the shareholders have

---

[14] We should note that the introduction of survivor bonds, perversely, provides the government with an incentive to introduce measures that reduce longevity amongst the aged, e.g. reducing medical expenditure and tobacco taxes on the elderly.

volunteered to bear the longevity risk. Some investors may be more risk tolerant than the typical taxpayer, and this could provide a more efficient means of risk-sharing. Nevertheless, while insurance company shareholders may indeed be more risk tolerant than the average taxpayer, it remains the case that no insurance company in the world has yet issued a single tradeable longevity bond.

Yet, insurance companies would appear, on the surface, to be natural issuers of such bonds, since they are in a position to hedge longevity risk with their other products: greater longevity raises the payouts on life annuities but lowers them on endowment policies. However, in practice, endowment policies provide a poor hedge for life annuities, since mortality improvements are not spread evenly across ages, but rather are concentrated at greater ages. To illustrate, the percentage improvement in mortality between the PMA80 and PMA92 tables (based on mortality experience for United Kingdom male annuitants in 1980 and 1992 respectively) was 12% at age 35, 9% at age 55, 23% at age 75 and 20% at age 95. Perhaps this is why insurance companies have chosen not to issue longevity bonds, despite there being no restrictions anywhere in the world preventing them from doing so.

It has been suggested that, since the market will price the bonds with an implied hazard rate that will coincide with expected longevity increases, the outcome should not differ from that of using a large insurance company, which provides annuities even if it does not sell longevity bonds. However, the forecasts of the market as a whole may not coincide with those of a particular insurance company and insurance companies can (and do) go bust, unlike governments (at least in advanced economies), so the outcome cannot be identical, except in the case of homogeneous expectations and zero bankruptcy costs.

The family itself provides an informal mechanism for the issuing of implicit longevity bonds between different generations of the same family, as implied by Kotlikoff and Spivak (1981), but the breakdown of the family in many countries makes this an increasingly unreliable mechanism.

Some (for example Dowd, 2003) have argued that private sector issuers, such as pharmaceutical companies or providers of long-term care homes, would be natural issuers of longevity bonds, since their cash inflows increase as people get older. But it is unlikely that such organisations could issue bonds in sufficient size to meet the potential demand. Further, such organisations are subject to substantial credit risk in respect of the distant coupon payments on these bonds.

Others argue that the state is the only realistic issuer of longevity bonds in any size (Blake, 2003). In much the same way as governments in a number of countries helped pension funds insure against inflation by issuing index bonds, the issuance of longevity bonds would help mature pension funds insure against the uncertainties involving an increasingly grey population. The reduction in cost loadings on annuities could be substantial.[15]

The world's first longevity bond was, in fact, announced by a supra-national organisation – the European Investment Bank – in November 2004. The bond was structured by BNP Paribas and the longevity risk was reinsured by Bermuda-based Partner Re. The proposed issue size was £540m and the term to maturity was 25 years. The bond did not attract sufficient investor interest and was later withdrawn. There were a number of reasons for this: the bond did not hedge inflation risk, pension fund trustees were reluctant to buy the bond (no one wanted to be the first to leap) and fund managers did not then have a mandate to manage longevity risk (Blake *et al.*, 2006).

9.5.4 Mortality-linked derivatives

Blake *et al.* (2006) propose a new class of mortality-linked derivatives, based on existing financial market derivatives.

One example is a *mortality* (or *longevity* or *surviver*) *swap* (Dowd *et al.*, 2006). A mortality swap is an agreement to exchange one or more cash flows in the future based on the outcome of at least one (random) survivor or mortality index. Mortality swaps have certain advantages over longevity bonds: they can be arranged at lower transaction cost than a bond issue and are more easily cancelled; they are more flexible and they can be tailor-made to suit diverse circumstances. They do not require the existence of a liquid market, just the willingness of counterparties to exploit their comparative advantages or trade views on the development of mortality over time. Mortality swaps also have advantages over traditional insurance arrangements: they involve lower transaction costs, are more flexible than reinsurance treaties, and so on.

---

[15] For example, US studies (e.g. Mitchell *et al.*, 1999; Poterba and Warshawsky, 2000), found that the deduction from the actuarially fair value of an annuity for a 65-year-old US male was 15% if the male was a typical member of the population as a whole (calculated using the mortality tables for the whole US male population) and 3% if the male was typical of the population buying annuities voluntarily (calculated using the select mortality tables for male annuity purchasers), implying a 12% deduction for the greater mortality risk.

Mortality swaps have a number of possible uses. One insurer, wishing to manage the risks on its annuity book, might be on one side of the swap, while on the other side of the swap might be a capital market institution wishing to acquire longevity risk exposure. Swaps are attractive because even where alternatives exist, swaps often offer the parties concerned less costly ways of managing their longevity risks, which can also be tailor-made to the users' requirements. Should circumstances change and one party later wish to change its desired exposure, a swap also gives it a much more flexible means of altering its exposure.

Other examples are mortality futures and options (which are based on the future path of survivor or mortality indices) and annuity futures and options (which are based on the future path of annuity rates).

As of 2006, the market in longevity bonds and mortality-linked derivatives has yet to develop, but it seems certain that it will. In 2006, a number of buy-out funds (e.g. Paternoster, Synesis, Pension Insurance Corporation) were established to buy up closed company pension funds. There is also a market developing in the closed annuity books of life offices (e.g. Canada Life purchased £4bn of Equitable Life's closed annuity book).

9.6   CONCLUSIONS

Risk management is becoming an increasingly important component of the overall management of a pension fund's assets and liabilities. The risks can be hedged on a temporary or continuous basis. Financial futures, options and swaps can be used to hedge interest-rate risk, currency risk and asset-price risk, typically on a temporary basis. A new class of mortality-linked instruments, such as longevity bonds, mortality swaps, mortality futures and options and annuity futures and options, has recently been proposed to hedge the longevity risk faced by pension funds and annuity providers on longer-term basis.

QUESTIONS

1. What are the objectives of risk management?
2. What are the rules for hedging with futures contracts?
3. What is a hedge portfolio?
4. What is the hedge ratio and how is it determined?
5. How are the number of contracts needed for a stock-index futures hedge determined?
6. What is a duration-based futures hedge?

7. How are the number of contracts needed for a duration-based futures hedge determined?
8. How are the number of contracts needed for a currency futures hedge determined?
9. When might an options hedge be used in preference to a futures hedge?
10. What are the rules for hedging with options contracts?
11. Discuss three different options strategies for hedging the downside risk in an individual shareholding.
12. What is a delta-neutral hedge?
13. What is a relative performance portfolio?
14. How can a synthetic short futures hedge be created using options?
15. Explain how an asset swap can be used to hedge the interest-rate risk in a bond portfolio.
16. What is longevity risk? How can it be hedged?
17. What arguments have been put forward to justify a role for the state in issuing instruments suitable for hedging longevity risk?
18. Longevity risk is a risk that cannot be effectively hedged by the private sector alone. Discuss.

REFERENCES

Arrow, K. and Lind, R. (1970) Uncertainty and the evaluation of public investment decisions. *American Economic Review*, **60**, 364–378.

Association of British Insurers (1997) *Insurance Statistics Year book 1986–1996*, Association of British Insurers, London.

Blake, D. (2000) *Financial Market Analysis*, John Wiley & Sons, Ltd, Chichester.

Blake, D. (2003) Reply to 'Survivor bonds: a comment on Blake and Burrows'. *Journal of Risk and Insurance*, **70**: 349–351.

Blake, D. and Burrows, W. (2001) Survivor bonds: helping to hedge mortality risk. *Journal of Risk and Insurance*, **68**, 339–348.

Blake, D., Cairns, A. and Dowd, K. (2006) Living with mortality: longevity bonds and other mortality-linked securities. *British Actuarial Journal*, forthcoming.

Cooper, R.W. (1972) An historical analysis of the Tontine Principle, *Monograph 1, S. S. Huebner Foundation*, Wharton School, University of Pennsylvania.

Dowd, K. (2003) Survivor bonds: a comment on Blake and Burrows. *Journal of Risk and Insurance*, **70**: 339–348.

Dowd, K., Blake, D., Cairns, A., Dawson, P. (2006) Survivor swaps, *Journal of Risk and Insurance*, **73**, 1–17.

Finkelstein, A. and Poterba, J. (2002) Selection effects in the United Kingdom annuities market, *Economic Journal*, **112**, 28–50.

Jennings, R.M. and Trout, A.P. (1982) The Tontine: from the reign of Louis XIV to the French Revolutionary Era, *Monograph 12, S. S. Huebner Foundation*, Wharton School, University of Pennsylvania.

Kotlikoff, L.J. and Spivak, A. (1981) The family as an incomplete annuities market. *Journal of Political Economy*, **89**, 372–391.

MacDonald, A. (1996) United Kingdom, in MacDonald, A. (Ed.) *The Second Actuarial Study of Mortality in Europe*, Groupe Consultatif des Associations D'Actuaires des Payes des Communautés Européennes, Oxford.

Mitchell, O., Poterba, J., Warshawsky, M., and Brown, J. (1999) New evidence on the money's worth of individual annuities, *American Economic Review*, **89**, 1299–1316.

Poterba, J. and Warshawsky, M. (2000) The costs of annuitising retirement payouts from individual accounts, in Shoven, J. (Ed.) *Administrative Aspects of Investment-Based Social Security Reform*, University of Chicago Press, Chicago.

10

Pension Fund Insurance

Pension fund insurance was discussed briefly in Chapter 3 and is discussed in much more detail in this chapter in the light of the establishment of the UK Pension Protection Fund (PPF) in 2005. The PPF was based on its US equivalent, the Pension Benefit Guaranty Corporation (PBGC), which was set up in 1974. To be successful, the PPF needs to learn not only the from the experience of the PBGC, but also from other types of financial institution and compensation scheme. We discuss the risks facing the PPF and how the PPF can deal with them.

10.1 THE PENSION PROTECTION FUND (PPF)

The 2004 Pensions Act established the Pension Protection Fund with the objective of protecting members of private sector defined benefit schemes whose sponsoring companies become insolvent with insufficient funds in their pension schemes, so they can be reassured they will still receive most of the pension benefits that they were expecting. The PPF came into operation in January 2005 and has a similar structure to the PBGC. The motivation for introducing the PPF was the experience of members of the ASW (Allied Steel and Wire) pension fund, who lost 80–90% of their pensions after 40 years' membership when ASW went bankrupt in July 2002. There are two criteria for entry into PPF: the sponsoring employer has become insolvent and the pension scheme has insufficient assets to buy out the PPF level of benefits with a life company. Once in, the scheme can never leave. Participation is mandatory.

The PPF offers two types of compensation. For DB schemes, the PPF protects 100% of the pension for members above scheme pension age, and 90% of the promised pension for members below scheme pension age (up to a maximum of £25 000), using a mixture of scheme individual rates and standardised rules. Pensions in payment are subject to limited price indexation (LPI) at 2.5%, while deferred pensions are subject to LPI at 5%. Survivors' benefits are also protected.

Compensation will be funded by taking on the assets of pension schemes with insolvent employers, and through a levy on defined benefit and defined benefit elements of hybrid schemes. The levy has three components:

- Pension protection levy
  - a 'scheme factors' element which depends on the number of members and the balance between active and retired members;
  - a 'risk factors' element (at least 80% of the total charge, although not raised in the first year of operation) which is linked to such factors as the level of underfunding, investment strategy and the sponsor's credit rating.
- Administration levy, covering set-up and ongoing costs of the PPF
- Fraud compensation levy

The governance and management of the PPF are in the hands of a board, which is responsible for: paying pension compensation, paying fraud compensation, determining the three levies, setting investment strategy and appointing at least two independent fund managers. The government has stated that it will not underwrite the PPF. Instead, it must survive on the basis of its powers to set levies, determine its own liabilities and borrow to smooth out differences in these.

10.2   WHAT THE PENSION PROTECTION FUND CAN LEARN FROM OTHER FINANCIAL INSTITUTIONS AND COMPENSATION SCHEMES

Financial regulators in the UK and elsewhere have moved towards a common risk-based framework of regulatory capital requirements for most of the institutions under their jurisdiction. The UK financial regulator, the Financial Services Authority (FSA), has introduced an integrated prudential sourcebook (PSB), based principally on the pre-existing one for banks, to cover all the institutions that it regulates: namely, banks, building societies, friendly societies, insurers and investment firms. A similar convergence has happened in the European Union (EU). The FSA and other regulators have recognised that the risk management practices of banks are well ahead of those of other institutions, and that this situation needs to be rectified as soon as possible.

The PSB contains rules and guidance on provisioning for liabilities and on capital requirements, with the aim of reducing the risk that a financial institution cannot meet its liabilities as they fall due as a result of insufficient funds. The purpose of the PSB is to enable the FSA to achieve its statutory objectives, specified in the Financial Services and Markets

Act 2000, of consumer protection and maintenance of confidence in the financial system.

We question why pension funds are not treated in terms of financial regulation in the same way as other financial institutions, including otherwise apparently similar long-term investing institutions, like life assurers. While the capital requirements of life assurers have moved closer to those of banks, UK pension funds are not regulated by the FSA at all, and, in addition, they do not have formal capital requirements: instead they operate on a prudent person principle.

We review the financial regulation of banks and life assurers and show how this has converged on a *three-pillar framework* involving *risk-based minimum capital charges*, *supervision* by the national financial regulator and *market discipline* via information disclosure. This rigorous approach to determining regulatory capital makes it easier to estimate the probability of, and expected loss in the event of, insolvency by banks and life assurers and hence to set the appropriate premiums for the insurance scheme that protects bank depositors and life office policyholders, namely the Financial Services Compensation Scheme. We contrast this with the much looser framework of regulating pension funds and the implications of this for the PPF. We show that the PPF will face the same four key risks as its US counterpart, the PBGC, namely moral hazard, adverse selection, systemic risk and political risk. We argue that the PPF will be severely weakened by the absence of a corresponding three-pillar framework for pension funds that would help it estimate default probabilities and losses in the event of default, since appropriate risk-based premiums cannot be reliably set for the UK's 90 000 pension schemes. Furthermore, we conclude that the extent of systemic risk is so great that even three pillars will not be sufficient to prevent the PPF seeking periodic bailouts from the government, despite the fact that the UK government has promised not to underwrite the PPF.

10.2.1   The financial regulation of banks

Banks were the first set of institutions to be subject to a formal set of regulatory capital requirements, namely the 1988 Basle Accord which came into force in 1992 (Basle Committee on Banking Supervision, 1988). The aim was to limit the credit risk (including off-balance sheet counterparty risk) that banks faced by imposing two minimum standards of capital adequacy: an assets-to-capital multiple and a risk-based capital ratio of 8% of risk-weighted on-balance sheet assets plus off-balance sheet exposures, irrespective of the maturity or volatility of the values of the assets held. Two types of capital were permitted: Tier 1, or core, capital (equity and non-cumulative perpetual preferred shares less goodwill), and Tier 2, or supplementary, capital (subordinated debt with an original maturity in excess of five years and cumulative perpetual preferred shares).

However, the Basle regime soon revealed itself to be both naive and inadequate (see, for example, Jackson *et al.*, 1997). On the one hand, netting of long and short positions in different but related markets (e.g. UK and US equities) was not permitted and holdings of short-dated corporate bonds were penalised much more than long-dated corporate bonds, and these restrictions put banks at a competitive disadvantage in comparison with securities houses, which had a more sophisticated approach to risk. On the other hand, banks' market risks, arising from their efforts to make trading profits by taking both long and short positions in bonds, equities, derivatives, foreign exchange and commodities, were not covered. In addition, the 8% capital ratio was set at an arbitrary level without any attempt to quantify the probability of insolvency implied by this level.

The market risk assumed by European banks and securities houses was dealt with by the 1996 EU Capital Adequacy Directive (CAD), which imposed minimum capital requirements on the trading books of these institutions. In 1998, the Basle Committee on Banking Supervision introduced an amended capital adequacy framework which now covered market risk, which became known as Basle 1 (Basle Committee on Banking Supervision, 1996). This permitted banks a choice of two models for determining their trading book capital: the *standardised model* and the *internal model*. It also allowed a third tier of subsupplementary capital (short-term subordinated debt with an original maturity in excess of two years) to be allocated against the market risk of the trading book.

Banks had to first allocate Tier 1 and Tier 2 capital to meet credit-risk capital requirements sufficient to cover 8% of risk-weighted assets. Then, Tier 3 capital was allocated to satisfy a second capital-assets ratio. The denominator of the new ratio is the sum of the risk-weighted assets and 12.5 times the market-risk capital charge (where 12.5 is the reciprocal of the minimum capital ratio of 8%). The numerator of the second ratio is the sum of the bank's Tier 1, Tier 2 and Tier 3 capital. Tier 3 capital could be used solely to meet the market-risk capital charge, while Tier 1 and 2 capital could also be used to satisfy the market-risk capital charge once the credit-risk allocation had been met in full. However, at least 50% of the bank's qualifying capital had to be Tier 1 (with term subordinated debt not exceeding 50%) and the sum of Tiers 2 and 3 capital allocated to market risk, not exceeding 250% of the Tier 1 capital allocated to market risk (so that at least 28.57% of market-risk capital had to be Tier 1). So, by 1998, banks had to satisfy three capital adequacy standards: a maximum assets-to-capital ratio of 20, a credit-risk capital charge of at least 8% of risk-weighted assets, both on- and off-balance sheet, and a minimum market-risk capital charge to cover traded instruments in the trading book on- and off-balance sheet (see, for example, Crouhy *et al.*, 1998).

Both the CAD and Basle standardised approaches determine a bank's regulatory capital as a percentage of its holdings in different asset classes, where the percentages depend on the price volatilities of the underlying asset classes. A weakness of both approaches is that the capital requirement is calculated for each asset class separately and then summed, a procedure that, by implicitly assuming unit correlations across all asset categories, ignores the benefits of diversification of both credit risk and market risk across asset classes. This approach penalises globally diversified banks in comparison with specialists trading only in single asset classes.

By contrast, the Basle 1 alternative approach allows banks to use the risk-based models that they had developed internally to measure the risk of given losses on their total portfolio or whole book. These models are generally based on the *value-at-risk* (VaR) approach established by J P Morgan in its RiskMetrics and CreditMetrics Models. The advantage of this approach is that the capital requirement is market-determined rather than prescriptive, in the sense that it is based on the banks' own assessment of their likelihood of insolvency and their desire to avoid this outcome.

The acceptance of internal risk-based (IRB) models for determining capital requirements was a revolutionary departure for supervisors, but it was driven, in part, by the underlying complexity of the products in bank portfolios and the proprietary expertise required by banks in pricing and trading these products. Even CAD and the Basle standardised approaches recognised that the capital requirements for banks' options and swap books could only be assessed sensibly by using the banks' own IRB models.

In order to be confident that the capital requirements are adequate, Basle 1 laid down standards for the IRB models that could be used. These involved both back tests and stress tests. For example, the model must calibrate the distribution of losses over a 10-day horizon using a minimum of 12 months of data and the capital required is that level sufficient to cover losses 99% of the time (on a one-sided test).

To assess the accuracy of the models, they must also be capable of performing back tests on a daily basis using the net trading losses that would have occurred if the book were held constant for the next day as well as the realised net trading losses for the next day. As an extra safeguard, Basle 1 set the capital requirement at the higher of the current VaR and a multiple of the average VaR over the previous 60 days. The multiplier, normally set at three, is designed as a hedge against model and parameter risk, inaccurate assessments of credit risks, operational risks and unusual market moves. The models also have to be the ones that are used in the daily risk management of the bank. Further improvements in the model are required if it fails to pass the tests, for example, when back testing produced too many days when trading losses exceeded the VaR (i.e. more than five days in the previous 250 days). The multiplier could be increased to 4 if the test was failed on ten or more days.

As Crouhy *et al.* comment (p. 16): 'Backtesting is a powerful process to validate the predictive power of a VaR model, without requiring the use of a benchmark model. It is a self-assessment mechanism which allows a bank to check the validity of its internal model on an ongoing basis, and challenges its key assumptions whenever the bank's actual trading results become inconsistent with the VaR numbers. It provides a natural framework to continuously improve and refine the risk modelling techniques'. Crouhy *et al.* (1998) demonstrate that, for their own bank (CIBC), use of an internal model reduced capital charges attributed to general market risk by between 60 and 85% over a six-month period.

Stress testing is designed to check the robustness of the VaR model by investigating the sensitivity of the VaR estimates to the key assumptions. This is achieved by generating extreme, low-probability events, such as a stock market crash, for which the underlying assumptions of the model might be violated. Stress testing should investigate the impact on the VaR estimates of the breakdown of previously stable relationships such as spreads, volatilities and correlations. In market crashes, for example, correlations across asset categories tend towards $+1$ or -1.

Despite the theoretically superior structure of the internal model compared with the standardised model, some regulators question the ability of the banks to correctly model the principal (directional, spread, curve and liquidity) risks contained in their portfolios (see, for example, Kupiec and O'Brien, 1995). Credit rating agencies such as Standard & Poors

(1996) also expressed concern that the amount of regulatory capital would fall as the high credit-risk charge under the 1988 Accord for on-balance sheet holdings of bonds and equities would be replaced by a much lower specific risk capital charge under Basle 1. S&P argued that the market risks of trading operations are swamped by other more difficult to quantify risks, such as operational risk (arising from systems failure and employee fraud), legal risk (arising from lawsuits from disgruntled clients), reputation risk, liquidity risk and operating leverage.

In 2007, a new IRB capital adequacy regime known as Basle 2 was introduced (see, for example, Basle Committee on Banking Supervision, 2003; Jackson, 2001, 2002). The objective is to further enhance the security of the global banking system by means of a three-pillar system of regulation that covers operational risk in addition to credit and market risk:

- Pillar 1 – sets minimum capital charges for credit, market and operational risks;
- Pillar 2 – involves supervision by national financial regulators;
- Pillar 3 – imposes market discipline via information disclosure.

The regulatory capital held under Pillar 1 must be sufficient to cover expected losses as well as unexpected losses. Again, banks can choose to use an internal or standardised model for measuring risk, but all banks must have a robust-risk identification structure in place by 2007 that categorises loans in terms of default bands.

The regulatory capital required for each loan will depend on the *probability of default* (PD) of the borrower (determined by the bank) and the *loss given default* (LGD) (determined by the bank if it uses the advanced approach and set by the regulator if the bank uses the standardised approach). The expected loss to the bank is equal to the product of PD and LGD and the bank needs capital to cover at least its expected losses.

However, there has been substantial criticism of the requirement to hold regulatory capital to cover expected losses, particularly by US banks, which argue that expected losses are a cost of doing business that should be incorporated into transaction prices and met from loan-loss provisions rather than covered in regulatory capital (see *Global Risk Regulator*, September 2003). The Basle regulators countered that it is hard to differentiate between expected and unexpected losses. Also, it is difficult to determine whether provisions are adequate to meet all expected losses, a necessary precondition for expected losses to be excluded from capital requirements.

US banks have proposed an alternative. Future margin income (FMI) should be used to offset the expected loss component of the capital charge; this would acknowledge that banks are pricing their products to cover expected losses. In addition, banks should be allowed to count 100% of loan-loss reserves as Tier 1 capital. They argue that Basle 2 already allows FMI to be offset against 75% of expected losses in the case of credit card debt, and this type of debt is not inherently different from other types of debt.

Regulators counter that banks cannot be confident that their transaction prices will fully cover expected losses and that FMI is more reliably forecast in the case of credit cards than in other types of credit. In any case, Basle 2 gives banks credit for the provisions that they make, allowing them to be offset against the expected loss portion of capital.

Pillars 2 and 3 have also been subject to criticisms by the banking community. The banks are concerned that the discretion of national supervisors under Pillar 2 might be used to undermine the level playing field upon which banks worldwide are supposed to play. In respect of Pillar 3, the main concern is with the costs of providing the additional information required, measured against its usefulness to investors and regulators (see *Global Risk Regulator*, September 2003).

Another issue is the accountancy rules established by the International Accounting Standards Board (IASB), which limit the extent to which banks are able to provision. While regulators want banks to have an adequate level of provisions to meet expected losses over a number of years ahead, the IASB want the true figures to be stated over the period of the current financial statement. Accounting rules will only recognise incurred losses or losses that are certain in the light of events. Banks, on the other hand, want to provision for losses that are statistically likely in the future, but have not yet happened. Accountants argue that this approach is used by the banks to smooth out fluctuations in profits, and therefore distorts the financial statement.

10.2.2   The financial regulation of life assurers

In June 2004, the Financial Services Authority published the *Integrated Prudential Sourcebook for Insurers* (PSB),[1] which introduced a new

---

[1] This section draws heavily on this document, together with Consultation Paper 195 (*Enhanced Capital Requirements and Individual Capital Assessments for Life Insurers*) released in August 2003.

set of risk-based capital requirements for with-profits life assurers that came into effect on 1 January 2005. The aim is to treat a life assurer's customers fairly through a combination of improved transparency, the holding of adequate capital for the firm's business mix and compliance with the Principles and Practices of Financial Management (PPFM) that the firm has disclosed. To achieve this aim, the FSA has adopted the same three-pillar approach to regulation as Basle 2.

The first pillar covers regulatory capital and the PSB introduces a 'twin peaks' standard for a life assurer's with-profits business that results in provisioning and capital requirements being more responsive to the way in which bonus payments are made to policyholders. As markets fall, so do both discretionary final bonuses and required provisions, and this raises the net assets available to meet capital requirements. The prudential cover of contractual and guaranteed contractual benefits is unchanged.

The first peak is defined as mathematical reserves plus a required minimum risk capital margin of at least 4% (the long-term insurance capital requirement, LTICR). This peak is necessary to ensure compliance with the EU Life Assurance Directive (known as Solvency 1).

Mathematical reserves are the assets backing the life assurer's liabilities, calculated as the actuarial value of its contractual and guaranteed benefits. Net cash flows from current in-force business (benefits paid less premiums received) are forecast and discounted (using a discount rate that depends on the expected rate of return on fund assets) to give a net present value reserving requirement. Allowances, known as 'margins for adverse deviation', are made to account for potential forecast errors. For example, asset returns are reduced to allow for reinvestment risk and counterparty default risk, while the 'net premium rule' permits expected future premiums to be reduced by an amount that reflects the payment of future discretionary bonuses.

The risk capital margin (RCM) is the additional capital that a firm needs in order to maintain cover of its with-profit liabilities, given a sequence of specified stresses in market risk (equity, interest-rate and property-price risk), credit risk (default by issuers of the firm's assets and non-payment by reinsurers), and persistency risk:

- Equity:
  - for UK equities, a fall of at least 10%, or if greater, the lower of:
    - a percentage fall in the market value of equities which would produce an earnings yield for the FTSE Actuaries All Share Index equal to 4/3 of the long-term gilt yield; and

- ▪ 25% less any percentage reduction between the current FTSE Actuaries All Share Index and its average over the last 90 days;
- – broadly equivalent test for overseas equities.
- • Interest rates: the more onerous of a fall or rise in yields on all fixed-interest securities by a percentage point amount equal to 20% of the long-term gilt yield (or comparable foreign government bond yield for foreign bonds).
- • Real estate: a fall in real estate values of a minimum of 10% and a maximum of 20%; the required fall increases as the ratio of the current value of an appropriate real estate index to the average value of that index over the three preceding financial years increases.
- • Credit risk:
  - – rated investment-grade corporate bonds:
    - ▪ increase in corporate bond yield spreads over equivalent risk-free rates from spreads prevailing at valuation date. Increase by differential between current average bond yield spread and specified maximum bond yield spread. Maximum bond yield spreads of 90–210 basis points above risk-free rates, according to credit grade of bond assets.
  - – rated, non-investment-grade corporate bonds:
    - ▪ increase in corporate bond yield spreads over equivalent risk-free rates from spreads prevailing at valuation date. Increase by differential between current average bond yield spread and specified maximum bond yield spread. Maximum bond yield spreads of 525–900 basis points above risk-free rates, according to credit grade of bond assets. For the lowest rated bonds, not in default, a fixed capital charge of 10% of the market value of the bonds.
  - – non-rated corporate bonds:
    - ▪ where the firm assesses the credit quality to be equivalent to that of a rated bond, according to the rating and the method for corporate bonds. In other cases, a fixed capital charge of 10% of the market value of the bonds.
  - – commercial mortgages and other non-rated assets:
    - ▪ where the firm assesses the credit quality to be equivalent to that of a rated bond, according to the rating and the method for corporate bonds. In other cases, a fixed capital charge of 10% of market value of the non-rated assets.
  - – reinsurance concentration:

- for material reinsurance arrangements,
  - ◆ where the reinsurer is rated, according to the credit rating of the reinsurer, and the method for corporate bonds;
  - ◆ where the reinsurer is not rated, a fixed capital charge of 10% of the value of the reinsurance assets.
- intra-group reinsurance is excluded, where both insurer and reinsurer are regulated in a designated state.
- − assets in default, that are specifically provisioned in accordance with accounting practice:
  - no credit stress required.
- − persistency:
  - termination rates in each year of projection of 50% of the termination rates assumed in realistic liabilities.

The RCM is the sum of the net losses for each of the above scenarios (i.e. in the cases where the assets fall by more than the fall in with-profit liabilities).

The resilience capital requirement was also modified. This requirement arises from a resilience test applied to the mathematical reserves. This test requires additional resilience capital to be set aside if stressed market conditions indicate that asset values will fall by more than the reduction in mathematical reserves. The modification is that the additional capital can come directly from shareholders' capital and need no longer be included in the mathematical reserves that are held in the life fund itself. In addition, the LTICR will be calculated with reference to mathematical reserves net of resilience capital.

The second peak is based on a realistic calculation of with-profits liabilities by life assurers. PSB permits firms to use one of two methods: the asset share approach and the prospective or bonus reserve approach. For the purposes of valuing contracts with guarantees and embedded options, PSB permits stochastic valuation and option-pricing models. If the second peak is higher than the first peak, additional capital (the with-profits insurance capital component, or WPICC) will be needed to cover expected discretionary bonus payments (such as annual increases in reversionary bonuses and the terminal bonus). The WPICC makes an allowance for adverse experience: the future values of realistic assets and liabilities might be respectively less or more than expected as a result of a firm's exposure to market, credit and persistency risks.

The FSA estimates that the required level of Pillar 1 capital (the capital resources requirement, or CRR) is the same as would attract a

Standard & Poors BBB rating. A BBB-rated insurer 'has *good* financial security characteristics, but is more likely to be affected by adverse business conditions than are higher rated insurers'. The FSA calculates that this equates to a 99.5% confidence level that the firm concerned will survive for a one-year period.

The second supervisory pillar is handled in the PSB by a framework of individual capital adequacy standards (ICAS). Each firm assesses the level of capital suitable for its own risk profile (the individual capital assessment, ICA) and this is then compared with the minimum capital requirements for with-profits business (established by the twin peaks standard) and the insurer's other life business.

The PSB provides general guidance on the risks to capital that life assurers should consider in relation to their individual capital needs. It also provides guidance on how the risks might be assessed by means of capital stress tests, scenario analyses or other models (such as economic capital models).

The FSA also offers individual capital guidance (ICG) in the light of a life assurer's individual capital assessments. To do this, the information set out in Table 10.1 needs to be submitted to the FSA.

Given this information, the FSA will confirm either that the firm's capital assessment is adequate or that a higher level of capital is required in the light of the FSA's judgement that the firm's business risks are greater than the firm has itself assessed.

The FSA needs to be confident that if the projected adverse financial situations materialise, firms will be able to pay their liabilities in full when they fall due. This requires that assets are valued at their liquidation value under the relevant scenarios and that liabilities are given a realistic value for their due date. The overarching aim is to ensure that a firm's customers are 'treated fairly'. This means that a firm must have sufficient resources to ensure that its customers' 'reasonable expectations' concerning terminal bonuses are fulfilled.

The PSB also takes account of the EU's 'Solvency 1' Life Directive in the following ways. The minimum capital requirement for life assurers is set at EUR 3 million and this will be updated in line with EU consumer price inflation. The capital resource requirement (or required margin of solvency) must be met at all times rather than just at the date of the last balance sheet. It can be met with ordinary shares without limit and with cumulative preference shares, subordinated debt and unpaid share capital up to specified limits (and in the last case with approval) – see Table 10.2.

Table 10.1   Information to be submitted to the FSA for individual capital
guidance

Item	Coverage
Summary	A summary of the financial position of the firm at the time the report is constructed and the risks to which the firm is subject.
Individual capital assessment (ICA)	The firm's proposed ICA, expressed as a proportion of its 'Pillar 1' capital resources requirement (CRR).
Background	Relevant historical development of the firm and any conclusions that can be drawn from that development which may have implications for the future of the firm.
Current business	The current business profile of the firm.
The future	The environment in which the firm expects to operate, and its projected business plans, projected financial position and future sources of capital.
Capital analysis	A detailed review of the capital adequacy of the firm. This analysis could include a commentary and opinion on the applicability of the CRR to the firm's own capital position and its appropriateness compared to its own capital assessment. It could involve an analysis of current capital levels and movements in solvency during past years, future capital requirements and general outlook.
Risk assessment	An identification of the major risks faced in each of the following categories: credit risk; market risk; insurance risk; operational risk and liquidity risk; and the extent to which the firm holds capital in response to each risk.
Stress and scenario tests	The quantitative results of stress and scenario tests carried out by the firm and the confidence level and key assumptions behind those analyses.
Other risks	Identification of any risks, for example systems and controls weaknesses, which, in the firm's opinion, are not adequately captured by the CRR. The firm's assessment of how it is responding to those risks, and, if through holding capital, the amount.
Capital models	If a more sophisticated modelling approach is used by the firm, we would expect a statement of the confidence level and other parameters that have been used in the model.

Source: FSA CP195, p. 48

Table 10.2

Tier of capital	Limit
Tier 1	
Core Tier 1	Unlimited but at least 50% of total Tier 1
Ordinary shares	
Reserves	
Non-ordinary shares	
Innovative Tier 1	15% of total Tier 1
Capital instruments	
Innovative instruments	
Implicit items	Waiver required
Tier 2	100% of total Tier 1
Upper Tier 2	
Perpetual cumulative preference shares	
Perpetual subordinated debt	
Lower Tier 2	25% of total capital resources
Long-term subordinated debt	
Other capital	Waiver required
Unpaid share capital	

Note: Characteristics of innovative instruments (FSA CP195, p. 63): treated as a liability in financial statements; coupon payments may be deferred with any deferred coupons payable only in shares; no specified redemption date but terms may include an issuer call, which may coincide with an increase in the coupon; normally ranks pari passu *with preference shares; loss absorbency usually achieved through conversion into shares at a predetermined trigger event.*
Source: FSA CP195, p. 62

Currently, future profits can be used to offset the capital requirement. Implicit items for future profits are restricted to 2/3 of the firm's LTICR (or to the level of the LTICR minus EUR 3 million, if less). By 2007, implicit items for future profits must be restricted to 25% of the lesser of the LTICR and its total (eligible) capital resources; and from 31 December 2009, they will no longer be allowed. Firms will be required to submit an actuarial report substantiating the emergence of the anticipated profits in future periods.

The PSB also changes the way in which capital resources are reported. The traditional approach measures the total of admissible assets less foreseeable liabilities. The new approach lists the components of capital. Both calculations give the same result, as shown in Table 10.3 (drawn from CP195: Table 2.2.10 G, Annex 6). This new approach

Table 10.3

Liabilities		Assets	
Borrowing	100	Admissible assets	350
Ordinary shares	200	Intangible assets	100
Reserves	100	Other inadmissible assets	100
Perpetual subordinated debt	150		
Total	550	Total	550

Traditional calculation of capital resources: eligible assets less foreseeable liabilities

Total assets	550
Less intangible assets	100
Less inadmissible assets	100
Less liabilities (borrowing)	100
Capital resources	250

New calculation of capital resources: components of capital

Ordinary shares	200
Plus reserves	100
Plus perpetual subordinated debt	150
Less intangible assets	100
Less inadmissible assets	100
Capital resources	250

is the same as that used by banks, building societies and investment firms.

The EU is introducing a 'Solvency 2' Life Directive in 2007, which will bring the regulation of life assurers even closer to the three-pillar Basle 2 framework of capital charges, supervisory review and information disclosure. It builds on recent developments in insurance, risk management, finance techniques and financial reporting.

In 2005, the International Accounting Standards Board introduced *fair value* international accounting standards. Insurers have to use the fair value standard for assets from 2005, while the fair value standard for liabilities (which replaces the book value measure) has to be used from 2007. The FSA believes that fair-value accounting is a necessary concomitant of risk-based solvency regulations: in order to ensure that firms match their capital more accurately to the risks they face, they need to measure both their assets and liabilities in a fair and transparent manner, in contrast with the opaque valuation methods that were commonly used.

Insurers have made the same sort of criticisms of the three-pillar system of regulations as the banks. In particular, they are concerned that the new rules will increase earnings volatility and, as a consequence, reduce equity investment (see *Global Risk Regulator*, September 2003).

10.2.3   Financial Services Compensation Scheme

The Financial Services Compensation Scheme (FSCS) came into operation on 1 December 2001. Although independent of the FSA, it developed out of the FSA's obligation to protect consumers. The scheme provides compensation to consumers if an authorised company becomes insolvent and is not able to pay its liabilities.

The FSCS replaced eight existing schemes that provided compensation if a firm collapsed owing money to depositors, policyholders or investors: the Deposit Protection Scheme, the Building Society Investor Protection Scheme, the Policyholders' Protection Scheme, the Friendly Societies' Protection Scheme, the Investors' Compensation Scheme, the Section 43 Scheme (which covers business transacted with listed money-market institutions), the Personal Investment Authority indemnity scheme and the arrangement between the Association of British Insurers and the Investor Compensation Scheme Ltd for paying compensation to widows, widowers and dependants of deceased persons.

There are three kinds of compensation, with different rules and limits:

- Deposit claims include deposits with banks, building societies and credit unions.
- Insurance claims include:
  - compulsory insurance (such as third party motor insurance);
  - noncompulsory insurance (such as home insurance);
  - long-term insurance (such as pension plans and life assurance).
- Investment claims include claims relating to bad investment advice or poor investment management, or where a firm has gone out of business and cannot return your investments or money.

The compensation limits for the new scheme are: deposits – £31 700 (100% of £2 000 and 90% of £33 000); long-term insurance – at least 90% of the value of the policyholder's guaranteed fund at the date of default; general insurance, compulsory – 100% of valid claim/unexpired premiums; general insurance, noncompulsory – 100% of the first £2 000 of valid claim/unexpired premiums and 90% of the remainder of the claim; investments – £48 000 (100% of £30 000 and 90% of the next £20 000).

The FSCS is funded by levies on the industry on a pay-as-you-go basis. There are two types of levy: a management expenses levy and a compensation costs levy. The former is determined annually in advance and covers 'base costs' (payable by all firms) and the 'specific costs' associated with paying compensation, which depends on the number of claims and types of default.

The compensation costs levy is also determined in advance on the basis of 'anticipated compensation costs for defaults expected to be declared in the 12-month period following the date of the levy'. These include 'the costs incurred in paying compensation, securing continuity of long-term insurance and safeguarding eligible claimants when insurers are in financial difficulties' (Financial Services Authority, 2001).

The FSCS is supported by the regulatory frameworks facing the institutions it covers. These determine the minimum regulatory capital needed to cover specified losses. This, in turn, enables the probability of loss and expected loss to be quantified and hence the insurance premium for the FSCS to be set on the basis of standard insurance principles. The FSCS is, therefore, likely to be an effective and reliable insurance scheme whose solvency is assured by the adequacy of its premium income.

10.2.4   The financial regulation of pension funds

Defined benefit pension schemes share many of the characteristics of with-profit policies. Both aim to deliver a predetermined benefit (a fixed minimum return in the one case, a fixed proportion of final salary in the other) despite investing in assets whose returns can be highly volatile. Yet, while the financial regulation of insurance companies is moving closer to that of banks, the financial regulation of pension funds remains very different.

The main difference between banks, life assurers and pension funds is that the first two are subject to a solvency standard whereas the last are subject to a funding standard. A solvency standard ensures that assets exceed liabilities. A funding standard involves setting a smooth path for contributions that enables the fund to pay the promised benefits over the long run. A funding standard is much weaker than a solvency standard. A pension fund can be fully funded but still be unable to pay its liabilities in full if the sponsor becomes insolvent. This is because a fully funded scheme depends on future sponsor contributions to make good any deficit.

The first attempt at financial regulation of pension funds was the Minimum Funding Requirement (MFR) introduced by the 1995 Pensions Act. The MFR (which came into effect on 6 April 1997) established a minimum level of funding for a defined benefit (DB) pension scheme (or for a defined contribution pension scheme which also provides salary-related benefits) and an associated schedule of contributions necessary to meet this minimum level of funding. The pension scheme's trustees were responsible for ensuring that this schedule was delivered. The MFR could be satisfied either by the minimum level of funding being met immediately or by having a schedule of contributions in place that would meet the minimum funding level within a specified time limit (a maximum of five years, subsequently extended to ten years).

A pension scheme has a 'deficiency' when it has insufficient assets to meet its liabilities, calculated on an MFR basis (where the discount rate for the liabilities depended on the return on a reference portfolio consisting of two statutory reference assets, UK equities and UK bonds, with the actual assets held by the pension fund 'allocated to' – i.e. treated as being equivalent to – one of the two reference assets). The schedule of contributions needed to make good the deficiency had to be agreed between the trustees and sponsor. A 'serious deficiency' occurred when the assets were valued at less than 90% of the value of the liabilities. To reduce the deficiency, the assets had to be increased to at least 90% of the liabilities, within one year (later extended to three years). This could be achieved either through a cash payment to the fund by the sponsor or by the sponsor giving a financial guarantee both to bring the scheme's assets up to at least 90% of the liabilities if the sponsor became insolvent and to maintaining the agreed contribution schedule. If either of these solutions were not feasible, the trustees had to inform the Occupational Pensions Regulatory Authority (OPRA) (the predecessor to The Pensions Regulator between 1997 and 2004) within 14 days, and scheme members within one month.

If the deficiency were less serious, with assets worth between 90% and 100% of the liabilities, the assets had to be increased to 100% of the liabilities by the end of the period covered by the schedule of contributions. Contributions might have had to be increased to achieve this. Such increased contributions could be spread evenly throughout the period covered by the schedule. It was also permissible for larger contributions to be paid early on in the period (this is called 'frontloading'), but the 'backloading' of contributions towards the end of the period was not permitted.

Following each MFR valuation, the trustees had to establish a schedule of contributions within twelve weeks. This showed the rates of contributions and the due dates on which the trustees had to receive the contributions. Each schedule covered a five-year period and might need to be revised during this period to ensure that the MFR continued to be met.

The schedule of contributions showed the contribution rates and due dates for all the contributions to be paid:

• by (or on behalf of) all active members (excluding additional voluntary contributions);
• by (or on behalf of) each sponsoring employer taking part in the scheme;
• by the sponsoring employer to rectify a serious shortfall in funding.

Even with this schedule of contributions, it would not necessarily be the case that the whole of a scheme's liabilities could be met in full if the scheme were to be wound up immediately. The MFR did not guarantee absolute security for pensions, since, unlike Basle 2 and Solvency 2, the MFR was a funding standard not a solvency standard. Mike Pomery, Chairman of the Pensions Board of the Faculty and Institute of Actuaries (FIA), speaking at the 2000 NAPF (National Association of Pension Funds) annual conference, stated that the MFR gave scheme members only a 'reasonable expectation' that they would get their full pension, not 'absolute security'. The FIA estimated that full funding for UK pension funds would cost an additional £100bn on top of assets valued at £830bn in 2000 (Faculty and Institute of Actuaries, 2000).

A pension fund that fully met the MFR might only have had funds sufficient to purchase around 70% of the pensions due to active members if the sponsor became insolvent. There were a number of reasons for this:

• The claims of retired members were met first.
• The insurance companies that provided both immediate and deferred pension annuities for members when a sponsoring company was wound up were likely to use lighter mortality assumptions than allowed for in the MFR regulations, and hence offer lower annuities for a given purchase price.
• Falling long-term interest rates since 1990 that raised the present value of scheme liabilities; even though the assets held by DB schemes,

mainly equities, had traditionally delivered high returns, they still failed to keep up with the growth in scheme liabilities (in large part due to increases in longevity) since the introduction of the MFR in 1997.

- It valued liabilities using the *current unit method with LPI revaluation*,[2] so did not take into account future earnings growth.

As many as one in six pension funds in 2000 were either at, or below, the MFR borderline of 90% funding. The weakness of the MFR was exposed in 2000 by the case of Blagden – a chemicals company whose pension fund fully satisfied the MFR, but which went into insolvency with funds sufficient only to meet two-thirds of its obligations to active members.

In March 2001, the H M Treasury-sponsored review of institutional investment chaired by Paul Myners, chief executive of Gartmore, was published. Its recommendations were immediately accepted in full by the government (Myners, 2001, see Section 7.9). The report called for a new approach to institutional investment, identified a series of current distortions to effective decision-making and suggested ways of tackling them.

One of the key features of the report was its proposal to replace the MFR with a long-term scheme-specific funding standard in the context of a strong regime of transparency and disclosure. The report also proposed a set of additional measures to strengthen protection:

- a recovery plan for returning schemes to full funding;
- a statutory duty of care on the scheme actuary;
- stricter conditions on the voluntary wind-up of a scheme where the employer remains solvent (e.g. the liabilities would have to include the actual cost of winding up the scheme and the actual cost of buying annuities to secure pensions in payment);
- an extension of the fraud compensation scheme: the level of compensation for fraud would be increased to cover not simply the MFR liabilities as at present, but the full cost of securing members' accrued benefits (or the amount of the loss from fraud, whichever is the lesser).

The government argued that: 'These proposals will provide protection for members of all defined benefit schemes and will encourage an intelligent and thought-through approach to planning investment and

---

[2] This is equivalent of the projected unit method with an LPI revaluation rate, see Equation (6.1).

contributions policy. They do not distort investment as the MFR does, because they do not involve the valuation of liabilities using statutory reference assets, which create artificial incentives for schemes to invest in those assets. Employers that wish to go on offering defined benefit schemes will find it easier to do so under these proposals. At the same time, the proposals will make it more difficult for those that wish to walk away from the pension promises that they have made'.

On 11 June 2003, the government announced that any solvent company which wound up its DB pension scheme had to do so, not on an MFR basis, but on a full buy-out basis with a life assurer (i.e. the fund had to have sufficient assets to buy immediate annuities for the scheme's pensioners and deferred annuities for active and deferred members).

The 2004 Pensions Act introduced the requirement for a *statutory funding objective*[3] (SFO) and a *statement of funding principles* (SFP) that presents the following information:

- the current value of the pension fund's assets and in what asset classes they are invested;
- the assumptions used to determine its liabilities;
- planned future contributions;
- its planned asset allocation for the following year or years;
- the assumed returns and assumed volatilities of those returns for each asset class sufficient to meet the liabilities;
- a justification by the trustees of the reasonableness of both their asset allocation and the investment returns assumed in the light of the circumstances of the fund and of the sponsor; and
- an explanation of the implications of the volatility of the investment values for possible underfunding, and a justification by trustees of why this level of volatility is judged to be acceptable.

The SFO must reflect the specific liabilities of the scheme. This means that the pension fund must invest in assets that match as closely as possible the liabilities of the scheme in terms of key features of the liabilities, such as the way that they change over time in response to earnings growth, changing interest rates and demographic factors, such as the maturity structure of the liabilities of the scheme.

UK pension funds are also subject to the European Union Pension Fund Directive (2003). This has adopted the Anglo-Saxon concept of

---

[3] This is what the Myners Report called the scheme-specific funding standard.

the 'prudent person'. As paragraph 31 of the Preamble states:

> Institutions are very long-term investors. Redemption of the assets held by these institutions cannot, in general, be made for any purpose other than providing retirement benefits. Furthermore, in order to protect adequately the rights of members and beneficiaries, institutions should be able to opt for an asset allocation that suits the precise nature and duration of their liabilities. These aspects call for efficient supervision and an approach towards investment rules allowing institutions sufficient flexibility to decide on the most secure and efficient investment policy and obliging them to act prudently. Compliance with the 'prudent person rule' therefore requires an investment policy geared to the membership structure of the individual institution for occupational retirement provision.

Despite its long history, the 'prudent person' principle is a rather vague and unquantifiable concept.

What is striking is the extraordinary level of detail associated with the financial regulation of banks, and especially life assurers, compared with pension funds, which by contrast are subject to a much vaguer framework of financial regulation. This clearly has important implications for an insurance scheme established to protect pension liabilities such as the Pension Protection Fund.

10.2.5   Pension Benefit Guaranty Corporation (PBGC)

The Pension Protection Fund is based, not on the FSCS, but on the US Pension Benefit Guaranty Corporation (PBGC).[4]

The PBGC was created by the Employee Retirement Income Security Act (ERISA) of 1974 to encourage the continuation and maintenance of DB pension plans in the US, provide timely and uninterrupted payment of pension benefits and keep pension insurance premiums at a minimum. The PBGC covers 44.3 million workers in 31 000 DB plans. It pays monthly retirement benefits to 459 000 retirees in 3287 pension plans that have ended and is responsible for the current and future pensions of about 934 000 people. For plans ended in 2004, workers who retire at age 65 can receive up to $44 386.32 a year.

The PBGC's premium revenue was $973 million in 2003. All single-employer pension plans pay a basic flat-rate premium of $19 per participant per year. Underfunded pension plans pay an additional variable-rate charge of $9 per $1000 (i.e. 0.9%) of unfunded vested benefits. The premium for smaller, multiemployer programmes is $2.60 per participant per year. The PBGC paid nearly $2.5 billion in benefits in 2003 and had a deficit in that year of $11bn. The 2005 deficit was $22.8bn.

---

[4] See the Pension Benefit Guaranty Corporation website http://www.pbgc.gov/

An interesting aspect of the PBGC is how the premium it charges has increased since 1974:

- 1974: flat-rate of $1 per participant
- 1978: raised to $2.60
- 1986: raised to $8.50
- 1988:
  - basic premium raised to $16
  - additional variable-rate premium was imposed on underfunded plans for a maximum total premium of $50 per participant.
- 1991:
  - basic premium raised to $19
  - maximum premium at $72 per participant for underfunded plans.
- 1994:
  - basic premium stays at $19
  - premiums increased for plans that pose greatest risk by phasing out maximum limit on premiums for underfunded plans
- 1997: maximum completely eliminated.

The premium is not explicitly risk-related (i.e. it is not higher for sponsors more likely to become insolvent). Although it is exposure-related (i.e. related to the level of the claim in the event of insolvency), it is not related to the probability of a claim being made. This means that, contrary to standard insurance principles, financially weak sponsors with underfunded schemes are not charged the full risk-adjusted premium.

There are three ways in which a pension plan can be taken over by the PBGC:

1. *Distress termination.* A company in financial distress may voluntarily terminate a pension plan if: a petition has been filed seeking reorganisation in bankruptcy; it has been demonstrated that the sponsor or affiliate cannot continue in business unless the plan is terminated; it has been demonstrated that the costs of providing pension coverage have become unreasonably burdensome solely as result of a decline in the number of employees covered by the plan.
2. *Involuntary termination.* The PBGC may terminate a pension plan if: the plan has not met minimum funding requirements; the plan cannot pay current benefits when due; a lump sum payment has been made to a participant who is a substantial owner of the sponsoring company; the loss to the PBGC is expected to increase unreasonably if the plan is not terminated.

3. *Standard termination.* A plan may terminate if the plan assets are sufficient to satisfy all plan benefits, e.g. through the purchase of annuities with an insurer. There have been 163 000 standard terminations since 1974.

The PBGC has experienced a number of cases in which companies have deliberately underfunded their pension plans in advance of their own bankruptcy. It has developed a number of ways of protecting against this.

The first is the Early Warning Program. The PBGC monitors certain companies that are financially distressed or have underfunded DB plans to prevent losses before they occur, rather than waiting to pick up the pieces.

The PBGC will contact a company if: (a) the company has a below-investment-grade bond rating and sponsors a pension plan with current liabilities over $25m or (b) the company (regardless of its bond rating) sponsors a pension plan that has current liabilities over $25m and that plan has unfunded current liabilities over $5m. It is particularly concerned about transactions that substantially weaken the financial support for a pension plan, such as the break-up of a controlled group, the transfer of significantly underfunded pension liabilities in connection with the sale of a business, or a leveraged buyout.

The PBGC has developed specialised tools, technology and financial expertise. Its staff use financial information services and news databases and technology. It also relies on information sharing among the Department of Labor, Internal Revenue Service and Securities and Exchange Commission.

Once the PBGC has identified a potential transaction that could jeopardise the pension insurance programme, it meets with corporate representatives to negotiate additional contributions or security. It will work with the company to find a settlement appropriate to the financial feasibility of the company. However, in the event of the company becoming insolvent and the PBGC taking over the plan liabilities, the PBGC can claim up to 30% of the company's net worth to cover a deficiency in the plan.

10.3   THE RISKS FACING THE PPF

Traditionally, pension schemes in the UK have operated on a prudent person principle and made promises not guarantees. This is the principal reason why they have not faced formal capital requirements, in contrast with, say, life assurers, which do offer guarantees. The PPF has changed all that. Speaking at the Labour Party annual conference on 1 October 2003, the Chancellor of the Exchequer Gordon Brown said the government will 'legislate for a new statutory pension protection fund. In future every worker contributing to a pension will have their pension protected and be *guaranteed* their pension rights'. This means that a *promise* made by a scheme sponsor is being *guaranteed* by the PPF, in effect, by all the other scheme sponsors. This will result in the PPF being subject to four key risks, which we now examine in turn.

10.3.1 Moral hazard

Moral hazard is one of the classic risks facing all insurance providers: people become more careless once they are insured and, in addition, they have an incentive to play 'games' against the insurer. The PPF provides scheme sponsors with an incentive to underfund their schemes and invest in assets with higher expected returns and risks (Utgoff, 1993). This is because the value of the PPF guarantee is greatest for 'those schemes where the sponsor is financially weak, the pension scheme is poorly funded, the equity exposure is high and contributions are low' (McCarthy and Neuberger, 2005). If the assets perform well, the deficit will be reduced. If the assets perform badly and the scheme becomes insolvent, the PPF will take over the pension liabilities. The PPF will increase the risk-based premium for an underfunded scheme. But this might not solve the problem and might only make matters worse for the sponsoring company, which is already in financial difficulty. For an employer near to insolvency, there is an immediate trade-off between pensions and jobs.[5]

Further, the existence of the PPF provides an incentive for financially weak companies to increase pension benefits rather than wage increases, since the latter have to be paid immediately, while the former might eventually be paid by the PPF. Other 'games' the PPF should become wary of are the early retirement of senior directors of a company taking substantial pension benefits with them, the sale of a subsidiary with an underfunded pension scheme to a financially weak buyer and

---

[5] Certainly for risk-based premiums to have the desired effect of increasing the funding level, the premium must be greater than the cost to the sponsor of borrowing funds to reduce the deficit.

pressure on the scheme actuary to change the actuarial assumptions in a way that lowers the reported deficit and reduces employer contributions (Gebhardtsbauer and Turner, 2004).

The PPF itself could fall into the same trap. It, too, has an incentive to take asset risk, since it can rely on future premiums and the implicit government underwrite: the government is unlikely to allow the PPF to go bust.

10.3.2   Adverse selection: bad drives out good

Adverse selection is another classic risk: only those most likely to claim take out insurance. As with all forms of insurance, strong schemes subsidise weak schemes. The costs of the PPF will provide a strong incentive for financially strong employers to close down their defined benefit schemes, leaving only the schemes of financially weak sponsors participating in the PPF. Although participation is mandatory if an employer has a DB scheme, there is no requirement for an employer to operate a DB scheme at all. Since the mid-1990s, firms have been switching away from DB schemes towards DC schemes, although on 11 June 2003, the government announced that solvent companies could not walk away from their DB obligations accrued before this date unless they were fully bought out by an insurance company by means of current and deferred annuities.

The government initially estimated that the levy would total £350m p.a. However, it has subsequently been estimated that the levy needs to be £600m for FTSE 100 companies alone. Given 8 million members of final salary schemes, this amounts to £80 per member. Since current administration costs per member are £90, administration costs could double. (Ralfe, 2004; *Economist* 2004).

10.3.3   Systemic risk

Insurance can work if the risks that the insurer covers are specific risks, i.e. risks that are uncorrelated across claimants. This is because specific risks can be pooled and total risk falls. Insurance does not work if the risks assumed are systemic. Total risk rises as additional policyholders join the insurance scheme.

McCarthy and Neuberger (2005) show that the risks facing the PPF are systemic. This is because insolvencies are cyclical. Claims arise when firms become insolvent and the claim size depends on the level

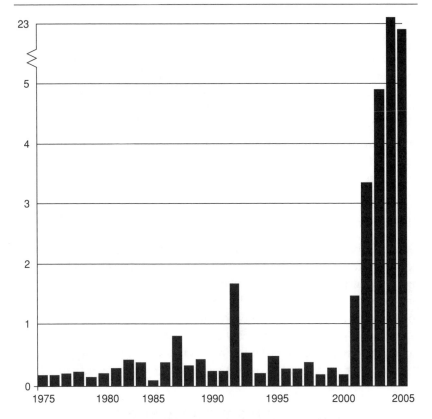

Figure 10.1   Claims on the PBGC 1975–2005 (single-employer plans) ($bn)

of underfunding. Since pension funds have a heavy equity exposure, underfunding is worst after sharp falls in stock markets and this is just when corporate insolvencies are likely to peak: Figure 10.1 shows the claims experience of the PBGC.

McCarthy and Neuberger use a simulation model in which pension funds invest two-thirds of their assets in equities, have a ten-year deficit amortisation period, guarantee 100% of their liabilities and premiums are set equal to the corresponding average annual breakeven claim rate of 0.3% of liabilities. They show that, over a 30-year period, given the volatility of equities, it is *likely* that there will be one year in which the claim rate is 1.2% and that it is *possible* (a 10% chance) that claims could equal 10% of liabilities. In other words, although, on average, the claims will be low, the PPF is likely to experience years when the claims will be very high 'when prolonged weakness in equity markets coincides with widespread corporate insolvencies' and 'the correlation of default risk across firms increases the skewness of the claims process'.[6]

The authors argue that it will be hard for the PPF to build reserves to cover claims of this size and therefore the PPF will need to raise premiums sharply after a prolonged market downturn, at the very time when all companies will be financially stretched. It is unlikely that this will be feasible. Yet, it is equally hard to believe that the PPF will be permitted to default. Consequently, the government will be forced to bail out the PPF in such circumstances (the PPF is permitted to borrow, but the government will be forced to guarantee the loan).

10.3.4 Political risk

Gebhardtsbauer and Turner (2004) point out that the PPF could face political pressures that reduce the effectiveness of its protection against moral hazard. One example is where financially weak companies exert pressures on the politicians in the constituencies where they are located to press for a reduction in the premiums that they face. A second is where the government limits contributions into the pension scheme in good economic times in order to limit its tax loss, and in doing so limits the surplus that provides a cushion against later falls in equity markets.[7]

10.4 DEALING WITH THESE RISKS

As Webb (2004) and Gebhardtsbauer and Turner (2004) point out, the PPF has a strong incentive to design the insurance scheme and to set the premium in a way that minimises the opportunities for pension funds to play games against it. With standard insurance, there are a number of ways of achieving this, which we now consider:

- the PPF could be permitted to convert its claim against the sponsoring company from a debt claim to an equity claim;
- having a maximum payout following a successful claim (i.e. co-insurance);
- permitting risk-based insurance premiums linked to the level of plan underfunding;

---

[6] Sweeting (2006) examines the correlation between pension scheme assets and firm values in greater depth and shows that ignoring these correlations (even if the volatility of pension scheme assets is allowed for) leads to a serious underestimation of the fair risk-adjusted PPF premium.

[7] The 1986 Finance Act did precisely this and limited pension scheme surpluses to 5% of liabilities.

- having a funding standard for schemes that will limit risk taking by the sponsoring company;
- close supervision and threatening the public exposure of companies that are underfunding their schemes.

10.4.1   An equity claim against the sponsoring company

This will not work in this case, as the sponsoring company that puts its pension scheme into the PPF will itself be insolvent.

10.4.2   A maximum payout

Although limiting the payout to a maximum proportion of the liabilities is generally a good way of reducing moral hazard, this too will not work here, as the 2004 Pensions Act specifies that the size of the payout will be independent of the assets in the fund.

Other restrictions might help in certain circumstances, however. For example, the PPF should not cover pension benefit withdrawals (especially by senior directors) or benefit increases made in a specified period (such as three years) prior to a scheme's insolvency. Nor should the PPF permit the sale of a subsidiary with an underfunded pension scheme to a financially weak buyer without a guarantee from the parent company.

10.4.3   Risk-based premiums linked to the level of underfunding

Again, these are usually a good way of dealing with moral hazard, but there are two problems with risk-based premiums in this case.

The first deals with assessing the correct level of default risk and, hence, premiums. Bodie (1996) shows that the default risk facing a pension fund insurer such as the PPF depends on the financial strength of the sponsoring company, the level of underfunding of the scheme and the extent of mismatch between the scheme assets and liabilities. The last two factors depend on the sponsor's contribution policy and the scheme's investment strategy, respectively. For example, an underfunded scheme might follow an aggressive equity-based investment strategy, hoping to rely on the equity risk premium to compensate for its inadequate contributions.

The insurance provided by the PBGC or PPF can be interpreted as a put option on the scheme's assets (see, for example, Sharpe, 1976; Treynor, 1977; Langetieg et al., 1982; Marcus, 1987 and Lewis and Pennacchi,

1999a, 1999b). These studies found that the insurance premiums charged by the PBGC, while correlated with the three factors identified by Bodie, significantly underestimated the true level of risk assumed by the PBGC, despite the fact that the basic premium had increased 19-fold since the PBGC was established. Vanderhei (1990) estimated the size of the insurance premiums the PBGC needed to charge to cover its costs. As shown above, this must equal the expected loss to the PBGC, which, in turn, is equal to the product of the probability of default (PD) of a pension scheme and the loss given default (LGD). Using data supplied by the PBGC, Vanderhei calculated the breakeven insurance premium for the PBGC using its own formula of a fixed premium per member and a variable premium per $1000 of underfunding. He found that the PBGC was undercharging on average, but also imposed significant cross-subsidies from strong to weak firms.[8]

The second problem is whether risk-adjusted premiums will have the desired effect. Both McCarthy and Neuberger (2005) and Gebhardtsbauer and Turner (2004) reject the view that risk-based premiums will, in this case, help to alleviate the problem of moral hazard. They argue that they will simply drive already weak schemes and companies to insolvency, since for companies already close to insolvency, the correct premium would almost equal the level of underfunding. And the attempt to get more solvent schemes to cross-subsidise the very weak schemes will push these schemes either towards insolvency or away from DB provision. Risk-related premiums could well increase the likelihood that the PPF is forced to look to the government to bail it out.

Gebhardtsbauer and Turner (2004) do, however, support the idea of premiums related to the size of underfunding, rather than to the risk. They put forward three reasons: it encourages firms to take seriously their commitment to funding their pension promise; it reduces the amount of cross-subsidy from strong to weak firms; and it is simple to understand in a way that more risk-based premiums might not be.

10.4.4   A funding standard for schemes

Both McCarthy and Neuberger (2005) and Gebhardtsbauer and Turner (2004) point out that the problem of moral hazard could be reduced by introducing tighter funding requirements. The immediate problem facing the PPF is that the same Act that established it also ended the

---

[8] The Marcus (1987) and Vanderhei (1990) models are explained in the appendix at the end of this chapter.

MFR, the nearest thing pension schemes had to a framework for determining 'regulatory capital'. The new funding standard (i.e. the SFO) that replaced the MFR, recognised some of its weaknesses: namely its inflexibility (one size fits all) and the distortion of the asset allocation of the fund assets towards the reference assets specified for setting the liability discount rate. However, to be effective, the SFO also needs to satisfy the following restrictions:

- the contribution rate needs to be set to remove a deficit over a short control period;
- the discount rate for determining liabilities needs to be based on the risk-free rate to remove the possibility of the equity risk premium being used to lower the contribution rate;
- limits should be placed on the equity weighting in the pension fund.

10.4.5 Close supervision and the public exposure of companies that underfund their schemes

Schemes with large deficits need to be watched and supervised very closely, along the lines of the PBGC's Early Warning Program. The potential reputational damage to a company of being exposed to its suppliers, creditors, workers and customers as having a large pension deficit should help to incentivise sponsors to remove the deficit.

The 2004 Pensions Act allows the Pensions Regulator to issue a *contribution notice* (CN) requiring a person who has been involved (within the previous six years) in a deliberate act to avoid pension liabilities to put money into a pension scheme up to a specified amount or to issue a *financial support direction* (FSD) requiring associated or connected persons to put financial support in place to guarantee the pension liabilities of an insufficiently resourced sponsor. A *clearance procedure* can be used to ensure that actions (called type A events) will not lead to the issue of a CN or FSD for schemes in deficit. Examples of type A events are the payment of a large dividend, a large sale buyback or the sale of the firm to another highly leveraged firm. These anti-avoidance powers are 'unprecedented in the history of company law and the lifting of the corporate veil should send a shiver down the spine of all irresponsible directors, their advisers and professional indemnity insurers' (Farr, 2005, p. 21). According to Farr, this should give comfort to trustees, who are likely to be the largest material unsecured creditors of the sponsoring firm. At the same time, Farr suggests that these trustees should also seek the advice of specialists in creditor negotiations.

10.4.6 Comment

What all this amounts to is a similar financial regulatory framework as the three-pillar model for banks and life assurers. And we should not be surprised at this.

What Sections 10.2 and 10.3 showed was the complexities involved in setting the appropriate level of regulatory capital, especially for life assurers, the nearest equivalent to pension funds. Yet, it is only once the appropriate regulatory capital is in place that the required premium for insurance protection can be determined. This is because the premium depends on both the probability of an insolvency occurring and the expected loss if one occurs, and these can only be assessed once the regulatory capital is in place. The situation with pension funds is actually more complicated than this, since the probability of insolvency of both the fund and the sponsor need to be taken into account.

One aspect that is different, however, is political risk. The PPF is likely to be subject to greater pressures than is likely to be the case in the banking and insurance world. The PPF must strongly resist political interference. In addition, in the presence of increasingly volatile global capital markets, the government should raise the contribution limits into schemes in order to help companies build up a cushion in good economic times.

10.5   CONCLUSIONS

Unlike banks and insurance companies, UK pension funds are not regulated by the FSA; moreover, they do not have formal capital requirements. Instead, they operate on a prudent person principle and make promises not guarantees. This explains why the current financial regulation of pension funds is so different from that of banks and life assurers.

However, the establishment of the Pension Protection Fund has radically altered the nature of the game by turning the promise of the scheme sponsor into a guarantee underwritten ultimately by the taxpayer. As we saw with banks and life assurers, a guarantee requires a much more stringent set of regulatory capital requirements than does a promise. Indeed, it requires the same three-pillar framework as for bank depositors and insurance company policyholders:

- Pillar 1 – sets minimum capital charges for the risks faced;
- Pillar 2 – involves supervision by The Pension Regulator;
- Pillar 3 – imposes market discipline via information disclosure.

There might even be a need for a fourth pillar – namely, barriers against political interference.

Yet, the very Act of Parliament that established the PPF also replaced the MFR with a much weaker scheme-specific funding standard (or Statutory Funding Objective). Rather than move towards the three- (or four-) pillar framework to support the PPF, the funding standard has been weakened. This, combined with the impact of systemic risk, spells potential disaster for the PPF: it is unlikely to survive without periodic government bailouts. Indeed the only way in which the PPF can survive is in circumstances in which it is not needed, namely that pension schemes are fully funded at all times.

Given that the average FRS17 funding level for the UK's top 350 companies is about 80%, these companies would need an extra £150bn to cover the PPF level of funding (*Pensions Week*, 25 April 2005). This indicates that in its first month after launch, the PPF was providing in excess of £150bn of insurance cover against annual levy premiums of just £300m. Standard & Poor's 2005 study of potential claims against the PPF, which was based on the default experience of the top 340 UK companies with different credit ratings since 1981, suggests that annual claims on the PPF will exceed £300m. Under the most optimistic assumptions, under which the PPF will recover 40% of the deficit from the defaulted sponsor, the annual claim on the PPF would be £670m. If the recovery rate was only 20%, a more realistic level for schemes below the top 340, the annual claim on the PPF would be £890m. However, limiting annual claims to £890m looks decidedly optimistic. In the first month of the PPF's existence alone, it received claims in excess of £1bn with the collapse of Turner & Newell (with liabilities of £875m) and Rover (with liabilities of £400m).

QUESTIONS

1. How does the PPF fund itself?
2. What is meant by regulatory capital?
3. What is an internal risk-based model? How is it used for regulatory purposes?
4. Describe the three-pillar system of financial regulation, known as Basle 2.
5. What role do 'probability of default' and 'loss given default' have in the determination of regulatory capital?
6. What is the Financial Services Compensation Scheme?

7. What is the difference between a solvency standard and a funding standard?
8. What is the difference between a promise and a guarantee?
9. What is meant by 'reasonable expectations'?
10. What does the Statement of Funding Principles show?
11. What is the PBGC?
12. Explain the three ways in which US pension plans can be taken over by the PBGC.
13. Explain the PBGC's Early Warning Program.
14. What is moral hazard and why should the PPF be concerned about it?
15. What is adverse selection and why should the PPF be concerned about it?
16. What is systemic risk and why should the PPF be concerned about it?
17. What is political risk and why should the PPF be concerned about it?
18. What possible ways have been proposed for dealing with the risks faced by the PPF?
19. Ideally, what restrictions should a Statutory Funding Objective satisfy?
20. Pension funds should have the same three-pillar framework of financial regulation as other financial institutions. Discuss.

APPENDIX: THE MARCUS (1987) AND VANDERHEI (1990) MODELS

Marcus (1987) was the first study to establish the fair value of the insurance provided by the PBGC using option theory. The value of the PBGC put is determined under two scenarios: (a) the pension plan is terminated when it is value-maximising for the sponsor, even though the sponsor remains solvent, and (b) the pension plan is terminated because the sponsor becomes insolvent. In the first scenario, the put option, is formally equivalent to an infinite maturity American option, which will be exercised when it is sufficiently in-the-money: the termination decision is an optimal timing problem. This value provides an upper bound to the value of PBGC insurance, since the plan will be terminated only when it is optimal for the firm to do so. In the second scenario, the pension plan is terminated only when the sponsor becomes insolvent. This will provide a lower bound to the value of PBGC insurance. This valuation is also consistent with the 11 June 2003 ruling in the UK that solvent companies could not walk away from their pension plan if it was underfunded.

Define:

A = value of accrued benefits
F = value of pension fund assets
E = net worth of the company
$S = F + 0.3E$ = liability of the company on termination (i.e. the value of the pension assets plus 30% of the net worth of the company)

The net proceeds to the firm on termination equal:

$$F - \min [A, S] = F - A + \max [A - S, 0]$$

Although the firm's net pension liability is $F - A$, at termination it can transfer its liability of A to the PBGC in exchange for only S.

Consider first the case of voluntary termination. Suppose the put option that the firm has against the PBGC is denoted $P^P(A, S)$. The boundary conditions for P^P are:

- at the point of exercise (when the firm terminates the plan voluntarily), the value of the put is $P^P = A - S$;
- the limit of P^P as S approaches infinity is zero;
- the limit of P^P as A approaches zero is zero;
- the voluntary termination decision is made to maximise the value of P^P.

Marcus shows that the value of the put is given by:

$$P^P(A, S) = (1 - K)A(S/A)^\varepsilon K^{-\varepsilon}$$

where

K = ratio of S/A at which the option is exercised.

$$\varepsilon = -\left[\left(\frac{C_S - C_A}{\sigma^2} - \frac{1}{2}\right)^2 - \frac{1}{2}\frac{C_A}{\sigma^2}\right]^{1/2} + \left[\frac{1}{2} - \frac{C_S - C_A}{\sigma^2}\right]$$

$$\sigma^2 = \sigma_A^2 + \sigma_S^2 - 2\rho\sigma_A\sigma_S$$

C_S = rate of firm contributions into the pension fund net of payments to retirees (as a proportion of S)
C_A = net growth rate in accrued benefits (increases as service increases and decreases as pensions are paid or retirees die)

σ_S^2 = variance of net growth rate in contributions as a result of investment returns, around a trend line growing at $C_S + r$, where r is the risk-free rate of return

σ_A^2 = variance of net growth rate in accrued benefits, around a trend line growing at $C_A + r$, where r reflects the unwinding of the liability discount

ρ = correlation between net growth rate in contributions and net growth rate in accrued benefits

The option value is maximised when K is set at:

$$K = \frac{\varepsilon}{\varepsilon - 1}$$

Now ε must be negative for K to be positive, which in turn implies that $0 < K < 1$, so the put will only be exercised for $S < A$, i.e. if fund assets plus 30% of the company's net worth are below the level of accrued benefits.

The value of the termination option increases with C_A and decreases with C_S: when the gap between the growth rates of accrued benefits (A) and the assets backing those benefits (S) increases, the expected proceeds from future exercise of the put option increase and the value to waiting also increases.

Marcus estimated the value of pension fund insurance for a plan capable of meeting its liabilities in full $(A = S = 1)$ for the case when $\sigma^2 = 0.05$, $C_S + r = 0$ (so assets are not changing) and $C_A + r = 0$ (so liabilities are not changing). Under these circumstances, the put is exactly at-the-money and has a value of 18% of the value of accrued liabilities. Even fully funded plans can pose a significant risk to the PBGC.

Now consider the case of plan termination due to sponsor insolvency. Suppose insolvency is declared when the value of the firm (V) falls below the value of the firm's debt obligations (D), i.e when $v = V/D < 1$. The PBGC inherits a liability of $A - F$, where F is the value of the funds in the pension plan. Since $E = 0$, the PBGC's claim against the firm $(0.3E)$ is worthless.

Suppose the put option that the firm has against the PBGC is denoted $P^P(v, F, A)$. The boundary conditions for P^P are:

- $P^P = A - F$ when $v = 1$;
- the limit of P^P as v approaches infinity is zero;
- the limit of P^P as A and F approach zero is zero;

Marcus shows that the value of the put in this case is given by:

$$P^P(v, F, A) = Av^{-\phi} - Fv^{-\theta}$$

where

$$\phi = \frac{L}{M} + \left[\left(\frac{L}{M} \right)^2 - \frac{2C_A}{M} \right]^{1/2} > 0$$

$$\theta = \frac{K}{M} + \left[\left(\frac{K}{M} \right)^2 - \frac{2C_F}{M} \right]^{1/2} > 0$$

$$K = -\frac{1}{2}\sigma_v^2 + \frac{1}{2}\sigma_D^2 - \sigma_{DF} + \sigma_{VF}$$

$$L = -\frac{1}{2}\sigma_v^2 + \frac{1}{2}\sigma_D^2 - \sigma_{DA} + \sigma_{VA}$$

$$M = \sigma_V^2 + \sigma_D^2 - 2\sigma_{DV} = \sigma_v^2$$

C_F = rate of firm contributions into the pension fund net of payments to retirees (as a proportion of F)

C_A = net growth rate in accrued benefits (increases as service increases and decreases as pensions are paid or retirees die)

σ_{DF} = covariance of rates of change between D and F, etc.

In determining its optimal funding decision for the pension plan, the firm faces a trade-off between maximising the value of pension fund insurance $P^P(v, F, A)$ (which increases as F decreases) and maximising the value of the tax shield (which increases as F increases – as pointed out by Bulow, 1981 and Harrison and Sharpe, 1983). This is shown in Figure 10.2. If v is sufficiently large, then the tax benefits of additional funding will dominate the reduced value of pension fund insurance. Otherwise, $P(v, F, A)$ is maximised when funding is minimised.

Suppose the firm's funding behaviour is determined as follows:

$$C_F = c_0 - c_1(D/V)$$

Figure 10.3 shows the value of the put, $P^P(v, F, A)$, as a function of the debt ratio, D/V, for a fully funded plan ($A = S = 1$) for three values of c_1 and for c_0 set at the value required to give a growth rate of plan assets to liabilities of 2% p.a. when $D/V = 0$. As D/V increases, the funding rate falls and eventually the ratio of plan assets to liabilities falls over time. For extreme values of the debt ratio, the value of the put falls to

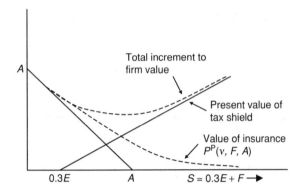

Figure 10.2 Optimal funding decision for the pension plan
Source: Marcus (1987). Reproduced from Bodie, Shoven and Wise (Eds) *Issues in Pension Economics*, University of Chicago Press.

zero. Since the plan is fully funded, the PBGC faces no liability, even if the firm becomes insolvent ($D/V = 1$). As the debt ratio tends to zero, so does the probability of insolvency, and so does the value of the put. For values of D/V in the middle, the value of the put can be quite high. For example, if $D/V = 0.6$ and $c_1 = 0.3$, the value of pension fund insurance can exceed 40% of the value of the liabilities, since assets are being drained from the fund at a very high rate.

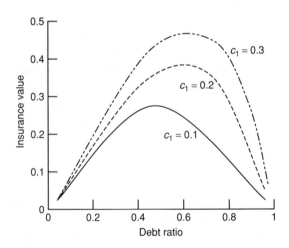

Figure 10.3 Pension-insurance value as a proportion of plan liabilities (fully funded plan, insolvency-only termination)
Source: Marcus (1987). Reproduced from Bodie, Shoven and Wise (Eds) *Issues in Pension Economics*, University of Chicago Press.

Vanderhei (1990) has criticised the Marcus put valuation model on the grounds of the difficulties of moving from the value of the put option to the calculation of fair value premium rates for pension insurance. Since fund termination dates are stochastic, the annual premiums that have the same expected present value as that of the PBGC obligations cannot be calculated easily. This is because they require an estimate of the expected time to termination of each company covered by the PBGC and a knowledge of the interest rate on each company's debt. The model also requires estimates of such parameters as the correlation between the fund's assets and the firm's value that are virtually impossible to determine. Marcus was, therefore, forced to use a standard set of 'reasonable guesses' for all the firms covered by his study.

Vanderhei uses a more direct approach to setting the premium, which equals the product of the probability of termination and the amount of exposure (or severity as he denotes it), given termination. This will provide the premium for a single year. To set multiperiod premiums, account must be taken of the volatility of asset and liability values.

The probability of termination was estimated using a logistic likelihood function:

$$\ell = \left(\frac{\alpha_p}{\alpha_s}\right) \sum_{n=1}^{N_1} \ln\left[\frac{\exp(\mathbf{X}'_{in}\boldsymbol{\beta})}{1 + \exp(\mathbf{X}'_{in}\boldsymbol{\beta})}\right] + \left(\frac{1 - \alpha_p}{1 - \alpha_s}\right) \sum_{n=1}^{N_0} \ln\left[\frac{1}{1 + \exp(\mathbf{X}'_{0n}\boldsymbol{\beta})}\right]$$

where

α_s = proportion of failed firms in the sample
α_p = proportion of failed firms in the population
N_1 = number of sample plans that terminated in the designated time period
N_0 = number of sample plans that did not terminate in the designated time period
$\mathbf{X}$ = vector of independent variables ($i = 0,1$)
$\boldsymbol{\beta}$ = vector of coefficients

Included in $\mathbf{X}$ are publicly available variables known to be significant in the prediction of corporate insolvency, with coefficients in parentheses (Altman *et al.*, 1977):

- Current assets/current liabilities (-1.46)
- Net income/total assets (-3.39)
- Log of total real assets (small companies have a higher failure rate) (-0.12)

Table 10.4

Years prior to termination	Average funding ratio of plans that terminated[*]
5	0.49
4	0.46
3	0.43
2	0.34
1	0.28
0	0.17

Note: [*]*As a proportion of the average funding ratio of all plans in the sample in the corresponding year*

- Capitalisation = FYRAVE/(FYRAVE + preferred stock + long-term debt) where FYRAVE is the five-year value of total market debt (−2.99)
- Dummy for primary metal industry (3.88).

The five-year probability of termination in the sample for Vanderhei's data period (1980–1984) was 0.063.

For the severity model, the starting point for calculating the PBGC's exposure is the size of the plan's unfunded vested liability. However, Ippolito (1989) has shown that many plans engage in extensive defunding prior to termination through the use of: funding waivers, modification of interest rates used for actuarial valuations, non-payment of required contributions, lump sum payouts to senior executives, increases in benefits instead of wage rises. This led to a reduction in the average funding ratio in the five years prior to termination and a claim on the PBGC (Table 10.4).

Given this, Vanderhei defines the severity of an insured plan as:

$$\text{Severity} = \max[0, 1 - (F - d)]L$$

where

L = plan liabilities for vested benefits
F = plan's current funding ratio for vested benefits
d = maximum expected deterioration in the funding ratio prior to termination

Vanderhei estimates $d = 0.506$, implying that over the sample period, the average plan that terminated reduced its funding ratio prior to

Table 10.5 Estimated risk-related premiums for the PBGC for 1985

	Total	Risk premium range maximums						
		$0.00	$10	$25	$50	$75	$100	$100+
Estimated Fair Premiums								
1. Number of plans	665	62.4%	15.9	4.2	3.4	2.8	1.5	9.6
2. Number of participants	2.4 m	68.1%	6.2	2.5	1.2	2.0	0.6	19.0
3. Risk-related premiums	$157.7 5m	0.0%	0.1	0.6	0.7	2.0	0.9	95.4
4. Exposure[1]	$4644	0.0	5436	2802	5196	8258	13 506	31 5603
5. Default risk per plan	9.8	7.5	3.0	8.7	9.8	14.8	9.6	34.8
6. Default risk[2] per participant	12.1	10.1	2.8	8.4	7.7	9.7	7.5	23.2
7. Average risk premium	$65.59	$0.00	2.18	16.35	37.05	60.38	87.03	753.05
PBGC Premiums								
8. Premiums[3]	$34.9m	49.0%	5.0	1.8	1.0	1.7	1.3	39.8
9. Absolute subsidy (%)	77.8	N.A.[4]	−788.0	33.7	69.7	80.5	68.9	90.7

[1] Per participant; includes a cushion for pretermination defunding.
[2] Per 1000.
[3] This includes a per-participant charge of $10.50.
[4] Since plans in the zero risk-premium category pay no risk premium, the amount of subsidy divided by zero is undefined.

termination by approximately 50 percentage points. The implication is that any plan with a funding ratio in excess of 1.506 would not have to pay a risk-related premium for that year (i.e. 1984).

Table 10.5 shows Vanderhei's estimates of the risk-related premium per plan member for the PBGC for 1985. A total of 62.4% of plans were so well-funded that no risk-related premium would be payable, while 9.6% of plans were so poorly funded that premiums averaging $753.05 per member (and adding up to more than 95% of total risk-related premiums) would be needed. The average exposure across all plans was $4644 per member, but this rose to $31 603 for the weakest plans, for which the average probability of termination on a participant-weighted basis was 23.2 per 1000, compared with 12.1 per 1000 for the whole sample. Total risk-related premiums amounted to $157.75m. This compares with the actual premiums collected of $34.9m, only 25% of the fair value. Those plans paying premiums below $10 (78% of the total) heavily subsidise the weaker plans.

REFERENCES

Altman, E., Haldman, R., and Narayan, P. (1977) ZETA analysis, a new model to identify bankruptcy risk of corporations. *Journal of Banking and Finance*, **1**, 29–54.

Basle Committee on Banking Supervision (1988) *International Convergence of Capital Measurement and Capital Standards*. Bank for International Settlements, Basle.

Basle Committee on Banking Supervision (1996) *Amendment to the Capital Accord to Incorporate Market Risks*. Bank for International Settlements, Basle.

Basle Committee on Banking Supervision (2003) *The New Basle Capital Accord*. Bank for International Settlements, Basle.

Bodie, Z. (1996) What the Pension Benefit Guaranty Corporation can learn from the Federal Savings and Loans Insurance Corporation. *Journal of Financial Services Research*, **10**, 83–100.

Bulow, J. (1981) *Pension Funding and Investment Policy*. Stanford University, mimeo.

Crouhy, M., Galai, D. and Mark, R. (1998) The new 1998 Regulatory Framework for Capital Adequacy: standardised models versus internal models, in Alexander, C. (Ed.) *Risk Measurement and Analysis. Vol. 1: Measuring and Modelling Financial Risk*, John Wiley & Sons, Ltd, Chichester.

Economist (2004) 'On the cheap,' 16 April.

European Union Pension Fund Directive (2003) Directive 2003/41/EC of the European Parliament and of the Council of 3 June 2003 on the Activities and Supervision of Institutions for Occupational Retirement Provision. *Official Journal of the European Union*, 23 September 2003.

Faculty and Institute of Actuaries (2000) *Review of the Minimum Funding Requirement*. Edinburgh and London, May.

Farr, R. (2005) The power of the new pensions regulator. *Pensions Week*, 9 May.

Financial Services Authority (2001) *Financial Services Compensation Scheme Funding Rules*. Policy Statement, September.

Financial Services Authority (2003) *Enhanced Capital Requirements and Individual Capital Assessments for Life Insurers*. Consultation Paper 195, August.

Financial Services Authority (2004) *Integrated Prudential Sourcebook for Insurers*, Policy Statement 04/16, June. (http://www.fsa.gov.uk/pubs/policy/ps04_16.pdf).

Gebhardtsbauer, R. and Turner, J. (2004) *The Protection of Pension Covered Workers and Beneficiaries: An Analysis of the UK Legislation Establishing the Pension Protection Fund*, prepared for Age Concern UK, March.

Harrison, J. M. and Sharpe, W. (1983) Funding and asset allocation for defined benefit pension plans, in Bodie, Z. and Shoven, J. (Eds) *Financial Aspects of the United States Pension System*. University of Chicago Press, Chicago.

Ippolito, R. (1989) *The Economics of Pension Insurance*. Irwin, Homewood, Illinois.

Jackson, P. (2001) Bank capital standards: the New Basle Accord. *Bank of England Quarterly Bulletin*, Spring, 55–63.

Jackson, P. (2002) Bank capital: Basle 2 developments. *Bank of England Financial Stability Review*, December, 103–109.

Jackson, P., Maude, D. and Perraudin, W. (1997) Bank capital and value-at-risk. *Journal of Derivatives*, Spring, 73–89.

Kupiec, P. and O'Brien, J. (1995) *The Use of Bank Trading Risk Measurement Models for Regulatory Capital Purposes*, FEDS Working Paper 95-11, Federal Reserve Board, Washington.

Langetieg, T., Findlay, M. and da Motta, L. (1982) Multiperiod pension plans and ERISA. *Journal of Financial and Quantitative Analysis*, **17**, 603–631.

Lewis, C. and Pennacchi, G. (1999a) The value of Pension Benefit Guaranty Corporation insurance. *Journal of Money, Credit and Banking*, **26**, 733–753.

Lewis, C. and Pennacchi, G. (1999b) Valuing insurance for defined benefit pension plans, in Boyle, P., Pennacchi, P. and Ricken, P. (Eds) *Advances in Futures and Options Research*, Volume 10, JAI Press, Stamford Connecticut, pp. 135–167.

Marcus, A. (1987) Corporate pension policy and the value of PBGC insurance, in Bodie, Z., Shoven, J. and Wise, D. (Eds) *Issues in Pension Economics*. University of Chicago Press, Chicago, pp. 49–76.

McCarthy, D. and Neuberger, A. (2005) The Pension Protection Fund. *Fiscal Studies*, **26**, 139–167.

Myners, P. (2001) *Institutional Investment in the United Kingdom: A Review*. H M Treasury, 6 March.

Ralfe, J. (2004) *Can the Pension Protection Fund Work?*, RBC Capital Markets Open Forum, 19 February.

Sharpe, W. (1976) Corporate pension funding policy. *Journal of Financial Economics*, **3**, 183–193.

Standard & Poors (1996) *Bank Ratings Comment: Market Capital Rules.* New York.

Standard & Poors (2005) *Study of Potential Claims on the PPF.* London.

Sweeting, P. (2006) Correlation and the Pension Protection Fund. *Fiscal Studies*, **27**, 157–182.

Treynor, J. (1977) The principles of corporate pension finance. *Journal of Finance*, **32**, 627–638.

Utgoff, K. (1993) The PBGC: a costly lesson in the economics of federal insurance, in Sniderman, M. (Ed) *Government Risk-Bearing*, Kluwer Academic, Norwell, MA, and Dordecht, pp. 145–160.

Vanderhei, J. (1990) An empirical analysis of risk-related insurance premiums for the PBGC. *Journal of Risk and Insurance*, **57**, 240–259.

Webb, D. C. (2004) *Sponsoring Company Finance, Investment and Pension Plan Funding*, London School of Economics.

Appendix A: Financial Arithmetic

This appendix covers some of the most important aspects of financial arithmetic that are be required in the book. It covers such issues as simple interest, compound interest, future values, present values, internal rates of return and time-weighted rates of return.

A.1 FUTURE VALUES: SINGLE PAYMENTS

The future value of a sum of money (the *principal*) invested at a given annual rate of interest will depend on:

- whether interest is paid only on the principal (this is known as *simple interest*), or, in addition, on the interest that accrues (this is known as *compound interest*);
- (in the case of compound interest) the frequency with which interest is paid (e.g. annually, semi-annually, quarterly, monthly, daily, continuously).

A.1.1 Simple interest

With simple interest, the future value is determined by:

$$F = P(1 + rT) \qquad \text{(A.1)}$$

where:

P = principal amount
F = future value (or end-of-period value or terminal value)
r = rate of interest (annual)
T = number of years.

For example, if $P = £1000$, $r = 0.1$ (10%) and $T = 2$ years, then:

$$F = 1000\,[1 + (0.1)(2)]$$
$$= 1200.00\,.$$

A.1.2   Compound interest: annual compounding

With compound interest, the future value (also known as the *compound value*) is determined by:

$$F = P(1+r)^T \qquad (A.2)$$

In this case, interest is earned on the interest that accrues. This can be seen by looking at the case when $T = 2$ years. After one year, the principal will have increased to $P(1 + r)$, the same as in the simple interest case. But in the second year, interest is earned on the accrued interest, so that at the end of the second year, the principal will have increased to:

$$F = P(1 + r)(1 + r)$$
$$= P(1 + r)^2$$

Using the information in the last example, the compound value after two years is:

$$F = 1000(1 + 0.1)^2$$
$$= 1210.00$$

which is £10 greater than with simple interest.

A.1.3   Compound interest: more frequent compounding

Sometimes compounding takes place more frequently than once a year. For example, if compounding takes place semi-annually, then an interest payment (equal to half the annual interest payment) will be made at the end of six months, and that interest payment will itself earn interest for the next six months. After two years, four interest payments will have been made.

In general, if compounding takes place m times per year, then, at the end of T years, mT interest payments will have been made and the future value of the principal will be:

$$F = P \left(1 + \frac{r}{m}\right)^{mT} \qquad (A.3)$$

For example, with semi-annual compounding, the future value of £1000 at the end of two years when the interest rate is 10% is:

$$F = P \left(1 + \frac{r}{2}\right)^{2T}$$

$$= 1000 \left(1 + \frac{0.1}{2}\right)^{(2)(2)}$$

$$= 1215.51$$

We can examine the effect of the frequency of compounding by examining the annualised interest-rate factors,

$$\text{Interest-rate factor} = \left(1 + \frac{r}{m}\right)^{m}$$

Assuming that $r = 0.1$ (10%):

Compounding frequency	Interest-rate factor
Annual	$(1 + r) = 1.100000$
Semi-annual	$\left(1 + \dfrac{r}{2}\right)^{2} = 1.102500$
Quarterly	$\left(1 + \dfrac{r}{4}\right)^{4} = 1.103813$
Monthly	$\left(1 + \dfrac{r}{12}\right)^{12} = 1.104713$
Daily	$\left(1 + \dfrac{r}{365}\right)^{365} = 1.105156$

Clearly, the more frequent the compounding, the greater the interest-rate factor.

The limit to this process occurs when interest is compounded continuously. This limit is derived as follows. Equation (A.3) can be rewritten:

$$F = P \left[\left(1 + \frac{r}{m}\right)^{m/r}\right]^{rT}$$

$$= P \left[\left(1 + \frac{1}{m/r}\right)^{m/r}\right]^{rT}$$

$$= P \left[\left(1 + \frac{1}{n}\right)^{n}\right]^{rT} \tag{A.4}$$

where $n = m/r$. As m, and hence n, approach infinity (and compounding becomes continuous), the expression in square brackets in (A.4) tends to the value known as e:

$$e = \lim_{n \to \infty} \left(1 + \frac{1}{n}\right)^n = 2.71828 \, .$$

Substituting this into (A.4) gives:

$$F = Pe^{rT} \tag{A.5}$$

in the case of continuous compounding.

In (A.5), e^{rT} is known as the *exponential function* of rT. It provides the continuously-compounded interest-rate factor. If $r = 0.1$ (10%) and $T = 1$ year, then:

$$e^r = (2.71828)^{0.1} = 1.105171 \, .$$

This is the limit to the process of more frequent compounding.

To illustrate continuous compounding, the future value of £1000 at the end of two years when the interest rate is 10% is:

$$F = 1000e^{(0.1)(2)}$$
$$= 1221.40 \, .$$

A.1.4   Flat and effective rates of interest

The *flat rate* of interest is the interest rate that is quoted on a deposit, loan, etc. But the *effective rate* of interest (sometimes called the *annual percentage rate* or APR) will be greater than the flat rate if compounding takes place more than once a year. The effective rate re is the compounded interest rate:

$$re = \left(1 + \frac{r}{m}\right)^m - 1 \tag{A.6}$$

For example, if the flat rate of interest is 10% and compounding takes place 12 times per year, then the effective interest rate is:

$$re = \left(1 + \frac{0.1}{12}\right)^{12} - 1$$
$$= 0.1047 \quad \text{(i.e. 10.47\%)} \, .$$

A.2   PRESENT VALUES: SINGLE PAYMENTS

If an amount F is to be received in T years' time, the *present value* of that amount is the sum of money P which, if invested today, would generate the compound amount F in T years' time. The process of finding present values is known as *discounting* and is the exact inverse of the process of finding future values.

A.2.1   Present values: annual discounting

With annual discounting, a sum of money F to be received in T years' time has a present value of:

$$P = \frac{F}{(1+r)^T}$$
$$= F(1+r)^{-T} \tag{A.7}$$

This is found by dividing both sides of (A.2) by $(1+r)^T$.

For example, the present value of £1000 to be received in five years' time when the interest rate is 10% is:

$$P = 1000(1+0.1)^{-5}$$
$$= 620.92.$$

This is because £620.92 invested for five years at 10% generates £1000. The rate of interest, r, involved in this calculation is known as the *discount rate* and the term $(1+r)^{-T}$ is known as the T-year *discount factor*, D_T:

$$D_T = (1+r)^{-T} \tag{A.8}$$

Hence, (A.7) can be written in the equivalent form:

$$P = F \times D_T \tag{A.9}$$

The five-year discount factor when the discount rate is 10% is:

$$D_T = (1+0.1)^{-5}$$
$$= 0.62092$$

A.2.2   Present values: more frequent discounting

If discounting takes place m times per year, then we can use (A.3) to derive the appropriate present value formula:

$$P = F\left(1 + \frac{r}{m}\right)^{-mT} \tag{A.10}$$

For example, with semi-annual discounting, the present value of £1000 to be received in five years' time when $r = 0.1$ (10%) is:

$$P = 1000 \left(1 + \frac{0.1}{2}\right)^{-(2)(5)}$$
$$= 613.91$$

The more frequent the discounting, the lower the present value. In the limiting case of continuous discounting, we can use (A.5) to derive the appropriate present value formula:

$$P = Fe^{-rT} \tag{A.11}$$

Using (A.11), the present value of the £1000 to be received in five years' time is:

$$P = 1000e^{-(0.1)(5)}$$
$$= 606.53$$

A.3   FUTURE VALUES: MULTIPLE PAYMENTS

So far we have considered the future value of a single payment. But we can also calculate the future value of a stream of payments. Initially we will assume that the stream of payments is an irregular one. Then we will consider the simpler case of a regular stream of payments.

A.3.1   Irregular payments

To calculate the future value of an irregular stream of payments, the appropriate future value formula is applied to each individual payment and the resulting individual future values are then summed. The formula for this is:

$$F = \sum_{t=1}^{T} d_t (1 + r)^{T-t} \tag{A.12}$$

where d_t = payment in year t (assuming the payment is made at the end of year). Since interest does not accrue until the end of each year, the first payment will accrue interest for $(T - 1)$ years, the second payment for $(T - 2)$ years, and so on.

To illustrate, the future value of the following stream of annual payments, $d_1 = 1000$, $d_2 = 1100$, $d_3 = 1200$, when the interest rate is

10% is:

$$F = 1000(1.1)^{3-1} + 1100(1.1)^{3-2} + 1200(1.1)^{3-3}$$
$$= 1210 + 1210 + 1200$$
$$= 3620.00$$

A.3.2   Regular payments

A regular stream of payments (for a given number of years) is called an *annuity*. (If the payments are made at the end of the year, as we are assuming here, the annuity is known as an *immediate annuity* or an *annuity in arrears*; if the payments are made at the beginning of the year, the annuity is known as an *annuity due* or an *annuity in advance*; if the annuity commences further than a year ahead, it is called a *deferred annuity*.) With an annuity, the payments d_t in (A.12) are identical and can be denoted as d. This allows the formula (A.12) to be simplified, as we shall now see. If $d_t = d$ for all t, then (A.12) becomes:

$$F = d \sum_{t=1}^{T} (1 + r)^{T-t} \tag{A.13}$$

If we multiply both sides of (A.13) by $(1 + r)$ and subtract the result from (A.13), we get:

$$F - (1 + r)F = d \left[\sum_{t=1}^{T} (1 + r)^{T-t} - \sum_{t=1}^{T} (1 + r)^{T-t+1} \right]$$
$$= -d[(1 + r)^T - 1] \tag{A.14}$$

which, on rearranging, yields:

$$F = d \left[\frac{(1 + r)^T - 1}{r} \right] \tag{A.15}$$

To illustrate this formula, we can calculate the future value of a three-year annuity, paying £1000 per year for three years, when the interest rate is 10%:

$$F = 1000 \left[\frac{(1.1)^3 - 1}{0.1} \right]$$
$$= 3310.00$$

As another example of the use of (A.15), we can calculate the size of an annuity necessary to accumulate a particular sum of money at a particular future date when the interest rate is known. An example of this would be the establishment of a pension fund of a particular size at some future date; the pension fund could then be used to provide a pension annuity to retired workers. The required size of the annuity is given by rearranging (A.15):

$$d = F \left[\frac{r}{(1+r)^T - 1} \right] \tag{A.16}$$

Suppose that a pension fund of £100 000 is required in 20 years' time. What should the annual pension contribution be if the rate of interest is 10%? Using (A.16):

$$d = 100\,000 \left[\frac{0.1}{(1.1)^{20} - 1} \right]$$
$$= 1745.96$$

A.4   PRESENT VALUES: MULTIPLE PAYMENTS

In a similar way, we can calculate the present value of a stream of future payments. Again, the solution depends on whether the future payments are regular or irregular.

A.4.1   Irregular payments

To calculate the present value of an irregular stream of payments, the appropriate present value formula is applied to each individual payment and the resulting individual present values are then summed. The formula for this is:

$$P = \sum_{t=1}^{T} d_t (1+r)^{-t} \tag{A.17}$$

where d_t = payment in year t (payment made at end of year).

To illustrate, the present value of the following stream of annual payments, $d_1 = 1000, d_2 = 1100, d_3 = 1200$, when the interest rate is 10% is:

$$P = 1000(1.1)^{-1} + 1100(1.1)^{-2} + 1200(1.1)^{-3}$$
$$= 909.09 + 909.09 + 901.58$$
$$= 2719.76$$

A.4.2   Regular payments: annual payments with annual discounting

The present value of an annuity is found very simply by finding the present value of (A.15):

$$
\begin{aligned}
P &= \frac{F}{(1+r)^T} \\
&= d\left[\frac{(1+r)^T - 1}{r}\right]\left[\frac{1}{(1+r)^T}\right] \\
&= d\left[\frac{1 - (1+r)^{-T}}{r}\right]
\end{aligned}
\tag{A.18}
$$

To illustrate this formula, we can calculate the present value of a three-year annuity, paying 1000 per year for three years when the interest rate is 10%:

$$
\begin{aligned}
P &= 1000\left[\frac{1 - (1.1)^{-3}}{0.1}\right] \\
&= 2486.85
\end{aligned}
$$

A.4.3   Perpetuities

An annuity that continues indefinitely is called a *perpetuity*. The future value of a perpetuity is obviously infinite, but its present value is easy to determine using (A.18), recognising that, as T tends to infinity, the term $(1+r)^{-T}$ tends to zero. This leads to:

$$
P = \frac{d}{r}
\tag{A.19}
$$

as the present value of a perpetuity.

An example of a perpetuity is an irredeemable bond, such as a 2.5% Consols, which pays £1.25 per 100 nominal every six months. On a coupon payment date when there is no accrued interest, the price of the bond when the rate of interest is 10% is:

$$
\begin{aligned}
P &= \frac{d/2}{r/2} \\
&= \frac{1.25}{0.05} \\
&= 25.00
\end{aligned}
$$

A.5   RATES OF RETURN

So far we have assumed that the rate of interest or the rate of return is given. But sometimes we do not know the rate of interest or the rate of return on an investment and it has to be calculated. There are several different ways of calculating such rates.

A.5.1   Single-period rate of return

The simplest way of measuring a rate of return is to do so over a single period. If, for instance, we buy a security today for P_0 and later sells it for P_1, then the return on holding that security from $t = 0$ to $t = 1$ is given by:

$$r = \frac{P_1 - P_0}{P_0}$$

$$= \frac{P_1}{P_0} - 1 \qquad (A.20)$$

For example, if an investor buys a security for 100 and sells it one week later for 110, his return over the week is:

$$r = \frac{110}{100} - 1 = 0.1 \quad \text{(i.e. } 10\%)$$

The ratio P_1/P_0 in (A.20) is known as the *price relative*. In many applications, the rate of return over a single period is calculated as a continuously-compounded rate of return, often known as the *log price relative*. This is given by:

$$r = \ln\left(\frac{P_1}{P_0}\right) \qquad (A.21)$$

If, for instance, an investor held a portfolio of shares comprising the FTSE 100 index, then the change in the level of that index over a period could be used to measure his return from holding the portfolio. Also, since the level of the index is continuously changing, it might seem reasonable to measure the return in terms of the log price relative. So, if the index is at 6141 (P_0) at the close of business on one day and falls to 5833 (P_1) by the close of business the next day, then, from (A.21), his return on the portfolio for that 24-hour period is:

$$r = \ln\left(\frac{5833}{6141}\right) \approx -0.051 \quad \text{(i.e. } -5.1\%).$$

A.5.2 Internal rate of return or money-weighted rate of return

One of the most common ways of measuring the return on an investment is the *internal rate of return* or the *money-weighted rate of return* (sometimes called the *yield to maturity*).

This is simple to calculate with single payments. Since $F = P(1 + r)^T$, the annual internal rate of return on an investment of P paying F in T years' time is the solution to:

$$(1 + r)^T = F/P$$

that is:

$$r = (F/P)^{1/T} - 1 \qquad \text{(A.22)}$$

For example, the annual internal rate of return on an investment costing 1000 today and returning 1500 in three years' time is:

$$r = (1500/1000)^{1/3} - 1$$
$$= 0.1447 \quad \text{(i.e. } 14.47\%)$$

With compounding taking place more frequently than once per year, the annual rate of return is the solution to:

$$\left(1 + \frac{r}{m}\right)^{mT} = F/P$$

that is:

$$r = m[(F/P)^{1/mT} - 1] \qquad \text{(A.23)}$$

Using the last example but with quarterly compounding, the annual internal rate of return is:

$$r = 4[(1500/1000)^{1/(4 \times 3)} - 1]$$
$$= 0.1375 \quad \text{(i.e. } 13.75\%)$$

The more frequent the compounding, the lower the internal rate of return.

With continuous compounding, the internal rate of return is the solution to:

$$e^{rT} = F/P \qquad \text{(A.24)}$$

In general, if $x^b = y$ then b is called the *logarithm* of y to the base x, i.e. $b = \log_x(y)$. In the case of (A.24), we have:

$$rT = \log_e(F/P) \qquad \text{(A.25)}$$

i.e. rT is the logarithm of (F/P) to the base e. Logarithms to the base e are known as *natural logarithms* and are denoted by $b = \ln(y)$. Therefore, (A.25) becomes:

$$r = \frac{1}{T} \ln(F/P) \qquad (A.26)$$

Using the last example, but with continuous compounding, the annual internal rate of return is:

$$r = \frac{1}{3} \ln(1500/1000)$$
$$= 0.1352 \quad (\text{i.e. } 13.52\%)$$

With multiple payments, an analytical solution for the internal rate of return does not generally exist. In general, the solution, r, to either:

$$F = \sum_{t=1}^{T} d_t (1+r)^{T-t} \qquad (A.27)$$

or:

$$P = \sum_{t=1}^{T} d_t (1+r)^{-t} \qquad (A.28)$$

has to be found numerically, i.e. by trial and error. This is true even if the payments are regular, as with an annuity.

Take, for example, the formula for the present value of an annuity:

$$P = d \left[\frac{1 - (1+r)^{-T}}{r} \right] \qquad (A.29)$$

Suppose we know that a three-year annuity of 1000 has a present value of £2465.12 and we want to find the internal rate of return. We begin with an estimate of the internal rate of return, say, $r = 0.1$ (10%). At $r = 0.1$ we find that $P = 2486.85$, which is greater than 2465.12. This implies that our estimate of r is too low. We should try a larger value for r, say $r = 0.11$ (11%). At $r = 0.11$, we find that $P = 2443.71$, which is less than 2465.12. The correct value of r must therefore lie between 10 and 11%. Suppose that we try $r = 0.105$ (10.5%). At this value of r we find that $P = 2465.12$ as required, so that the internal rate of return is 10.5%.

Only in the case of a perpetuity is the internal rate of return easy to calculate. From (A.19), we see that the internal rate of return is simply:

$$r = \frac{d}{P} \tag{A.30}$$

If the present value of a perpetuity of £5 per year is £41.67, then the internal rate of return is:

$$r = \frac{5}{41.67}$$
$$= 0.12 \quad \text{(i.e. } 12\%\text{)}.$$

A.5.3   Time-weighted rate of return or geometric mean rate of return

The *time-weighted rate of return* or the *geometric mean rate of return* takes into account the value of earlier payments at the time that the next payment in the series arises. If P is the initial value of an investment, F is the final value, d_t is the payment received by the investment in year t and V_t is the value of the investment when the payment is received, then the time-weighted rate of return is calculated as follows:

$$(1 + r)^T = \left(\frac{V_1}{P}\right) \left(\frac{V_2}{V_1 + d_1}\right) \left(\frac{V_3}{V_2 + d_2}\right) \cdots \left(\frac{F}{V_{T-1} + d_{T-1}}\right) \tag{A.31}$$

But $(V_1/P) = (1 + r_1)$, one *plus* the return on the investment in the first period, $[V_2/(V_1 + d_1)] = (1 + r_2)$, one *plus* the return on the investment in the second period, etc., so that this equation can be rewritten:

$$(1 + r)^T = (1 + r_1)(1 + r_2) \cdots (1 + r_T) \tag{A.32}$$

or, solving for r:

$$r = [(1 + r_1)(1 + r_2) \cdots (1 + r_T)]^{1/T} - 1 \tag{A.33}$$

From (A.33), it is clear that the time-weighted rate of return is the geometric mean of the individual period returns.

To illustrate, consider the case of an investment beginning with £100, attracting £50 at the end of year 1 (when the value of the investment was £110), and at the end of year 2 the value of the investment was £225.

The time-weighted rate of return is calculated as:

$$r = \left[\left(\frac{110}{100}\right)\left(\frac{225}{110 + 50}\right)\right]^{1/2} - 1$$
$$= [(1.10)(1.406)]^{1/2} - 1$$
$$= [1.5469]^{1/2} - 1$$
$$= 0.2437 \quad (24.37\%).$$

The comparable money-weighted rate of return is given by the solution to the following calculation:

$$225 = 100(1 + r)^2 + 50(1 + r)$$

implying a money-weighted rate of return of 27.07%.

Appendix B: Yields and Yield Curves

Bonds, with their regular and generally reliable stream of payments, are often considered to be natural assets for pension funds to invest in. In this appendix we consider some of the key yield measures on bonds. We also examine different types of yield curve.

B.1 YIELDS

B.1.1 Current yield

The simplest measure of the yield on a bond is the *current yield* (or *flat yield, interest yield, income yield* or *running yield*). This is defined as:

$$rc = \frac{d}{P} \tag{B.1}$$

where:

rc = current yield
P = clean price.

For example, if the clean price of the bond is 95.30 and the coupon is 8.75, then the current yield is:

$$rc = \frac{8.75}{95.30}$$
$$= 0.0918 \quad (9.18\%).$$

B.1.2 Yield to maturity

The *yield to maturity* (or *redemption yield*) is the most frequently used measure of the return from holding a bond. It takes into account the pattern of coupon payments, the bond's term to maturity and the capital gain or loss arising over the remaining life of the bond. The yield to maturity is equivalent to the *money-weighted rate of return* or the *internal rate of return* on the bond (see Section A.5.2).

The yield to maturity (rm) is calculated by solving the following equation:

$$P_d = \left[\frac{1}{\left(1 + \dfrac{rm}{2}\right)^{N_{tc}/182.5}} \right] \times \left\{ \frac{d}{2} + \frac{d/2}{\left(1 + \dfrac{rm}{2}\right)} + \cdots \right.$$

$$\left. + \frac{d/2}{\left(1 + \dfrac{rm}{2}\right)^{S-1}} + \frac{B}{\left(1 + \dfrac{rm}{2}\right)^{S-1}} \right\}$$

$$= \left[\frac{1}{\left(1 + \dfrac{rm}{2}\right)^{N_{tc}/182.5}} \right] \times \left\{ \sum_{t=0}^{S-1} \frac{d/2}{\left(1 + \dfrac{rm}{2}\right)^{t}} + \frac{B}{\left(1 + \dfrac{rm}{2}\right)^{S-1}} \right\}$$

$$= \left[\frac{1}{\left(1 + \dfrac{rm}{2}\right)^{N_{tc}/182.5}} \right] \times \left\{ \frac{d}{rm}\left[\left(1 + \frac{rm}{2}\right) - \frac{1}{\left(1 + \dfrac{rm}{2}\right)^{S-1}} \right] \right.$$

$$\left. + \frac{B}{\left(1 + \dfrac{rm}{2}\right)^{S-1}} \right\} \tag{B.2}$$

where:

$P_d = P + AI$ = dirty bond price (clean price *plus* accrued interest since last coupon payment)

B = par value of bond

$d/2$ = semi-annual coupon payment

rm = yield to maturity

N_{tc} = number of days between current date t and next coupon payment date c

S = number of coupon payments before redemption (if T is the number of *complete* years before redemption, then $S = 2T$ if there is an even number of coupon payments before redemption, and $S = 2T + 1$ if there is an odd number of coupon payments before redemption).

Equation (B.2) uses rm to discount the bond's semi-annual cash flows back to the date of the next coupon payment (the term in curly brackets {.}) and then discounts the present value at that date back to the current date (the term in square brackets [.]) The rm will be the yield to maturity if the value so achieved equals the dirty price of the bond at date t. In other words, rm is the *internal rate of return* that equates the present value of the discounted cash flows on the bond to the current dirty price of the bond (if date t is the current date). The solution for rm cannot be found analytically and has to be found through numerical iteration using a computer or a programmable calculator.

To illustrate, suppose a bond has a dirty price of 96.50, an annual coupon payment of 8.75, and there is exactly one year before maturity. In this case, (B.2) becomes:

$$96.50 = \frac{4.375}{\left(1 + \dfrac{rm}{2}\right)} + \frac{104.375}{\left(1 + \dfrac{rm}{2}\right)^2}$$

Since this is a quadratic equation there will be two solutions, only one of which gives a positive rm. The positive solution is $rm = 12.58\%$.

B.2   YIELD CURVES

In this section we shall examine the relationship between various yield measures and bonds that have different maturities but are otherwise similar. The relationship between a particular yield measure and a bond's maturity is called the *yield curve* (or *term structure of interest rates*) for that particular yield measure. To construct a yield curve correctly, only bonds from a homogeneous group should be included: for example, only bonds from the same risk class or with the same degree of liquidity. We would therefore not expect a yield curve to be constructed using both government and corporate bonds, since these would be from different risk classes. We consider the following types of yield curve: the yield to maturity yield curve, the coupon yield curve, the par yield curve, the spot yield curve, the forward yield curve, the annuity yield curve and the rolling yield curve.

B.2.1   The yield to maturity yield curve

The most familiar yield curve is the *yield to maturity* (YTM) *yield curve*. This is a plot of the yield to maturity (derived from (B.2) above) against term to maturity for a group of homogeneous bonds. Three different shapes of yield curve are shown in Figure B.1.

There are several problems with the YTM yield curve. Implicit in the definition of YTM is the assumption that coupon payments are reinvested

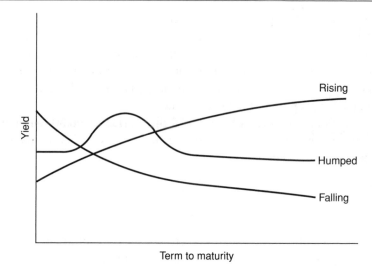

Figure B.1   Yield to maturity yield curves

at the YTM. As market rates of interest vary over time, it becomes difficult to achieve this, a feature known as *reinvestment risk*. The only type
of bond devoid of reinvestment risk is a zero-coupon or pure discount
bond. Another problem is that the YTM yield curve does not distinguish
between the different payment patterns of low-coupon bonds and high-
coupon bonds with the same maturity. With the latter, the payments are
concentrated in the early years of their lives, while with the former, they
are concentrated in the later years. Yet this is not taken into account in
the YTM curve, which assumes a flat payments pattern. In other words,
the cash payments on the bond are not discounted at the appropriate
interest rate. For reasons such as these, bond analysts have devised a
number of other types of yield curve.

B.2.2   The coupon yield curve

The *coupon yield curve* is a plot of the yield to maturity against term
to maturity for a group of bonds with the same coupon. A typical set
of coupon yield curves is presented in Figure B.2, indicating that high-
coupon bonds trade at a discount (have higher yields) relative to low-
coupon bonds, because of reinvestment risk and tax reasons. There is
a chance that interest rates will fall during the life of the bond and this
reduces the reinvestment return from reinvesting the coupon payments

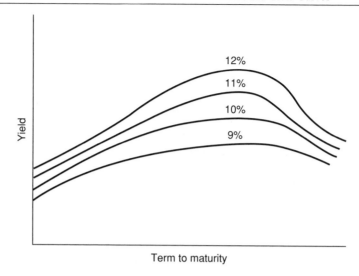

12%

11%

10%

9%

Yield

Term to maturity

Figure B.2   Coupon yield curves

(which is a greater risk for high-coupon compared with low-coupon bonds) and high-rate taxpayers prefer to have a return in the form of capital gains rather than coupon income, since capital gains tax can be deferred (whereas income tax cannot). It is clear that yield can vary quite considerably with coupon for the same term to maturity, and with term to maturity for different coupons. In other words, different coupon curves not only have significantly different levels, but may also have significantly different shapes. Therefore, the kinds of distortion that can arise in the YTM curve if no allowance is made for coupon are obvious.

As an alternative to the two-dimensional representation depicted in Figure B.2, we can construct a three-dimensional *yield plane* of coupon against yield to maturity against term to maturity (see Figure B.3).

B.2.3   The par (or swap) yield curve

The *par* (or *swap*) *yield curve* is a plot of the yield to maturity against term to maturity for bonds priced at par. The par yield is therefore equal to the coupon rate for bonds priced at or near par (since the YTM for bonds priced at par is equal to the coupon rate). The par yield curve is used to determine the required coupon on a new bond that is to be issued at par.

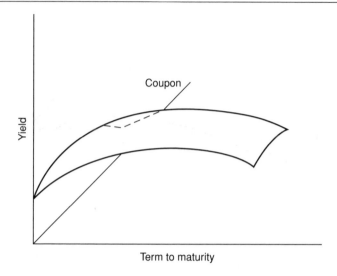

Figure B.3   Yield plane

Suppose that the current par yields on bonds that will mature in one, two and three years' time are given respectively by 10, 10.25 and 10.75%. This suggests, for example, that a new two-year bond issued at par would have to have a coupon of 10.25% and that for a three-year bond with annual coupons trading at par the following equality holds:

$$100 = \frac{10.75}{1.1075} + \frac{10.75}{(1.1075)^2} + \frac{110.75}{(1.1075)^3}$$

demonstrating that the YTM and the coupon are identical when a bond is trading at par.

B.2.4   The spot (or zero-coupon) yield curve

The *spot* (or *zero-coupon*) *yield curve* is a plot of spot yields (or zero-coupon yields) against term to maturity.

Spot yields satisfy the following equation (assuming annual coupons and the calculation is made on a coupon payment date so that $AI = 0$):

$$P_d = \sum_{t=1}^{T} \frac{d}{(1 + rs_t)^t} + \frac{B}{(1 + rs_T)^T}$$

$$= \sum_{t=1}^{T} d \times D_t + B \times D_T \tag{B.3}$$

where:

rs_t = the spot or zero-coupon yield on a bond with t years to maturity
$D_t = 1/(1 + rs_t)^t$ = the corresponding discount factor.

In (B.3), rs_1 is the current one-year spot yield, rs_2, the current two-year spot yield, and so on.

The spot yield for a particular term to maturity is the same as the yield on a zero-coupon bond of the same maturity (hence the alternative name). The spot yields can be derived from the par yields as follows.

The derivation is based on the interpretation of a bond as a composition of an annuity (which provides the coupon stream) and a zero-coupon bond (which provides the principal repayment) represented by (using (B.3) with $P_d = B = 100$ and $d = 100 \times rp_T$):

$$100 = 100 \times rp_T \times \sum_{t=1}^{T} D_t + 100 \times D_T$$
$$= 100 \times rp_T \times A_T + 100 \times D_T \qquad (B.4)$$

where rp_T is the par yield for a term to maturity of T years, the discount factor D_T is the fair price of a zero-coupon bond with par value of 1 and a term to maturity of T years, and where:

$$A_T = \sum_{t=1}^{T} D_t = A_{T-1} + D_T \qquad (B.5)$$

is the fair price of an annuity of 1 per year for T years (with $A_0 = 0$ by convention). Substituting (B.5) into (B.4) and rearranging gives the expression:

$$D_T = \frac{1 - rp_T \times A_{T-1}}{1 + rp_T} \qquad (B.6)$$

for the T-year discount factor.

For one-year, two-year and three-year par yields given by 10, 10.25 and 10.75%, respectively, we get the following solutions for the discount factors:

$$D_1 = \frac{1}{1 + 0.10} = 0.9091$$
$$D_2 = \frac{1 - (0.1025)(0.9091)}{1 + 0.1025} = 0.8225$$
$$D_3 = \frac{1 - (0.1075)(0.9091 + 0.8225)}{1 + 0.1075} = 0.7349$$

It is easy to verify that these are the correct discount factors. Substituting them back into (B.4), we get, respectively, for the one-year, two-year and three-year par value bonds:

$$100 = 110 \times (0.9091)$$
$$100 = 10.25 \times (0.9091) + 110.25 \times (0.8225)$$
$$100 = 10.75 \times (0.9091) + 10.75 \times (0.8225) + 110.75 \times (0.7349).$$

Now that we have found the correct discount factors, it is easy to calculate the spot yields. From Equation (B.3):

$$D_1 = \frac{1}{(1 + rs_1)} = 0.9091, \quad \text{implying } rs_1 = 10.0\%$$

$$D_2 = \frac{1}{(1 + rs_2)^2} = 0.8225, \quad \text{implying } rs_2 = 10.26\%$$

$$D_3 = \frac{1}{(1 + rs_3)^3} = 0.7349, \quad \text{implying } rs_3 = 10.81\%$$

An alternative procedure for calculating the spot yields is to equate Equations (B.3) and (B.4) for each T and solve for the unknown spot yield rs_T. For example, when $T = 2$ (and given that $rp_1 = rs_1 = 10\%$ and $rp_2 = 10.25\%$), we have:

$$\frac{10.25}{1.1025} + \frac{110.25}{(1.1025)^2} = 100 = \frac{10.25}{(1.10)} + \frac{110.25}{(1 + rs_2)^2}$$

which solves for $rs_2 = 10.26\%$. Similarly for $T = 3$ (and given that $rp_3 = 10.75\%$), we have:

$$\frac{10.75}{(1.1075)} + \frac{10.75}{(1.1075)^2} + \frac{110.75}{(1.1075)^3} = 100$$
$$= \frac{10.75}{(1.10)} + \frac{10.75}{(1.1026)^2} + \frac{110.75}{(1 + rs_3)^3}$$

which solves for $rs_3 = 10.81\%$.

In (B.3) we are discounting the t-year cash flow (coupon payment and/or principal repayment) by the corresponding t-year spot yield. In other words, rs_t is the *time-weighted rate of return* on a t-year bond (see Section A.5.3). Thus, the spot yield curve is the correct method for pricing or valuing any cash flow (whether regular or irregular) because it uses the appropriate discount factors. This contrasts with the YTM procedure, shown in (B.2), in which *all* cash flows are discounted by the *same* yield to maturity.

B.2.5   The forward yield curve

The *forward* (or *forward-forward*) *yield curve* is a plot of forward yields against term to maturity. Forward yields satisfy:

$$P_d = \frac{d}{(1 + {}_0rf_1)} + \frac{d}{(1 + {}_0rf_1)(1 + {}_1rf_2)}$$

$$+ \cdots + \frac{B}{(1 + {}_0rf_1)\ldots(1 + {}_{T-1}rf_T)}$$

$$= \sum_{t-1}^{T} \frac{d}{\prod_{i=1}^{t}(1 + {}_{i-1}rf_i)} + \frac{B}{\prod_{i=1}^{T}(1 + {}_{i-1}rf_i)} \qquad (B.7)$$

where:

$_{i-1}rf_i$ = implicit forward rate (or forward-forward rate) on a one-year bond maturing in year i.

Comparing (B.3) and (B.7), we can see that the spot yield is the *geometric mean* of the forward yields:

$$(1 + rs_t)^t = (1 + {}_0rf_1)(1 + {}_1rf_2)\ldots(1 + {}_{t-1}rf_t) \qquad (B.8)$$

This implies that:

$$(1 + {}_{t-1}rf_t) = (1 + rs_t)^t/(1 + rs_{t-1})^{t-1} = D_{t-1}/D_t \qquad (B.9)$$

For the spot yields given above, we can derive the implied forward yields from (B.9): ${}_0rf_1 = 10\%$, ${}_1rf_2 = 10.53\%$ and ${}_2rf_3 = 11.92\%$. This means, for example, that, given the current spot yields, the market is expecting the yield on a one-year bond maturing in three years' time to be 11.92%.

The relationship between the par yields, spot yields and forward yields is given in Table B.1. This relationship is also shown in Figure B.4 (in the case of rising yield curves) and Figure B.5 (in the case of falling yield curves).

Table B.1   The Relationship Between Par Yields, Spot Yields and Forward Yields

Year	Par yield (%)	Spot yield (%)	Forward yield (%)
1	10.00	10.00	10.00
2	10.25	10.26	10.53
3	10.75	10.81	11.92

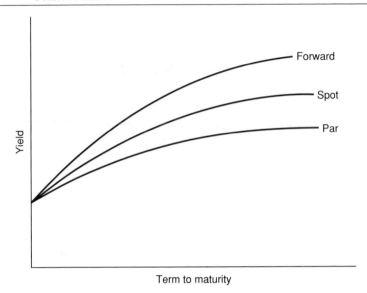

Figure B.4   Rising par, spot and forward yield curves

The relationship between par yields and spot yields can be shown using the following example. Suppose that a two-year bond with cash flows of £10.25 at the end of year 1 and £110.25 at the end of year 2 is trading at par (i.e. has a par yield of 10.25%) and hence a terminal value

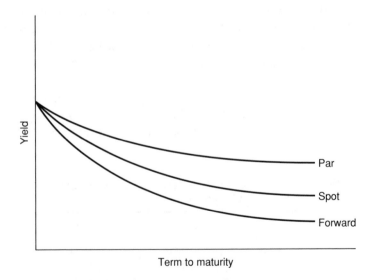

Figure B.5   Falling par, spot and forward yield curves

of:

$$10.25 \times (1.1053) + 110.25 = 121.57$$

where the first year's coupon payment (10.25) is invested at the one-year forward rate for year 2 (10.53%). To be regarded as equivalent to this, a pure discount bond (making a lump sum payment at the end of year 2 with no year 1 payment) would require a rate of return of 10.26% (the spot yield), i.e. for the same investment of 100, the maturity value would have to be:

$$100 \times (1.1026)^2 = 121.57$$

As another example, if we know the spot yields, then we can calculate the coupon required on a new bond if it is to be issued at par using:

$$100 = \frac{d}{(1.10)} + \frac{d}{(1.1026)^2} + \frac{d + 100}{(1.1081)^3}$$

This gives $d = 10.75$, the same as the three-year par yield.

The relationship between spot yields and forward yields is shown in (B.8). If the spot yield is the *average return*, then the forward yield can be interpreted as the *marginal return*. If the marginal return between years 2 and 3 increases from 10.53 to 11.92%, then the average return increases from 10.26% to

$$\left[(1.1026)^2(1.1192)\right]^{1/3} - 1 = 0.1081 \quad (10.81\%)$$

The relationship between forward yields and par yields can be explained as follows. Suppose a three-year bond pays coupons equal to the corresponding forward rates; such a bond is similar to a floating-rate note in the sense that the current forward rates are the market's best expectation of what the future spot rates will be. This bond will trade at par, since (discounting using spot rates):

$$100 = \frac{10.00}{(1.10)} + \frac{10.53}{(1.1026)^2} + \frac{111.92}{(1.1081)^3}$$

A corresponding fixed-income bond, which also trades at par, will pay a fixed annual coupon equal to the three-year par yield, since (again discounting using spot yields):

$$100 = \frac{10.75}{(1.10)} + \frac{10.75}{(1.1026)^2} + \frac{110.75}{(1.1081)^3}$$

So the par yield is the constant or flat yield corresponding to a given set of forward yields.

B.2.6 The annuity yield curve

The *annuity yield curve* is a plot of annuity yields against term to maturity.

An *annuity yield* is the implied yield on an annuity where the annuity is valued using spot yields. In (B.4) above, we decomposed a bond into an annuity and a pure discount bond. We used the spot yield to price the discount bond component. Now we are concerned with the pure annuity (or pure coupon) component.

The value of the annuity component of a bond is given by:

$$A_T^* = \sum_{t=1}^{T} \frac{d}{(1 + rs_t)^t}$$

$$= \sum_{t=1}^{T} d \times D_t \qquad (B.10)$$

$$= d \times A_T$$

where rs_t and D_t are defined in (B.3) and A_T is defined in (B.5). But A_T, the fair price of an annuity of 1 per year for T years, is given by the standard formula (see Equation (A.18)):

$$A_T = \frac{1}{ra_T} \times \left[1 - \frac{1}{(1 + ra_T)^T} \right] \qquad (B.11)$$

where ra_T is the annuity yield on a T-year annuity.

Suppose that we have a three-year bond with annual coupon payments of 10.75. The value of the annuity component is given by (B.10):

$$A_3^* = \frac{10.75}{(1.10)} + \frac{10.75}{(1.1026)^2} + \frac{10.75}{(1.1081)^3}$$

$$= 26.51$$

This implies that $A_3 = 2.47$ (i.e. 26.51/10.75). Solving for ra_3 in (B.11) gives a three-year annuity yield of $ra_3 = 10.48\%$.

The relationship between the spot and annuity yield curves is shown in Figure B.6. With an upward-sloping spot yield curve, the annuity yield is below the end-of-period spot yield ($10.48 < 10.81$); with a falling spot yield curve, the annuity yield curve lies above it.

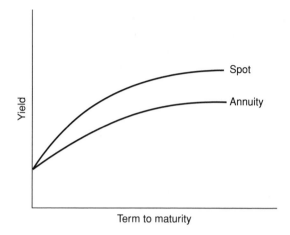

Figure B.6   Spot and annuity yield curves

B.2.7   Rolling yield curve

The *rolling yield curve* is a plot of rolling yields against term to maturity (see Figure B.7).

The one-year *rolling yield* is the yield on a bond when the holding period is one year but the prices of bonds are assumed to remain constant

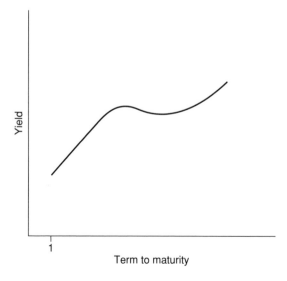

Figure B.7   Rolling yield curve (one-year horizon)

during the year. For example, an investor could buy a ten-year bond, hold it for one year and receive the coupon, and then sell it for the current price of a nine-year bond with the same coupon. The rate of return on this investment would be the one-year rolling yield for a term to maturity of ten years.

The one-year rolling yield is given by:

$$rr_T = \frac{d + P_{T-1}}{P_T} - 1 \tag{B.12}$$

where:

rr_T = one-year rolling yield on a T-year bond
P_T = dirty price on a T-year bond
P_{T-1} = dirty price on a T-1-year bond with the same coupon (d).

For example, suppose that the price of a ten-year 10% bond is 107.25 and the price of a nine-year 10% bond is 106.75. The one-year rolling yield on a ten-year bond is:

$$rr_{10} = \frac{10.0 + 106.75}{107.25} - 1$$
$$= 0.0886 \quad (8.86\%).$$

Appendix C: Duration and Convexity

This appendix discusses different ways of measuring the *interest rate risk* from holding bonds. Interest rate risk is the risk that bond prices will fall if market interest rates rise. It is the main form of market risk for bonds paying fixed coupons. There are two principal measures of interest-rate risk that we will consider: duration and convexity.

C.1 DURATION

The measure of interest rate risk typically used by bond analysts is called *duration*, which was invented by Macaulay (1938). Duration is defined as the weighted average maturity of a bond using the relative discounted cash flows in each period as weights. If we assume annual coupons, then (see Chua, 1984):

$$D = \frac{d}{P_d} \times \sum_{t=1}^{T} \frac{t}{(1+rm)^t} + \frac{B}{P_d} \times \frac{T}{(1+rm)^T}$$

$$= \frac{d}{P_d} \times \left[\frac{(1+rm)^{T+1} - (1+rm) - (rm)(T)}{(rm)^2(1+rm)^T} \right] + \frac{B}{P_d} \times \frac{T}{(1+rm)^T}$$

$$\text{(C.1)}$$

where:

D = duration (measured in years)
d = annual coupon
B = par value of bond
P_d = dirty price of bond (i.e. clean price plus accrued interest)
t = time in years to tth cash flow
T = time in years to maturity
rm = yield to maturity.

In (C.1), $d/(1+rm)^t$ is the discounted value of the tth cash flow and so $d/P_d(1+rm)^t$ is the relative discounted value of the tth cash flow; similarly with the terminal value.

Example of duration. A 10% annual coupon bond is trading at par with three years to maturity, so $P_d = B = 100$, $d = 10$, $rm = 10\%$, $T = 3$ years. Therefore, duration is given by:

$$D = \frac{10}{100}\left[\frac{1}{(1.1)} + \frac{2}{(1.1)^2} + \frac{3}{(1.1)^3}\right] + \frac{100}{100}\left[\frac{3}{(1.1)^3}\right]$$

$$= \frac{10}{100}\left[\frac{(1.1)^4 - (1.1) - (0.1)(3)}{(0.1)^2(1.1)^3}\right] + \frac{100}{100}\left[\frac{3}{(1.1)^3}\right]$$

$$= 2.74 \text{ years}$$

which implies that the average time taken to receive the cash flows on this bond is 2.74 years (see Figure C.1).

We can examine some of the properties of duration. Duration is always less than (or equal to) maturity. This is because some weight is given to the cash flows in the early years of the bond's life and this helps to bring forward the average time at which cash flows are received. In the above example, the coupon element contributes 0.5 years to duration, while the principal element contributes 2.24 years. Duration also varies with coupon, yield and maturity.

For a zero-coupon bond, duration equals the term to maturity. This is obvious from the definition of a zero-coupon bond and also from (C.1) given that for a zero-coupon bond $d = 0$ and $P_d = B/(1 + rm)^T$. For a perpetual bond, duration is given by:

$$D = \frac{1 + rc}{rc} = \frac{1}{rc} + 1 \tag{C.2}$$

where $rc = (d/P_d)$ is the current yield. This follows from (C.1) as $T \to \infty$, recognising (from Equation (B.2) in Appendix B) that, for a perpetual bond, $rm = rc$.

Equation (C.2) provides the limiting value to duration. For bonds trading at or above par (so that $rm \leq rc$), duration increases with maturity and approaches this limit from below. For bonds trading at a discount to par (so that $rm > rc$), duration increases to a maximum at around 20 years and then declines towards the limit given by (C.2). So, in general, duration increases with maturity (see Figure C.2).

Duration increases as coupon and yield decrease, as shown in Figure C.3. As the coupon falls, more of the relative weight of the cash flows is transferred to the maturity date and this causes duration to rise.

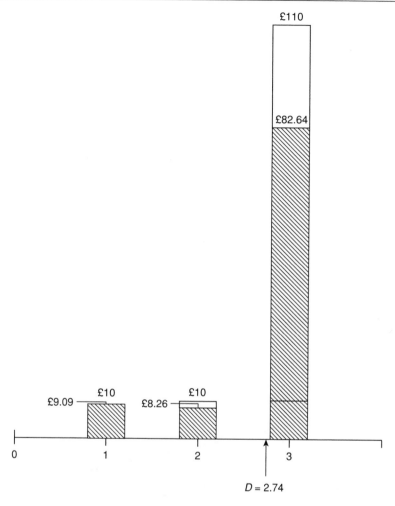

Figure C.1   Duration as the weighted average maturity of a bond

As yield increases, the present values of all future cash flows fall, but the present values of the more distant cash flows fall relatively more than those of the nearer cash flows. This has the effect of increasing the relative weight given to nearer cash flows and hence of reducing duration. Because the coupon on index-linked gilts is much lower than on conventional gilts, this means that the duration of index-linked gilts will be much higher than for conventional gilts with the same maturity.

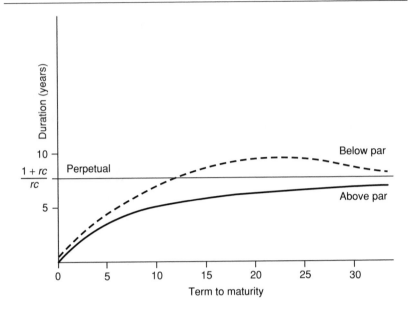

Figure C.2   Duration against maturity

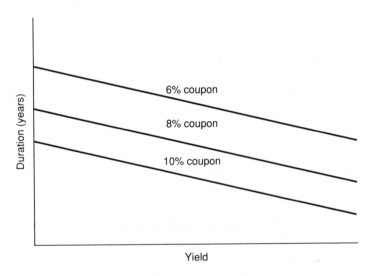

Figure C.3   Duration against coupon and yield

That duration is a measure of interest rate risk is demonstrated as follows. The present value equation for an annual coupon bond is given by:

$$P_d = \sum_{t=1}^{T} \frac{d}{(1+rm)^t} + \frac{B}{(1+rm)^T} \qquad (C.3)$$

Differentiating this equation with respect to $(1 + rm)$ gives:

$$\frac{\Delta P_d}{\Delta(1+rm)} = -d \times \sum_{t=1}^{T} \frac{t}{(1+rm)^{t+1}} - B \times \frac{T}{(1+rm)^{T+1}} \qquad (C.4)$$

where Δ means 'a small change in'. Multiplying both sides of (C.4) by $(1 + rm)/P_d$ gives:

$$\frac{\Delta P_d/P_d}{\Delta(1+rm)/(1+rm)} = -\frac{d}{P_d} \times \sum_{t=1}^{T} \frac{t}{(1+rm)^t} - \frac{B}{P_d} \times \frac{T}{(1+rm)^T}$$
$$= -D \qquad (C.5)$$

The LHS of (C.5) is the elasticity of the bond price with respect to (one *plus*) the yield to maturity, $\varepsilon[P_d, (1+rm)]$, where:

$$\varepsilon[P_d, (1+rm)] = \frac{\Delta \ln P_d}{\Delta \ln(1+rm)}$$
$$= \frac{\Delta P_d/P_d}{\Delta(1+rm)/(1+rm)} \qquad (C.6)$$

The RHS of (C.5) is (the negative of) duration. So, duration measures the interest-rate elasticity of the bond price, and is therefore a measure of interest-rate risk. The lower the duration, the less responsive is the bond's value to interest-rate fluctuations.

Figure C.4 shows the present-value profile for a bond. There is a negative-sloping and convex relationship between (the natural logarithm of) the price of the bond and (the natural logarithm of) one *plus* the yield to maturity. The slope of the present-value profile at the current bond price and yield to maturity is equal to the (negative of the) duration of the bond. The flatter the present-value profile, the lower the duration and the lower the interest-rate risk.

Example of first-order interest-rate risk. A 10% annual coupon bond is trading at par with a duration of 2.74 years. If yields rise from 10 to

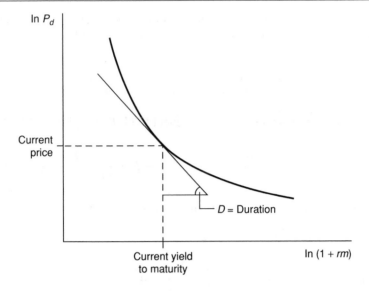

Figure C.4 Present-value profile and duration

10.5%, then the price of the bond will fall by:

$$\Delta P_d = -D \times \frac{\Delta(rm)}{1+rm} \times P_d$$

$$= -2.74 \times \frac{0.005}{1.1} \times 100$$

$$= -1.25$$

to £98.75.

The UK markets use a concept called *modified duration* (also known as *volatility*), which is related to duration as follows:

$$MD = \frac{D}{1+rm} \qquad (C.7)$$

where MD = modified duration in years. This means that the following relationship holds between modified duration and bond prices:

$$\Delta P_d = -MD \times \Delta rm \times P_d \qquad (C.8)$$

For example, if $D = 2.74$ years and yields are 10% then:

$$MD = \frac{2.74}{1.1}$$

$$= 2.49 \text{ years}$$

Market practitioners also use a concept called *basis point value* (BPV) (which is sometimes referred to as *risk*). It is related to modified duration as follows:

$$BPV = \frac{MD \times P_d}{10\,000} \tag{C.9}$$

While modified duration gives the percentage change in the price of a bond, BPV gives the money change in the price of a bond in response to a one-basis-point change in yield: from (C.8) it is clear that:

$$BPV = -\frac{\Delta P_d}{\Delta rm} \times \frac{1}{10\,000}$$

Some practitioners in the financial markets (an example is Bloomberg, suppliers of online financial information) calculate duration and modified duration using numerical approximations to the first-order derivative given in (C.5). For example, modified duration can be calculated using the following expression:

$$MD = \frac{10^4}{2}\left(\frac{|\Delta P_d''|}{P_d} + \frac{|\Delta P_d''|}{P_d}\right), \tag{C.10}$$

where:

$|\Delta P_d'|$ = absolute value of the change in dirty price if the yield increases by 1 basis point (0.01%); i.e. by one *BPV*.

$|\Delta P_d''|$ = absolute value of the change in dirty price if the yield falls by 1 basis point (0.01%); i.e. by one *BPV*.

The scaling factor 10^4 is explained by the fact that the price difference is calculated on the basis of a 100th of 1% change in yield, whereas the price level is based on 100% of par value.

To illustrate this we can use the same bond as in the above example of duration. If the yield increases from 10.00 to 10.01% then, using (C.3) above and Equation (A.18) in Appendix A, the price of the bond will fall to:

$$P_d' = \frac{10}{(0.1001)}\left[1 - \frac{1}{(1.1001)^3}\right] + \frac{100}{(1.1001)^3}$$
$$= 99.9751359$$

or by $\Delta P'_d = -0.0248641$. If the yield falls to 9.99%, the price of the bond will rise to:

$$P''_d = \frac{10}{(0.0999)} \left[1 - \frac{1}{(1.0999)^3} \right] + \frac{100}{(1.0999)^3}$$

$$= 100.0248729$$

or by $\Delta P''_d = 0.0248729$. Therefore:

$$MD = \frac{10^4}{2} \left(\frac{0.0248641}{100} + \frac{0.02489729}{100} \right)$$

$$= 2.49.$$

C.2   CONVEXITY

Duration can be regarded as a first-order measure of interest-rate risk: it measures the *slope* of the present-value profile. *Convexity*, on the other hand, can be regarded as a second-order measure of interest-rate risk: it measures the *curvature* of the present-value profile.

A second-order Taylor expansion of the present-value equation (C.3) gives:

$$\frac{\Delta P_d}{P_d} = \frac{1}{P_d} \times \frac{\Delta P_d}{\Delta rm} \times (\Delta rm) + \frac{1}{2P_d} \times \frac{\Delta^2 P_d}{\Delta rm^2} \times (\Delta rm)^2$$

$$= -MD \times (\Delta rm) + \frac{C}{2} \times (\Delta rm)^2 \qquad (C.11)$$

where:

MD = modified duration
C = convexity

Convexity is the rate at which price variation to yield changes with respect to yield and, as is clear from (C.11), it is found by taking the second derivative of Equation (C.3) with respect to rm and dividing the result by P_d. Blake and Orszag (1996) show that this expression for convexity can be simplified as follows:

$$C = \frac{1}{P_d} \times \frac{\Delta^2 P_d}{\Delta rm^2}$$

$$= \frac{d}{P_d} \times \sum_{t=1}^{T} \frac{t(t+1)}{(1+rm)^{t+2}} + \frac{B}{P_d} \times \frac{T(T+1)}{(1+rm)^{T+2}}$$

$$= -\frac{d}{P_d} \left\{ \frac{(T+1)(T+2)\left(\dfrac{1}{1+rm}\right)^{T+2}}{rm} \right.$$

$$+ \frac{2\left[(T+2)\left(\dfrac{1}{1+rm}\right)^{T+2} - \left(\dfrac{1}{1+rm}\right)\right]}{rm^2}$$

$$\left. + \frac{2\left[\left(\dfrac{1}{1+rm}\right)^{T+2} - \left(\dfrac{1}{1+rm}\right)\right]}{rm^3} \right\} + \frac{B}{P_d} \times \frac{T(T+1)}{(1+rm)^{T+2}}$$

(C.12)

Convexity can also be approximated by the following expression for the numerical second-order derivative:

$$C = 10^8 \left(\frac{\Delta P_d'}{P_d} + \frac{\Delta P_d''}{P_d} \right)$$

(C.13)

where:

$\Delta P_d'$ = change in dirty bond price if yield increases by 1 basis point (0.01%); i.e. by one *BPV*.

$\Delta P_d''$ = change in dirty bond price if yield decreases by 1 basis point (0.01%); i.e. by one *BPV*.

Example of convexity. A 10% annual coupon bond is trading at par with three years to maturity, so $P_d = B = 100$, $d = 10$, $rm = 10\%$, $T = 3$ years. Therefore, using the second line of (C.12), convexity is given by:

$$C = \frac{10}{100} \left[\frac{2}{(1.1)^3} + \frac{6}{(1.1)^4} + \frac{12}{(1.1)^5} \right] + \frac{100}{100} \times \frac{12}{(1.1)^5}$$

$$= 8.76$$

We get the same answer if we use the numerical approximation to the second-order derivative (C.13). We know that if the yield increases from 10.00 to 10.01%, the price of the bond will fall by $\Delta P_d' = -0.0248641$, while if the yield falls to 9.99%, the price of the bond will rise by

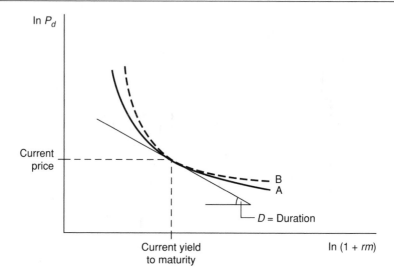

Figure C.5   Present-value profile and convexity

$\Delta P_d'' = 0.0248729$. Therefore:

$$C = 10^8 \left(\frac{-0.0248641}{100} + \frac{0.0248729}{100} \right)$$
$$= 8.76$$

It can be shown that convexity increases with the square of maturity. It decreases with both coupon and yield. Index-linked bonds are more convex than conventional bonds.

That convexity is a second-order measure of interest-rate risk is demonstrated in Figure C.5. This figure shows the present-value profiles for two bonds A and B, trading at the same price and yield to maturity, and having the same duration. Bond B, however, is more convex than bond A. B is clearly more desirable than A, since B will outperform A whatever happens to market interest rates. If yields rise, the price of B falls by less than the price of A, while if yields fall, the price of B rises by more than that of A. High convexity is therefore a desirable property for bonds to have.

When convexity is high, the first-order approximation for interest-rate risk, (C.5) or (C.6), will become increasingly less accurate as the change in yield becomes large. This is clear from Figure C.5. Duration is a linear approximation to the present-value profile. For small changes in yield, the linear approximation will be reasonably good; but for large jumps in yield, the linear approximation will become very poor if convexity is high. It will overestimate the risk (i.e. overestimate the price adjustment) when convexity is positive and underestimate risk and price adjustment when convexity is negative (which is the case, for example, with callable bonds near par). So, for large jumps in yield, the quadratic approximation to the present-value profile given by (C.12) or (C.13) is preferred.

Example of second-order interest-rate risk. A 10% annual coupon bond is trading at par with a modified duration of 2.49 and convexity of 8.76. If yields rise from 10 to 12%, the price of the bond will fall by:

$$\Delta P_d = -MD \times (\Delta rm) \times P_d + \frac{C}{2} \times (\Delta rm)^2 \times P_d$$

$$= -(2.49) \times (0.02) \times 100 + \frac{8.76}{2} \times (0.02)^2 \times 100$$

$$= -4.98 + 0.18$$

$$= -4.80$$

to £95.20. The first-order approximation overestimates the fall by £0.18.

REFERENCES

Blake, D. and Orszag, J. M. (1996) A closed-form formula for calculating bond convexity. *Journal of Fixed Income*, **6**, 88–91.

Chua, J. (1984) A closed-form formula for calculating bond duration. *Financial Analysts Journal*, **40**, 76–78.

Macaulay, F. (1938) *Some Theoretical Problems Suggested by the Movement of Interest Rates, Bond Yields, and Stock Prices in the US since 1856*, National Bureau of Economic Research, New York.

Index

A

Aberdeen Asset Management, 317
ABN AMRO, 41
absolutely mispriced bond, 246
absolute return benchmark, 274, 299
accrual factor, 194, 252
accumulation units, 17
ACD, *See* authorised corporate direct
active risk, 231, 240, 304
activism, 278
actuarial deficit, 212
actuarial surplus, 212
actuarial valuations, 212
actuary, 212
adjustable annuity, 148
age premium, 157
aggressiveness, degree of, 92
agricultural land, 21
Alliance Capital, 41
Allied Steel and Wire pension fund, 367
ALM strategies
cash flow matching, 266–267
horizon matching, 267
immunisation, 260–266
liability driven investing, 267–274
multi period immunisation, 266
alpha, 41, 240
transfer, 241

Alternative Investment Market, 11
alternative investments
private market or private equity strategies, 44–47
public market strategies, 38–44
alternatively secured pension (ASP), 151
Alzheimer's Disease, 183
American option, 26
annual charge equivalent, 141
annual percentage rate (APR), 414
annuities
in advance, 417
in arrears, 417
with capital protection, 147
charges, 154–155
due, 148, 417
factor, 108
with minimum guarantee, 147
with minimum guarantee and overlap, 147
with proportion, 147
yield curve, *See* yields
anomaly switches, 245
appropriate benchmarks, 279
A1/P1 quality, 3
arbitrage-free pricing model, 24
arbitrage fund, types of
basis trading or basket trading or portfolio trading, 43